THE
PROFESSIONAL
WINE
REFERENCE

THE
PROFESSIONAL
WINE
REFERENCE

REVISED EDITION

Frank E. Johnson

BEVERAGE MEDIA LTD., NEW YORK

1817

HARPER & ROW, PUBLISHERS, New York

Cambridge, Philadelphia, San Francisco, London
Mexico City, São Paulo, Sydney

THE PROFESSIONAL WINE REFERENCE
IS PUBLISHED IN COOPERATION WITH
BEVERAGE MEDIA LTD.
161 AVENUE OF THE AMERICAS
NEW YORK, NEW YORK 10013

Designed by: Bennett Glazer / Graphic Image, Inc.

Library of Congress Cataloging in Publication Data

Johnson, Frank E., 1948

The professional wine reference.

1. Wine and wine making—Dictionaries. 1. Title.

TP 546.J64 1983   641.2′22′0321   83-47561

ISBN 0-06-091087-9 (Harper & Row: pbk.)

83 84 85 86 87 10 9 8 7 6 5 4 3 2 1

Contents

Maps of World Wine Regions

Preface

I discovered *The Professional Wine Reference* back when it was first published in 1977, and said then and feel as strongly now that it's as necessary to wine merchants and restaurateurs as their liquor license. I've never come across another book on the subject that is as complete, concise, accurate and interesting to read.

I welcome this new revised edition, which addresses itself to the major developments in the wine industry over the last half-dozen years—the multiplying varieties of European wines imported to this country from France, Italy, Germany, Spain and other regions; and, of course, our own American wines evidenced especially by the remarkable progress and growth that continues to take place in California.

The wine market has evolved to the point where America now has the widest ranging, most sophisticated choice of wines available anywhere in the world. This would not have been possible were it not for the American consumer. It's a testament to the American wine enthusiast's developing taste and sophistication. So it's especially appropriate that *The Professional Wine Reference*, long a bible of the wine industry, will now find its way into the consumer's hands.

PAUL KOVI
Co-proprietor, The Four Seasons, New York
Co-author, *The Four Seasons Cookbook*

Introduction to the Revised Edition

Condensing so much information into so small a space is a challenge one doesn't want to confront too often in life, but now, as we put the last touches on this revision and the years of work it represents, we admit we feel very good about it and not a little bit proud.

The wine market has undergone important changes in the five years that have elapsed since the first edition of *The Professional Wine Reference* was printed. Not only has the world market expanded to make hundreds of new imported wines available, but new wineries have cropped up each year, supplanting certain traditional names and labels, and thousands of acres of new vineyards have been planted in the United States and abroad.

There was a lot of useful information on wine and related subjects we wanted to add to this revision, and we tried to do it without sacrificing our traditional and most basic aims—clarity, completeness, impartiality and easy readability.

The Professional Wine Reference has been designed to put a vast wealth of information right at your fingertips. There are some 950 individual articles organized alphabetically so you can quickly find precise answers to questions about wine. But it is our hope that you will also browse through the book, opening it to any page and embarking on a journey, spurred from article to article by our system of cross-referencing that enables you to investigate, in depth, a whole range of interesting subjects. (Cross references in each article are identified in the text by SMALL CAPITAL LETTERS.)

Because the book is international in perspective, each entry is followed by a short pronunciation guide.

When no pronunciation guide is given, it means the word can be pronounced as it would be in English.

Those looking for American wineries, please note that wineries are listed under the county or state where they are located, rather than in alphabetical order, both for reasons of space and as an aid to location. Note too the sections in the back of the book on grape varieties and varietal wines, and the wine character chart, which give you at a glance the characteristics of the most popular wines and grapes.

As we send this new edition to press, we do so with the certain knowledge that more new factors in wine production and trade will prove to be influential in the years to come. It is our intention to continue to keep *The Professional Wine Reference* up to date so that it remains the best standard reference work in the field for the wine trade and consumers alike.

Abboccato *(Ah-bo-ka′-tow)*: Italian for "semi-dry."

Abruzzi *(Ah-broot′-zee)*: Mountainous region in east-central Italy, bordering the Adriatic Sea; also called Abruzzo. Red wine of the region, made from the Montepulciano grape, is called Montepulciano di Abruzzo; the white is made from Trebbiano. Both are rated D.O.C.

Acescense *(Ah-see′-sans)*: The disagreeable scent of acetic acid or vinegar in spoiled wine; also called volatile acidity.

Acidity: In relation to wine there are two basic kinds of acidity, fixed and volatile. Fixed acidity refers to the natural fruit acids normally present in wine; the most important are citric, lactic, malic and tartaric. Volatile acidity, however, is not a desirable component of sound wine. It is an alternate term for acetic acid or ACESCENSE, which is formed when air and Acetobacter microbes enter wine during or after fermentation. It is called "volatile" because it is given off in the bouquet. There is usually a small amount of acetic acid in all wines, but when detectable in the bouquet it is an indication of spoilage.

Aglianico del Vulture *(Ahl-yan′-ee-co del Vool′-too-ray)*: Fine red wine of the Basilicata region east of Naples, Italy. Made from Aglianico grapes grown on the slopes of the Monte Vulture, an extinct volcano, it is considered to be one of the region's best wines, and is rated D.O.C.

Ahr *(Are):* Tributary of the Rhine River south of Bonn, Germany; also a wine region or AN-BAUGEBIET. The second smallest of the eleven German wine regions, the Ahr specializes in light red wines produced from Spätburgunder (Pinot Noir), popular in Germany but not widely exported; there are some 1,200 acres of vineyard, all within a single BEREICH (sub-region), Walporzheim/Ahrtal. In a few places unsuited to Spätburgunder, some Riesling, Portuguieser and Müller-Thurgau is grown. Villages within the Bereich include Neuenahr, Bachem, Ahrweiler, Walporzheim, Altenahr, and Marienthal; annual production amounts to some 500,000 cases of wine.

Alameda *(Al-ah-mee'-da):* County on the eastern shores of San Francisco Bay, California; historically famous for winegrowing. Alameda still has some 2,000 acres of vineyard, but much of the land is threatened by housing developments. The county includes part of the fertile Livermore Valley, a viticultural area noted for its special gravelly soil, and some of the major producers include: Wente Bros., a noted white wine producer; Concannon Vineyards, a leading producer of table wines since 1883; Villa Armando, primarily a bulk wine producer; Stony Ridge Winery in Pleasanton, and Weibel Vineyards near Fremont. Livermore Valley Cellars and Channing Rudd are two new wineries in the Livermore area.

Albana di Romagna *(Al-bahn'-na dee Romon'-ya):* White wine produced in the EMILIA-ROMAGNA district, north-central Italy, from the Albana grape; entitled to D.O.C. In its most basic forms Albana di Romagna may be dry, but a semi-sweet version is also made—occasionally the wine may be slightly sparkling *(frizzante),* or fully sparkling *(spumante).* At present, the still dry wine seems to be most popular in the U.S.

Alcamo *(Al'-ca-mo)*: Good quality red and white wines produced west of the city of Palermo on the island of SICILY, recently awarded a D.O.C. rating. Produced predominantly from the Catarrato bianco grape, Alcamo bianco (white) is a popular dry white wine in Sicily, and exports are increasing.

Aleatico *(Ahl-yah'-tee-co)*: Red Muscat grape variety used for making a fairly sweet wine in central and southern Italy.

Algeria: Presently the seventh largest wine-producing country in the world, Algeria is steadily improving the quality of her table wines, which became famous in 19th century France during the period of colonial occupation. After independence from France in 1962, the Algerian government delimited several of the best wine regions under the laws of *appellation d'origine garantie*, which are similar to the French APPELLATION CONTRÔLÉE laws. The most important regions are: Coteaux de Mascara, near the city of Mascara and famous for rich, full-bodied red wines; Medea, near Algiers and noted for good reds and whites; Tlemcen near Oran, another good red and white wine zone; and Dahra, further east near the Mediterranean coast, celebrated for reds. There are now some 520,000 acres of vineyard in Algeria, restricted by law to the traditional producing zones in order to assure the quality of wine exports.

Alicante-Bouschet *(Al-uh-con'-tay Boo-shay')*: High-yield, red HYBRID grape variety, developed in the 19th century by L. and H. Bouschet in France and now an important variety in the Central Valley wine district of California. Known as a "teinturier" (dyer) variety because of the intensely dark color of its pulp, Alicante-Bouschet now covers over 4,900 acres in the state. It is grown primarily for blending purposes, but a few wineries have tried releasing it on its own as a varietal.

Aligoté *(Ah-lee-go-tay')*: Secondary grape variety used for the lesser white wines of Burgundy, which are called "Bourgogne Aligoté." Very pleasant when consumed young, Bourgogne Aligoté is often mixed with Cassis liqueur to make the popular aperitif KIR.

Aloxe-Corton *(Ahl-oss' Cor-tawn')*: Picturesque hillside town in the northern CÔTE DE BEAUNE, Burgundy, named for its excellent red wine CORTON. Wine from the Corton vineyard, and also a very fine white wine from the famous CORTON-CHARLEMAGNE vineyard, is rated Grand Cru (Great Growth). Other renowned vineyards include the CLOS DU ROI, BRESSANDES, Pougets, and Renardes. The area under vines in the Aloxe-Corton commune is about 600 acres, and the average annual production is approximately 72,300 cases.

Alsace *(Ahl'-zass)*: A part of France that has retained Germanic dialects and wine-growing tendencies, Alsace today is a major French wine district, rapidly developing an identity with quality wines. The vineyards extend over some 30,000 acres, located on the eastern slopes of the Vosges Mountains along the border with Germany. Viticultural Alsace includes the two departments of Bas-Rhin and Haut-Rhin, which acknowledge the Rhine River that forms the border with Germany and imparts its own influence to the area. The limits of the region lie near the city of Strasbourg to the north, and Mulhouse to the south.

Alsace is a unique French wine region in that the grape variety exceeds the growing area in importance. Certain select sites in the wine district are better than others; but in general, the essential character of Alsace wines relates to the informing grape variety. By law, 100% of the indicated grape variety must be used,

ALSACE

Shaded area indicates vineyards

and the wines must be bottled in the green, fluted bottle reserved solely for Alsace wines.

Another major quality factor in Alsace wines is the shipper. Some firms have been in business for over a century, and each have their own quality standards, many of them more stringent than the law requires. The largest shippers own their own vineyards and produce what they sell, while others act as *négociants* (merchants), selecting what will be marketed under their own label. Among the major firms are: Hugel, F. E. Trimbach, Schlumberger, A & O Muré (Mure-Ehrhard), Dopff & Irion, Léon Beyer, Willm, Klug, J. Lorenz, Weinbach, and Klipfel.

Among the grapes grown in Alsace, two varieties stand out: Riesling and Gewürztraminer. Also grown in Germany and Austria, these grapes give special results in Alsace. The wines are usually totally dry, with slightly more alcohol than their Germanic counterparts, yet preserve all of their varietal character. Gewürztraminer originally was selected in Alsace as a CLONE or subvariety of Traminer, which is grown all over Europe.

Two other varieties produce "grand vin" in Alsace: Muscat, the same white Muscat grown in the FRONTIGNAN and Canelli districts, and Tokay d'Alsace, which is the same as Pinot Gris or Ruländer. Both produce slightly drier wines from these grapes than are usually seen elsewhere, yet retain their varietal identity. Other good grapes include Pinot Blanc (Weissburgunder), Pinot Noir (grown for light red wines and rosés), and Sylvaner. A basic, economical Alsace wine is EDELZWICKER, a blend of the four "cépages nobles": Riesling, Gewürztraminer, Tokay, or Muscat, which is usually the carafe wine of the region.

Normally, Alsace wines are totally dry; but when conditions permit, growers take pride in producing LATE HARVEST wines that resemble similar wines made in Germany and Austria.

Originally known as *vendange tardive*, or late harvest, these lusciously sweet wines are now called "sélection des grains nobles"—literally, a selection of only the ripest berries. They are similar to the BEERENAUSLESEN of Germany.

The vineyards of each Alsace wine town form a "route du vin" that extends southward from Strasbourg to Mulhouse. Among the more famous wine towns are: Ribeauvillé, Riquewihr, Turckheim, Colmar, Eguisheim, Rouffach, Guebwiller, Wintzenheim, and Westhalten. A few growers market select wines identifying a special vineyard where they were grown, like the Clos St. Hune of Trimbach, the Clos St. Landelin of Muré, and the Clos Gaensbroennel of Willm, which sell for higher prices than the basic shippers' wines. To qualify for the special distinction of *grand cru*, a quality grade formally established in 1975, an Alsace wine must attain a minimum alcoholic content, be grown in one of the leading wine villages, and be made only from Gewürztraminer, Riesling, Muscat, or Tokay d'Alsace.

Alto Adige *(Al′-tow Ah′-dee-gee)*: Mountain river valley in the northern Italian Tyrol near the Austrian border; located around Lake Caldaro (Lago di Caldaro), Alto Adige is an important wine region. It is considered part of TRENTINO; Bolzano and Merano are its two most important towns.

Because Alto Adige is so close to Austria and much of its population is German-speaking, its wines often bear German labels—Lago di Caldaro is also known as *Kalterersee*. Much wine is exported to Germany and Switzerland, but a good deal is sent to the U.S. Red wine produced from the Schiava grape near Lake Caldaro is called CALDARO and is rated D.O.C.; SANTA MADDALENA, grown near Bolzano and also made from the Schiava, is considered the best Alto Adige red wine. Cabernet, Pinot Noir and Merlot are also grown, and are known by their varietal names. Among the

7

Alto Adige white grape varieties, Pinot Blanc, Sauvignon Blanc, Chardonnay, Riesling, Pinot Grigio and Traminer all give excellent results.The region is also famous for Lagarino, a rosé made from Lagrein grapes.

Alto Douro *(Al'-tow Doo'-roe):* The "Upper Douro," in Portuguese; specifically, the delimited zone on the Douro River where grapes used in making PORT are grown. The Port is first made here on the estate or QUINTA, then brought downstream to Vila Nova de Gaia where it is blended and aged.

Amador: Historic county and winegrowing area in the foothills of the Sierra Nevada mountains, California; noted as an area for growing especially rich, intense Zinfandel wines. Presently the area has over 1,100 acres of vineyard, much of it planted in Zinfandel. The oldest winery in the area, d'Agostini Winery in Plymouth, was founded in 1856; the Deaver Vineyard has been supplying the Sutter Home Winery in Napa with quality grapes for years. Two excellent wineries in close proximity in Amador are Monteviña and Shenandoah Vineyards, both located near the town of Plymouth and both specializing in high-quality Zinfandel. Other promising new wineries include: Amador Foothill Winery, Amador Winery in Amador City, Baldinelli Shenandoah Valley Vineyards, Beau Val, Karly, Kenworthy Winery, and Santino Wines.

Amarone *(Ah-ma-roe'-nay):* A special type of VALPOLICELLA, for which selected grapes from the uppermost part of the bunches are left to dry on racks after picking, so that the resulting wine is fuller and more concentrated. The term is used with RECIOTO Valpolicellas to indicate that the residual sugar in this normally sweet wine has been fermented, to yield a dry wine. It fetches a much higher price than regular Valpolicella, and ages better.

Amontillado *(Ah-mon-tee-ya'-doe)*: A dry SHERRY of the FINO type, usually fuller and darker in color than most Finos, with a pronounced "nutty" flavor.

Anbaugebiet *(On'-bough-ge-beet)*: German for "region under cultivation." The 1971 German Wine Law authorized eleven specific viticultural areas in Germany as Anbaugebiete: AHR, BADEN, FRANKEN (Franconia), HESSISCHE BERGSTRASSE, MITTELRHEIN, MOSEL-SAAR-RUWER, NAHE, RHEINGAU, RHEINHESSEN, RHEINPFALZ (Palatinate), and WÜRTTEMBERG. The exact legal terminology is "bestimmtes Anbaugebiet" (b.A.) or "designated region." See QUALITÄTSWEIN.

Anjou *(Ahn-zhoo')*: Old French province, now part of the department of the Maine-et-Loire, near Angers on the lower Loire River. Red wines made from the Cabernet Franc grape are called Cabernet d'Anjou; this grape variety is also used for excellent rosés that may be either dry or semi-sweet. Anjou's white wines, produced from the Chenin Blanc, are superior. To the north, the Coteaux de la Loire includes the district of SAVENNIÈRES, one of the best dry Loire wines from the Chenin Blanc; to the south, the COTEAUX DU LAYON is known for sweet, luscious white wines, for which the QUARTS DE CHAUME and BONNEZEAUX vineyards are celebrated. SAUMUR is noted for its good whites and also its sparkling wines, made by the Champagne process.

Appellation Contrôlée *(Ah-pell-ah'-syon Kontroll-ay')*: In French, "controlled place name": the legal authorization for the name of a vineyard or wine region. It is outlined by the Institut National des Appellations d'Origine Contrôlée (I.N.A.O.), the official French government regulatory agency for wines and spirits.

The French wine laws are designed to protect the reputation of a famous wine area and also serve to protect the consumer. The words "appellation contrôlée" on a wine label are apt to be an indication of superior quality, because by law the wine *has* to come from the specified vineyard or wine district. This legislation has been in effect for about 40 years, and it has succeeded in reducing the incidence of wine frauds.

Besides defining the geographical origin of a wine, the laws also specify the approved grape varieties best suited to the area, minimum alcoholic strength of the wine, limits on yield per hectare, and pruning methods. These provisions work to defend quality by discouraging overproduction.

Appellation d'Origine (*Ah-pell-ah'-syon Dor'-re-zheen*): In French, "place name of geographic origin"; also, the laws regulating the use of these place names and restricting them to the better wine regions.

A quality hierarchy entitles France's most famous wines to APPELLATION CONTRÔLÉE: there are over 200 of these, each one identifying a superior wine in its class. Next come the "Vins Délimités de Qualité Supérieur" (V.D.Q.S.), whose quality does not quite measure up to appellation contrôlée. These wines must conform to certain standards, however, and are usually well-made: they carry a government seal on their labels. At the bottom of the scale are the "vins de pays" (regional wines). Though quality standards for them are not rigorous, they must come from the region indicated on the label, and are relatively inexpensive.

Apulia (*Ah-pool'-ya*): Wine district in southern Italy, the "heel" of the Italian "boot." The equivalent of 110 million cases of wine is produced in Apulia each year. Much is used in bulk in the manufacture of VERMOUTH, but there are many fines wines sold under their own names: SAN SEVERO and Castel del Monte, red, white or rosé wines produced near the town of Foggia, are perhaps the most famous and are entitled to D.O.C.

Arbois *(Are'-bwah):* Town located in eastern France near the Swiss border, in the JURA Mountains. Arbois is the best-known of several Jura APPELLATION CONTRÔLÉES that all produce similar wines (see CHÂTEAU-CHALON). It is famous for *vin jaune*, a white wine made from the Savagnin grape, that undergoes a transformation in cask similar to SHERRY; a process of air-drying the grapes to concentrate them prior to vinification is also used for VIN DE PAILLE. A rosé called Rosé d'Arbois is very popular; both this and a red Arbois is made from the Pinot Noir grape. Average production of all wine types is 245,000 cases.

Argentina: Argentina is one of the world's largest wine-producing countries, with more than 750,000 acres under vines; per capita consumption is on the order of ten cases of wine a year. With mass production in giant wineries (BODEGAS), the domestic need for top-quality wine is not great, but many of Argentina's better wines that are exported to the U.S. are excellent value. Red wines are generally more popular than the whites.

Seventy-five percent of Argentina's vineyards lie near the Chilean border, to the west. The climate is very dry, and irrigation is necessary in many vineyards. Principal vineyard areas are in MENDOZA and San Juan provinces, and the Rio Negro territory.

As Americans see them, Argentinean wines are known by their VARIETAL names, of which the most important are Cabernet Sauvignon, Merlot, Malbec (or Malbeck) and Barbera for red wines; Riesling, Chardonnay, Traminer, Pinot Blanc and Sémillon for whites.

Aroma: The fruity, "grapey" scent in a young wine. Aroma should not be confused with BOUQUET, a more complex scent in mature

11

wines, which is achieved through the process of bottle aging.

Asti: Town in PIEMONTE, Italy, east of Torino (Turin). It is famous for Asti *Spumante*, a very popular sweet sparkling wine made from Muscat grapes; also, good red wines made from Barbera, Grignolino, Nebbiolo and Freisa grapes.

Aszú *(Ahs'-zoo):* A superior sweet grade of Hungarian TOKAY, made only in the best vintages.

Aube *(Ohb):* French department in the southern and secondary part of the Champagne region.

Aude *(Ode):* The second largest wine-producing department in France, after the HÉRAULT. Though chiefly a region of ordinary wines, the Aude has several APPELLATION CONTRÔLÉES, including FITOU and Blanquette de Limoux, and V.D.Q.S. wines such as CORBIÈRES and part of the MINERVOIS.

Aurora *(Aw-raw'-ra):* White French HYBRID grape variety; one of the earliest and most successful crossings developed by M. Albert Seibel at the turn of the century; known officially as Seibel 5279. It is the most widely planted French hybrid in the Finger Lakes district of New York State, and also one of the oldest. While some of its wines may be on the neutral side, it has shown to be valuable in the preparation of sparkling wine cuvées. Significantly, it is quite resistant to frost and develops fruit rapidly during the growing season, factors that are important in cool winegrowing areas.

Ausbruch *(Ouse'-brook):* Special quality grade for Austrian wines, relating to select wines produced from overripe grapes harvested especially late in the season. Under the Austrian Wine Law, a wine labeled Ausbruch falls into a category between Beerenauslese and Trockenbeerenauslese: by law it must have a minimum MUST WEIGHT, expressed in degrees KMW, of 27°. Such wines can only be produced in vintages when there is a high incidence of the "noble mold" (BOTRYTIS CINEREA); they have a special flavor, character and luscious sweetness that distinguishes them, and the wines fetch high prices.

Auslese *(Ouse'-lay-zeh):* German for "selection." As outlined in the 1971 German Wine Law, a wine labeled Auslese is made from particularly ripe selected grape bunches from which all unripe grapes have been discarded. The legal minimum MUST WEIGHT must be about 90 (varies by area). Auslese wines are usually sweeter and more concentrated than SPÄTLESE, and are more expensive. They are only made in better vintages.

Ausone, Château *(Oh-zone'):* Famous classified Premier Grand Cru (First Great Growth) of SAINT-ÉMILION, considered one of the very best wines of BORDEAUX; it is celebrated for its body and bouquet. Its name is derived from Ausonius, a Roman poet and consul; about 2,800 cases are made each year. The vineyard is owned jointly by the Dubois-Challon and Vauthier families, and the wines have recently shown great improvement.

Australia: The vine is not native to Australia, and so it was only in 1788 that the first vineyards were planted by British settlers at Sydney. Since then, Australia has become a major wine-producing nation; much is consumed on the home market, but the export of wines to the U.S.—and their quality—is increasing. Whereas Australia previously concentrated on making dessert and FORTIFIED WINES, her emphasis now is on quality table wines.

Most of Australia's 60,000 acres of vineyard lie in the south of the continent. The most important wine-producing state is South Australia, which produces two-thirds of the nation's wine; the vineyards surround Adelaide, the state's capital. A notable area for table wine is the Hunter River Valley, north of Sydney in New South Wales; the balance of wine production is largely furnished by Victoria.

In the past, Australia's wines had GENERIC labels, like "claret" or "burgundy," after their European counterparts. Though such practices persist, quality wines are now apt to be designated by their VARIETAL name, such as Cabernet Sauvignon and Hermitage (Shiraz) for red wines. Riesling is the most important white wine variety, but the true Riesling is known as "Rhine Riesling" in Australia, and wine labeled "Riesling" is usually made from Sémillon. In addition, some good sparkling wine is made in Victoria.

Austria: Winemaking in Austria reflects a 1,000-year-old tradition for quality, combined with an ideal area for viticulture in the eastern half of the country, and a national love for wine. Besides vineyards encircling the capital city of Vienna, which provide the capital and account for the popularity of the wine taverns known as *Heurigen,* important vineyards can be found along the Danube River valley in the WACHAU district, to the northeast in Retz and Langenlois, in the fertile BURGENLAND district along the Hungarian border, and in the Steiermark district to the south. Currently over 125,000 acres are in production, and exports are increasing.

Three-fourths of all Austrian wine is white, and most of it is produced from the Grüner Veltliner grape—a variety unique to Austria that typifies the lively, fresh qualities of Austrian wine. White Riesling is also popular, although in Austria it is called Rhine Riesling and plays a secondary role in comparison to a related but more productive grape, Welsch Riesling. Pinot Blanc (Weissburgunder), Gewürztraminer, Muskat Ottonel and Müller-Thurgau do well in the sunny climate of Burgenland, whose warm autumns often encourage the production of late-harvested, high-quality sweet wines. These are the speciality of the town of RUST.

On a more limited basis, fragrant and lively reds are produced from Pinot Noir—known as Blauer Spätburgunder in Austria—or from Blaufränkisch, Portugieser, and St. Laurent. The white wines of GUMPOLDSKIRCHEN, south of Vienna, are particularly famous, as are those of KREMS and Dürnstein in the Wachau.

Fourteen growing areas have been delimited for wine production in Austria, which fall into four larger, more general regions. *Niederösterreich* (lower Austria): Krems, Langenlois, Klosterneuburg, Wachau, Falkenstein, Retz, Gumpoldskirchen, Vöslau. *Burgenland*: Rust-Neusiedler See, Eisenberg. *Steiermark* (Styria): Sudsteiermark, Weststeiermark, Klöch-Oststeiermark. *Wien* (Vienna).

Although Austrian wines are often compared to those of her neighbor Germany, the vast majority are fermented out to dryness and are somewhat higher in alcohol than German wines. Sweeter, rarer wines from great vintages are comparable to some of the world's best, and can live for decades.

Auxey-Duresses *(Oak'-say Dew-ress')*: Small hillside town in Burgundy's CÔTE DE BEAUNE, to the west of MEURSAULT. There are 370 acres of vineyard that produce good, light red wine; the best vineyards are rated Premier Cru (First Growth) and include: Les Duresses, Le Val, and Reugné. Annual production amounts to some 50,000 cases.

Avelsbach *(Ah'-vuhls-bock)*: Wine commune near the RUWER district, Germany; since 1971 officially part of the district of TRIER. Its wines are not well-known outside of Germany, but can be outstanding in good vintages. The vineyards (EINZELLAGEN) are Hammerstein, Altenberg, and Herrenberg.

15

Ayl *(I'll)*: Wine village in the SAAR district, Germany, with some 178 acres of vineyard, mostly planted in Riesling. Ayl often makes some of the Saar's finest wines; the most famous vineyards (EINZELLAGEN) are Kupp, Scheidterberg, and Herrenberger.

Baco Noir *(Bah'-co Nwar)*: Red HYBRID grape variety, developed at the turn of the century by François Baco from a cross between Folle Blanche and an American species, Riparia. Officially known as Baco No. 1, Baco Noir was one of the first French-American hybrids to be brought to the United States. Moderately resistant to frost, it gives very full-bodied red wines with a characteristic flavor. Another Baco variety, called 22 A, is used for Armagnac brandy production in France.

Badacsony *(Bad'-ah-chony)*: Wine area located on the north shore of Lake Balaton, Hungary; named after Mount Badacsony, an extinct volcano. Primarily white wines are produced, such as Riesling, which is called Badacsonyi Rizling, and two specialities: Badacsonyi Szürkebarat *(Soor-kee-ba-rat')*, a medium-dry white wine with an earthy bouquet, and Badacsonyi Keknyelu *(Kek'-nyuh-lew)*, a light dry wine.

Baden: Situated in southwestern Germany along the Rhine River, Baden is that country's third largest wine region. Previously, only tourists who visited Baden's famous Black Forest knew the delights of the wines, but Baden is now taking an active interest in exports and is moving in the direction of high-quality wines. Some 90% of all Baden wine comes from the Z.B.W. wine cooperative in Breisach.

The 1971 German Wine Law delimited Baden into several sub-districts or BEREICHE: *Bodensee*, along Lake Constance, noted for a light red wine called "Seewein"; MARKGRÄFLERLAND, to the south of the city of Freiburg, where the Gutedel (Chasselas) variety predominates; *Kaiserstuhl-Tuniberg*, named for the KAISERSTUHL, a volcanic hill where some of Baden's best wines are made from Ruländer (Pinot Gris); *Breisgau*, famous for a light rosé called WEISSHERBST; *Ortenau*, the home of Affenthaler, a local red wine shipped in an amusing "monkey bottle"; *Bergstrasse-Kraichgau*, around the city of Heidelberg; and *Badisches Frankenland*, further inland near the region of FRANKEN, which ships its wines in the squat BOCKSBEUTEL flask native to Franken. There are over 30,000 acres of vineyard in Baden; one-fourth of the wines are red, made mostly from Spätburgunder (Pinot Noir)—rare in Germany.

Bandol *(Bahn'-dol):* Located just to the west of Toulon on the French Mediterranean coast, Bandol is one of the better wines of PROVENCE, and it is rated APPELLATION CONTRÔLÉE. Also a resort area, the region produces red, white and rosé wines—the latter are perhaps the most famous. Principal grape varieties used in making red and rosé Bandol wines are Grenache and Mourvèdre; for white, Clairette and Ugni Blanc. The area under vines is 300 acres, and the average annual production is about 173,000 cases.

Banyuls *(Bahn-yulz'):* Sweet French FORTIFIED WINE produced south of Port-Vendres on the Mediterranean coast, near the Spanish border. One of several sweet wines (vins de liqueur) made within the area of Grand Roussillon, Banyuls is considered to be the best. It is grown on very steep, rocky hills extending over 6,920 acres.

Barbaresco *(Bar-ba-ress'-co):* Fine, full-bodied red wine from the district of PIEMONTE, Italy; produced from the Nebbiolo grape grown east of the city of Alba along the banks of the River Tánaro. Barbaresco is similar in style to its neighbor BAROLO, except that it is usually lighter and is apt to mature sooner. Under D.O.C. law, Barbaresco must have a minimum alcoholic strength of 12.5% and must be aged for a minimum of two years before release; if aged for three years or more, it may be sold as a *Riserva*. With an average annual production of 11,000 cases, producton of Barbaresco is only a fraction of Barolo's, making the wine relatively rare and fairly expensive.

Barbera *(Bar-bear'-ah):* Good-quality red wine grape, widely used in northern Italy and also in California, where some 20,400 acres have been planted. In PIEMONTE, where it is most successful, the wines entitled to D.O.C. are called Barbera d'Asti, Barbera di Monferato, and Barbera di Alba.

Bardolino *(Bar-do-leen'-o):* Attractive light red wine produced on the eastern shore of Lake Garda near Verona, Italy. Made from a blend of Corvina, Rondinella and Molinara grapes, like its neighbor VALPOLICELLA, it is best when consumed quite young—usually before it is three years old. Over a million cases a year are produced.

Barolo *(Ba-roll'-lo):* Outstanding red wine from the district of PIEMONTE, northern Italy; possibly the finest and richest of those produced from the Nebbiolo grape. A robust red wine that takes on delicious subtleties with age, Barolo is produced predominantly in the townships of Barolo, Castiglione Falletto and Serralunga d'Alba, within the province of Cuneo in southern Piemonte; by law it must attain a minimum alcoholic strength of 13%. Under D.O.C. law, Barolo must be aged at least three years prior to release, with at least two years in cask; if aged four years or more, it is allowed to be called *Riserva*. From 24,700 acres of vineyard, some 300,000 cases of Barolo are produced each year; many of the best Riservas are not normally consumed until a decade later.

Barsac *(Bar'-sack):* Commune in Bordeaux famous for its sweet white wines—the northernmost part of the district of SAUTERNES. Although Barsacs are legally entitled to the name Sauternes, most wines from this equally famous commune will bear the name Barsac.

In comparison to wines from Sauternes, Barsacs tend to be a bit drier. They are fine naturally sweet wines made from Sémillon, Sauvignon Blanc and Muscadelle grapes that have gained sweetness from the action of the "noble mold" (POURRITURE NOBLE).

The most famous Barsac estates or CHÂTEAUX are Coutet and Climens, classified as First Growths (Premiers Crus) in 1855. The Barsac châteaux rated Second Growth (Deuxième Cru) include Myrat, Doisy-Daëne, Doisy-Vedrines, Broustet, Nairac, Caillou, and Suau. Annual production of all Barsac averages about 183,000 cases per year.

Bâtard-Montrachet *(Bah'-tarr Mon-rah-shay'):* One of the best white wines of the CÔTE DE BEAUNE, Burgundy. Made from the Chardonnay grape, the wine often rivals even MONTRACHET, which is more famous. The Grand Cru (Great Growth) vineyard is 29 acres large, divided equally between the adjoining communes of PULIGNY- and CHASSAGNE-MONTRACHET; there are some 4,400 cases made each year.

Beaujolais *(Bo'-zho-lay):* Popular French wine, produced in the southern BURGUNDY district; almost all of the growing area is in the department of Rhône, although a small northern section lies in the department of Saône-et-Loire. Because of its early-maturing qualities, Beaujolais has become the ideal wine for

19

grover and consumer alike: it drinks best during its first year, and rapidly loses its fresh, fruity qualities with age. Like a number of light red wines, it is best served slightly chilled.

Red Beaujolais is produced from the Gamay grape, grown in a delimited area between the cities of Mâcon and Lyon. A very small quantity of white Beaujolais, known as Beaujolais Blanc, is produced from Chardonnay in the northernmost areas where the soil tends to be different. Because of the great world demand for the red wine—much of which is exported—production of Beaujolais Blanc only amounts to about 5% of the red.

The character and charm of Beaujolais derives in large part from the grape variety used, where it is grown, and the techniques used in production. The most important of these is known as "whole berry fermentation," or *macération carbonique* (carbonic maceration), which gives Beaujolais its characteristic, aromatic bouquet. Instead of being crushed, ripe grape bunches are left to ferment in a sealed tank, with the skins unbroken, for a period of about a week. After this initial fermentation, the grapes are pressed immediately and the juice is drawn off with a minimum of skin contact. This technique results in a soft, supple red wine with a full bouquet, but because the juice has very little contact with the skins, the wine is characteristically light and is deliberately produced for early consumption.

In terms of this early-maturing trait, the most popular form of Beaujolais is the NOUVEAU, or "vin de l'année"—the wine consumed in the same year it is made. Prior to the early 1970s this wine was primarily consumed only in local restaurants in the Lyon and Paris regions, but with the advent of rapid container transport and air freight, export of Beaujolais Nouveau soon became feasible. The wine is also known as Beaujolais *Primeur*, meaning that it is destined for immediate consumption, with the result that the terms nouveau and primeur have become interchangeable. This type of wine drinks best in its initial months and is not produced with any intent towards shelf life, but the best Beaujolais Nouveau keeps its fruity freshness for at least six months after release.

Basic grades of Beaujolais must attain a minimum alcoholic strength of 9%. If it has 10% alcohol it may be labeled "Beaujolais Supérieur." The most productive zone for Beaujolais is in the southern tier of the district, immediately west of Lyon, known as Bas-Beaujolais. The best wine is produced in the north, where the granitic soil and the rolling hills make for a longer-lived wine. Thirty-five townships or communes in this area are entitled to the appellation "Beaujolais-Villages"; their wines are superior because the vineyards produce less per acre, and the requirements for production are more stringent.

The finest Beaujolais, however, is not sold as Beaujolais at all, but goes under the name of nine *crus* (growths), which may legally be sold as Burgundies. Each represents an outstanding area within the Beaujolais-Villages, which produces fuller, finer and more expensive wine: BROUILLY, CÔTE DE BROUILLY, CHÉNAS, CHIROUBLES, FLEURIE, JULIÉNAS, MORGON, MOULIN-À-VENT, and SAINT-AMOUR. Unlike ordinary Beaujolais, wine from the crus tends to improve with age but will still mature faster than most other red Burgundies.

The Beaujolais region as a whole is one of the most productive wine districts in France. From some 42,000 acres of vineyard, almost 10 million cases of wine are produced annually—wine from the *grands crus* amounting to about one-tenth of the total.

Beaumes-de-Venise *(Bome duh Ven-neese'):* Famous vineyard area in the southern CÔTES-DU-RHÔNE district, France, extending over some 390 acres in the department of Vaucluse. The area produces one of the most celebrated

French FORTIFIED WINES, known as a *vin doux naturel*, prepared by adding spirit to partially fermented Muscat wine: it is sold as "Muscat de Beaumes-de-Venise." By law, the minimum alcoholic content must be 15%. Served chilled, the wine is lusciously sweet and has an extraordinary depth of flavor; although rare and costly, it is among the best of its type. Good examples are distributed by Jaboulet Aîné, Prosper Maufoux, and others recently introduced to the U.S. market.

In addition, the area also produces some dry red wine, sold under the name Beaumes-de-Venise.

Beaune (*Bone*): Picturesque city of some 20,000 in the department of CÔTE D'OR, France; the headquarters of the BURGUNDY wine trade. A charming city whose medieval character has been carefully preserved, Beaune gives its name to the CÔTE DE BEAUNE, the southern section of the Côte d'Or, and many of Burgundy's most important shippers have their cellars there. The city is also famous for a charity hospital, the HOSPICES DE BEAUNE or Hôtel de Dieu, which derives its income from a number of vineyard holdings. Each November, a general auction is held of the wines of the Hospices that tends to establish prices for the Burgundies of that vintage.

There are some 1,327 acres of vineyard in Beaune, most of them planted in Pinot Noir and devoted to red wine production, but a small amount of white wine is also grown from Chardonnay. The best vineyards, located above the city on a single, well-exposed hillside, are rated Premier Cru (first growth). Two of the most famous are the Fèves and GRÈVES vineyards, owned in part by the Hospices; the CLOS DES MOUCHES produces some superior white wine. Other excellent vineyards include CLOS DU ROI, BRESSANDES, Marconnets, Les Cent Vignes, Clos de la Mousse, Les Avaux, Theurons, Champ Pimonts (or Champimonts), Les Aigrots, Épenottes, Boucherottes, Les Couchereaux, and Les Chouacheux. Annual production amounts to 115,000 cases.

Beerenauslese *(Bearen-ouse'-lay-zeh)*: German for "berry selection." As specified in the 1971 German Wine Law, a wine labeled Beerenauslese is a special AUSLESE made from individually selected, fully ripened grapes affected by the "noble mold" (EDELFÄULE) and picked berry by berry. The resulting wine is rich and high in residual sugar; the legal minimum MUST WEIGHT must be about 120 (varies by area). Though rare and rather expensive, Beerenauslesen are among the world's greatest wines.

Bereich *(Buh-ryke')*: German for "area" or "region." As outlined in the 1971 German Wine Law, a Bereich is a sub-region within a larger ANBAUGEBIET (region under cultivation). It may extend over several wine-producing villages and vineyard areas within the Anbaugebiet that produce wines of similar type; however, these wines never carry the name of a single vineyard. See GROSSLAGE, EINZELLAGE.

Bergerac *(Bear'-shair-ack)*: City and viticultural area in the Périgord region, southwestern France, situated some 60 miles to the east of BORDEAUX. Whie most of Bergerac's wine is ordinary and is apt to be consumed locally, there are two exceptions: PÉCHARMANT, located to the north of the city and known for its red wines, and MONBAZILLAC, famous for its old château, which produces sweet white wines similar to SAUTERNES. The most basic wines are reds produced from Cabernet Sauvignon, Merlot, and Cabernet Franc, and white wines from Sauvignon Blanc or Sémillon, sold under the Bergerac appellation.

Bernkastel *(Beam'-cast'l)*: World-famous wine village in the MOSEL district, Germany, with some 500 acres of vineyard; linked by a bridge to its neighboring twin, Kues, across the Mosel. One of the largest towns on the Mosel and

23

possibly the most celebrated, Bernkastel extended its name considerably under the 1971 German Wine Law, to assist growers in marketing their wines. It is therefore important to understand the difference between wines actually grown in Bernkastel, and the regional "Bernkastelers" in general distribution.

Under the 1971 Wine Law, Bernkastel became a BEREICH or sub-region, extending throughout the Mittel-Mosel. While popular in the trade, the "Bernkasteler Rieslings" commonly encountered may be produced from any one of dozens of villages along the Mosel. More specific to Bernkastel are the two collective sites (GROSSLAGEN) that relate to vineyards in closer proximity to the town of Bernkastel itself: Bernkasteler Kurfürstlay and Bernkasteler Badstube. The latter site is superior, because it is restricted solely to the town of Bernkastel.

The finest wines generally come from the individual sites (EINZELLAGEN) in Bernkastel-Kues. The most famous of these, and usually among the most costly of all German wines, is Doktor, directly above the village. Other good Einzellagen include: Graben, Lay, Bratenhöfchen, Matheisbildchen, Johannisbrünnchen, Schlossberg, and Stephanus-Rosengärtchen; and, near Kues, the Einzellagen Rosenberg, Kardinalsberg, and Weissenstein.

At their best, the wines of Bernkastel are spicy, scented, and especially well-balanced; they are among the very finest wines produced from the Riesling grape. To be sure of getting the best, one should buy an estate-bottled wine (ERZEUGER-ABFÜLLUNG) from one of the more reliable producers or shippers.

Bienvenue-Bâtard-Montrachet *(Be-an-vay-noo' Bah'-tarr Mon-rah-shay')*: Excellent small vineyard (6 acres) in the commune of PULIGNY-MONTRACHET, in Burgundy's CÔTE DE BEAUNE. Until recently it was part of BÂTARD-MONTRACHET, but now the wines are sold separately. Like its neighbor, it is rated Grand Cru (Great Growth) and is in the same noble class; about 1,430 cases are made each year.

Bingen: Situated at the mouth of Germany's NAHE River where it meets the Rhine, Bingen is the most western part of the RHEINHESSEN region. Its soft, full-flavored white wines are among the best of the region, especially those produced near the Scharlachberg (scarlet mountain), a particularly well-exposed promontory overlooking the Rhine. Under the 1971 German Wine Law, Bingen also became the name of a BEREICH (sub-region), extending over many different villages, but some of the best wines come from approximately 800 acres around the city of Bingen itself. A number of major German exporters have their headquarters in Bingen, as there are extensive rail and shipping facilities. The leading individual vineyards (EINZELLAGEN) include: Scharlachberg, Schlossberg-Schwätzerchen, Kirchberg, Kapellenberg, Pfarrgarten, Bubenstück, Osterberg, and Schwarzenberg; one of the best growers is Weingut Villa Sachsen in Bingen, which produces a wide variety of quality wines from Riesling and other grape varieties.

Blagny *(Blahn'-yee):* Small hamlet (hameau) in the CÔTE DE BEAUNE, Burgundy, located on the boundary between PULIGNY-MONTRACHET and MEURSAULT. Both red and white wines are made in Blagny; the whites, made from the Chardonnay grape, are better-known. Under French law, wine from the section in Meursault is called "Meursault-Blagny" or just plain "Blagny"; in Puligny-Montrachet, "Puligny-Montrachet, Hameau de Blagny." The former is more common in the U.S.

Blanc de Blancs *(Blawn duh Blawn'):* A white wine produced exclusively from white grapes. Technically it is significant only in the French CHAMPAGNE country in the CÔTE DES BLANCS, where Chardonnay grapes are grown. Most

Champagne is made from Pinot Noir, a black grape (see BLANC DE NOIRS), and Champagnes made only from the Chardonnay are delicate, very distinguished and generally more expensive than those made from Pinot Noir.

In recent years, "Blanc de Blancs" has been used to label many white wines from other areas without any real justification, since outside the Champagne district almost all white wines are made from white grapes only.

Blanc de Noirs (*Blawn duh Nwar'*): A white wine made from black grapes. The term applies principally to French CHAMPAGNE, most of which is made from the juice of black grapes (Pinot Noir) removed from the skins and fermented separately so that the alcohol produced during fermentation does not extract any color from the skins.

Commercially, most French Champagne is a blend of Blanc de Noirs with some BLANC DE BLANCS to add delicacy, although there are some Champagnes made by small producers that are totally Blanc de Noirs. In the U.S., many producers use "Blanc de Noirs" to identify a sparkling wine made from Pinot Noir according to the traditional French Champagne process.

Blanc Fumé (*Blawn Foo-may'*): Local name for the Sauvignon Blanc grape grown in the district of Pouilly-sur-Loire in France's LOIRE River valley; the wine that it gives is called POUILLY-FUMÉ or "Pouilly-Blanc Fumé," to be distinguished from the region's more common wines that are made from the Chasselas and are known as Pouilly-sur-Loire.

To avoid a conflict with the French growers by calling their wine Pouilly-Fumé, Californian wineries often use the term Blanc Fumé to identify a VARIETAL wine made from the Sauvignon Blanc that is similar to the French.

Blaye (*Bly*): Viticultural district of Bordeaux, situated on the right bank of the GIRONDE estuary opposite the MÉDOC. The better wines of Blaye are red, and are called Premières Côtes de Blaye; they are fruity, supple, and generally inexpensive. In addition, a large quantity of lesser-quality white wine is produced, called Côtes de Blaye or "Blayais." Superior wine is made on estates or CHÂTEAUX, the best-known being Châteaux Barbé, Lescadre, Segonzac, and Le Menaudat.

Boal: see BUAL.

Bocksbeutel *(Bocks'-boy-tul):* The rounded, flask-shaped green bottle used for the white wines of FRANKEN (Franconia), Germany. The name is allegedly derived from the scrotum (Beutel) of a goat (Bock). Similarly-shaped bottles are used in Chile, Australia and Portugal.

Bodega *(Bo-day'-ga):* Spanish for "wine cellar," although in Spain a "cellar" is usually located above ground. In many Spanish-speaking countries, the term also applies to a large winery.

Body: The degree of concentration or substance in a wine, referring to the presence of alcohol and flavors. Rich red wines are generally full-bodied, but this is not always a distinction in certain white wines (such as those of the MOSEL), for they are prized for their light body and any unexpected fullness might be considered a defect.

Bonnes-Mares *(Bawn Marr'):* One of the very greatest red wines of the CÔTE DE NUITS, Burgundy, rated Grand Cru (Great Growth). Full and with a great depth of flavor, a good Bonnes-Mares takes on considerable complexity with age, and is long-lived. The vineyard extends over 37 acres, with 32 acres located in the commune of CHAMBOLLE-MUSIGNY and 5 acres in MOREY-ST. DENIS, to the north, where it borders the CLOS DE TART. About 5,400 cases are made each year.

Bonnezeaux *(Bonn-zo′):* Wine region in the CÔTEAUX DU LAYON district, near the LOIRE River. Bonnezeaux and nearby QUARTS DE CHAUME are considered the best white wine districts of the Côteaux du Layon, and have their own APPELLATION CONTRÔLÉES. Both are made from the Chenin Blanc, and in good vintages the grapes are harvested late, yielding fine, naturally sweet wines. About 250 acres are under vines in Bonnezeaux; there are some 12,000 cases of wine made each year.

Bordeaux *(Bor-doe′):* Important seaport city in southwestern France, situated on the GARONNE River; to the north, the Garonne meets the DORDOGNE River to form the GIRONDE, a tidal estuary and also the name of the department (administrative region) in which Bordeaux is located. The vineyard area entitled to the appellation Bordeaux is immense. One-third of all French wine exported to the United States comes from Bordeaux; from about 250,000 acres under vines, the average wine production is over 30 million cases.

Bordeaux produces a wide variety of red and white wines, though it is perhaps best-known for its reds, known popularly as "clarets." The most famous red wine district of Bordeaux is the MÉDOC, located to the north of city; the central portion is called the HAUT-MÉDOC, which consists of four principle communes; from north to south, they include: SAINT-ESTÈPHE, PAUILLAC, SAINT-JULIEN, and MARGAUX. Fine red wines are also made in GRAVES to the south of the city, and in the adjoining regions of SAINT-ÉMILION and POMEROL 25 miles to the east. The secondary red wine districts include BOURG and BLAYE, located on the right bank of the Gironde opposite the Mèdoc; FRONSAC, near Pomerol, and Premières Côtes de Bordeaux south of the city.

The best red Bordeaux wines from great vintages are slow to mature, and need several years of aging in bottle. They are made pri-

BORDEAUX

Shaded area indicates vineyards

marily from the Cabernet Sauvignon grape, a late-ripening variety that gives full, elegant wines, or the closely-related Cabernet Franc. The Merlot, an early-ripening grape prized for the soft, scented wines that it produces, is used principally in Saint-Émilion and Pomerol. Other red varieties include the Malbec and the Petit-Verdot. It is customary for most red Bordeaux to be made from a blend of these varieties, depending on the soil and the region in which they are grown.

Bordeaux is also noted for its white wines; the famous white Graves are very dry, while the regions of SAUTERNES and BARSAC near Graves specialize in sweet wines. The secondary white wine regions include CÉRONS and SAINTE-CROIX-DU-MONT close to Sauternes, and ENTRE-DEUX-MERS, "between two seas," located east of Bordeaux in the area between the Garonne and Dordogne Rivers.

The principal grape varieties used in making white Bordeaux are the Sauvignon Blanc and the Sémillon, which are used to make either the crisp, dry wines of Graves or the rich, sweet wines of Sauternes and Cérons. To make sweet wines, the grapes are harvested late when they are overripe. A third variety, the Muscadelle, is also used in the sweet wine districts but is less widely grown.

Almost any wine from Bordeaux is likely to be well-made, but superior wine bears the name of a specific region in Bordeaux from where it comes—the more information given on the label, the better the wine. The best Bordeaux wines are produced on estates called CHÂTEAUX. When the wine is bottled at the estate and not by a shipper in Bordeaux, its label will read: "MIS EN BOUTEILLE AU CHÂTEAU"—château-bottled—which is equivalent to ESTATE-BOTTLED wine in other districts. This system assures the authenticity of fine Bordeaux wines, and also controls quality; most of the great Bordeaux are château-bottled, but there are a few exceptions.

Botrytis Cinerea *(Bo-treet'-iss Sin-uh-ray'-uh)*: The botanical term for what is known as POURRITURE NOBLE in French and EDELFÄULE in German: "noble mold." It is found in many of the world's wine regions, but only in certain climates and under certain conditions is its action "noble," for rotting of the grapes is a constant fear of wine-growers. In the fall, following a period of warm weather and high humidity, the mold gathers on the skins of the grapes but does not rot them—instead, it causes the skins to shrink and the juice to become concentrated and high in sugar and extracts. It is essential to the manufacture of the best naturally sweet wines, which include the SAUTERNES and BARSACS of Bordeaux, the AUSLESEN of Germany, and the TOKAYS of Hungary. See also LATE HARVEST.

Botrytis is beneficial only to white grapes, most notably the Riesling, Sémillon, Sauvignon Blanc, and Chenin Blanc. During the 1970s, a number of excellent wines were produced from grapes affected by Botrytis in the United States.

Bouchet *(Boo-shay')*: The local name for the red Cabernet Franc grape in the SAINT-ÉMILION and POMEROL districts of Bordeaux.

Bouquet: The scent of a mature wine, to be distinguished from AROMA, which is given off by young wines. Chemically rather complex, bouquet is a product of bottle age, and most good wines will develop it to a certain degree if allowed to mature. It is created by slow oxidation of the alcohol, fruit acids and other compounds in the wine as it ages—this produces new compounds such as esters and aldehydes.

Wines will generally best display their bouquet if swirled in an appropriate glass, so that the volatile compounds may evaporate. Certain mature wines generally possess more bouquet than others, most notably those of MARGAUX (red) or the MOSEL (white).

31

Bourg: see CÔTES DE BOURG.

Bourgeois *(Boor'-zhwah):* French for "common" or "middle class." Though this term is legally applied to a grade of Bordeaux wine (Cru Bourgeois), most notably in the MÉDOC region, from the quality standpoint it is somewhat misleading. Wine from a Cru Bourgeois CHÂTEAU (or the slightly higher rank, Cru Bourgeois Supérieur) may not be common wine at all—in fact, from a good château in a fine vintage, the wine may occasionally be quite impressive, if not equal in quality to a CLASSIFIED GROWTH château.

Bourgogne *(Boor-gon'-yuh):* French for BURGUNDY. Bourgogne is also an APPELLATION CONTRÔLÉE, the legal designation for ordinary red or white wine produced within the specified area of Burgundy. Although these wines are not entitled to a COMMUNE appellation and are therefore not as good as other Burgundies from a more specific region, they are generally inexpensive. In poor vintages, or when there is over-production, many more famous Burgundies may have to be de-classified and given the simpler name "Bourgogne" if they do not meet the standards that apply to them. Wine with the appellation Bourgogne may be given the following designations:

—*Bourgogne.* Red or white wines produced exclusively within the region of Burgundy. The red wines must have a minimum alcoholic strength of 10%; the whites, 10½%.

—*Bourgogne Ordinaire* or *Bourgogne Grand Ordinaire.* Red, white or rosé wines, either declassified or else not meeting the standards for Bourgogne. The minimum alcoholic strength for red wines must be 9%; for whites, 9½%.

—*Bourgogne Aligoté* (white wines only). Wines from the secondary regions, made principally from the Aligoté grape and not the more distinguished Chardonnay, although some Chardonnay may be used. Minimum alcoholic strength: 9½%.

32

—*Bourgogne Passe-Tout-Grains* (red wines only). Wines made from Gamay and Pinot Noir grapes vatted together, with at least one-third Pinot Noir. Because in northern Burgundy the Gamay is more productive and produces lesser wines than the Pinot Noir, wines cannot be made entirely from the Gamay with good results, but as inexpensive table wine Passe-Tout-Grains serves a useful purpose. Minimum alcoholic strength: 9½%.

Bourgueil *(Boor-goy')*: Town and viticultural district of TOURAINE (a former province) on France's LOIRE River. The district includes two neighboring townships, Bourgueil and St. Nicolas-de-Bourgueil; the latter, being situated on hillier country with a higher concentration of chalk in the soil, is apt to produce better wine.

Along with CHINON to the south, Bourgueil generally makes the best red wines of the Loire. Both regions use the Cabernet Franc grape—called Breton locally—which is also used to make a lesser quantity of rosé. Often possessing a fine bouquet of raspberries, Bourgueils may be drunk young but the best improve with some bottle age.

Bouzy *(Boo-zee')*: Village in the French CHAMPAGNE district, located in the northern portion known as the MONTAGNE DE REIMS. In addition to being considered one of the best vineyard areas in the Montagne de Reims for growing red Pinot Noir grapes that are used in making Champagne, Bouzy is also celebrated for its still red wine, called Bouzy Rouge; fine and delicate, it is comparable to a light red Burgundy. Red Bouzys enjoy considerable local fame and are also very popular in Paris; recently some have been shipped to the U.S.

Brachetto *(Bra-kett'-o)*: Sparkling red wine from the region of PIEMONTE in northern Italy, named after the grape variety from which it is made. Superior Brachetto is produced near the

33

town of Acqui and is called Brachetto d'Acqui; it is entitled to D.O.C.

Brauneberg *(Brown'-uh-bairg):* Celebrated wine village of the MOSEL River valley, Germany. There are some 550 acres of vineyard around Brauneberg, four-fifths of them planted in Riesling. The wines are among the Mosel's best; they often rival those of BERNKASTEL, which lies four miles to the east. The leading vineyards (EINZELLAGEN) are: Juffer (the best-known), Juffer-Sonnenuhr, Hasenläufer, Kammer, and Klostergarten.

Bressandes *(Bres-sond'):* One of the fine red wines of the commune of ALOXE-CORTON, in Burgundy's CÔTE DE BEAUNE. The Bressandes vineyard extends over 42½ acres and lies near the famous CORTON vineyard; because the two land parcels share similar exposure and soil, the wines are sold either as "Corton Bressandes" or "Corton." They are scented and full-flavored Burgundies, slower to mature than most Côte de Beaune red wines.

There is also a Bressandes vineyard in the commune of BEAUNE to the south, rated Premier Cru (First Growth). It is not so well-known as Corton Bressandes but often produces similar wine.

Brix: Scale used in the U.S. to determine the MUST WEIGHT, or sugar content, of ripe grapes. Also known as "Balling," the Brix scale is based on the principle that a sugar solution has a higher density or specific gravity than the same quantity of distilled water. In establishing must weight, Brix is determined by the number of grams of sugar in solution per 100 grams of water, and may also be expressed as a percentage. In the vineyard, a small quantity of crushed grapes is placed in a calibrated HYDROMETER, known as a saccharometer, to enable the winegrower to determine if the grapes are ready to harvest. Since alcoholic fermentation will convert a given quantity of sugar into a known quantity of alcohol and carbon dioxide, the degree of Brix at harvest time also gives the winegrower an estimate of the eventual alcoholic content of the finished wine.

Brouilly *(Broo-yee′)*: Red wine district in the BEAUJOLAIS region, southern Burgundy, extending over some 2,160 acres. Officially classified as one of the nine *crus* (growths)—those areas that usually produce the best Beaujolais—Brouilly is the southernmost of these, and consists of five associated communes: Odenas, Saint-Lager, Cercié, Quincié, and Charentay. The center of Brouilly is a hill known as the CÔTE DE BROUILLY, a separate district.

Generally quick to mature, Brouillys are among the best-known and most attractive Beaujolais. Their fresh, fruity qualities make them most enjoyable rather soon after they are made. Over 750,000 cases are produced annually.

Brunello di Montalcino *(Brew-nel′-lo dee Mawn-tal-chee′-no)*: Rare, exquisite red wine from the district of TUSCANY, Italy; among the most costly of all Italian red wines. Named for the Brunello grape, a CLONE or sub-variety of Sangiovese, Brunello di Montalcino is produced from some 800 acres of vineyard around the little village of Montalcino in southern Tuscany; less than 125,000 cases are made each year. By law, the wine may not be sold until it is at least four years old, and must have a minimum of 12.5% alcohol prior to release. With five or more years aging, Brunello di Montalcino may be sold as a *Riserva*. The wine has a rich, dark color in good vintages, and enough tannin to assure development in bottle for decades. The wine's great fame is due in large part to the Biondi-Santi family in Montalcino, who were originally responsible for isolating the Brunello grape in the 1880s and encouraging its cultivation. Today their estate, "Il Greppo," is among several fine producers, including the Colombini family (Fattoria di

Barbi), Constanti, Poggia alla Mura, Silvio Nardi, Tenuta Argiano, Val di Suga, and other notable wineries. The wine was among Italy's first to achieve the coveted *garantita* (D.O.C.G.) status in 1980.

Brut *(Brute):* French for "natural" or "unrefined," employed in the CHAMPAGNE district to designate the driest wines. Brut is drier than "Extra Dry," although the latter is often incorrectly assumed to indicate the driest Champagnes.

When a Champagne is ready for market, it normally receives a small amount of sugar solution prior to being shipped: the "liqueur d'expédition." Brut Champagnes receive a minimum amount of sweetening, and are therefore the driest. In the trade, the term Brut is used for both vintage and non-vintage Champagnes, as well as other sparkling wines.

Bual (also **Boal**): A sweet type of MADEIRA, with a fragrant bouquet and a golden color. It is generally served as a dessert wine.

Bulgaria: Although Bulgaria is one of the world's oldest wine-producing areas, many centuries of Moslem rule prohibited wine drinking and frustrated large-scale vineyards until quite recently. After World War II, with a nationalized wine industry and modern winemaking techniques, Bulgaria rose to sixth place among the world's wine exporting nations. Presently there are over 422,000 acres of vineyards, most of them located in the central plains east of Sofia, the capital.

Bulgarian wines are usually named after the grape varieties from which they are made. White wines are produced from Chardonnay, Italian Riesling, Dimiat, and a local variety of Muscat known as Misket. The red wines include Cabernet, Pamid, Gamza, and two uniquely Bulgarian specialties: Mavrud, a dark, flavorful wine, and Melnik, a strong, full-bodied wine made near the town of the same name.

Burgenland *(Boor'-gen-lond):* Major Austrian wine district, located around the Neusiedlersee (Lake Neusiedl), south of the city of Vienna along the Hungarian border. Lake Neusiedl's shallow depth, combined with its protected location and special climate, encourages the production of high-quality wines: it was here that the first late-harvested wines, known as AUS-BRUCH, were produced in the 16th century. There are some 39,000 acres of vineyard in Burgenland; traditionally the most famous wine town is RUST, on the western shores of Lake Neusiedl, with comparable wines produced in the villages of Oggau and Mörbisch, immediately to the north and south of Rust. Other notable Burgenland wine towns include: St. Margarethen, Siegendorf, Mattersburg, Pöttelsdorf, Apetlon, Donnerskirchen and Podersdorf.

Burgundy (French, **Bourgogne**): Historic old French province, now divided into smaller separate districts or departments, each of them a producer of wine. Specifically, Burgundy refers only to these regions in France; elsewhere, "burgundy" is used loosely as a GENERIC term to indicate red wine of almost any type. But Burgundy also makes white wines that are among the world's greatest.

The Burgundy vineyards extend over 160 miles south from Auxerre in the department of the Yonne practically down to the city of Lyon. CHABLIS in the Yonne, renowned for its fine white wines, is Burgundy's most northerly wine region. The center of Burgundy is the CÔTE D'OR, to the north and south of the city of BEAUNE, an area that produces some of the region's most famous wines. In the Côte d'Or fine red wines are made in the CÔTE DE NUITS, the northern section, and red and white wines are produced in the southern section—the CÔTE DE BEAUNE.

37

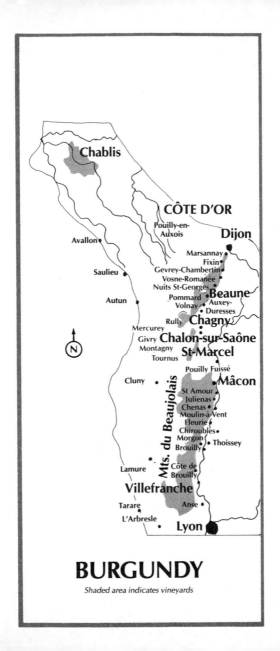

BURGUNDY

Shaded area indicates vineyards

South of the Côte d'Or is the CHALONNAIS region, named after the city of Chalon-sur-Saône. It consists of four vineyard areas: RULLY, MERCUREY, GIVRY, and MONTAGNY. Further south, the viticultural region of MÂCON, called "Mâconnais" in French, yields some excellent white wines; POUILLY-FUISSÉ is perhaps the most famous, with POUILLY-LOCHÉ, POUILLY-VINZELLES, and SAINT-VÉRAN close equals. White Mâcon (Mâcon blanc) comes from a much larger area. The vineyards of BEAUJOLAIS are located principally in the department of the Rhône north of Lyon, and mark the southern limit of the Burgundy region. In all, Burgundy has about 76,600 acres of vineyard, most of them under their own APPELLATION CONTRÔLÉES.

Though soil and climate are largely responsible for Burgundy's excellent wines, the grape varieties used in making them are equally important. Burgundy's best red wines are usually made only from the Pinot Noir, especially in the Côte d'Or, where it gives full, fruity and vigorous wines. Although the Gamay is a secondary variety in the Côte d'Or, it thrives in the Beaujolais and there it gives better wine than the Pinot Noir. The Chardonnay (or Pinot Chardonnay) is a noble variety grown nearly everywhere in Burgundy, where it gives the best white wines. Secondary white wines are made from the Aligoté.

Good, authentic Burgundy, despite its considerable fame, is a relatively rare wine. Grown in a cool inland climate, much of it comes from small scattered vineyards whose quality and output varies greatly from year to year. Thus, the more specific information indicated on the label, the better the wine, because its origins can be identified more precisely. This applies to all wines, but because of the diversity of the vineyards, it has special significance in Burgundy.

Cabernet Franc (*Cab'-air-nay Fronc*): Fine red grape variety, widely cultivated in the BORDEAUX region. The Cabernet Franc is a close relative of the famous Cabernet Sauvignon, and shares many of its noble characteristics; as its wine is slightly softer, it is usually blended with Cabernet Sauvignon to give balance to Bordeaux wines. In the SAINT-ÉMILION and POMEROL districts of Bordeaux, it is called Bouchet. The Cabernet Franc is also grown in the LOIRE River valley, where it is known locally as Breton. Important new plantations have recently been made in California.

Cabernet Sauvignon (*Cab'-air-nay So'-vin-yawn*): Premium red grape variety, one of the most important of several grape varieties used in blends to make the fine red wines of BORDEAUX, especially those of MEDOC and GRAVES. Though it ripens relatively late and its yield is small, the wine that it gives has a great deal of strength and character. When it is young, wine made from Cabernet Sauvignon has considerable tannin and astringency, and usually requires some aging in cask and in bottle. Depending on the vintage, good Cabernet Sauvignons can mature for decades.

Although Cabernet Sauvignon is not planted extensively in France outside of the Bordeaux region, it adapts well to different climates and gives fine results in Chile, Australia, Italy, Argentina, and the United States. It gives outstanding wines in California, where some 22,800 acres have been planted, and is one of the top varietals there.

Cahors *(Kah-or')*: City and wine district in southwestern France, located along the River Lot, which eventually flows into the GARONNE. The rich, dark red wines of Cahors, still as yet little known even in France, are celebrated *vins noirs*, or "black wines"; they are made predominantly from the Malbec grape, known locally as Cot or Auxerrois, to which Merlot and a local variety, Tannat, is customarily added for complexity. The best Cahors have a deep, dark color and plenty of tannin to assure long life. They mature beautifully after a few years in bottle.

Long considered worthy of only V.D.Q.S. status, the region of Cahors became an APPELLATION CONTRÔLÉE in 1971, after showing considerable improvement in quality over several decades. The vineyard area presently covers some 8,000 acres, but only about a tenth of the potential acreage is now under vines. Some 200,000 cases of Cahors are produced each year; the best wines are CHÂTEAU-BOTTLED, from better growers such as Georges Vigouroux (Château de Haute-Serre), Jean Jouffreau (Clos du Gamot, Château du Cayrou), Baldès (Clos Triguedina), Tesseydre, Pontié, Bouloumie, and several others. On a much larger scale, there are some cooperative cellars that collectively vinify over a third of the region's total production.

Cailleret *(Ky'-uh-ray)*: French for "clot" or "curdle"; also the name of several vineyards in the CÔTE DE BEAUNE, Burgundy. The most famous is in the commune of VOLNAY and is known as Volnay Caillerets; made from the Pinot Noir grape, it is one of the best red wines of the Côte de Beaune.

There are also two other vineyards named Cailleret in PULIGNY-MONTRACHET and CHASSAGNE-MONTRACHET to the south; planted in white Chardonnay grapes, both vineyards are noted for their wine. The name Cailleret is said to originate from Burgundian humor, so bawdy that it can turn wine into vinegar.

Calabria (*Ka-la'-bree-ah*): The southern-most part of the Italian mainland—the "toe" of the Italian "boot." With its hot, dry climate, Calabria is primarily a producer of ordinary wines, but there are two exceptions. CIRÒ, a red, white or rosé wine, is rated D.O.C. Greco di Gerace, a rare sweet white wine made from Greco grapes, has been famous since Roman times. Calabria as a whole produces the equivalent of 12 million cases of wine a year.

Caldaro (*Cal-dar'-o*): Small town in the ALTO ADIGE region, northern Italy; also a lake (Lago di Caldaro) three miles to the south. Two D.O.C. wines may carry this name: Caldaro, a light red wine made from the Schiava grape, and Lago di Caldaro; the latter is apt to be somewhat finer. Because of Alto Adige's large German-speaking population, Caldaro and Lago di Caldaro may sometimes be called Kalterer and Kalterersee, respectively.

California: America's most important wine-producing state, both in terms of vineyard acreage (over 684,000 acres, about half planted in wine grapes), and their contribution to our total consumption. Winemaking in California reflects a heritage more than two centuries old; during the 1970s there was a virtual explosion of new wineries in the state, many of them only now beginning to release their wines on the market for the first time.

Most of California is ideal for vineyards. The state as a whole benefits from a mediterranean climate, and only in certain areas to the north is it too cold or rainy for the highest quality wines. The industry got its start in the 18th century, when Franciscan missionaries brought vines from Mexico, to supply the chain of missions in what was then Spanish-held territory. After California achieved statehood in 1850, Hungarian-born entrepreneur

Agoston Haraszthy, often called "the father of California winemaking," helped establish a number of wineries and in the 1860s was commissioned to import hundreds of thousands of vines from Europe, to formally establish the California wine industry. Thus, although California has some wild grapes of her own, it was really the importation of the VINIFERA grape varieties of Europe that established the state as a wine producer.

Until the 1960s, the production in California of sweet DESSERT WINES outclassed that of table wines, reflecting a modest public demand for "port" and "sherry" that could be produced inexpensively in the state. In the past few decades this trend was dramatically reversed, and dessert wine production continues to diminish in favor of table wines. Public preference for high-quality table wines, combined with the "white wine boom" of the 1970s, encouraged the largest wineries to expand their output considerably, as it prompted many others to establish new wineries in areas where grapes had never been planted before.

Since California initially looked to Europe for quality standards, the wines originally were sold with GENERIC labels, identifying a "class" or type of wine, as opposed to one from a specific geographical area—such as sauterne, rhine, or burgundy. Until very recently, this form of labeling continued because winemakers believed that consumers could not otherwise identify the wines they wanted. In the 1940s some California wineries first released wines under VARIETAL labels, identifying the grape variety used, and as the industry grew after World War II, there was less need for generic labeling. In January, 1983, minimum requirements for varietal wines increased from the old standard of 51% to 75%, in efforts towards uniformity among various producers and also to increase the overall quality of wines sold under a varietal label.

Generic labeling is steadily being phased

43

Mendocino

Lake

Sonoma

Napa

Solano

Marin

Contra Costa

San Francisco

San Mateo

San Jose

Santa Cruz

Monterey • Salinas

COAST

Sacramento

Stockton

San Joaquin

Modesto

RANGES

Alameda

Santa Clara

San Benito

Me

N

**CALIFORNIA
(Northern)**

Sa
Ob

S

Shaded area indicates vineya

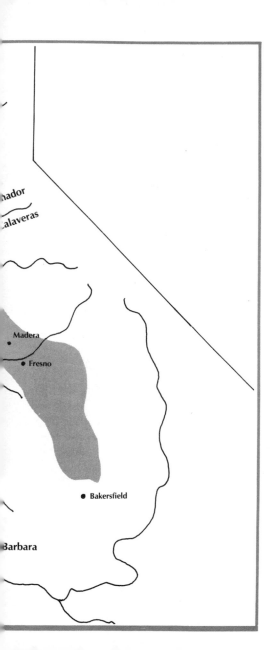

mador
Calaveras

• Madera

• Fresno

• Bakersfield

Barbara

out by many of California's better wineries. Instead, their most basic products bear proprietary labels like "classic white," "premium red," or even, simply, "white table wine"; varietal labeling is reserved for their finest releases. The new minimum varietal labeling requirements will not pose a hardship for most California producers, because they already meet or exceed federal standards.

Since California has so many different wine regions, not all grapes are right for a specific location or climate. In the 1930s, specialists at the University of California at Davis prepared a system for classifying regions for grape-growing, by which five regions were devised according to the degree of sunshine they received in a typical growing season (see DEGREE DAY). The highest-quality table wines come from cooler climates, identified as regions I and II, where more temperate heat and rainfall patterns produce the highest-quality fruit. Other grape varieties do better in warmer growing areas, such as regions III and IV, where they may be assisted to a certain extent by different vine training methods, or irrigation.

California's finest wines have been produced from grape varieties that are traditional in Europe's most famous winegrowing regions: for whites, Chardonnay, Sauvignon Blanc, Johannisberg (White) Riesling, and Gewürztraminer; for reds, Cabernet Sauvignon, Pinot Noir, and Merlot. When grown in cooler growing districts in California, their quality often rivals Europe's best. California's unique red wine grape, Zinfandel, produces a very individual red wine; its origins may be uncertain but its reputation is unquestionable. Other varieties, in the past called "standard varietals" because they were usually used for inexpensive wines, have shown excellent results when grown in certain select areas and vinified correctly. White varieties include Chenin Blanc, French Colombard, Ugni Blanc (St. Emilion), Folle Blanche, Green Hungarian and Sylvaner; red varieties include Barbera, Carignane, Gamay, and Petite Sirah. Very often, wines from these grapes, in certain vintages, outclass the so-called premium varietals.

In California's warmest growing districts, it is often very difficult to develop proper color in red grapes, or acidity in whites. In response, scientists at the University of California developed a series of new grapes, by crossing vinifera varieties with one another. The earliest were Ruby Cabernet (red) and Emerald Riesling (white), followed by Flora, Carnelian, Centurion, and Carmine. So far only a few of these grapes have been released varietally, their production being destined for commercial blends, but in certain climates they show considerable promise.

Tremendous strides have been made in California to increase the quality of sparkling wine production. The best sparkling wines are produced by the classical method of bottle fermentation used in the French CHAMPAGNE district, but good results can be obtained with other methods that do not require so much time to produce. Several French Champagne producers promoted ventures in the 1970s to make high-quality sparkling wines under license in California. While these are not sold under the name Champagne, they are clearly among the best of their type.

California has greatly expanded vineyard acreage in many counties during the past few years. In the "North Coast Counties" around San Francisco, vineyards are already at their maximum state of development, and the expansion of housing poses a constant problem. Now, many grape growers are looking further to the south and to the north. Recent growing areas that have already contributed to increased wine production are in AMADOR, LAKE, SAN LUIS OBISPO, SAN BENITO, SANTA BARBARA, Santa Maria and TEMECULA.

But the traditional growing areas still play a dominant role in high-quality wine produc-

47

tion in California. The "North Coast Counties" collectively make up quite a large vineyard area, and recently efforts have been made to designate specific, unique viticultural zones within each county, in a move towards more exact place-names under which the wines are to be sold. Currently, the most important include MENDOCINO, NAPA, SONOMA, ALAMEDA, SANTA CLARA, SANTA CRUZ, and MONTEREY. These wine districts are strongly influenced by the Coast Range mountains and typically have a fairly cool climate during the growing season, which results in highest quality wines.

A vast majority of the most basic California wines is produced in the wide, fertile CENTRAL VALLEY, where major corporations employ the latest in winemaking technology to produce consistently affordable wines of remarkably good quality, for everyday use. Many of the most familiar of these bear generic labeling, but good-quality varietal wines are becoming increasingly popular in this category. In the past, the overly warm, dry climate posed severe limitations for the best wines, but refrigeration and temperature control in many wineries overcome many of the problems associated with too much heat, and newer grape varieties give excellent results in these areas. In this respect, California is a model for other wine districts to follow.

The associated table and raisin grape industry plays a major role in California's economy, and for many years it was difficult to determine the direction that many California grape growers wanted to take, with possible outlets in the table grape and raisin industries for their products. The present demand tends to keep each industry separate, with its own requirements for production and marketing, and under these circumstances the wine industry is sure to continue its rapid growth.

In California, as in many other wine regions in the United States, the name of a winery essentially becomes that of a brand name, which tends to surpass area of origin in importance. A complete roster of each California winery would fill many pages, and therefore they are listed in connection with the county or area where they are located.

Caluso Passito (*Ca-loo'-so Pah-see'-toe*): Sweet white dessert wine made near the town of Caluso in PIEMONTE, northern Italy. To make the wine, white Erbaluce grapes are dried on indoor racks during the winter to concentrate their sugar, and in the following spring are made into wine. Caluso Passito, which is rated D.O.C., is not normally sold until after five years.

Campania (*Cam-pahn'-ee-ah*): Wine region in southwest Italy, with an annual production totaling more than 30 million cases of wine a year. Its principal city is the port of Naples (Napoli); in the region's predominantly volcanic soil, the vine today is as abundant as it was in Greek and Roman times, and Campanian wines have strength and character.

Traditionally, a famous Campanian wine is LACRIMA CHRISTI, grown on the slopes of Mt. Vesuvius, which may be red, white or rosé; the name means literally "Christ's Tears." The wines of the little island of ISCHIA in the Bay of Naples can often be good; particularly the whites, which are rated D.O.C. The neighboring island of Capri to the south also produces a fine white wine of the same name, made from Greco grapes. One of the best Greco wines comes from further inland, near the little town of Tufo; connoisseurs consider the fine GRECO DI TUFO to be among Italy's best whites. TAURASI, a robust red wine made from Aglianico grapes, is produced nearby; some excellent Greco di Tufos and Taurasis are made by the Mastroberardino family, who also produce the rare white wine Fiano di Avellino. Gragnano, a light red wine produced near Naples, is pleasant to drink but not widely exported. Though

49

not officially rated D.O.C., the wines of RAV-ELLO, grown on a peninsula between Salerno and Capri, are occasionally exported.

Canada: The cold North American continental climate limits grape-growing in Canada to those areas where mountain barriers or large water bodies protect the vineyards from temperature extremes. But Canada's close association with French culture naturally involved an interest in winemaking, and the industry dates back as early as 1811. The country presently has over 30,000 acres of vineyard, spread out in different sections of the nation, and along with domestic consumption, exports are increasing.

Over three-fourths of Canada's wine is produced in the Niagara Peninsula between Lake Erie and Lake Ontario, where the lakes temper the cold north winds. Traditionally, native American grape varieties (Concord, Catawba) have been grown there, but they are being supplanted by French-American hybrids, which combine winter hardiness with improved taste characteristics. Vineyards have also been planted in the Okanagan Valley in British Columbia, and when sufficiently protected from winter cold, even the VINIFERA varieties give good results. Ontario is another important wine district, especially for sparkling wine. The nation has over thirty bonded wineries, and as their output increases, so will their reputation.

Cantenac (*Cahnt'-nack*): Red wine commune in the HAUT-MÉDOC, north of BORDEAUX. Cantenac adjoins MARGAUX and its wines are entitled to this appellation; the commune is sometimes called Cantenac-Margaux. There are many famous wine estates or CHÂTEAUX; the ones that were officially ranked in the 1855 Bordeaux classification include Châteaux Brane-Cantenac, Kirwan, d'Issan, Cantenac-Brown, Boyd-Cantenac, Palmer, Pouget, and Prieuré-Lichine.

Cantina *(Can-tee'-na):* Italian for "winery" or "cellar." A "cantina sociale" is a wine growers' cooperative.

Capsule: The seal over the mouth of a corked wine bottle. It may be made of lead or aluminum foil, or, most recently, plastic.

Carbonic Maceration: Method of alcoholic fermentation commonly employed in the BEAUJOLAIS district of France; also called "whole berry" fermentation. The French term is *macération carbonique.* Instead of the usual procedure of crushing red grapes so that the fermenting juice stays in contact with the skins, ripe grape bunches are left in sealed tanks without being crushed, for a period of about seven days. Fermentation takes place very slowly in the tank, under a blanket of carbon dioxide. After a week the grapes are pressed and the juice is allowed to continue fermenting to dryness. Since very little tannin and extract is available though carbonic maceration, the method is usually performed only on wines destined to be consumed during their first or second year, and also on wines produced from light red grapes like Gamay, whose fruit is enhanced considerably by the process.

Carignan *(Cahr'-reen-yahn):* Productive red grape variety, grown extensively in the French MIDI also in Algeria, Spain and California. Though not a noble variety, it is well-suited to warm climates, and generally produces sound, sturdy wines. After Zinfandel, it is the second most widely planted red grape variety in California, where it is called Carignane: over 25,000 acres have been planted.

Case: A wooden or cardboard container of bottled wine, as prepared for shipment and distribution. A case of standard-sized bottles contains 9 liters of wine, bottled in 12 bottles of 750 ml (25.4 oz) each; this corresponds to 2.38 U.S. gallons, the older liquid measure used in the American wine trade before metric standards took effect on January 1, 1979. Other sizes are half-bottles (375 ml), which come 24 to the case, and magnums (1.5 liters, or 50.7 oz), which come 6 to the case. The two largest case containers are those with 3-liters (12 liters to the case), or the large 4-liter bottles (16 liters to the case), which replace the older gallon sizes. In this dictionary, because bottle sizes vary, production statistics for various wine regions have been converted into cases, rather than bottles, for simplicity.

Cases containing non-standard bottle sizes that were assembled prior to January 1, 1979 may be imported and distributed in this country, provided that they be accompanied by an official bottling certificate, issued by the producer, stating that the wine was bottled prior to the time metric sizes became standard in the U.S.

Cask: Rounded wooden vessels in which wine has traditionally been fermented and aged. The size of a cask varies by country and also by region, ranging from the diminutive *feuillette* of the CHABLIS region (equivalent to 15 cases) to the huge *Doppelstück* of the Rhine (equivalent to 275 cases). In BORDEAUX, the standard cask is the *barrique* (equivalent to 24 cases), which is similar to the *pièce* of BURGUNDY. Four barriques comprise a TONNEAU—the traditional measure of production in Bordeaux.

Of the various woods used for casks, oak is acknowledged to be the best, as it imparts an agreeable flavor to the wine. Recent experiments have shown that the type of oak used is highly important to the quality of the finished wine.

While wood casks are still the best containers in which to age fine wine, stainless steel fermenting tanks allow better temperature control and are rapidly replacing wood fermenting tanks in many parts of the world.

Cassis *(Cas-seese')*: Charming little seaport town in PROVENCE, southern France, on the

Mediterranean coast; also the name of the wines made in its environs. An important fishing village, Cassis produces red, white and rosé wines, but the whites are the most famous. They are made principally from the Ugni Blanc grape, though other varieties may be used. The Cassis vineyards lie to the north of the town and extend over some 370 acres; average annual wine production amounts to over 57,000 cases, white wine accounting for about one-third of the total.

Cassis is also the name of a sweet liqueur made from blackcurrants, produced in the BURGUNDY region in France. It is mixed with a light white wine to make the aperitif KIR.

Castelli di Jesi (*Cas-stell'-ee dee Yay'-zee*): Wine district in the region of MARCHE, central Italy, west of the town of Ancona. It is the principal production zone for the white wine VERDIC-CHIO, and many Verdicchios are labeled "Verdicchio dei Castelli di Jesi" to be distinguished from the less well-known "Verdicchio di Matelica," which is made south of the Castelli di Jesi region. Both wines are rated D.O.C.

Castelli Romani (*Cas-stell'-ee Ro-mahn'-nee*): Italian for "Roman Castles"; also the general term for the many good white wines made in the hilly country to the south of Rome. Not all of them are exported or even bottled, but those that are usually are well-made and represent good value; they tend to be semi-dry or *abboccato*. The best and most famous is FRASCATI; notable Castelli Romani wines entitled to D.O.C. include COLLI ALBANI, Marino, Colli Lanuvini, Zagarolo, and several others.

Catalonia (*Cat-ah-loon'-ya*): Region in northeastern Spain, of which Barcelona is the principal city. Catalonia is spelled Cataluña in Spanish and its native language is Catalan; the limits of the region are said to be defined by the extent to which Catalan is spoken.

Catalonia has four principal wine districts.

53

To the north of Barcelona is Alella, Spain's smallest wine region, located along the Mediterranean coast. Alella is known primarily for its excellent white wines. South of Barcelona is the much larger Penedés region, where there is an important concentration of sparkling wine production: the city of San Sadurni de Noya is the home of some of Spain's largest and most famous sparkling wine producers: Codorniu, Freixenet, and Segura Viudas. Each specializes in bottle-fermented wines according to the traditional Champagne process. Nearby, in Villafranca del Penedés, is the famous producer Torres, established in 1870 and now a major supplier to the U.S. market. Their traditional branded red wines ("Sangre de Toro" and "Coronas"), and the white "Vina Sol," have recently been supplanted by some especially good wines produced by the traditional French varieties: Pinot Noir, Cabernet Sauvignon, Cabernet Franc, Gewürztraminer, Muscat, Riesling, and Merlot. The success of these wines, based on the initiative of winemaker Miguel Torres, should serve as a model for other Catalonian growers to follow.

Tarragona, both the name of a Catalonian province and an important city, produces a sweet fortified wine. The Priorato, a small mountainous region northwest of the city of Tarragona, is famous for its very rich, concentrated red wine. Catalonia has some good traditional grape varieties, such as Ull de Llebre, Parellada and Monastrell, in addition to Carignan (Cariñena) and Grenache (Garnacha); the success of the new European varieties in the area, however, may prompt a changeover in the near future.

Catawba (*Ca-taw'-ba*): Native American pink grape of the species LABRUSCA, widely used to make wine and grape juice in the eastern United States, especially in the New York Finger Lakes district and Ohio. Named after the Catawba River in North Carolina, it was first

54

cultivated in 1823 and quickly became a leading grape variety in several eastern states. It is also an important variety for sparkling wines.

Although technically a red grape, the Catawba is used to make red, white or rosé wines. It generally gives better white wine than red, and in making white Catawba wine the skins are removed prior to fermentation. White Catawba wine usually tends to be sweet or semi-sweet, with a characteristic flavor.

Cave *(Cahv)*: French for "cellar."

Central Valley: General term for the large, fertile area surrounding the San Joaquin Valley in California, beginning near Sacramento and extending south practically to the city of Los Angeles. The region is extremely productive: although rainfall is blocked by the mountain barrier of the Coast Range bordering the Pacific Ocean, irrigation makes the Central Valley the nation's foremost area for table and raisin grape production. Seven counties collectively make up the vineyard area; from north to south, they include Sacramento, San Joaquin, Merced, Stanislaus, Fresno, Tulare, and Kern, with a total of 462,000 acres of vineyard, much of them recently planted in wine grapes. Major Central Valley producers include: Ernest & Julio Gallo, Guild, Bear Mountain (M. Lamont), East Side, Franzia, and United Vintners.

Centrifuge: Device employed in many wineries to clarify crushed grape juice (must), or finished wine, using the principle of centrifugal force to rapidly precipitate solid matter out of suspension. A cylindrical vessel is rotated at high speed, and purified material is drawn from the top of the vessel once it slows down. A centrifuge has an advantage over conventional filters in that it does not subject wine to pressure or foreign matter that might be present in filter media, and it is a valuable tool in ridding wine from harmful bacteria or yeast

55

remainders that could act on wine following its release from the winery. See FILTRATION.

Cépage *(Say-pahj′)*: French for "grape variety." This term is often specified when several different grape varieties are employed in a vineyard—as is the practice in BORDEAUX.

Cérons *(Say-rawnss′)*: White wine region of BORDEAUX, located north of BARSAC on the left bank of the GARONNE River. The neighboring districts of Podensac and Illats lie within the delimited region of Cérons. Like Barsac, Cérons produces sweet white wines made from Sauvignon Blanc, Sémillon and Muscadelle grapes—except that the wines of Cérons tend to be less sweet than most Barsacs. Some dry Cérons is also made. Cérons wines are well-known in France, and they are also increasingly popular in America. The leading estates or CHÂTEAUX include Châteaux Haut-Mayne, de Cérons, Lamouroux, Haut-Rat, Grand-Enclos du château de Cérons, and Madère.

Chablis *(Shab-lee′)*: Small town in northeastern France, in the department of the Yonne, Burgundy; also the name of its famous white wine. Although "chablis" is produced in many other parts of the world—this GENERIC name describing virtually any dry white wine regardless of origin—the true Chablis of France is relatively rare. There are approximately 10,919 acres of vineyard under this appellation in Chablis; only about half are in full production, and output is often curbed by spring frosts. But a good Chablis ranks with the world's finest white wines.

Chablis may be produced from only one approved grape variety, the Chardonnay (which is called "Beaunois" in Chablis). The Chablis vineyards are located in 20 different communes on the banks of the Serein River, the central and most important being: Chablis, Maligny, La Chapelle-Vaupelteigne, Poinchy, Milly, Fyé, Chichée, and Fleys. The wines of Chablis are ranked according to quality:

—*Chablis Grand Cru.* The best Chablis, which is always identified by the names of seven vineyards: Bougros, Les Preuses, Vaudésir, Grenouilles, Valmur, Les Clos, and Blanchot. (La Moutonne, the proprietary name of a small vineyard parcel between Vaudésir and Les Preuses, is also rated Grand Cru but is relatively rare). Minimum alcoholic strength must be at least 11%; average production is about 45,000 cases.

—*Chablis Premier Cru.* This designation may appear by itself, or with a vineyard name added. (Note: Since 1966 several Premier Cru vineyards have been allowed to use the name of a more famous vineyard in close proximity. Though this usage is optional, many producers employ it, and in the following list the more famous vineyards are marked with an asterisk—subsequent names without asterisks are legally entitled to this name. The Premier Cru vineyards on the right bank of the Serein, near the Grand Crus, are considered superior.) *Right bank of the Serein:* Monts de Milieu*, Montée de Tonnerre*, Pied d'Aloup, Chapelot, Fourchaume*, Vaulorent, Côte de Fontenay, Vaupulent, L'Homme Mort, Vaucoupin*, Les Fourneaux*, Morein, Côtes des Près Girots. *Left bank of the Serein:* Vaillons*, Beugnons, Châtains, Séché, Les Lys, Montmains*, Les Forêts, Butteaux, Côte de Lechet*, Beauroy*, Troesmes, Vosgros*, Vaugiraud, Mélinots*, Roncières, Les Epinottes. Minimum alcoholic strength must be at least 10½%; average production is about 180,000 cases.

—*Chablis.* Wine from the designated communes of Chablis, which is never identified with a vineyard name. In poor vintages, Grand Cru or Premier Cru Chablis may have to be declassified to this category if it does not meet minimum standards. Minimum alcoholic strength must be at least 10%; average production is about 350,000 cases.

—Petit Chablis. Lesser wine from the outermost vineyards near the district boundary; not always bottled or exported. Minimum alcoholic strength must be at least 9½%; average production is the equivalent of 100,000 cases.

Chai *(Shay):* French for a storage place for wine above ground, as opposed to a CAVE, or cellar, which is usually located underground.

Chalonnais *(Shall-lon-nay'):* Vineyard area in central BURGUNDY, France. The Chalonnais region (or Côte Chalonnaise) lies to the west of the city of Chalon-sur-Saône, from which its name is derived. The region is noted for its good red wines, made from the Pinot Noir, and fine white wines made from the Chardonnay: in addition some rosé and sparkling wine is also produced. There are four principal wine districts that are entitled to APPELLATION CONTRÔLÉE, which are, from north to south: RULLY a producer of red and white wines, though the whites are better-known and amount to four-fifths of all the wine produced; MERCUREY, just to the south, famous for its red wines that are usually the best of the entire Chalonnais region; GIVRY, a source of equally good red and white wines, and finally MONTAGNY, the southernmost limit of the Chalonnais region, which is noted for its fine white wine.

Chambertin *(Shawm'-bear-tan):* World-famous vineyard in the northern COTE DE NUITS, Burgundy. It has been producing wine for over 1,000 years and is rated Grand Cru (Great Growth)—the highest classification for a Burgundy. Planted entirely in red Pinot Noir vines, the Chambertin vineyard extends over 32 acres; another great vineyard, the CLOS DE BÈZE (which because of its close proximity, and the similarity of its fine wines, is called Chambertin-Clos de Bèze) adjoins it just to the north. Surrounding the two Chambertin vineyards are several others, also rated Grand Cru but considered to be not quite in the same class:

LATRICIÈRES-CHAMBERTIN, CHARMES-CHAMBER-TIN, MAZOYÈRES-CHAMBERTIN, MAZIS-CHAMBER-TIN, CHAPELLE-CHAMBERTIN, GRIOTTE-CHAM-BERTIN, and RUCHOTTES-CHAMBERTIN. Each of these vineyards has legally attached the name Chambertin to show their relationship to their noble neighbor, as has the town of Gevrey to the north, which since 1847 has been called GEVREY-CHAMBERTIN. All of these vineyards lie within the Gevrey-Chambertin commune.

A Chambertin from a fine vintage is one of Burgundy's very greatest red wines—sturdy and full-bodied, with considerable character. About 3,600 cases are made each year.

Chambolle-Musigny (*Shawm'-boll Mooz'-een-ye*): Picturesque little hillside town and wine commune in the CÔTE DE NUITS, Burgundy, with some 432 acres of vineyard. Chambolle-Musigny takes its name from the great vine-yard MUSIGNY, one of Burgundy's best, which is rated Grand Cru (Great Growth); the commune's other Grand Cru, BONNES-MARES, is scarcely less famous. Two very fine Premier Cru (First Growth) vineyards, practically in the same class, are Les Amoureuses and Les Charmes, which lie close to Musigny. Chambolle-Musigny is renowned for its delicate and scented red wines made from the Pinot Noir, with the exception of a small amount of white wine, Musigny Blanc, which is made from the Chardonnay. Average annual production is about 40,000 cases.

Champagne (*Sham-pain'*): Of all the world's wines, Champagne is unquestionably the best-known, traditionally a beverage associated with festivity and gaiety. More precisely, Champagne is a uniquely French product, although its illustrious name has been borrowed by makers of sparkling wines all over the world who use the same process.

Despite its world-wide fame, French Champagne comes from a rather small area in northeastern France, and is made by a slow, methodical process. While sparkling wines are made elsewhere in France, they are called "vins mousseux" (sparkling wines) and if they are made by the same process as Champagne, "méthode champenoise," but not Champagne. See CRÉMANT.

The delimited area entitled to the appellation Champagne extends over 54,362 acres in the Marne River valley, within the departments of the Marne, Aube, Aisne and Seine-et-Marne. The department of the Marne is the most important area and produces 81% of all Champagne; it includes the famous "Champagne towns," Reims and Épernay, and has three principal vineyard areas. The northern section, which produces fine, full-bodied wines, is called the Montagne de Reims. The middle area, the Vallée de la Marne, lies on the right bank of the Marne River. Its vineyards have a southern exposure and yield soft, rounded wines. The southern area near Épernay is known as the "Côte des Blancs" because it is largely planted in white Chardonnay grapes; the Montagne de Reims and Vallée de la Marne are mainly planted in black grapes: Pinot Noir or Pinot Meunier, the only approved varieties.

Virtually all Champagne is white; a much lesser amount of still red and white wine, and pink Champagne, is made. Most of the white wines used in making Champagne come from black grapes; the Pinot Noir (or Pinot Meunier) grapes are pressed immediately after they are picked, yielding white juice (see BLANC DE NOIRS). A lesser amount of wine from Chardonnay is used, which is either blended with Pinot Noir to add finesse, or else is used exclusively on its own for especially light, delicate Champagnes (see BLANC DE BLANCS).

Each village in the Champagne district has been ranked according to the quality of its wines, by *crus* (growths). At harvest time, a committee of growers and merchants decides

N

REIMS •

Beaumont-
sur-Vesle
Sillery •
Puisieux •
• Verzenay
• Mailly

Forêt de la Montagne
de Reims

Louvois •
• Bouzy

VALÉE DE LA MARNE

Ambonnay

Ay •

Épernay •
Tours-sur-Marne

• Cramant
• Avize
La Côte des Blancs

CHAMPAGNE

Shaded area indicates vineyards

the price for one kilo of grapes, based on the quality of the vintage and market conditions. The highest-ranked villages, the Grands Crus, are rated 100%, which means that their grapes receive the full price. Next come the Premier Cru villages, rated 99% to 90%, which receive the corresponding fraction of the full price. Though lacking in finesse, the wines from the lesser communes are useful for adding strength to the blends. The towns rated Grand Cru (100%) are:

—*Montagne de Reims*: Beaumont-sur-Vesle, Mailly, Puisieulx, Sillery, Verzenay (Verzy: 99%).

—*Vallée de la Marne*: Ambonnay, Ay, Bouzy, Louvois, Tours-sur-Marne (Tauxières-Mutry: 99%).

—*Côte des Blancs*: Avize, Cramant (Le Mesnil-sur-Oger, Oger, and Oiry: 99%).

Most Champagne producers do not grow all their own grapes; instead, they buy direct from local vineyard owners who have holdings in the various communes. Each proprietor is paid according to the location of his holdings. When the grapes are taken to the presses, a record is kept of where they came from—this is vitally important later on, when the wines are blended.

At the harvest, the grapes are picked and the bunches examined so as to eliminate any unripe or sick berries (see ÉPLUCHAGE). They are then brought to the presses, and the expressed juice is taken to fermenting tanks where it turns into wine.

During the winter, Champagne is treated like any other still wine, but in the spring, when the process of blending or CUVÉE takes place, the Champagne process begins. Various blends are selected according to the "style" of the maker—which is the same each year—and are then given a precisely measured sugar and yeast solution: the LIQUEUR DE TIRAGE. This solution will ferment to produce alcohol and carbon dioxide gas, but because the wine is kept in tightly closed, heavy glass bottles, the gas is contained and the wine becomes sparkling. The bottles are then left in the chilly subterranean cellars to mature.

When the wines are ready for shipment, the sediment that was introduced during the secondary fermentation has to be removed. The process of removal is called REMUAGE. The bottles are placed in racks *(pupitres)* that can be tilted in order to collect the sediment at the cork. The bottles are given a slight twist periodically by skilled workmen, and after about 90 days all the sediment is collected on the cork, ready to be removed by the process of "disgorging" (DÉGORGEMENT). The bottles are then placed neck down into a freezing brine solution, and when uncorked, the sediment pops out in a frozen mass, leaving the wine perfectly clear.

Since some wine is lost during disgorging, this is replaced, along with another dose of sugar solution for shipment: the "shipping dosage" (LIQUEUR D'EXPÉDITION). Most Champagne is austerely dry, and the amount of shipping dosage relates to taste preferences in the country where the wine will be shipped. *Brut,* the driest, ranges from 0 to 1½% dosage; *Extra Dry,* from 1–2%; *Dry (Sec,* in French), from 2–4%; *Demi-Sec,* from 4–6%; and *Doux,* from 8—10%. (Demi-Sec and Doux Champagnes are generally too sweet for the U.S. market, and are mostly shipped to Latin America.) The English have traditionally preferred drier Champagnes, and some Brut Champagnes are labeled "prepared for the English market" to indicate extreme dryness.

Vintages vary in Champagne as they do in many other fine wine regions, but because all Champagne is blended, vintage years do not mean as much as they do elsewhere; in addition, up to 20% of a wine from a specified vintage may legally be wine from other vintages. Following an exceptional harvest, a vintage may be declared by the producers during the process of *cuvée* in the spring, but because only a few years produce vintage Champagnes, only superior wine will bear a vintage date; the other wines will be blended into non-vintage Champagne, the most important commercial grade.

The following list identifies the major Champagne producers with a nation-wide U.S. distribution. There are hundreds of different Champagne producers, but not all export their wines outside of France. Leading firms (*maisons*) are: Ayala, Billecart-Salmon, Bollinger, Canard-Duchêne, A. Charbaut & Fils, Veuve Clicquot-Ponsardin, Deutz & Geldermann, Delbeck, Henriot, Charles Heidsieck, Heidsieck Monopole, Jacquesson, Krug, Lanson, Laurent-Perrier, Mercier, Moët & Chandon, G. H. Mumm, Perrier-Jouët, Piper-Heidsieck, Pol Roger, Pommery & Greno, Louis Roederer, Ruinart Père & Fils, and Taittinger.

Champigny (*Shawm'-peen-ye*): Village in the LOIRE River valley, France, located southeast of SAUMUR in the district of ANJOU. Made from the Cabernet Franc grape, Champigny's fine red wines are Anjou's best. They are similar to the wines of CHINON upstream, except that Champignys are perhaps a bit lighter. Because Champigny's vineyards extend into the region of Saumur, the wines are often labeled Saumur-Champigny.

Chancellor Noir (Seibel 7053): Red HYBRID grape variety, originally developed in France by crossing two Seibel varieties, S. 5163 and S. 800. Chancellor Noir is one of the oldest of the French-American hybrids; it is grown primarily in non-appellation districts in southern France, but in the New York Finger Lakes district it has become one of the principal red varieties. Its medium-bodied wines recall a claret and are quite popular.

64

Chapelle-Chambertin (*Sha-pell' Shawm'-beartan*): Famous vineyard in the northern CÔTE

DE NUITS, Burgundy, rated Grand Cru (Great Growth). It extends over 13 acres, bounded on the west by the great CHAMBERTIN-CLOS DE BÈZE vineyard and on the south by GRIOTTE-CHAMBERTIN. Planted exclusively in Pinot Noir, Chapelle-Chambertin produces about 2,400 cases of excellent red wine annually.

Chaptalisation (*Shap-tally-zah'-see-yon*): The addition of sugar to grape must in order to increase the alcoholic strength of the wine. Chaptalisation (called *Gallization* in German) is named after a Frenchman, Dr. Jean Antoine Chaptal (1756–1832), minister of agriculture under Napoleon I, who wanted to simultaneously increase sugar beet acreage and improve the quality of wines made in years when the grapes do not ripen fully. It is a common practice in the making of red BURGUNDY wines, but the amount of sugar added may not exceed 3 kg. per hectoliter of must (6.6 lbs per 26.4 gallons). It is also permitted in BORDEAUX, though usually only in poor vintages. In Germany, sugaring of grape musts is performed regularly for ordinary wines (see TAFELWEIN, QUALITÄTSWEIN) but never for the best grades. Chaptalisation is not allowed in California, but it is permitted elsewhere in the U.S. where weather variations could affect the quality and the quantity of wine.

Charbono (*Shar-bo'-no*): Red wine grape, probably of Italian origin, which is grown primarily in the Napa Valley, California. The Charbono is very similar to the Barbera, and gives a robust, flavorful red table wine.

Chardonnay (*Shar'-doe-nay*): Outstanding white wine grape, used in making the best white wines of Burgundy in France (see MONTRACHET, MEURSAULT, CHABLIS, and POUILLY-FUISSÉ) and for the BLANC DE BLANCS of CHAMPAGNE. Transplanted from its home ground, it has proved to be one of America's best white wine grapes; when grown in cool climates, outstanding wines have been produced from Chardonnay, particularly in California, where over 17,000 acres have been planted: many California Chardonnays compare with the world's best. The grape's yield is small and it does not grow well in all locations, but the wines that it gives have incomparable finesse and elegance. While it is often called "Pinot Chardonnay," grape specialists (ampelographers) maintain that the Chardonnay technically is not a member of the Pinot family, so it is more correct to simply call it Chardonnay.

Charmat (Bulk) Process: A method of producing sparkling wines more quickly than by the laborious process used in the French CHAMpagne region; also called *"cuve close."* Still wine is introduced into closed tanks, where it is artificially aged before sugar and yeast is added to make the wine sparkling. No wines made by the Charmat process may be called Champagne in France, and U.S. law requires the lable "Bulk Process" on any sparkling wines made by this method.

Charmes-Chambertin (*Sharm Shawm'-beartan*): Excellent red wine vineyard in the northern CÔTE DE NUITS, Burgundy, rated Grand Cru (Great Growth). It adjoins MAZOYÈRES-CHAMBERTIN, another Grand Cru, and wines from the latter vineyard may legally be called Charmes-Chambertin; however, wines from the Charmes-Chambertin vineyard may not be labeled Mazoyères-Chambertin.

The name of both vineyards derives from the incomparable CHAMBERTIN vineyard, which borders Charmes-Chambertin to the west; LATRICIÈRES-CHAMBERTIN lies to the west of Mazoyères-Chambertin. Together, Charmes- and Mazoyères-Chambertin comprise some 78 acres and produce about 11,400 cases of fine, sturdy red wine annually.

Chassagne-Montrachet (*Sha-sign' Mon-rah-shay'*): Famous wine commune in the CÔTE DE

BEAUNE, Burgundy; noted for its extremely fine white wines made from the Chardonnay grape, in addition to excellent reds made from the Pinot Noir. Chassagne-Montrachet adjoins PULIGNY-MONTRACHET to the north, and both communes are named after the magnificent MONTRACHET—the leading Grand Cru (Great Growth) white wine vineyard of Burgundy. Part of the scarcely less famous Grand Cru BÂTARD-MONTRACHET also lies in Chassagne-Montrachet; yet another Grand Cru, CRIOTS-BÂTARD-MONTRACHET, is exclusive to the commune. Two excellent vineyards, RUCHOTTES and CAILLERETS, produce fine white wine that is rated Premier Cru (First Growth).

There are about 860 acres of vineyard in Chassagne-Montrachet; despite its many famous white wines, the commune actually produces almost twice as much red wine as white—the most eminent red wine vineyards are MORGEOT, Clos St. Jean, and La Boudriotte. About 134,000 cases of wine are made in Chassagne-Montrachet annually.

Chasselas (*Shass'-la*): Fine quality white table grape, used for wine in many parts of Europe. In northern France it gives light and attractive white wines, of which the best-known are POUILLY-SUR-LOIRE of upper Burgundy and CRÉPY of Savoy. In Germany the Chasselas is called GUTEDEL and it is widely grown in BADEN; in Switzerland near Lake Geneva it is called FENDANT in the canton of VALAIS and DORIN in the canton of VAUD, where it yields some of the best white wines of these regions.

Château (*Shot-toe'*): French for "castle"; specifically, in the BORDEAUX region, a wine estate in which a house (château) is associated with a vineyard. Under French law, the name of the château applies to the vineyard and the wines it produces, as well as the house (see CRU), but only if the vineyard and the house are mutually involved in wine production.

In many parts of Bordeaux the château is

67

a residential building without wine-making facilities, normally separate from the winery and storage area—the CHAI. Wine that is bottled by the proprietor at the estate is said to be CHÂTEAU-BOTTLED.

Château-Bottled: In the BORDEAUX region, a wine made by an estate or CHÂTEAU that has been bottled directly at the property. The system of bottling wines at the château assures their authenticity through guarantee of origin. Elsewhere, wines bottled at the property are said to be ESTATE-BOTTLED; some indication of château-bottling should usually appear on the label of a superior Bordeaux wine. If the wine has been so bottled, it will be labeled "Mis en Bouteilles au Château" or "Mis du Château."

Château-Chalon *(Shot-toe' Shall'-lawn)*: Rare, exceptionally long-lived white wine from the JURA district, France. Château-Chalon is not a CHÂTEAU-BOTTLED wine, but derives its name from the town where it is produced. Made from the Savagnin grape, the wine is kept in cask for at least six years, and matures through the action of FLOR yeast—the same kind found in Spain's SHERRY district. The French term for this special kind of wine is "vin jaune," and a unique bottle, the *clavelin*, is reserved exclusively for the vin jaunes of the Jura. Château-Chalon is a great rarity in the U.S. import trade, since less than 2,300 cases are produced annually.

Châteauneuf-du-Pape *(Shot-toe-nuff' dew Pop')*: World-famous wine of the southern RHÔNE valley, France. Châteauneuf-du-Pape, which means "new castle of the pope" in French, was named after the papal residence at Avignon during the 14th century. The region was the first in France to enact laws relating to wine-making practices—a move that led to the APPELLATION CONTRÔLÉE laws promulgated in 1935.

The vineyards of Châteauneuf-du-Pape extend over some 6,600 acres in the department of Vaucluse. The coarse, pebbly soil retains the sun's heat to ripen the grapes fully, yielding a wine with the highest minimum alcoholic strength (12.5%) of any French wine. 99% is red, but a little white wine is also made. Up to 13 grape varieties may be blended together to make the red wine; the most important is Syrah, but Mourvèdre, Grenache, Picpoul and Cinsault are other leading varieties.

The best Châteauneuf-du-Pape is generally made on estates that bottle their own wine; Chateau des Fines-Roches, Château Fortia, Domaine de Mont-Redon, Château de la Gardine, Château de Vaudieu, etc. Typically, the region as a whole produces over 750,000 cases of wine annually.

Chavignol *(Shav'-een-yawl)*: White wine commune in the upper LOIRE valley, near the village of SANCERRE. Planted exclusively in Sauvignon Blanc, Chavignol's vineyards lie within the area of Sancerre and are entitled to this appellation; in fact, one of the best Sancerre vineyards, Les Monts Damnés, is located in Chavignol.

Chelois *(Shel'-wah)* or Seibel 10878: Red HYBRID grape variety, originally developed in France at the turn of the century by crossing two Seibel hybrids, S. 5163 and S. 5593. An early-ripening variety, Chelois is planted predominantly in the New York State Finger Lakes district, in the midwest and in parts of Canada. It gives a good-quality red wine, in the style of a Burgundy.

Chénas *(Shay'-nah)*: Red wine district in the BEAUJOLAIS region, extending over some 300 acres. Chénas is the smallest of the nine Beaujolais *crus*—those districts that generally make superior wine. Part of Chénas is included within the more famous area of MOULIN-À-VENT to the south; under its own appellation, Chénas annually produces over 140,000 cases

69

of sturdy, full-bodied wine, among the slowest to mature of the Beaujolais.

Chenin Blanc *(Shay'-nan Blawn)*: Excellent white wine grape, responsible for the famous white wines of the LOIRE River valley, France; these include VOUVRAY, SAVENNIÈRES, QUARTS DE CHAUME, and others. Wines made from the Chenin Blanc may be either dry or semi-dry, depending on autumn harvest weather and methods of vinification. Occasionally called Pineau de la Loire (or, incorrectly, white Pinot), the Chenin Blanc is also grown successfully in California, where almost 33,000 acres have been planted. It is a productive variety that gives fresh and attractive wines, frequently with an agreeable trace of sweetness.

Cheval-Blanc, Château *(Shev'-al Blawn')*: Superb red BORDEAUX wine, from the district of SAINT-ÉMILION. Cheval-Blanc, which means "white horse" in French, is considered, along with Château AUSONE, the leading wine of Saint-Émilion and both wines are rated Premier Grand Cru (First Great Growth). The vineyard extends over about 80 acres, and production amounts to some 12,000 cases annually of fruity, scented and full-bodied red wine. It is owned by the Fourcaud-Laussac family.

Chevalier-Montrachet *(Shev-al-yay' Mon-rah-shay')*: Superb white wine vineyard in the CÔTE DE BEAUNE, Burgundy, rated Grand Cru (Great Growth)—the highest rank for a Burgundy. Made from the Chardonnay grape, the wine of Chevalier-Montrachet is one of Burgundy's very best, often the equal of the magnificent MONTRACHET. The latter vineyard adjoins Chevalier-Montrachet further down the slope.

Chevalier-Montrachet's 18 acres of vineyard lie wholly within the commune of PULIGNY-MONTRACHET; production averages about 1,800 cases annually of very fine, scented and flavorful white wine.

Chianti *(Key-ahn′-tee):* Famous red wine from the region of TUSCANY, Italy; traditionally associated with the squat, straw-covered flask or FIASCO (plural: fiaschi) in which it was bottled. For years, the fiasco bottle was popular in the district because it could be hand-blown, and kept from breakage by a protective mat of straw around its sides, but because of higher labor costs it is seen only infrequently today.

Chianti's strong association with the fiasco has its drawbacks. Regular bottles can be laid horizontally for storage, which fiaschi cannot, so finer quality Chiantis are normally not put into fiaschi. Instead, they are shipped in brown bottles similar to those used for BORDEAUX wines, called *bottiglia bordolesi.*

Under Italian law, the place-name Chianti is unique to a specific, delimited part of Tuscany, extending between the cities of Florence (Firenze) and Siena. Because of the wine's great popularity, many wines—including those produced outside of Italy—were previously sold as Chianti, but by law only the region of Tuscany may produce wines under this name in Italy. Likewise, there used to be a white Chianti wine, but with the enactment of the D.O.C. laws this was suppressed: white wines in the district are now known as "Bianco di Toscana." (see also GALESTRO).

Red Chianti is made from a blend of several grape varieties, in which white grapes are added to make the wines more accessible in their youth. Baron Bettino Ricasoli, the 19th century proprietor of Castello di Brolio in Chianti, ordained a specific formula for the grapes that later became a model for all Chianti growers to follow: 50-80% Sangiovese, 10-30% Canaiolo, 10-30% white Malvasia and Trebbiano, and 5% Colorino. Growers nowadays are limiting the amount of white grapes to be added, since the area occasionally has a problem with overproduction and in the past many of the wines were too light.

Less expensive grades of Chianti often have

71

a faint sparkle, which results from the process of GOVERNO: a small amount of unfermented must from dried grapes is added to the new wine, causing a slight secondary fermentation that is said to add freshness. Since wines treated in this manner are often unstable, Chiantis treated by the *governo* method are becoming rare in the U.S. wine trade. For the finer *Riserva* grades, which may only be released for sale after several years in cask and in bottle, the governo process is incompatible.

The D.O.C. region of Chianti covers an irregular area between Florence and Siena, and defines two different styles of wines. Six growing areas produce basic Chianti, sometimes marketed under a more specific name: Colli Senesi near Siena, Colli Fiorentini near Florence, and Colli Arentini near Arezzo all have minor differences in their wines, while Chianti Rufina and Chianti Montalbano are softer, and Chianti Pisane generally the coarsest. Many growers in these areas have banded together in a voluntary organization known as the CONSORZIO, and collectively the wines belonging to this association are called "Chianti Putto." They are subject to inspection and analysis before being sold, and may be identified by a special neck seal showing a cherub from a Della Robbia painting.

The central and best portion of the Chianti area lies in hilly country practically on a line between Florence and Siena. This is the CLASSICO district, which includes the famous wine towns of Radda, Castellina, Gaiole, Fonterutoli, and Greve. Because of the area's superior climate and soil, the finest Chiantis have traditionally come from the Classico area, and they normally sell for higher prices. Since 1924, many of the producers have joined the Consorzio for Chianti Classico, the original model for similar organizations all over Italy. The seal of the Chianti Classico Consorzio may be recognized by a black rooster *(il gallo nero)*, surrounded by backdrops of red or gold, as quality and age increases. Because certain minimum standards must be met, the *gallo nero* is usually an indication of quality, although membership in the Consorzio is not obligatory for all growers, and a number of producers who originally joined the Consorzio have dropped out.

A Chianti Classico will usually be slightly higher in alcohol than ordinary Chianti, and will possess greater aging potential. If it has been aged a minimum of three years prior to release, it may be sold as Riserva; if the alcohol is 1% higher than usual, it may be called Riserva *Speciale*.

The Chianti area as a whole is very productive; the Classico district alone has some 90,000 acres of vines, and produces several million cases a year. The wine's popularity is world-wide, and although other winegrowing nations adopt this name occasionally for wines that are similar in style, few—if any—can match it in quality.

Chiaretto *(Key-ah-rett'-o):* Fine Italian rosé wine produced on the western shores of Lake Garda (Riviera del Garda), in the region of LOMBARDY. Called Chiaretto del Garda, the wine is made principally from Gropello grapes and is rated D.O.C.; ideally it should be enjoyed when very young. Sometimes the term Chiaretto also applies to a light red wine.

Chile: Wine has been produced in Chile since the 16th century, but it was not until 1851 that French wine-makers first came to Chile to practice their trade, a move that precipitated large-scale planting of vineyards in noble European grape varieties. With some 271,800 acres of vineyard, Chile is the second largest wine-producing country in Latin America, exceeded only by her neighbor Argentina.

The climate is ideal for grape-growing in most of Chile between the 30th and 40th parallels. There are three principal regions where grapes are grown. In the north near Coquimbo, table grapes and raisins are produced

73

under irrigation in a very dry climate. In the south near Valdivia, the climate is very humid and a lesser grape variety, the Pais, is grown primarily for use in brandy distillation. The central region near Santiago, the capital, has the greatest reputation for quality wines. It is cleaved by four rivers that course down from the Andes—Aconcagua, Maipo, Cachapoal, and Teno—each of which has vineyards on its fertile alluvial soil. One particularly fine wine region is the Maipo basin (Llano del Maipo) southwest of Santiago.

The best Chilean red wine is generally made from Cabernet Sauvignon, vinified according to the traditions of French immigrants from BORDEAUX, who also brought with them such noble varieties as Merlot, Malbec (often spelled Malbeck in Chile) and Petit-Verdot. Other good red wines are made from Pinot Noir and Barbera. White wine varieties include Sauvignon Blanc, Sémillon, Chardonnay and Riesling; the latter usually makes the best white Chilean wines and is normally shipped in squat BOCKSBEUTEL bottles.

Because of their very high quality and relatively low price, Chilean wines have been very popular on the U.S. market. Some are among the best wines made in Latin America.

Chinon (Shee'-nawn): Red wine district in the LOIRE River Valley, France, in the old province of TOURAINE. Made from the Cabernet Franc grape (locally called the Breton), Chinon is among the Loire valley's finest red wines. It is often drunk young but the best wines improve with some bottle age; they are sturdy and full-bodied, often with a scent of violets. Chinon's 2,000 acres of vineyard include the communes of Beaumont-en-Véron and l'Ille Bouchard; there are some 171,500 cases made each year.

74   **Chiroubles** (Shee-roo'-bluh): Red wine commune in the BEAUJOLAIS district; southern Burgundy, with some 650 acres of vineyard. Chiroubles is one of the nine Beaujolais *crus*—

the regions that generally produce the best wine. Its vineyards adjoin FLEURIE to the east, and its scented and fruity red wines are similar; much Chiroubles is consumed directly from the cask during its first year and gains little with age, but a considerable quantity is bottled and exported. The equivalent of 182,000 cases is produced annually.

Chorey-Les-Beaune *(Shor'-ray Lay Bone')*: Red wine commune of secondary importance, located to the north of BEAUNE, Burgundy, with some 400 acres of vineyard. Its wines may be sold either under the name Chorey-Les-Beaune or "CÔTE DE BEAUNE-VILLAGES."

Chusclan *(Shuss'-clawn)*: Village in the southern RHÔNE River valley, France, located west of the city of Orange. Its red and rosé wines are entitled to the appellation CÔTES-DU-RHÔNE, and are usually labeled "Côtes-du-Rhône Chusclan."

Cinqueterre *(Chink'-way-tair'-ray)*: Italian for "five lands"; specifically, five towns (Biassa, Corniglia, Monterosso, Riomaggiore, and Vernazza) located between the cities of Chiavari and La Spezia on the Italian Riviera, in the region of LIGURIA. The golden white wine of Cinqueterre has been famous since medieval times; it may be dry or quite sweet, depending on methods of vinification. In recognition of its long heritage of fine wines, Cinqueterre received a D.O.C. rating in 1973.

Cinsault *(San'-so)*: Fine quality red grape variety, one of the principal grapes used in the production of CHÂTEAUNEUF-DU-PAPE and other red wines of the southern CÔTES-DU-RHÔNE district. Also spelled Cinsaut, the grape adds important color, softness and scent to blends with Grenache and Mourvèdre in the Rhône region. Grown in the Republic of South Africa, it makes some of that country's best red wines.

Cirò (*Chee'-ro*): Small coastal town in the region of CALABRIA, southern Italy, with over 4,600 acres of vineyard. The fine red, white and rosé wines of Cirò are among Calabria's best, and are rated D.O.C. The reds and rosés are made from a local grape variety, the Gaglioppo, which yields full-bodied wines that age well. The whites are made from Greco Bianco; they are high in alcohol (over 13.5%) and like the reds are apt to be full-bodied.

Clairette (*Clair-rett'*): White wine grape grown extensively in southern France. There are three wines rated APPELLATION CONTRÔLÉE that are made from the Clairette: Clairette de Bellegarde, a soft, dry white wine produced south of the city of Nîmes in the department of Gard; Clairette de Die, a sparkling or semi-sparkling white wine to which some Muscat is normally added, produced southeast of the city of Valence in the RHÔNE River valley; and finally Clairette du Languedoc from the department of HÉRAULT, a full-bodied, golden white wine produced from semi-dried grapes. Though a few are exported, Clairettes are generally rare outside of their production zone.

Claret: A term used in English-speaking countries to designate light, dry red wines similar to those produced in BORDEAUX, France. The word *claret* originated from the medieval term "clairet," meaning either a light red wine or one to which some white wine was added. The English called clairet "claret," which has applied unofficially to Bordeaux wines ever since.

Legally, however, there is no precise definition for "claret"; this word is almost never seen on a bottle of Bordeaux wine, although in many other parts of the world it indicates a light, dry red wine.

Clarete (*Clar-ate'-ay*): Spanish for "light red wine."

Clos (*Clo*): French for "walled vineyard." In France, many good examples of a clos can be found in BURGUNDY, for monastical orders who tended the vineyards during the Middle Ages often built walls around their holdings. However, a number of clos exist outside of Burgundy. The use of the word "clos" is now restricted by French law to a specific vineyard, though it need not be surrounded by a wall.

Clos de Bèze *(Clo duh Bezz')*: World-famous vineyard in the northern CÔTE DE NUITS, Burgundy. The Clos de Bèze makes one of Burgundy's finest red wines, rated Grand Cru (Great Growth). It lies alongside the equally celebrated CHAMBERTIN vineyard and hence is officially called Chambertin-Clos de Bèze, although historically it is several centuries older than Chambertin. The vineyard is 37 acres large; about 5,800 cases of Chambertin-Clos de Bèze are produced each year.

Clos du Chapitre *(Clo dew Sha-peet'-ruh)*: The name of two fine vineyards in the region of BURGUNDY, France. The first lies in the commune of FIXIN in the northern CÔTE DE NUITS; 11½ acres large, it produces a very good red wine rated Premier Cru (First Growth). The second is further south, located in the commune of VIRÉ near MÂCON; planted in white Chardonnay grapes, the vineyard makes an excellent white wine—one of the best of the Mâcon region.

Clos des Lambrays *(Clo day Lawm'-bray)*: Excellent red wine vineyard in the commune of MOREY-ST. DENIS, in Burgundy's CÔTE DE NUITS. Rated Grand Cru (Great Growth), it is planted entirely in Pinot Noir grapes and extends over about 15 acres. Clos des Lambrays is the proprietary name for Les Larreys, as the vineyard is officially called; it lies adjacent to the famous CLOS DE TART vineyard and like the Clos de Tart it belongs to a single owner (see MONO-POLE). The wine of the Clos des Lambrays is an especially rich and fine red Burgundy.

Classico *(Class'-ee-co):* Italian for "classic"; when preceded by the name of a wine, it indicates that the wine comes from the central and best part of the region (CHIANTI Classico, SOAVE Classico, VALPOLICELLA Classico, etc.).

Classified Growth (French, *cru classé):* In BORDEAUX, France, a wine estate or CHÂTEAU that has been officially ranked or classified, based on the price of the wines and their reputation in the trade.

The first official Bordeaux wine classification took place in 1855 in preparation for the Paris Exposition of that year, and two wine districts—the MÉDOC and SAUTERNES—were officially classified into groups of CRUS (growths). Other leading wine regions of Bordeaux were classified about a century later. Owing to many changes that have taken place since the 1855 classification, a major revision in the near future remains a distinct possibility.

Climat *(Clee'-ma):* French for "climate." In the region of the CÔTE D'OR in BURGUNDY, France, a climat is a single, specific vineyard or CRU (Growth), distinguished from its immediate neighbors. Each climat differs from others around it through variations in soil, exposure to the sun, the slope of the land, soil drainage, and suitability for certain grape varieties. Because of these subtle differences—and because Burgundy's vineyards are likely to be shared by a number of different proprietors—the Burgundians like to think in terms of climats rather than "vineyards."

Clone: A group of individual plants, reproduced asexually from a common ancestor. Selected clones of noble grape varieties can now be planted in many of the world's vineyards, resulting in a dramatic improvement in the quality of the wine.

Clos des Mouches *(Clo day Moosh'):* Celebrated vineyard in the CÔTE DE BEAUNE, Burgundy, extending over 61 acres within the

78

commune of BEAUNE. The Clos des Mouches is planted in both red Pinot Noir and white Chardonnay grapes; the red wine is in more general distribution. It is a typical Beaune, graceful and fairly soon to mature. The rare *blanc* (white) Clos des Mouches, which is mostly produced by the famous Burgundy shipper Joseph Drouhin, is a particularly delectable white Burgundy and fetches high prices in the trade.

Clos de la Perrière *(Clo duh la Pair-yair')*: Fine red wine vineyard in the commune of FIXIN, in the northern CÔTE DE NUITS, Burgundy. Planted in Pinot Noir, the vineyard's 12 acres produce what many experts regard as Fixin's best wine, rated Premier Cru (First Growth). There is an unrelated white wine vineyard in the commune of MEURSAULT to the south, in Burgundy's CÔTE DE BEAUNE, called "Clos des Perrières." Also rated Premier Cru, the wine is excellent but not well-known in the U.S.

Clos de la Roche *(Clo duh la Rawsh')*: Outstanding red wine vineyard in the commune of MOREY-ST. DENIS, in the CÔTE DE NUITS, Burgundy. The Clos de la Roche is rated Grand Cru (Great Growth) and is one of Burgundy's best red wines; its qualities are similar to the great CHAMBERTIN produced nearby, which is much better-known. The Clos de la Roche vineyard extends over some 38 acres; average annual production is about 4,500 cases of sturdy, full-bodied red wine.

Clos du Roi *(Clo dew Rwah')*: The name of two fine red wine vineyards in the CÔTE DE BEAUNE, Burgundy. The more famous of the two occupies about 25 acres in the commune of ALOXE-CORTON; it is officially part of the Grand Cru (Great Growth) vineyard CORTON and is usually sold as "Corton-Clos du Roi." The other Clos Du Roi vineyard lies in the commune of BEAUNE to the south and is somewhat larger (34 acres); its similarly fine red wines, rated Premier Cru (First Growth), are among the best of Beaune.

Clos Saint-Denis *(Clo San Duh-nee')*: Excellent red wine vineyard in the CÔTE DE NUITS, Burgundy, rated Grand Cru (Great Growth). The name of this famous vineyard became legally associated with the town of Morey in 1927, in which it lies, which is now known as MOREY-SAINT-DENIS. The Clos Saint-Denis is some 16 acres large; production averages about 2,000 cases of fine, full-bodied red wine annually.

Clos Saint-Jacques *(Clo San Zhack')*: Outstanding red wine vineyard in the commune of GEVREY-CHAMBERTIN, in the northern CÔTE DE NUITS, Burgundy. Its wine, rated Premier Cru (First Growth), is similar to the Grand Cru (Great Growth) CHAMBERTIN, but the Clos Saint-Jacques vineyard is located some distance away from Chambertin on a different slope—hence the distinction in rank. Its 16 acres of vineyard are ideally located, and produce a fine, rich red Burgundy.

Clos de Tart *(Clo duh Tarr')*: Fine red wine vineyard in the CÔTE DE NUITS, Burgundy, rated Grand Cru (Great Growth). Its 18 acres of Pinot Noir vines lie in the commune of MOREY-ST. DENIS and adjoin BONNES-MARES, another famous Grand Cru vineyard. The Clos de Tart is the exclusive property of J. Mommessin, a Burgundy shipper; the vineyard produces about 2,300 cases of excellent red wine annually.

Clos de Vougeot *(Clo duh Voo'-zho)*: World-famous red wine vineyard in the CÔTE DE NUITS, Burgundy. Originally the property of Cistercian monks prior to the French Revolution, the Clos de Vougeot presently consists of 125 acres planted in Pinot Noir vines—the largest vineyard in the Côte de Nuits. It produces red wine exclusively, rated Grand Cru (Great Growth), except for a small section planted in white Chardonnay grapes rated Premier Cru (First Growth): this is the rare Clos Blanc de Vougeot, the exclusive property of the Burgundy shipper L'Héritier-Guyot.

A venerable old building rising up in the heart of the vineyard, the Château du Clos de Vougeot is presently used for the banquets of the Confrérie des Chevaliers du Tastevin, Burgundy's wine fraternity, though wine is no longer made at the château. Today about sixty proprietors own different parts of the vineyard, and so the wines tend to vary more than most other Burgundies. At its best, a good Clos de Vougeot is one of Burgundy's best red wines—scented, complex, and with a glorious aftertaste. Currently some 16,000 cases of Clos de Vougeot are made each year; one should not confuse a Clos de Vougeot with lesser wines simply labeled VOUGEOT, which are pleasant but not in the same class.

Colares *(Co-lahr'-resh):* One of the best red wines of Portugal, produced west of Lisbon near the town of Sintra. The vineyards of Colares border the Atlantic Ocean and are planted in unusually thin, sandy soil. Red Colares wine is produced from the Ramisco grape, which is said to have been imported from France, and after years of cask aging becomes subtle and interesting. Some white Colares is made, but only in small quantities. Colares wines became quite famous during the 19th century, but the vineyards are very hard to work and the wines are now becoming rare.

Colheita *(Cawl-hate'-ah):* Portuguese for "vintage," or "wine with the date of harvest." This word has special significance in the district where PORT is made, as it describes a select grade of Port that has been aged a minimum of seven years in cask before being bottled, sold with a vintage date. These wines differ from true Vintage Port in that they lose their sediment in cask, and consequently some of their color and body as well. Although col-

81

heita Ports are sold with a vintage date, they tend to be somewhat less expensive than true Vintage Ports, and have a lighter character relating to the time spent in cask.

Colli Albani *(Coll'-ee Ahl-bahn'-ee):* Italian for "Alban Hills," the fertile uplands 15 miles to the southeast of Rome, which have furnished wine for the capital since the days of the Roman Empire. Today, Colli Albani is the name of a dry or semi-dry white wine entitled to D.O.C., produced within six communes in the region of LAZIO (Latium). The wine is made principally from Malvasia and Trebbiano grapes; it is apt to be consumed directly from the cask when very young, but a considerable quantity is bottled and exported.

Colombard *(Coll'-um-bar):* High-yield, good quality white wine grape grown in the Cognac district, France, where its pale and rather acidic white wines are used for brandy distillation. The Colombard produces better wine in warmer climates, and is grown extensively in California where it is called "French Colombard"; there, its wine is light and fruity. Originally used principally in the making of GENERIC wines like "chablis," it is now increasingly sold on its own as a good, inexpensive VARIETAL wine. Over 44,000 acres have been planted.

Color: The color of a wine indicates its age, concentration, and quality. The best way to assess a wine's color is to put it in a clear, stemmed glass that can be tipped easily, and hold it up to the light or against a white background. When viewed this way, the wine should be clear and brilliant.

Red and rosé wines derive their color from pigments in the grape skins that are dissolved by the alcohol produced during fermentation. Dark red wines contain more extracts, and are likely to be fuller in flavor. Light white wines from cool regions are palest in color; sweet white wines are usually darker in color than dry white wines, and are correspondingly darker when old.

During the aging process, the color of a wine changes through contact with oxygen (see OXIDATION). Initially oxidation helps mature the wine, but too much over too long a period of time is harmful. Exposure to heat will also damage a wine and make it change color.

Red wines are usually deep purple when young, then become brick-red when mature. When brownish-red, they are generally too old. White wines begin clear yellow or greenish, then turn golden with age. Brownish white wines are overly oxidized and unpleasant to drink. Rosé wines are pale pink when young, then develop a warm orange hue with age. An overly pronounced red or orange color in a rosé is a defect.

Combettes (*Cawm-bett'*): Excellent white wine vineyard in the commune of PULIGNY-MON-TRACHET, in Burgundy's CÔTE DE BEAUNE. Rated Premier Cru (First Growth), the Combettes vineyard extends over 16½ acres planted in Chardonnay, and produces racy white wines noted for their bouquet and finesse.

Commune (*Cawm'-yoon*): French for "township" or "parish"; a specific town or village and the surrounding land.

Complex: A complex wine has a multitude of pleasing flavors that are difficult to describe. Such a wine is exciting and very fine.

Concord: Native American red wine grape, named for the town of Concord, Massachusetts, where it originated. Of the species LA-BRUSCA, the Concord is widely grown in the eastern United States, the midwest, and Canada. It is an important table grape and makes good grape juice, but it has to be heavily sugared to make wine; wine made from the Concord has a pronounced "foxy" (grapey) aroma and flavor, which many people nevertheless

83

seem to enjoy. The most widely planted grape variety in New York State, the Concord is essential in the making of Kosher wines and also "Cold Duck"—a blend of champagne and sparkling burgundy.

Condrieu (*Cawn-dree-yuh'*): Rare and exquisite white wine of the RHÔNE River valley, France, produced south of the city of Vienne on the river's steep banks. The vineyards of Condrieu include the tiny Château-Grillet, only 4 acres large—the smallest vineyard in France with its own APPELLATION CONTRÔLÉE. A wine that is most enjoyable when young, Condrieu is made from the Viognier grape, a variety exclusive to the Rhône valley, which is also used in making the red CÔTE ROTIE produced just to the north. Condrieu is largely consumed locally and until recently very little was exported.

Consorzio (*Con-sorts'-ee-o*): Italian for "consortium" or "guild": a regulatory agency for an Italian wine region that functions to oversee the region's wine production and set standards for quality. The most famous consorzio is probably that of CHIANTI, the "Consorzio Vino Chianti Classico," whose offices are in Florence. The Consorzio provides that its members identify their wines by a "Gallo Nero" (black rooster) seal banded on the neck of the bottle. The Gallo Nero indicates that the wines have been made by traditional methods and have passed rigorous tests before being released to the public. In existence since 1924, the Chianti Classico Consorzio has set the pace for fine wine standards in Italy, and its Gallo Nero is almost always an indication of superior quality.

Cooperative (French, *Co-oh'-pair-ah-teev'*): A winery owned and managed jointly by a number of different growers. Cooperatives are a convenient way for the smaller producers to share the cost of expensive wine-making equipment and also be in a better position to market their wines. For these reasons, cooperatives are increasing in number in Europe and the U.S.

Corbières *(Cor-be-yair')*: Wine region in southern France, extending over some 86,500 acres in the department of the AUDE. Corbières produces red, white and rosé wines under the V.D.Q.S. label; if they reach 12% alcohol they may be called Corbières Supérieur. The red Corbières are quite popular; made from Carignan, Grenache or Cinsault grapes, they are generally inexpensive and quite good. One of the best red Corbières, FITOU, has its own APPELLATION CONTRÔLÉE. The equivalent of over 6.8 million cases of Corbières is produced annually.

Cornas *(Cor'-nahss)*: Fine, full-bodied red wine from the RHÔNE River valley, France. Made exclusively from the Syrah grape, Cornas is usually the sturdiest of the Rhône red wines and takes time to mature, but becomes distinctive with age. The steep, terraced vineyards of Cornas lie west of the city of Valence near the famous wine region of HERMITAGE, and the wines are similar; being less well-known, Cornas wines are often exceptional value. About 18,000 cases are produced each year.

Corsica: France's largest island, Corsica has had vineyards for centuries but the wines are not well-known on the U.S. market. Located in the Mediterranean Sea off the coast of Italy, Corsica acknowledges its proximity to Italy with many wines made from grape varieties indigenous to the Italian mainland: the most important are Vermentino, Aleatico, Genovesella and Moscato.

There are several APPELLATION CONTRÔLÉES in Corsica, all granted rather recently. "Vin de Corse" (Corsican Wine) is the most general; wines from more specific regions bear this label, followed by the name of the production

85

zone. All apply to red, white or rosé wines. Patrimonio, one of the best rosés of Corsica, is produced in the north on the peninsula of Cap Corse; Coteaux d'Ajaccio, named for Ajaccio, Corsica's largest city, was with Patrimonio the first Corsican appellation contrôlée. Sartène in the southwest is famous chiefly for its strong and lively red wine; the coastal vineyards of Calvi lie near those of Patrimonio. While there are several others, they are not likely to be exported.

Cortese *(Cor-tay'-zay):* White grape variety grown extensively in PIEMONTE, northern Italy. It gives fresh and attractive white wines best enjoyed in their youth; an especially good one is made around the town of GAVI and is called "Gavi Cortese." Considered to be the best white wine of Piemonte, Gavi Cortese was awarded a D.O.C. rating in late 1974.

Corton *(Cor-tawn'):* Famous red wine of the CÔTE DE BEAUNE, Burgundy, produced near the little village of Aloxe, which has assumed the name of this illustrious vineyard to become ALOXE-CORTON. Rated Grand Cru (Great Growth), the noble red wine of Corton is the finest of the Côte de Beaune and the only Grand Cru red wine. The vineyard extends over 193 acres and combines a number of different parcels, each of which is legally entitled to the Corton APPELLATION CONTRÔLÉE; among the most famous are Corton-CLOS DU ROI, Corton-BRESSANDES, Corton-Pougets, and Corton-Renardes. An exceptionally fine white wine of Aloxe-Corton, also rated Grand Cru, is called CORTON-CHARLEMAGNE. About 35,500 cases of Corton are produced annually.

Corton-Charlemagne *(Cor-tawn' Sharl-man'):* Outstanding white wine of the CÔTE DE BEAUNE, Burgundy, rated Grand Cru (Great Growth). Located in the commune of ALOXE-CORTON, the Corton-Charlemagne vineyard adjoins the equally famous red wine vineyard

CORTON, and is planted exclusively in white Chardonnay grapes. Corton-Charlemagne is named after the great emperor Charlemagne (742-814 A.D.), who was one of its owners. It is one of Burgundy's very finest and rarest white wines; the vineyard extends over 61 acres, and production averages about 14,000 cases of superb, scented white wine annually.

Corvo di Casteldaccia (*Cor'-vo dee Cas-tell-datch'-ya*): Good red and white wines produced near the little town of Casteldaccia south of the city of Palermo, on the island of Sicily. While not rated D.O.C., the wines of Corvo di Casteldaccia are among Sicily's best and are internationally famous; the vineyards are owned by the estate of the Dukes of Salaparuta.

Côte (*Coat*): French for "hill" or "slope"; the plural is *côtes*. In the wine regions, vineyards are likely to be located on slopes for proper drainage and optimum exposure to the sun.

Côte de Beaune (*Coat duh Bone'*): The southern half of Burgundy's CÔTE D'OR, the Côte de Beaune derives its name from the city of BEAUNE—the wine metropolis of Burgundy. Excellent red wines made from the Pinot Noir account for about four-fifths of the total annual production (about 800,500 cases); the exquisite white wines made from the Chardonnay are without peer anywhere in the world.

The Côte de Beaune consists of about 7,400 acres, blessed with the perfect combination of the right soil and exposure that makes great wines. The best of them, rated Grand Cru (Great Growth) under the French law of APPELLATION CONTRÔLÉE, are listed under separate headings in this dictionary (example: MONTRACHET). Next come wines rated Premier Cru (First Growth), a much larger group including most of the remaining classified vineyards, the most important of which also appear under separate headings (ex.: PULIGNY-

MONTRACHET Les COMBETTES). Wine from un-classified vineyards within the Côte de Beaune communes is entitled to a communal appellation (ex.: Puligny-Montrachet); the quality of commune wines is more variable than the Grand or Premier Crus, but their quality standards are still among the highest in France. Wines that do not meet the minimum standards for their category—such as in a poor vintage or when there is overproduction—must be declassified (see BOURGOGNE).

The Côte de Beaune begins in the north near LADOIX-SERRIGNY and continues south for about 15 miles. It includes the major wine communes of ALOXE-CORTON, Beaune, POM-MARD, VOLNAY, MEURSAULT, PULIGNY-MON-TRACHET, CHASSAGNE-MONTRACHET, and SANTENAY. The secondary wine communes of the Côte de Beaune include PERNAND-VERGE-LESSES, SAVIGNY-LES-BEAUNE, CHOREY-LES-BEAUNE, MONTHÉLIE, AUXEY-DURESSES, SAINT-ROMAIN, SAINT-AUBIN, Sampigny-Les-Mar-anges, Cheilly-Les-Maranges, and Dezize-Les-Maranges. Wines from the secondary com-munes may either be labeled after the name of the commune, or appear as CÔTE DE BEAUNE-VILLAGES.

Côte de Beaune-Villages (*Coat duh Boné Villahj'*): A general term describing a wine or a blend of two or more wines from secondary communes within the CÔTE DE BEAUNE, Burgundy. Only red wines with a minimum of 10.5% alcohol are entitled to this appellation. The wines used for blending must be characteristic of their area of origin. Côte de Beaune-Villages wines are entirely different from those labeled "Côte de Beaune," which are ordinary wines produced in vineyards near Beaune but without right to that appellation.

88 **Côte des Blancs** (*Coat day Blawn'*): The southern portion of the French CHAMPAGNE country south of the city of ÉPERNAY, so named because it is planted in white Chardonnay grapes. Avize and Cramant are its two highest-ranked towns but Le Mesnil-sur-Oger, Oger, and Oiry also produce outstanding wines.

Côte de Brouilly (*Coat duh Broo-yee′*): The center of the red wine district of BROUILLY in the BEAUJOLAIS country, southern Burgundy. The middle of the Côte de Brouilly is a hill surrounded by vineyards, the Mont de Brouilly, at the top of which is a chapel that annually receives a pilgrimage prior to the harvest, in anticipation of a good vintage. Made from the Gamay grape, the wines of the Côte de Brouilly are similar to Brouilly's, with perhaps a bit more fruit and concentration. There are some 495 acres of vineyard; production averages about 169,000 cases of fine red wine each year.

Côte de Nuits (*Coat duh Nwee′*): The northern half of Burgundy's CÔTE D'OR, the Côte de Nuits is celebrated chiefly for its incomparable red wines made from the Pinot Noir—though there are a few isolated white wine vineyards planted in Chardonnay. The region takes its name from the medieval town of Nuits, the largest on the Côte, which is now called NUITS-ST. GEORGES. The total area under vines in the Côte de Nuits is a scant 3,460 acres.

Under the French law of APPELLATION CON-TRÔLÉE, the greatest wines are rated Grand Cru (Great Growth). As an indication of the excellence of the Côte de Nuits vineyards, all but one of the 23 Grand Cru red Burgundies come from this region. Each Côte de Nuits Grand Cru is listed individually in this dictionary (example: CHAMBERTIN). The other leading vineyards in the Côte de Nuits are rated Premier Cru (First Growth), and can frequently produce some of the best Burgundies (Ex.: GEVREY-CHAMBERTIN CLOS SAINT-JACQUES). The unclassified vineyards in the Côte de Nuits produce wine entitled to a communal appellation, which in so renowned an

89

area can still be very fine (ex.: Gevrey-Chambertin). When the wines do not meet minimum standards, they are declassified (see BOURGOGNE), but on the Côte de Nuits this is quite rare.

The Côte de Nuits begins a few miles south of the city of Dijon, and continues south past world-famous wine communes: Gevrey-Chambertin, MOREY-ST. DENIS, CHAMBOLLE-MUSIGNY, VOUGEOT, FLAGEY-ÉCHEZEAUX, VOSNE-ROMANÉE, Nuits-St. Georges, and PRÉMEAUX. The secondary wine communes of the Côte de Nuits, located at the northern and southern extremes of the Côte, include FIXIN, Brochon, Prissy, Comblanchien, and Corgoloin. In the past, wine from the secondary communes received the appellation "Vins Fins de la Côte de Nuits," but they are now labeled CÔTE DE NUITS-VILLAGES.

Côte de Nuits-Villages *(Coat duh Nwee Villahj')*: A general appellation for a wine or a blend of two or more wines from five secondary communes at the northern and southern extremes of the CÔTE DE NUITS, Burgundy. This new appellation replaces the former classification for red wines of at least 10.5% alcohol from communes whose wines share similar characteristics—"Vins Fins de la Côte de Nuits." While not representative of the best wines the Côte de Nuits has to offer, Côte de Nuits-Villages wines are generally inexpensive and often good value.

Côte d'Or *(Coat Dor)*: The "slope of gold," in French, the Côte d'Or is both an administrative region in France (department) and also the most famous wine region in BURGUNDY. It consists of a narrow strip of vineyard, located along a chalk-marl slope beginning south of the city of Dijon and continuing southwest for almost 30 miles. The Côte d'Or is divided into two principal sections: the northern part, the CÔTE DE NUITS, begins near the town of FIXIN and ends 12 miles south, near the town of

PRÉMEAUX. The southern half, the CÔTE DE BEAUNE, begins near the town of ALOXE-CORTON and extends down to the village of SANTENAY some 15 miles to the south. There are two minor vineyard areas in the hilly country to the west, the "Hautes Côtes de Nuits" and the "Hautes Côtes de Beaune," but they produce lighter, less distinguished wines that are rarely exported.

Two noble grape varieties thrive in the Côte d'Or; while they are grown elsewhere, in few regions do they produce wines with such a high degree of finesse. Rich, robust reds are made from the Pinot Noir, while racy, scented whites are produced from the Chardonnay. In general, the Pinot Noir is predominant in the Côte de Nuits and the Chardonnay is more widely grown in the Côte de Beaune, though the Côte de Beaune actually produces more red wine than white and some white wine vineyards do exist in the Côte de Nuits.

Some vineyards in the Côte d'Or are superior to others, and have been classified by the French laws of APPELLATION CONTRÔLÉE. Outstanding vineyards are rated Grand Cru (Great Growth); other leading vineyards, only slightly less celebrated, are rated Premier Cru (First Growth). Vineyards that have not been classified but lie within a delimited township or commune produce wine entitled to a commune appellation.

Some towns in the Côte d'Or have adopted a peculiar practice of adding their name to that of the most famous vineyard nearby. Thus the village of Aloxe in the Côte de Beaune is now ALOXE-CORTON. A few villages have not hyphenated their name because their vineyards are not as famous, but under the system one should always remember that "Aloxe-Corton" applies to any wine produced within that commune; Aloxe-Corton Les Chaillots to a particular vineyard rated Premier Cru; and COR-TON to a single, outstanding vineyard rated Grand Cru. The Grand Crus never take the

91

name of their commune and are always sold under their own name.

Over the years, many vineyards in the Côte d'Or were sold to different owners, and few vineyards presently belong only to one proprietor. Scores of different owners may have holdings in only one vineyard, which means that the wines will vary—even though they all come from the same source. Some owners sell their wines to a shipper (see NÉGOCIANT); others sell it themselves. A wine that is produced and bottled by the same person is said to be ESTATE-BOTTLED; the French equivalent is "Mis en Bouteilles au Domaine." Though estate-bottling is a key to authenticity in any wine region, it is particularly important in the Côte d'Or because of the fragmented nature of Burgundy's vineyards.

Côte Rotie (*Coat Ro-tee'*): The "Roasted Slope" in French, Côte Rotie is a famous wine region in the northern RHÔNE River valley, France. The scented, slow-maturing red wine of Côte Rotie has been celebrated for nearly 2,000 years. It is produced near the town of Ampuis; the vineyard area includes the nearby commune of Tupin-et-Semons. Grown on steep, terraced vineyards, the Syrah grape produces four-fifths of the wine of Côte Rotie, with white Viognier constituting the remainder; the latter is used to soften the red wine and make it less astringent. Two principal sections of the Côte Rotie, the "Côte Brune" (Dark Slope) and the "Côte Blonde" (Fair Slope) are normally blended together to make the finished product. There are some 148 acres of vineyard, shared between many different proprietors; annual production is about 40,000 cases.

Coteau (*Co-toe'*): French for "hill" or "hillside"; the plural is *coteaux*.

Coteaux Champenois (*Ko'-toe Shom'-pen-wa*): French for "Champagne hillsides." New AP-PELLATION CONTRÔLÉE, issued in 1974, for the still red, white and rosé wines produced in the French CHAMPAGNE district, without the normal Champagne process of secondary fermentation (see MÉTHODE CHAMPENOISE).

Still wines have been produced in Champagne for centuries, but because they tended to be eclipsed by the illustrious sparkling wine of the district, they were rarely exported. They bore the name "Vin Nature de la Champagne." Because French Champagne requires the intervention of man to make it sparkle, authorities reasoned that the word "nature" was incompatible with a still wine produced without the second fermentation, and subsequently created the appellation Coteaux Champenois: the first wines sold under this name were released to the U.S. market in 1975.

Since practically all of the wine grown in the Champagne district is made sparkling, Coteaux Champenois wines remain a rarity on the market. Some of the better producers reserve a small amount of high-quality still wine for the export market: one of the most famous is the estate-grown "Saran Nature," produced by Moët & Chandon. Similar wines are produced by Laurent-Perrier, Bollinger, A. Charbaut & Fils, and Jacquesson. In some instances, producers may use the Coteaux Champenois appellation for wines from the second pressing (see CUVÉE).

Coteaux du Layon (*Co-toe' dew Lay-awn'*): White wine district in the region of ANJOU, on the lower LOIRE River, France. Named for the River Layon, a tributary of the Loire, the APPELLATION CONTRÔLÉE Coteaux du Layon includes the villages of Rochefort-sur-Loire, Beaulieu-sur-Layon, and Thouarcé. The famous wine regions of BONNEZEAUX and QUARTS DE CHAUME, noted for their sweet white wines made from late-picked Chenin Blanc grapes, are located within the Coteaux du Layon. The region as a whole extends over some 9,900 acres.

Coteaux du Tricastin (*Co'-toe dew Tree'-castan*): Wine region in southern France, east of the RHÔNE River valley in the department of Drôme, that achieved APPELLATION CONTRÓLÉE status in 1973 as a result of a dramatic improvement in quality. The red wines are produced primarily from Grenache, Cinsault and Syrah grapes; they are similar in quality to basic CÔTES-DU-RHÔNES but are much less well-known outside of France. A few properties like O. and H. Bour produce an exceptionally good red wine from 100% Syrah, which is superior to basic Coteaux du Tricastins and more closely recalls northern Rhône valley reds.

Côtes-Canon-Fronsac: see FRONSAC.

Côtes de Bourg (*Coat duh Boor*): Wine region north of the city of BORDEAUX, France, facing the MÉDOC on the right bank of the GIRONDE estuary. The light red wines of the Côtes de Bourg district are popular; they tend to mature earlier than most other red Bordeaux, and most of them are still fairly inexpensive. They are produced from the same Merlot, Cabernet Franc and Cabernet Sauvignon grapes as other red Bordeaux, and some CHÂTEAU-BOTTLED wines can, on occasion, be extraordinary.

There are three associated APPELLATION CONTRÓLÉES in the Bourg region: Bourg, Bourgeais, and Côtes de Bourg, but the latter includes most of the best estates or châteaux: de Barbe, Laurensanne, de la Grave, La Grolet, Mille-Secousses, La Croix-Millorit, Caruel, Rousset, du Bousquet, etc. Similar wines are produced in the associated district of BLAYE to the north.

Côtes-de-Fronsac: see FRONSAC.

Côtes de Provence (*Coat duh Pro-vawnss'*): Vineyard area in southern France near the Mediterranean Sea, in the old province of PROVENCE. The Côtes de Provence vineyards produce red, white and rosé wines, for many years sold under the V.D.Q.S. seal until their promotion to APPELLATION CONTRÔLÉE status in 1977-78. Comprising the present-day departments of Bouches-du-Rhône and Var, the region has been acclaimed primarily for its excellent rosés, sold in special amphora-shaped bottles. In some cases, finer wines will be sold as Côtes de Provence "Cru Classé" (classified growth), followed by the name of the vineyard, to indicate outstanding quality. Coteaux d'Aix-en-Provence, a much smaller delimited area near the city of Aix, was also restricted to V.D.Q.S. status for many years but often produced excellent wines: this was finally promoted to appellation contrôlée in 1982.

Traditionally, the Carignan grape variety has been the mainstay of wine production in the Côtes de Provence, supplemented to a certain extent by Grenache, although Cabernet Sauvignon is rapidly gaining favor with many growers. Better vinification techniques are producing finer and fresher white wines, and especially full and sturdy reds—the rosés go well with the seafood specialties of the Mediterranean district.

The best wines from the Côtes de Provence are generally sold under their own names. These include: CASSIS, known for its white wines; BANDOL, famous for its reds and rosés; and PALETTE, celebrated both for its red and white wines. The white wines of Bellet, produced just north of Nice, are also famous locally but are rarely seen outside their production zone.

Côtes-du-Rhône (*Coat dew Rone'*): The general term for the red, white and rosé wines produced in the RHÔNE River valley, France. There are two principal areas of production: the northern Rhône district, between the cities of Vienne and Valence, in the departments of Drôme, Ardèche and Loire, and the southern Rhône district near the cities of Orange and Avignon, in the departments of Vaucluse

95

and Gard. The total vineyard area extends over some 96,000 acres.

Côtes-du-Rhône is an APPELLATION CONTRÔLÉE for the fine, generally inexpensive wines produced throughout the entire Rhône region; if they come from a smaller area, whose wines are similar, they can be labeled "Côtes-du-Rhône-Villages." Better wines are made in delimited communes whose name is specified along with Côtes-du-Rhône: Côtes-du-Rhône CHUSCLAN, Côtes-du-Rhône VACQUEYRAS, etc. The best wines of the Côtes-du-Rhône have their own appellation contrôlée and are sold under their own name. The northern Rhône includes world-famous wines like CÔTE-ROTIE, CONDRIEU, HERMITAGE, CROZES-HERMITAGE, CORNAS, SAINT-JOSEPH and SAINT-PÉRAY; the southern Rhône includes equally renowned wines of CHÂTEAUNEUF-DU-PAPE, TAVEL, LIRAC, GIGONDAS, and BEAUMES-DE-VENISE. CÔTES DU VENTOUX, a large vineyard area in the southern Rhône region, has recently been granted an appellation contrôlée.

Côtes du Ventoux *(Coat dew Von-too')*: Wine district in southern France, near the city of Orange in the southern RHÔNE region. Named for the Mont de Ventoux, a dramatic mountain peak some 6,200 ft. high, the vineyards cover some 25,000 acres and produce a number of good red, white and rosé wines; the reds are particularly good and, as they are fairly inexpensive, make an important contribution to the wine trade. They are produced primarily from the Grenache grape, and being fairly soft and fruity, are popular "vins de comptoir," or bar wines—best suited to early consumption. Formerly known only locally in the area around Orange, the region achieved APPELLATION CONTRÔLÉE status in 1974 as a result of the wines' steady improvement.

Cotnari *(Cot-narr'-ee)*: One of the best white wines of Romania, Cotnari has been famous for centuries, although nowadays it is less well-known. Produced in the northeastern corner of the country near the city of Iasy, in the province of Moldavia, Cotnari is a fine, naturally sweet dessert wine made primarily from grape varieties indigenous to Romania—Grasa de Cotnari, Feteasca, and Tamîioasa. Scented and with a great depth of flavor, Cotnari is a distinctive and interesting dessert wine.

Crémant (*Cray'-mawn*): French term for a sparkling wine, produced outside the CHAMPAGNE district, that in 1975 became incorporated into the laws of APPELLATION CONTRÔLÉE. Formerly a term used broadly to describe a wine that was not entirely sparkling, Crémant now relates to a wine produced in a delimited vineyard area, that may only be made by the classic MÉTHODE CHAMPENOISE system of bottle-fermentation that originated in Champagne. Three principal appellations are now in effect: in Burgundy, the Crémant de Bourgogne (see BOURGOGNE), which augments the name "Bourgogne Mousseux" for sparkling Burgundy; Crémant de Loire (see LOIRE), where many wines of this type are produced; and the remarkable "Crémant de Cramant," named for the little village of Cramant in the Côte des Blancs area in Champagne, which produces an exceptionally fine, delicate Champagne predominantly from Chardonnay grapes.

Crépy (*Cray-pee'*): Light white wine produced south of Lake Geneva in northeastern France, near the town of Douvaine in the department of Haute-Savoie. Made from the Chasselas grape, Crépy is entitled to APPELLATION CONTRÔLÉE; more often than not it is faintly sparkling or *pétillant*, which makes it refreshing. There are about 148 acres of vineyard; some 22,900 cases are made each year.

Criots-Bâtard-Montrachet (*Cree'-o Bah'-tarr Mon-rah-shay'*): Fine white wine produced in the CÔTE DE BEAUNE, Burgundy, rated Grand

Cru (Great Growth). Located in the commune of CHASSAGNE-MONTRACHET, the vineyard of Criots-Bâtard-Montrachet used to be part of the great BÂTARD-MONTRACHET, but the wines are now sold separately. A suave, scented white wine, Criots-Bâtard-Montrachet is relatively rare because of the vineyard's small size (3½ acres); production averages less than 600 cases.

Crozes-Hermitage *(Crows Air´-me-tahj):* Good red and white wines produced in the northern RHÔNE River valley, France. Crozes-Hermitage is the APPELLATION CONTRÔLÉE for the wines made in 11 communes surrounding the famous vineyards of HERMITAGE; being sturdy and full-bodied, the wines are similar but generally lighter and less fine than Hermitage. About 90% of Crozes-Hermitage is red, made from the Syrah grape; the remainder is white wine produced from the Marsanne or Roussanne. Including Hermitage, the vineyards extend over some 1,230 acres; production averages over 100,000 cases annually.

Cru *(Crew):* French for "growth." Under the law of APPELLATION CONTRÔLÉE, a cru is a specific vineyard—and the wine that it gives—that has been classified according to its quality. When officially classified, the vineyard and the wine is said to be *cru classé.*

Cuvaison *(Kew´-vay-zawn):* From the French word *cuve,* meaning "tank": the essential practice of letting red wines ferment on their skins so as to extract color and tannin. The length of time required, or *cuvage,* is related to the degree of color and tannin desired.

Cuvée *(Kew-vay´):* From the French word *cuve,* meaning "tank": the contents of a vat of wine. There are three different meanings of cuvée, depending on the regions where this term is used. The first relates to the initial pressing of the juice from the grapes in the French CHAMPAGNE country—wine made from the first, light pressing is called "vin de cuvée," which will be

98

superior to wine made from subsequent pressings. Another meaning of cuvée is the annual process of blending the finished wines to be made into Champagne. A third and rather ambiguous meaning of cuvée has until recently prevailed in BURGUNDY, where it referred to a vineyard and its wine. Since cuvée is by its very nature a cellar term and therefore not applicable to a vineyard, the APPELLATION CONTRÔLÉE law now designates Burgundy's vineyards by the more appropriate rating of CRU (growth). The greatest vineyards are called Grand Cru (Great Growth); other leading vineyards, Premier Cru (First Growth).

Cyprus: The third largest island in the Mediterranean Sea, Cyprus lies off the south coast of Turkey and wine constitutes over 7% of her exports. Most of the island is arid, but the lofty Troödos Mountains rise up in the west center to attract rainfall and provide an ideal setting for the vine; currently there are over 98,000 acres of vineyard.

Despite her close proximity to Turkey, Cyprus' ethnic and viticultural traditions are distinctly Greek. The Knights Templar settled in Cyprus in the 12th century, and their order at Limassol made a sweet, liquorous wine that later grew famous under the name Commandaria. This fine dessert wine is still made today. Cyprus also produces a wide variety of good red and white wine, and a large quantity of FORTIFIED WINES called "Cyprus sherry." Most wine for export is made by four large Limassol firms: Keo, Sodap, Etko, and Loel.

Dão (*Downg*): Wine region in north-central Portugal, situated some 50 miles southeast of the city of Oporto. The town of Viseu is Dão's center, both viticulturally and economically. The hard, granitic soil produces good white wines and especially fine, full-bodied reds made from the same grape varieties used for making PORT. White Dão is best consumed young, but the red wine ages well and continues to develop for a decade or longer. Increasingly popular in the U.S., Dão is one of Portugal's best red wines and represents exceptional value.

Debröi Hárslevelü (*Deh'-broy-ye Harsh'-level-yuh*): Good quality white wine produced northeast of Budapest, Hungary, on the slopes of the Matra Mountains. Debroi Hárslevelu takes its name from the Hárslevelu grape, an indigenous variety, and may be either dry or semi-sweet, depending on the vintage.

Decant: To transfer the contents of one wine bottle to another container. Generally a glass wine decanter is used, though a clean, washed bottle may be substituted for a decanter.

The idea of decanting is twofold: aeration during the decanting process allows the wine to "breathe" and gain in bouquet; separation of the wine from its sediment will allow it to be served perfectly clear, without any harshness imparted by the sediment or the cloudiness it creates when stirred up.

Many red wines throw a sediment as they age, and have to be decanted; white wines can also be decanted, but as they are usually served chilled, directly from the bottle, most white wines do not benefit from decanting. To decant a wine that has sediment, stand it upright a day or so in advance so that the sediment collects at the bottom. Then, gently transfer the contents near a light source so that when sediment is seen trickling into the decanter, the operation can be stopped.

de Chaunac (*Seibel 9549*): Red French HYBRID grape variety, grown to a wide extent in New York's Finger Lakes district and in the Niagara Peninsula in Canada; produces full-bodied red wines with plenty of color. Named for the Canadian enologist Adhemar F. de Chaunac, the grape is of uncertain origin but was one of a number of crosses developed by M. Albert Seibel around the turn of the century. The wines that it gives can be good, provided that skin contact is kept relatively short; too much skin contact often results in unpleasant vegetal flavors in the finished wine.

Dégorgement (*Day'-gor-zha-mawn*): French for "disgorging": the process used in the French CHAMPAGNE country for removing sediment introduced by a secondary fermentation. After REMUAGE or "riddling," the sediment collects on the cork and is removed (disgorged) by placing the neck of the bottle in a freezing brine solution, and then allowing the frozen sediment to pop out under pressure when the bottle is opened.

Degree Day: A unit of measurement of heat summation, determined by the difference in degrees above 50° F. (10° C.), multiplied by the number of days at which the change in degrees occurred. The normal growing season for the vine depends on temperatures greater than 50° F., and the degree day system may be used to classify viticultural growing zones. Using an annual total of degree days, scientists have determined five principal winegrowing zones in California: Region I, the coolest, with

101

2,500 degree days or less; Region II, 2,501–3,000 degree days; Region III, 3,001–3,500 degree days; Region IV, 3,501–4,000 degree days; and Region V, the warmest, with more than 4,000 degree days. Premium wine grape varieties generally do best in Regions I and II; table grapes and raisins are best suited for Regions IV and V.

Deidesheim *(Die'-dess-heim)*: Fine wine area in the RHEINPFALZ (Palatinate), Germany. Located in the central portion of the Rheinpfalz called the Mittel-Haardt, Deidesheim's vineyards extend over approximately 950 acres and usually produce some of the finest white wines of the Rheinpfalz; the best of them are planted exclusively in Riesling. The leading vineyards or EINZELLAGEN are: Hergottsacker, Hohenmorgen, Leinhöhle, Grainhübel, Kieselberg, Letten, Paradiesgarten, and Maushöhle.

Delaware: Native American pink grape of the species LABRUSCA, named not for the state of Delaware but the town of Delaware, Ohio. Widely planted in New York State and Ohio, the Delaware is valuable both as a table grape and as an ideal wine grape, for it has a high sugar content when ripe. Though pink, it yields white juice, and is especially good for making sparkling wine.

Demijohn: An oversized wine container, usually in the form of a straw-covered glass flagon, with a capacity ranging from one to ten U.S. gallons. Inexpensive Spanish wines are often bottled in demijohns.

Demi-Sec *(Dem'-mee Seck')*: French for "semi-dry"; officially, a grade of sweetness employed in the French CHAMPAGNE country. Like EXTRA DRY, this term is somewhat misleading because it really indicates a sweet Champagne with up to 6% sugar syrup solution added by the "shipping dosage" (LIQUEUR D'EXPÉDITION).

Only those Champagnes labeled DOUX (sweet) are sweeter.

Denominazione di Origine Controllata *(Dee-nommy-nots-ee-oh'-nay dee Aw-ree'-gin-ay Cawn-trol-lah'-ta)*: Italian for "controlled denomination of origin," the law specifying approved place-names for Italian wines. Similar to the French laws of APPELLATION CONTRÔLÉE, the Denominazione di Origine Controllata (D.O.C.) laws were enacted in 1963 and have assisted a marked improvement in the quality of Italian wines. The words Denominazione di Origine Controllata on a wine bottle are an indication of superior quality.

The 1963 Italian wine law authorized three denominations:

—*Denominazione di Origine Semplice* (simple). Ordinary wines produced in Italy's traditional wine regions. No quality guarantee accompanies these wines.

—*Denominazione di Origine Controllata* (controlled). Quality wines originating from delimited wine regions, produced from approved grape varieties, and made by traditional practices. The vineyards producing D.O.C. wines are listed in an official register.

—*Denominazione di Origine Controllata e Garantita* (controlled and guaranteed). Particularly fine wines sold in bottles with less than 5 liters (1.32 gallons) capacity, bearing a government seal stating that the wines have conformed to certain standards.

In addition, the laws outline production limits, labeling practices and quality inspection procedures, and provide for penalties to violators.

Dessert Wine: In U.S. wine trade usage, a wine that has been fortified over 14% alcohol (sherry, port, madeira, etc.) by having brandy or spirits added to arrest fermentation, so that residual sugar remains. However, not all fortified wines are sweet, nor are all sweet wines fortified; a less ambiguous definition of a des-

103

sert wine would simply mean a sweet wine to be served with dessert. See FORTIFIED WINE.

Dézaley *(Day'-zuh-lay)*: Fine white wine region in the canton of the VAUD, western Switzerland, situated on the north shore of Lake Geneva east of the city of Lausanne. Planted in Chasselas grapes (locally called Dorin), the Dézaley vineyards produce some of Switzerland's best white wines; one particularly fine vineyard, the Clos des Abbayes, is the exclusive property of the city of Lausanne.

Dhron *(Drone)*: Attractive little town on the MOSEL River, Germany, located between PIESPORT and TRITTENHEIM. One of the oldest wine villages in Germany, Dhron is named after the Dhron River, a tributary of the Mosel, and the town's best vineyards lie along its banks. Dhron lies just to the north of NEUMAGEN, another famous wine village, and the community is called Dhron-Neumagen. The leading vineyards or EINZELLAGEN are: Hofberger (also called Dhronhofberger), Engelgrube, Laudamusberg, Roterde, and Rosengärtchen.

Dienheim *(Deen'-heim)*: Town and vineyard area in the RHEINHESSEN region, Germany, located south of OPPENHEIM. With well-exposed vineyards largely planted in Silvaner, Dienheim is one of the lesser-known wine towns of Rheinhessen and its wines are often exceptionally good value. There are over 900 acres of vineyard in Dienheim; the leading vineyards or EINZELLAGEN include: Paterhof, Falkenberg, Herrenberg, Kreuz, and Tafelstein.

D.O.C.: see DENOMINAZIONE DI ORIGINE CONTROLLATA.

Dolceacqua *(Dole-chay-ack'-wa)*: Italian for "sweet water"; a good red wine produced near the town of San Remo on the Italian Riviera, the region of LIGURIA, Italy. Made from the Rossese grape, Dolceacqua may sometimes be called Rossese di Dolceacqua; the wine has been famous for centuries, and was awarded D.O.C. status in 1972.

Dolcetto *(Dole-chet'-toe):* Red grape grown in the region of PIEMONTE, northern Italy, and the name of the good red wine that it produces. Fragrant and fruity, Dolcetto is usually the quickest to mature of the red Piemonte wines. Four areas that produce Dolcetto were granted D.O.C. status in 1974: Dolcetto di Diano d'Alba, Dolcetto d'Asti, Dolcetto delle Langhe Monregalesi, and Dolcetto d'Alba.

Dôle *(Dole):* One of the best red wines of Switzerland, produced in the canton of VALAIS in the upper RHÔNE River valley. Dôle is made from both the Pinot Noir and Gamay grapes in equal proportions; sometimes Petite Dôle, made only from the Pinot Noir, is also produced. Generally quite full-bodied, Dôle has a deep, dark color, and ages well.

Domaine *(Doe-main'):* French for "wine estate." In the region of BURGUNDY, the estate may include vineyards owned in part or entirely by one owner. If the wines are bottled at the property by the owner, they are entitled to be labeled "Mis en Bouteilles au Domaine" (see ESTATE-BOTTLED). In BORDEAUX, the word domaine may be used as a property name for a wine, but only if the wine was actually produced on that property (see CHÂTEAU).

Dordogne *(Dor-doyn'-yuh):* Major river in southwestern France; also the name of an administrative region or department. The Dordogne joins the GARONNE River north of the city of BORDEAUX to form the GIRONDE, a tidal estuary. Several wine regions are located further inland on the Dordogne; the most important are BERGERAC, MONBAZILLAC, and PÉCHARMANT. Closer to Bordeaux, the region of FRONSAC also lies on the Dordogne.

Dorin *(Daw-ran')*: The local name for the white Chasselas grape in the canton of VAUD, Switzerland.

Dosage *(Doe-sahj')*: In the French CHAMPAGNE country, the process of adding an extra sugar solution, the LIQUEUR D'EXPÉDITION, to Champagnes before final corking and shipment. All Champagnes are very dry before the dosage, and the amount of dosage relates to customer taste preferences in the region where the wine is to be shipped. Normally, the dosage consists of a mixture of old wine, cane sugar and occasionally brandy, in a carefully measured solution. See CHAMPAGNE.

Doux *(Doo)*: French for "sweet." In the French CHAMPAGNE region, a wine labeled doux is always the sweetest (and usually not the best) Champagne that has received the maximum amount (8–10%) of sugar solution or DOSAGE prior to shipment. Doux Champagnes are popular in warm countries, but are relatively rare in the U.S.

Dry: The opposite of sweet. A dry wine contains only a little residual sugar; a sweet wine has considerable residual sugar. A wine becomes dry when all the sugar is completely fermented into alcohol.

Dubonnet *(Dew-bawn-nay')*: The proprietary name of a wine-based French apéritif to which plant extracts have been added, also manufactured under license in the U.S. in Fresno, California. Two types are produced: red Dubonnet, a semi-sweet wine, and white Dubonnet, which is drier.

Dürkheim *(Deerk'-heim)*: Vineyard town in the RHEINPFALZ (Palatinate) region, Germany, located in the central section known as the Mittel-Haardt. Because of its famous mineral spas, the town is officially called Bad Dürkheim but the wines are known as Dürkheimers. With some 2,000 acres under vines, this is one of the largest wine communities in Germany. A considerable amount of red wine made from the Portuguiser grape is produced in Bad Dürkheim, but the white is superior—particularly if made from the Riesling—and accounts for 75% of the total. The most common vineyard names are Feuerberg, Hochmess and Schenkenböhl, but under the 1971 Wine Law these have become composite vineyards or GROSSLAGEN; the leading single vineyards (EINZELLAGEN) are: Fuchsmantel, Michelsberg, Fronhof, Abtsfronhof, Spielberg, Hochbenn, Herrenberg, Herrenmorgen and Rittergarten.

Earthy: The unmistakable flavor of soil in a wine, usually caused by planting a vineyard in clayey or alluvial soil. If present to a marked degree, it can be most unpleasant. The French term for this is *goût de terroir*; in German it is called *Bodengeschmack*.

Échezeaux *(Esh'-shay-zo):* Fine red wine of the CÔTE DE NUITS, Burgundy, rated Grand Cru (Great Growth). The commune of FLAGEY-ÉCHEZEAUX in which it is produced is named after Échezeaux, though there is actually no vineyard of this name; wines labeled Échezeaux will come from about ten different vineyards extending over some 76 acres, whose wines are entitled to this famous appellation. The especially fine vineyard of GRANDS-ÉCHEZEAUX which lies nearby covers 22½ acres and is considered superior to Échezeaux, yet both wines are prized for their scent and delicacy. Production of both Grands-Échezeaux and Échezeaux averages about 12,600 cases.

107

Edel *(Aid'-ll):* German for "noble"; when applied to wine, a very great one, with considerable class and substance.

Edelfäule *(Aid'-ll-foy-luh):* German for "noble mold," the fungus that collects on grape skins and concentrates the juice without rotting the grapes. See BOTRYTIS CINEREA.

Edelzwicker *(Aid'-el-tsvik-er):* In the region of ALSACE, France, a wine blended from several different grape varieties; often from second pressings or grape must close to the lees. The wines were formerly known as "Zwicker," and varied considerably in quality; it was recently declared that the term Zwicker shall be superseded by "Edelzwicker," recalling the German word *Edel*, or "noble"—in order to identify the mandatory blending of the *cépages nobles* used in the preparation of Edelzwicker: Riesling, Gewürztraminer, Tokay d'Alsace (Pinot Gris), and Muscat. Although some Edelzwicker can be quite pleasant, they represent the most basic grade of Alsace wine a shipper or grower has to offer, and consequently should never be too expensive.

Égrappage *(Eh'-grap-pahj):* French for "destemming," the process of removing the stalks from grapes before they are crushed and fermented, necessary to avoid an excess of tannin or astringency caused by the stalks. Formerly performed by hand, the process in many places is now carried out by a special machine, an *égrappoir*, which removes the stalks.

Egri Bikavér *(Eh'-gree Beek'-ah-vair):* Famous red wine produced near the town of Eger, Hungary, in the northeastern part of the country. Egri Bikavér, which means "Bull's Blood of Eger" in Hungarian, is made principally from a local red grape variety, the Kadarka, usually with some Pinot Noir and Merlot added. Generally rather full-bodied, Egri Bikavér ages well and is quite long-lived.

Ehrenfelser *(Air′-ren-fel-ser)*: New white grape variety, recently developed at the Geisenheim Viticultural Institute in Germany; a cross between Riesling and Silvaner. Optimized to produce better-quality fruit and higher yields in a short growing season, Ehrenfelser is becoming increasingly popular in the cooler German wine districts—particularly the RHEIN-GAU. It is named for the Ehrenfels ruins overlooking the Rhine near RÜDESHEIM.

Einzellage *(Ein′-tse-log-uh)*: German for "single vineyard." Under the 1971 German Wine Law, an Einzellage is an individual vineyard parcel at least 5 hectares (12 acres) large, located within a specific wine community or WEIN-BAUORT. The smallest geographical unit under the German Law, an Einzellage is a single, unbroken part of a composite vineyard or GROSS-LAGE, and will usually produce superior wine.

Eiswein *(Ice′-vine)*: German for "ice wine"; a rare, special and intensely sweet wine, produced very late in the season from grapes harvested in a frozen state. Officially one of the grades of QUALITÄTSWEIN MIT PRÄDIKAT, Eiswein recently became a more restricted quality category: from 1982, a select wine of BE-ERENAUSLESE grade only, made from overripe grapes harvested berry by berry. Previously, Eisweine could be made in any applicable *Prädikat* category.

Vintners have attempted to salvage frozen grapes since the earliest times; but only recently, with the introduction of modern presses that can quickly and precisely express the rich juice, has Eiswein production been possible on an expanded basis. Late in the growing season, when conditions permit, German vintners allow a few vines to mature well past the normal picking date. During a heavy frost, in the early morning hours when the temperature is at its lowest, the unripe berries within a grape bunch will freeze solid, but the ripest of these will remain only partially frozen, because their

109

higher sugar content has a lower freezing point. If picked quickly and taken to the winery right away to be pressed, a rich, luscious juice will be expressed, allowing an especially sweet and concentrated wine to be made.

Eisweine are essentially a German specialty; but they are also produced in Austria, and a number of American vintners have produced similar wines. They differ from other LATE HARVEST wines in that their high concentration of sugar is the result of freezing, and in addition, their acidity is very high. Consequently the wines take a long time to mature, and very often, can be produced with good results in vintages when the remainder of the crop is disappointing. Because of their very limited production, the wines are extremely costly and are hard to come by.

Eitelsbach (*l'-tells-bock*): Wine community in the RUWER region, Germany; since 1971 officially part of the district of TRIER. Eitelsbach is celebrated chiefly for its leading vineyard, the Karthäuserhofberg, which belonged to Carthusian monks during the Middle Ages and is now administered by Herr Werner Tyrell, president of the German Vintners Association. The property extends over 45 acres, and is divided into five sections or *lagen*: Kronenberg, Sang, Burgberg, Orthsberg, and Stirn; on the unusual little label the specific *lage* will be identified, preceded by the words "Eitelsbacher Karthäuserhofberg." In good vintages, the wines are prized for their bouquet and finesse.

Besides the Karthäuserhofberg, Eitelsbach has another individual vineyard or EINZEL-LAGE, Marienholz, which belongs to several different owners.

Eltville (*Elt'-villa*): Important wine town in the RHEINGAU district, Germany; headquarters of the State Wine Domaine (Staatsweingut) in addition to the famous producers Langwerth von Simmern and Graf Eltz. There are 514 acres of vineyard, the best of them located behind the town away from the Rhine front. Though not considered the greatest of the Rheingaus, Eltville's wines are very consistent and charming, especially in great vintages; the leading vineyards (EINZELLAGEN) include: Sonnenberg, Langenstück, Taubenberg, Rheinberg, and Sandgrub.

Emerald Riesling: A HYBRID grape developed in 1946 by Dr. Harold Olmo of the University of California at Davis. Optimized to produce quality white wines in warm climatic regions, the Emerald Riesling is a cross between the Johannisberg Riesling (White Riesling) and the Muscadelle. In recent years it has proven quite successful, and its acreage—particularly in California's fertile Central Valley—is increasing.

Emilia-Romagna *(Eh-mee'-lee-ah Ro-mon'-ya):* Wine region in central Italy, bounded in the north by the Po River and in the south by the Apennine Mountains. There are three principal wine areas in Emilia-Romagna: the first, near the city of Modena, is the center for the famous sparkling red wine LAMBRUSCO; further west, near the town of Piacenza, is the D.O.C. region of GUTTURNIO, a fine red wine; the southernmost part of Emilia-Romagna, near the little republic of San Marino, is renowned for a golden, semi-sweet white wine, ALBANA DI ROMAGNA, and a dry red, the Sangiovese di Romagna. Both wines are famous locally but the white seems to be better known in the U.S.

Entre-Deux-Mers *(Awn'-truh Duh Mair'):* French for "Between Two Seas"; specifically, an important wine district in the BORDEAUX region, France. The Entre-Deux-Mers vineyards lie between the GARONNE and DORDOGNE Rivers east of the city of Bordeaux, hence the derivation of the name. There are few important wine estates or CHÂTEAUX in Entre-Deux-Mers, but a number of well-estab-

111

lished wine cooperatives produce good dry white wines entitled to the appellation Entre-Deux-Mers; some red wine is made in the region, but it is only allowed the appellation Bordeaux. There are over 3,200 acres of vineyard; more than 1 million cases of wine are made yearly.

Épenots (*Eh'-pen-no*): Fine red wine vineyard in the commune of POMMARD, in Burgundy's CÔTE DE BEAUNE. One of Pommard's best vineyards, Épenots extends over 25 acres; Petits-Épenots, a larger vineyard nearby occupying 50 acres, is not considered to be in the same class, but both vineyards produce fine and graceful red wines, rated Premier Cru (First Growth). The vineyard plot continues into the adjoining commune of BEAUNE to the northeast, and there it is called Beaune Épenottes. This vineyard also produces good red wine, but the Pommard section is superior.

Épernay (*Eh'-pair-nay*): City in the French CHAMPAGNE region, with a population of some 30,000. Situated in the Marne River valley, Épernay forms the northern extreme of the CÔTE DES BLANCS, a slope of vineyard largely planted in white Chardonnay grapes; Moët & Chandon, Pol Roger, Perrier-Jouët, Mercier, and A. Charbaut & Fils are important Champagne producers with offices in Épernay.

Épluchage (*Eh-ploo-shahj'*): A process employed in the French CHAMPAGNE country, by which grape bunches are carefully inspected after picking, and any sick or unripe berries discarded, before being taken to the press house and made into wine.

Erbach (*Air'-bock*): Village in the RHEINGAU district, Germany, with 470 acres of vineyard. Erbach is renowned primarily for a single vineyard, the MARCOBRUNN. Planted in Riesling vines near the Rhine River front, this remarkable vineyard used to be called "Marcobrunner," but since the enactment of the 1971 German Wine Law its wines are called "Erbacher Marcobrunn."

Besides Marcobrunn, Erbach has other superior vineyards or EINZELLAGEN, the most famous being: Siegelsberg, Schlossberg, Steinmorgen, Michelmark and Hohenrain.

Erben *(Airb'-en)*: German for "heirs." When preceded by a proper name, this indicates that the estate's wines are sold under the original family name, and that the estate is managed by the present generation.

Erden *(Aird'-en)*: Small wine village on the MOSEL River, Germany. Celebrated for its excellent wines, Erden lies on the right bank of the Mosel, and its best vineyards or EINZELLAGEN face south on an extraordinary steep slope; the most famous is Treppchen ("little staircase," in German), but Prälat, Busslay and Herrenberg also produce good wine. There are some 200 acres of vineyard in Erden, most of them planted in Riesling.

Erzeuger-Abfüllung *(Air-tsoy'-ger Ab'-foolung)*: German for "Producer Bottling." Authorized under the German Wine Law of 1971, Erzeuger-Abfüllung replaces "Original-Abfüllung," which is no longer allowed on a German wine label. It indicates that the wine has been ESTATE-BOTTLED by a single producer, and not by a shipper. "Aus Eigenem Lesegut," which means "From the Producer's Own Harvest," means essentially the same thing, and may also appear in connection with Erzeuger-Abfüllung.

Escherndorf *(Esh'-shern-dorf)*: Wine village in the region of FRANKEN (Franconia), Germany with some 195 acres of vineyard, most of them planted in Silvaner and Riesling. Escherndorf is one of Franken's leading wine communes; its wines are traditionally shipped in the squat BOCKSBEUTEL bottle native to the region. The most famous vineyards (EINZELLAGEN) are: Lump, Berg, and Fürstenberg.

Estate-Bottled: A term signifying that a wine was produced and bottled by the same person, and not sold in bulk to a shipper. By guaranteeing origin and authenticity, estate-bottling usually indicates a superior wine.

In the region of BORDEAUX, France, an estate-bottled wine is said to be CHÂTEAU-BOTTLED. In BURGUNDY, an estate-bottled wine is officially labeled "Mis en Bouteilles au Domaine" (Domaine-Bottled) or "Mis en Bouteilles à la Proprieté" (Bottled at the Property). These terms are sometimes accompanied by the English translation on the same label.

Some French wines, however, seem to be estate-bottled when in fact they are not; thus the terms "Mis en Bouteilles dans Nos Caves" (Bottled in Our Cellars) "Mis en Bouteilles dans la Région de Production" (Bottled in the Region of Production) and "Mis en Bouteilles par les Vignerons" (Bottled by the Wine-Growers) legally do not mean estate-bottled in French. "Produced and Bottled," written in English on a French wine label, likewise does not mean estate-bottled. While the wines may be quite acceptable, their labels officially do not mean what they imply.

Elsewhere, the 1971 German Wine Law authorizes ERZEUGER-ABFÜLLUNG to indicate estate-bottling, and in California, an estate-bottled wine by law must be made exclusively from grapes grown by the proprietor.

Est! Est! Est!: Good white wine produced in the region of LAZIO, Italy, north of Rome near the town of Montefiascone. Tending to be semi-dry, Est! Est! Est! is made chiefly from Trebbiano and Malvasia grapes, and is rated D.O.C.

Estufa *(Esh-too'-fa):* The process by which the wines of MADEIRA are heated slowly, at high temperature, so as to take on a caramel color and characteristic flavor.

Etna *(Et'-na)*: Fine red, white and rosé wines produced in 20 communes on the slopes of Mount Etna, Sicily, a volcanic peak 10,741 ft. high. Sometimes spelled Aetna, the wines of Etna are among Sicily's best, and are entitled to D.O.C. The whites, called Etna Bianco, are made from a local grape variety, the Carricante; the reds and rosés are produced principally from the Nerello. Some particularly fine Etna reds can improve for a decade or more.

Extra Dry *(French, Extra-Sec)*: A grade of sweetness employed in the French CHAMPAGNE region. Though a wine labeled Extra Dry will be fairly dry, this term usually does not mean what it implies; Champagnes labeled BRUT are actually drier than Extra Dry. Officially, an Extra Dry Champagne contains between 1 and 2% sugar solution from the LIQUEUR D'EXPÉDITION (shipping dosage) added before shipment.

Fass *(Fahss)*: German for "barrel" or "cask," a term used most frequently in the Rhine region. Officially, a Fass has no specific capacity; the *Halbstück* of 600 liters (68.6 cases) is the preferred cask size in the RHEINGAU.

Faugères *(Fo-zhair')*: Wine region in the department of HÉRAULT, southern France, north of the city of Béziers. Both red and white wines entitled to the V.D.Q.S. seal are produced in Faugères; the reds, made from Carignan and Grenache grapes, are superior. Generally well-made and inexpensive, the wines of Faugères are becoming popular in the U.S.

Fendant *(Fawn'-dawn):* The local name for the Chasselas grape in the canton of VALAIS, Switzerland.

Fermentation: The conversion of grape sugar to ethyl alcohol and carbon dioxide by the action of yeasts, which use an enzyme, ZYMASE, to convert the grape sugar by a complex series of biochemical reactions. Fermentation usually stops when 14-15% alcohol is reached, but a different process, MALOLACTIC FERMENTATION, occurs in some wines after the initial fermentation takes place.

Fiasco *(Fee-ass'-co):* Italian for "flask"; specifically, the squat, straw-covered flask in which the wines of CHIANTI and ORVIETO have traditionally been bottled. The plural is *fiaschi*.

Filtration: The process of clarifying a wine by passing it through a filter. A wine filter is usually constructed of several porous layers sandwiched together, through which the wine is pumped under pressure.

Besides removing sediment that might make the wine cloudy, filtration is helpful in removing yeast, bacteria and other unwanted substances so as to stabilize the wine and protect it from spoilage. Essentially an absorption process, filtration should not be confused with FINING, a technique by which colloidal substances are added to the wine to remove particles in suspension.

Finger Lakes: Important wine region in NEW YORK STATE, named for four lakes: Canandaigua, Keuka, Seneca, and Cayuga. The first two lakes are the most significant in terms of leading wineries and total vineyard acreage; Widmer, Taylor, Pleasant Valley Winery, Gold Seal, Bully Hill and Vinifera Wine Cellars are representative Finger Lakes wineries.

Fining: The addition of a precipitating agent (fining agent) to a wine in order to remove small, suspended particles. When the fining agent is added, the particles cling to it and settle to the bottom; the clarified wine is subsequently transferred to another container.

Called *collage* in French, fining is traditionally performed with colloidal fining agents such as egg whites, isinglass, gelatin, or even ox-blood, but nylon powder and bentonite are often substituted nowadays. Traditionally performed at least six months after the vintage, fining assists in stabilizing wines prior to bottling. It is an older method than FILTRATION, but it is equally helpful in removing suspended particles; many wineries presently use both fining and filtration in order to render their wines free of sediment.

Fino *(Fee'-no):* The palest and driest kind of SHERRY, which has matured through the action of FLOR yeast.

Fitou *(Fee'-too):* Excellent red wine produced in the region of CORBIÈRES, in the department of AUDE, France. The Fitou vineyards are planted chiefly in two red grape varieties, Carignan and Grenache, which must constitute at least 75% of the wine. One of the best wines of Corbières, Fitou is entitled to APPELLATION CONTRÔLÉE; by law it must be aged in cask for two years prior to sale. Generally inexpensive, Fitou is often excellent value; about 670,000 cases are produced annually.

Fixin *(Feex'-san):* Red wine commune in the CÔTE DE NUITS, Burgundy. The most northerly village of consequence in the Côte de Nuits, Fixin lies just to the north of GEVREY-CHAMBERTIN and its best wines show a close similarity to those of that famous commune. Fixin's three most important vineyards are rated Premier Cru (First Growth); they include CLOS DE LA PERRIÈRE, CLOS DU CHAPITRE, and Les Hervelets. There are about 106 acres under vines in Fixin; production averages about 10,000 cases annually.

Flagey-Échezeaux *(Flah-zhay′ Esh′-shay-zo):* Town in the CÔTE DE NUITS, Burgundy, named after the great red wine ÉCHEZEAUX, rated Grand Cru (Great Growth). Another Grand Cru vineyard, GRANDS-ÉCHEZEAUX, is considered to be even better, and usually produces one of Burgundy's very finest wines. The vineyard commune of Flagey-Échezeaux lies just to the north of VOSNE-ROMANÉE, and most of its wines are usually sold as Vosne-Romanées, as there is no Flagey-Échezeaux APPELLATION CONTRÔLÉE. Some 150 acres of vineyard lie within the commune boundaries.

Fleurie *(Flur-ree′):* Wine village in the BEAU-JOLAIS district, southern Burgundy, and its fine red wine. Officially one of the nine Beaujolais *crus* (growths), those areas that generally produce the best Beaujolais, Fleurie is one of the most famous *crus.* The wine is prized for its early-maturing, fruity qualities—hence the name, which means "flowery." There are 1,729 acres of vineyards in Fleurie; annual production amounts to some 465,000 cases.

Flor *(Floor):* Spanish for "flower"; specifically, a special kind of yeast, *Mycodermi vini,* found only in certain wine regions—most notably, the SHERRY and MONTILLA districts of Spain, and in the JURA, France. The yeast collects as a thick film on the surface of the wine in the cask and protects it from oxidation; in addition, it imparts an agreeable taste, which is characteristic of the best dry FINO Sherries. In the United States, sherries that have been made by the action of flor yeast are often called "flor sherries," to distinguish them from ordinary sherries that have been "baked" by exposure to high temperature, without the beneficial action of flor yeast.

118

Flora: A white HYBRID grape variety, recently developed by Dr. Harold Olmo of the University of California at Davis. Made from a cross between the Gewürztraminer and the Sémillon, the Flora combines many desirable characteristics of both varieties. Several California wineries have already produced VARIETAL wines from the Flora, and the grape is also well-suited to the making of sparkling wines.

Foch (full name: *Maréchal Foch*, or *Kühlmann 188.2*): Red French HYBRID grape variety, grown extensively in the eastern United States, produced from a riparia-rupestris cross with Goldriesling. Among the red French hybrids that give better-quality wine, Foch is quite winter hardy and ripens early; it gives fairly sturdy red wines reminiscent of a burgundy.

Folle Blanche (*Fall Blawnsh'*): White wine grape, known under several different names. Because of the low alcoholic strength and high acidity of its wines, the Folle Blanche used to be the principal grape variety in the French Cognac district, but now comprises less than 3% of the total vineyard acreage because of its susceptibility to various diseases. Known under the name Picpoul, the Folle Blanche is widely grown in the Armagnac district and in other parts of southern France, where it makes light dry wines; one of the best, Picpoul de Pinet, is rated V.D.Q.S. In the lower LOIRE River valley, the Folle Blanche is called Gros Plant; another wine rated V.D.Q.S., Gros Plant du Pays Nantais, is produced near the city of Nantes and is occasionally exported.

On a limited basis, the Folle Blanche has found a good environment in California; there, its inherently high acidity is lessened, and it is used either for sound and generally inexpensive still white wines, or in blends for better-than-average sparkling wines.

Forst: Famous wine town in the RHEINPFALZ (Palatinate) region, Germany, with some 495 acres of vineyard. Forst is located on a rare basalt outcropping, and largely for this reason, its vineyards are among the most valuable in the Rheinpfalz. Three-fourths of the best sites are planted in Riesling, and in good vintages especially ripe, scented wines are made. The leading vineyards (EINZELLAGEN) are: Kirchenstück, Jesuitengarten, Ungeheuer, Freundstück, Elster, Musenhang, and Pechstein.

Fortified Wine: A wine to which brandy has been added, either to arrest fermentation so as to retain sweetness, or to increase the alcoholic content. Examples of fortified wines include SHERRY, PORT, and MADEIRA. U.S. law does not allow wines of this type to be labeled "fortified wine," and so they must be called DESSERT WINES.

France: Quality wine has an intimate and traditional association with French culture, history and lifestyles. After grain and cereal production, winegrowing is France's second most valuable agricultural product, employing about 15% of the work force; and throughout modern history, French wines essentially define the quality standards to which almost all other great wines are compared.

The quality tradition in France relates in large part to many favorable grape-growing areas throughout the country where climate, rainfall and sunshine combine with the soil to produce high-quality grapes. Certain areas in France are ideal for this, and because of the high value of their products, these areas have become well-established on the export market. France has a long history of selecting only her best representatives to enhance her image of quality wines. But for many years the average Frenchman knew—or cared—very little about the great wines produced in his own country. Well over four-fifths of all French wine is sold in bulk for everyday consumption, and much of this *vin ordinaire* is not even bottled. Many Americans are unaware that, despite France's great reputation for fine food and wines, the average Frenchman is not apt to be a wine connoisseur, although he does consume over thirteen times as much wine as his American counterpart.

In modern France, the old regions and provinces of France are now divided into some ninety-five *départements* or administrative districts, and most of these have vineyards. Each department is listed in alphabetical order, and the numerical sequence of each department also defines the official postal zones and automobile license plates in France. The accompanying chart may be used to determine France's principal winegrowing districts:

Vineyard Acreage In France, By Department

On the accompanying chart, each department is listed in alphabetical sequence, along with a number in the exact sequence that the department is listed. In France, this department number is an invaluable guide in determining location; the first two digits of a postal code relate to the number of the department, and the last two digits on an automobile license plate identify the department in which the vehicle is officially registered.

In the 1970s, postal department numbers in France took on a new meaning in wine labeling. Certain less expensive grades of wines, carrying no specific identification of area of origin, have now appeared on the American market with department code numbers. On the capsule, stamped code numbers identify the district in which the wine was bottled; on the label, a code number is now substituted for the most ordinary grades of wines that by law may not be sold with an indication of place-name. This came in response to many non-appellation wines bottled in famous wine districts, that contained little if any of the actual products of those districts; the new restrictions strengthen the laws of appellation contrôlée in many of France's finest wine districts.

01	Ain	3,877
02	Aisne	3,800
03	Allier	4,485
04	Alpes de Hautes-Provence	4,381
05	Alpes (Hautes-)	1,789
06	Alpes-Maritimes	909
07	Ardèche	35,810
08	Ardennes	2

09	Ariège	1,544
10	Aube	8,856
11	Aude	285,791
12	Aveyron	5,614
13	Bouches-du-Rhône	48,837
14	Calvados	0
15	Cantal	57
16	Charente	116,461
17	Charente-Maritime	143,078
18	Cher	6,771
19	Corrèze	2,343
20	Corse	58,353
21	Côte d'Or	20,475
22	Côtes-du-Nord	0
23	Creuse	2
24	Dordogne	48,209
25	Doubs	67
26	Drôme	41,639
27	Eure	0
28	Eure-et-Loir	0
29	Finistère	0
30	Gard	214,339
31	Garonne (Haute-)	18,916
32	Gers	71,792
33	Gironde	247,236
34	Hérault	365,503
35	Ille-et-Vilaine	0
36	Indre	5,668
37	Indre-et-Loire	30,554
38	Isère	6,368
39	Jura	4,354
40	Landes	18,090
41	Loir-et-Cher	28,599
42	Loire	4,151
43	Loire (Haute-)	638
44	Loire-Atlantique	46,798
45	Loiret	1,782
46	Lot	17,401
47	Lot-et-Garonne	29,187
48	Lozère	208
49	Maine-et-Loire	52,363
50	Manche	0
51	Marne	47,893
52	Marne (Haute-)	255

53	Mayenne	0
54	Meurthe-et-Moselle	432
55	Meuse	89
56	Morbihan	0
57	Moselle	158
58	Nièvre	2,244
59	Nord	0
60	Oise	0
61	Orne	0
62	Pas-de-Calais	0
63	Puy-de-Dôme	4,885
64	Pyrénées-Atlantique	8,350
65	Pyrénées (Hautes-)	4,670
66	Pyrénées-Orientales	138,705
67	Rhin (Bas-)	12,328
68	Rhin (Haut-)	18,253
69	Rhône	50,601
70	Saône (Haute-)	255
71	Saône-et-Loire	25,528
72	Sarthe	1,441
73	Savoie	4,796
74	Savoie (Haute-)	660
75	Paris	0
76	Seine-Maritime	0
77	Seine-et-Marne	22
78	Yvelines	2
79	Sèvres (Deux-)	7,035
80	Somme	0
81	Tarn	45,452
82	Tarn-et-Garonne	28,048
83	Var	105,151
84	Vaucluse	135,480
85	Vendée	15,935
86	Vienne	12,684
87	Vienne (Haute-)	111
88	Vosges	309
89	Yonne	7,255
90	Belfort	0
91	Essone	0
92	Hauts-de-Seine	2
93	Seine-St. Denis	0
94	Val-de-Marne	0
95	Val-d'Oise	0
	TOTAL ACREAGE	2,686,126

DEPARTMENTS

FRANCE

In the decade since these statistics were originally compiled, a number of French wine districts lost acreage. In the past century, in fact, thousands of acres of vines in France have been abandoned, for various reasons. Part of this decline was caused by the inexorable advance of housing, especially in areas near major cities, but many of the lesser-known winegrowing regions cannot sell their products for a fair price that realistically offsets the high cost of production. To make up for these losses, the more traditionally famous areas produce much greater yields per acre than before, and with modern land management and production techniques, the cost of producing wine today is far less than it used to be.

The French government is keenly aware that the traditional fame of French wines is founded on quality. France's most famous regions lie in cool, temperate climates where production is considerably less than in more southerly regions. In addition to considerable taxes levied on wine consumption, strict controls are enforced concerning the production of wine destined for sale to the consumer. As vineyards and climates vary substantially throughout France, it is important to know where the wines are produced; and, if they bear the name of a famous wine region, that the wines are totally authentic and unblended with anything else. First enacted in 1935, the laws of APPELLATION CONTRÔLÉE (controlled place-name) relate to France's highest quality wines from the most famous wine-growing districts, and guarantee the origin and authenticity so that the buyer is assured of getting exactly what he pays for. Appellation contrôlée laws are enforced by the Institut National des Appellations d'Origine (I.N.A.O.), a governmental agency, and the laws are periodically revised and amended as needed.

France's wine laws establish several quality levels. The most basic wine bears no geographical designation, other than its source in

France—the wine is merely graded according to its alcoholic content. Wines sold with an alcoholic strength under 14% are known as *vins de table* (table wines), which, when sold without any indication of area of origin, is generally a producer's most basic and least expensive offering. Much wine is sold under a brand name (*vin de marque*) and is bottled in large-sized containers, for everyday consumption.

The regional wines (*vins de pays*), produced in fairly large growing areas subject to less stringent controls over production, are on a higher quality level. In 1974 the French government authorized 44 regions from which *vins de pays* could originate. The wines are labeled according to their area of origin and the name of the department or administrative region where they were made. A glance at the chart will show where some of the more popular vins de pays are produced. Many such wines are given VARIETAL labels indicating the grape variety or *cépage* from which they were made, and a number of these have become quite popular in recent years, since they are usually well-made and rarely very expensive.

A large number of good French wines are classified as "Vins Délimités de Qualité Supérieur" (V.D.Q.S.), which are subject to official controls before being released for sale. V.D.Q.S. wines must be made from approved grape varieties, grown in delimited regions with a restricted yield per acre. The quality of some V.D.Q.S. wines is quite high, and the law provides that certain areas that have consistently shown an improvement in quality can someday be elevated to the highest quality category: appellation contrôlée.

Appellation contrôlée wines include all of the most famous wines of France. The scope of this category is such that it delimits vineyards ranging from thousands of acres in size down to tiny plots of only a few acres. In addition to regulating winegrowing practices in the vineyard, certain restrictions in the appellation contrôlée laws also regulate what goes on in the cellar. A new measure enacted in 1978 establishes the average production per acre for an area in a given year, and is designed to eliminate lighter, less representative wines that are the result of overproduction. Only the production up to the maximum established in that year may be sold under the appellation; the excess loses the right to the appellation and is said to be "declassified." Few countries have passed such comprehensive wine laws.

Vineyards grow in many areas in France, but not everywhere. An invisible barrier winds across France, above the Loire River; north of this "limit of the vine," centuries of experience have determined that quality wines cannot be consistently produced from vintage to vintage. But south of this barrier, vineyards abound in most regions where they are suited. The more important wine regions include: CHAMPAGNE, the source of the world's most renowned sparkling wine; ALSACE, along the border with Germany, where many good white wines are made; BURGUNDY, the home of some of the world's most famous red and white wines; the RHÔNE River valley, with its noble red wines prized for their strength; PROVENCE, an area steadily gaining in reputation; the MIDI to the south, traditionally an area of bulk wine production but with an increasing number of excellent new appellations; BORDEAUX, one of France's most famous wine regions; and the LOIRE River valley, with a whole chain of quality vineyards following its course across France. An indication of the wide range of excellent French wines can be gleaned by their extensive representation in this encyclopedic dictionary.

Franken *(Frank'-en):* German for "Franconia," an important wine region (ANBAUGE-BIET) in the upper Main River valley, Germany. There are some 7,700 acres of vineyard in Franken, most of them planted in white grape varieties. Some of the best wines of Fran-

128

ken are made from the Silvaner—normally a secondary variety in other parts of Germany— and the wines are traditionally shipped in the squat, green BOCKSBEUTEL bottles native to Franken. The region's center is the city of WÜRZBURG, which has the most famous vineyards, but the neighboring villages of ESCHERNDORF, IPHOFEN and RANDERSACKER are equally acclaimed for their wines. Franken normally produces over 2.2 million cases of wine annually.

Frascati *(Fras-cah'-tee):* Fine white wine from the region of LAZIO (Latium), Italy, produced south of the city of Rome. Made chiefly from Malvasia and Trebbiano grapes, Frascati is one of the best wines of the CASTELLI ROMANI district. Three types are produced: dry, semi-dry, and *cannellino* (sweet); the dry is more popular in the U.S. The wine has been famous since the days of the Renaissance, and is rated D.O.C.

Frecciarossa *(Frech-ya-ross'-ah):* Italian for "red arrow," the proprietary name for red, white and rosé wines produced near the town of Casteggio in the region of LOMBARDY, Italy. Frecciarossa is made by the estate of Dr. Giorgio Odero, who labels the red *(rosso)* "Grand Cru," the white *(bianco)* "La Vigne Blanche," and the rosé "St. George."

Free Run: The free-flowing wine after fermentation, as opposed to the solid residue or POMACE. After the free run wine is drawn off, the pomace can be pressed to extract PRESS WINE, which contains more tannin and coloring. Called *vin de goutte* in French, free run wine usually makes up four-fifths of the total volume of fermented wine.

Normally, free run wine is superior to press wine and many producers bottle it separately, but press wine is often blended with free run wine for a balanced product.

129

Freiherr *(Fry'-hair):* German for "baron." The nobility still own many wine estates in Germany, and this term occasionally appears on a German wine label.

Freisa *(Fray'-za)*: Red wine grape grown extensively in PIEMONTE, northern Italy; also the name of its wine. One of the best of Piemonte's lesser-known wines, Freisa may be either dry or semi-sweet, and is sometimes slightly sparkling or *frizzante*. Two Freisa wines bear the D.O.C. seal: Freisa di Chieri (usually the best and most famous), produced east of the city of Turin in the Monferrato Hills, and Freisa d'Asti. A third, Freisa delle Langhe, has not yet received D.O.C. status.

Friuli-Venezia Giulia *(Free-oo'-lee Ven-etts'-ee-ah Julia)*: Wine region in the extreme northeast corner of Italy, bordering Austria and Yugoslavia. Friuli-Venezia Giulia produces a great variety of wines; not many are exported, but some are excellent value. There are several D.O.C. wines; the most famous is Collio Goriziano (or Collio), a golden, dry white wine. Collio may be produced from several varieties; the most important is occasionally indicated on the label. Colli Orientali del Friuli, another D.O.C., comes from the eastern hills of Friuli in the province of Udine; this district is famous for Picolit, a rare and exquisite sweet white wine. The region's third D.O.C. is Grave del Friuli, named for the region of Grave between the towns of Udine and Pordenone. The average annual production for the region as a whole is over 14 million cases of wine.

Frizzante *(Fritz-sahn'-tee)*: Italian for "semi-sparkling"; said of some Italian wines that are occasionally bottled early, allowing a slight secondary fermentation to develop.

Fronsac *(Frawn'-sack)*: Town in the BORDEAUX district, France, located along the DORDOGNE River. The fine, sturdy red wines of Fronsac are not well-known, but are among the best values in Bordeaux wines. As the region is hilly, wines from this district used to be sold as "Côtes de Fronsac" or "Côtes Canon-Fronsac," but to simplify matters two new APPELLATION CONTRÔLÉES were recently issued by the French government, in which the word "côtes," meaning hillsides, has been suppressed.

—*Fronsac*, the first new appellation, applies only to red wines produced on the right bank of the Dordogne River, near the city of Libourne. It lies to the north of the smaller district of Canon-Fronsac and the wines are similar, although Canon-Fronsac has the more traditional reputation. The leading estates (CHÂTEAUX) include La Dauphine, Rouet, La Croix, des Tonnelles, La Rivière, and La Valade; production annually amounts to some 300,000 cases of full, slow-maturing red wine.

—*Canon-Fronsac*, the second new appellation, relates to a smaller area of vineyards located closer to the Dordogne River, named for its most famous wine estate, Château Canon. Production is less than one-half that of the larger district of Fronsac, and the wines tend to be fuller and finer than most Fronsacs. The leading estates include Châteaux Canon, Canon-de-Brem, Bodet, Toumalin, du Gaby, Pichelebre, and Junayme.

Frontignan (*Frawn'-teen-yawn*): French wine region and town on the Mediterranean coast, north of the city of Sète. Frontignan is famous for its golden sweet wine made from the Muscat Doré grape, called Muscat de Frontignan. Officially rated APPELLATION CONTRÔLÉE, Muscat de Frontignan is a FORTIFIED WINE to which brandy is added to arrest fermentation and retain sweetness; its minimum alcoholic strength is 15%. Bottled with a special seal, the wine is similar to SHERRY, and is very popular in France as an apéritif. The Frontignan vineyards extend over 865 acres; three-fourths of the annual production of 228,700 cases is produced by the Frontignan wine cooperative.

Fuder *(Foo'-der)*: German for "barrel" or "cask." Originally a Fuder was a tun (tonne), an old measure of cooperage; nowadays it is an oak cask used in the MOSEL region, with a capacity of 1,000 liters (114 cases).

Fumé Blanc *(Foo-may Blawn')*: The inverted version of BLANC FUMÉ, the local name for the Sauvignon Blanc grape variety grown in the upper LOIRE River valley in France. Essentially a term used in California by some wineries, Fumé Blanc relates to a drier style of Sauvignon Blanc; alternately, Sauvignon Blanc may be used to describe a slightly sweeter wine, although at present there seems to be no specific criterion for use.

Funchal *(Foon'-shal)*: The largest town on the island of MADEIRA, and the headquarters of the Madeira wine trade, where the shippers' offices (lodges) are located.

Furmint *(Foor'-mint)*: The grape variety grown in the TOKAY district, Hungary, and in other Hungarian wine regions.

Fürst *(Foorst)*: German for "prince."

Gaillac *(Guy'-yak)*: Wine region in southwestern France, located around the town of the same name in the department of Tarn. There are two Gaillac APPELLATION CONTRÔLÉES, Premières Côtes de Gaillac and Gaillac, which apply to red, white or rosé wines. It is primarily the sweet or semi-sweet wines of Gaillac, which are occasionally made sparkling *(mousseux)*, that have made the region famous. Sparkling Gaillacs may be produced either by the Champagne process or by merely bottling the wine early, when residual sugar and yeast are still present. The area under vines in Gaillac is 2,700 acres; production amounts to the equivalent of 686,000 cases of wine annually.

Galestro (*Gal-less'-tro*): White wine produced in the region of TUSCANY, Italy; a recent addition to the growing number of dry white wines from that region. Produced primarily on the initiative of the Antinori family in Tuscany, Galestro is made from Trebbiano and Malvasia grapes, that in the past would have normally been used to lighten up red CHIANTI wines. Since Tuscan producers now wish to produce a fuller and finer Chianti without the previous addition of white grapes, Galestro represents an ideal solution to the surplus from existing white wine vineyards in the area. Besides Antinori, production of Galestro now includes many other firms and is increasing.

Gamay (*Gam'-may*): Red wine grape grown extensively in the BEAUJOLAIS district, southern Burgundy. The zesty, generous red wines that it gives are prized for their quick-maturing, fruity qualities. There are several varieties of Gamay, some of which give red juice; the *Gamay Noir à jus blanc*, which gives white juice, is the only one permitted in Beaujolais. This grape is a secondary variety in the CÔTE D'OR to the north, where it is often used in blends with Pinot Noir, which are called "Bourgogne Passe-Tout-Grains" (see BOURGOGNE). The Gamay is also grown in other parts of France and in Switzerland.

In California, Gamay has presented a problem as to what it should really be called. Almost 5,000 acres of Gamay have been planted in northern California, where it is also called "Napa Gamay"; generally these wines do not resemble French Beaujolais, although recently some producers have succeeded in making good wines in the same, fruity style. For years, a related variety was grown in California and its wines were marketed under the name "Gamay Beaujolais," since the grape was thought to be the original Gamay grown in France. Recently, grape specialists (ampelographers) determined that Gamay Beaujolais was actually a CLONE, or sub-variety, of Pinot Noir, and that the "Napa Gamay" now grown in California is not the real Gamay at all, as was commonly believed; latest findings identify it as Valdiguié, an obscure variety still cultivated in southwestern France. As the science of grape identification becomes more precise in California, there will hopefully be less confusion on the marketplace in years to come.

Gambellara *(Gam-buh-larr'-ah)*: Light white wine produced in the region of VENETO, northeast Italy. The D.O.C. region of Gambellara lies east of the city of Verona, and adjoins the more famous white wine district of SOAVE; the wines are similar and are made from identical grape varieties, but Gambellara is generally a lighter wine and is much less well-known.

Garganega *(Gar-ga'-nay-ga)*: White grape variety used in making the wines of SOAVE, and other good white wines of northern Italy.

Garonne *(Gar-rawn')*: Major river in southwestern France, drawing its source in the foothills of the Pyrénées and draining into the GIRONDE estuary north of the city of BORDEAUX. The wine regions of GRAVES, SAUTERNES, and Premières Côtes de Bordeaux lie near the Garonne.

Garrafeira *(Gahr-ra-fay'-ra)*: Portuguese for "private cellar," a term roughly equivalent to the Spanish *Reserva*; used to describe a select lot of wines from better vintages, aged longer in cask or in bottle prior to release. When seen on a label, garrafeira may indicate a particularly fine lot, set aside for further aging, which is released in limited quantity at a higher price than a grower's normal production. Some of Portugal's finest wines fall into this group.

Gattinara *(Got-tee-nar′-rah)*: Excellent red wine produced in the region of PIEMONTE, northern Italy. Made from the Nebbiolo grape, Gattinara is one of the very finest Italian red wines— rich, pungent, and slow to mature. It is produced in the section of Piemonte known as the Novara Hills, just southwest of Lake Maggiore; in this district, the Nebbiolo is also known locally as the Spanna, and sometimes a bottle of Gattinara will be labeled Spanna. Gattinara must be aged at least four years before being sold; about 29,000 cases are produced annually.

Gavi *(Gah′-vee)*: Little town in the region of PIEMONTE, northern Italy, famous for its white wine. See CORTESE.

Geisenheim *(Guy′-zen-heim)*: Town and wine region in the western portion of the RHEINGAU district, Germany. The location of a famous school of viticulture, Geisenheim has several good vineyards planted in Riesling, though not many of its white wines are widely known outside of Germany. The entire Geisenheim commune officially has over 1,000 acres suitable for cultivation, though only about half are presently under vines. The leading vineyards (EINZELLAGEN) are: Rothenberg, Mäuerchen, Kläuserweg, Mönchspfad, Kilzberg, Fuchsberg, and Schlossgarten.

Gemeinde *(Ge-mine′-duh)*: German for "community" or "municipality," a delimited township and the surrounding land. This term is roughly equivalent to the French COMMUNE.

Generic *(Jen-nair′-ick)*: A wine labeled according to a particular class or type, as opposed to place of origin. Under U.S. labeling law, a generic wine is named after a wine region that has ceased to have any significance of geographical origin—chablis, sauterne, cham-

135

pagne, etc. Originally these names were used by American winemakers to label their products, for lack of better names. But since many nations have codified wine laws restricting the use of place names, there has been considerable pressure on the U.S. to prohibit generic labeling. This could only come about with great difficulty, however, since these names are in such widespread use.

In the U.S. wine trade nowadays, a generic wine usually falls into the lower quality categories, and most wineries prefer to use VARIETAL labeling for their premium wines, specifying the grape variety used. However, U.S. law permits generic labeling for any wine, so long as the true place of origin is clearly indicated on the label.

Germany: German winegrowers not only produce some of the world's most distinctive and scented white wines, they succeed in producing them in what is probably the most northerly winegrowing area in the world—a climate located on the same latitude as Labrador and Winnipeg, Canada, with only a short, cool growing season. While the uncertain climate in Germany makes production of wine inconsistent from vintage to vintage, it also produces wines with a delectable acid balance that assures longevity, and delicate nuances and scents that contribute to the fame of Germany's wines world-wide.

In 1982 Germany had some 220,000 acres of vineyard, spread out largely in the south-central part of the country, and 85% of these vineyards are devoted to white wine production. Red wines cannot give consistently good results in such a cool, northerly climate, and so they play a secondary role. Many of the best vineyards are located close to rivers, where water bodies hold down fluctuations in temperature, and give off heat and humidity to assist the vines during the growing season. The vineyards also tend to have a southerly ex-

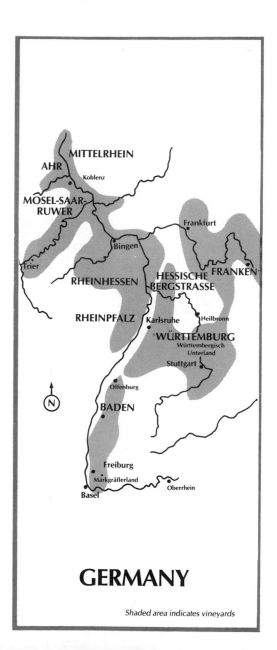

MITTELRHEIN

AHR

Koblenz

MOSEL-SAAR-
RUWER

Frankfurt

Bingen

Trier

RHEINHESSEN   HESSISCHE   FRANKEN
                      BERGSTRASSE

RHEINPFALZ   Karlsruhe   Heilbronn

WÜRTTEMBURG
Württembergisch
Unterland

Stuttgart

Offenburg

N

BADEN

Freiburg

Markgräflerland   Oberrhein

Basel

GERMANY

Shaded area indicates vineyards

posure, so that they receive as much sunshine during the day as possible.

Traditionally, German wines are mild, low in alcohol, and slightly sweet, a style best exemplified in the popular LIEBFRAUMILCH—probably Germany's most famous wine. This slight sweetness is intended to offset the wines' characteristically high acid content. More recently, German vintners are devoting an increasingly large portion of their production to drier wines—the so-called "TROCKEN" (dry) and "HALBTROCKEN" (semi-dry) wines. These wines reflect a change in public tastes towards a wine that can be enjoyed with food rather than on its own, and they first appeared in quantity on the U.S. market in the 1970s. Whether they will be successful here remains to be seen, however, since less expensive dry wines from other countries are more readily available, and the consumer still expects German wines to be slightly sweet.

German wines would certainly be more successful in the U.S. if the average consumer were not so wary of long, unpronounceable names and labels with ornate German script lettering. Exporting firms are adapting labels and selection to the market's requirements—but the key to understanding a German wine label is its logic. In addition to listing the producer's name and the vintage year, a German wine label usually indicates the town or growing district where it was made and, if the wine is superior, the name of the vineyard. The town and vineyard name are always included together, in that order (e.g., Rauenthaler Baiken, Piesporter Goldtröpfchen).

To protect the quality of German wines, the government adopted a comprehensive set of wine laws in 1971 that set forth quality standards for growing, production, and labeling. Wine laws have been in effect in Germany for decades, but the 1971 German Wine Law is one of the world's most complete and comprehensive sets of wine legislation. Because the vine is near its northern limit in Germany, the law recognizes the need to add sugar to grape juice or must (see CHAPTALISATION), but only to increase alcohol and not to sweeten the wine. In addition, the law also limits the addition of sugar to only the most basic wines, not the highest-quality wines that are the pride of German viticulture.

The 1971 Wine Law recognizes several distinct quality categories for German wines. The most basic is called TAFELWEIN, or table wine; *Deutscher Tafelwein* may only be made from German wine, although in some vintages European Economic Community (E.E.C.) wines may be blended for proper balance. Some German Tafelwein is exported, but most of it is produced for home consumption. An important addition to the German Wine Law in 1982 was the enactment of a new category for German regional wines, or LANDWEIN. Qualitatively, these are a step above Tafelwein, but as they include the most basic blends they are still best suited to the interior market.

Most German wine in the export trade falls into the category of QUALITÄTSWEIN (quality wine), which is produced in designated growing districts or ANBAUGEBIETE. There are two groups of Qualitätswein: the most basic is Qualitätswein bestimmter Anbaugebiete (quality wine from designated growing regions), which may be produced with sugar added. When released for sale, the wine is subject to government inspection; under the Wine Law, all Qualitätswein must bear an official government certification number *(Amtliche Prüfungsnummer)*, which identifies the region, the winery, the particular lot of wine, and the year the wine was certified. This system is designed to insure quality control, and to protect the buyer.

The best German wines are made from fully-ripened grapes that need no addition of sugar: QUALITÄTSWEIN MIT PRÄDIKAT (quality wine with distinction). All of Germany's best wines belong to this group (see KABINETT, SPÄT-LESE and AUSLESE). Each category of *Prädikat* wines has legal minimum MUST WEIGHT standards for ripeness and sugar content (as noted in the table below), and all Prädikat wines receive the official tasting approval and certification before being released for sale.

For centuries, German wines have been closely identified with a single, outstanding grape variety that thrives in the cool climate—the Riesling. In select locales, Riesling yields the ideal combination of flavor, acid balance and ability for aging that has lead to the great

Minimum Oechsle Reading (Must Weight) for German Wines	Ahr	Baden	Franken	Hessische Bergstrasse	Mittelrhein
Kabinett					
Riesling	70	75	76	73	70
Müller-Thurgau & Silvaner		72	76		
All other whites	73	75	76	73	73
All reds	73	78	80	78	
Spätlese					
Riesling	76	85		85	76
Ruländer/Traminer	80	88	90	85	81
All other whites	80	85	85	85	80
All reds	85	91	90	90	80
Auslese					
Riesling	83	98	100	95	83
All other whites	88	101	100	100	88
All reds	88	101	100	105	
Beerenauslese					
All varieties	110	124	125	125	110
Trockenbeerenauslese					
All varieties	150	150	150	150	150

This chart, derived from the 1971 German Wine Law, shows the legal minimum Oechsle readings for each category of Qualitätswein mit Prädikat. It gives an idea of the amount of sunshine each wine region (Anbau-

renown of German wines. Also known as White Riesling or Johannisberg Riesling, this grape is ideal for the technique of late-harvesting (see LATE HARVEST), because it has the ability to ripen steadily and retain acidity.

But Riesling is not suited to all areas and soils; and traditionally the Silvaner (Sylvaner) has been planted in other regions, for greater production. Now the Silvaner is being phased out in many areas, in favor of a new grape crossing, Müller-Thurgau, now the most widely cultivated grape in Germany. Although not as winter hardy as Riesling, Müller-Thurgau can

Mosel-Saar-Ruwer	Nahe	Rheingau	Rheinhessen	Rheinpfalz	Württemberg	Minimum Oechsle Reading (Must Weight) for German Wines
						Kabinett
70	70	73	73	73	72	Riesling
	73		73	73	72	Müller-Thurgau & Silvaner
73	76	73	76	76	75	All other whites
	76	80	76	76	75	All reds
						Spätlese
76	78	85	85	85	85	Riesling
	85	85	85	85	85	Ruländer/Traminer
80	82	85	85	85	85	All other whites
	90	90	90	90	90	All reds
						Auslese
83	85	95	92	92	95	Riesling
88	92	100	95	95	95	All other whites
	100	105	100	100	95	All reds
						Beerenauslese
110	120	125	120	120	124	All varieties
						Trockenbeerenauslese
150	150	150	150	150	150	All varieties

gebiet) normally receives, as well as the grape varieties grown in each region. In the north it is more difficult to make an Auslese; the minimum Oechsle readings are equivalent to a Spätlese in the south.

be counted on for productivity and regularity. Produced by crossing Riesling with Silvaner, Müller-Thurgau introduced a whole new science to world viticulture: the creation of new grape varieties that can be optimized to specific climates and requirements.

Produced in institutes for grape-growing and grape-breeding in Geisenheim, Siebeldingen and Weinsberg, a host of these new grape-breedings *(Neuzüchtungen)* is being planted in many areas, although the best and most famous vineyards will continue to be planted in Riesling. There are dozens of successful new grape varieties; some of the better known include Scheurebe (S-88), Bacchus, Faber, Siegerrebe, Huxelrebe, Kanzler, Morio-Muskat, and Ortega. Three of the most promising new German grapes are Ehrenfelser, Kerner, and Optima (see); they ripen earlier than Riesling, give a more reliable production, and still retain much of the same flavor. Very exciting possibilities are afforded by the Neuzüchtungen, so long as they allow the wines to reflect the vineyard and growing area, and not the taste of the grape. For this reason, the more neutral varieties are preferred, for the best wines.

Of the eleven designated Anbaugebiete, four border the Rhine River, one of Europe's most important waterways. Probably Germany's most famous wine district is the RHEIN-GAU, extending west from Hochheim to Assmannshausen. Produced mostly from Riesling, Rheingau wines are characteristically ripe and full-flavored, particularly in great vintages. To the south is the RHEINHESSEN district, the largest wine region, probably better known for Liebfraumilch than the other outstanding wines it produces. Away from the Rhine plain to the south is the RHEINPFALZ (Palatinate), Germany's most productive wine region; its center, the Mittel-Haardt, is a particularly noted wine district. The MITTELRHEIN, Germany's most northern wine region, extends south from Bonn to Bingen; some good wines are made, but their production is limited. The same applies to the HESSISCHE BERGSTRASSE, the country's smallest wine region, located between the cities of Heidelberg and Darmstadt.

Two important tributaries of the Rhine, the MOSEL and NAHE Rivers, also have outstanding vineyards. The Mosel in turn has two tributaries, the SAAR and RUWER rivers, which produce some exceptional wines; the designated Anbaugebiet is Mosel-Saar-Ruwer. Their wines are prized for their scent and delicacy; Nahe wines, not as yet well-known in the U.S., recall some of the better Rheingaus. The little district of the AHR, to the north, produces some light red wine from the Spätburgunder (Pinot Noir), most of which is destined for home consumption.

The three remaining districts are all further to the south. BADEN, the most southerly, extends along the French border north from Lake Constance (Bodensee). Its wines are steadily gaining in reputation. To the northwest, WÜRTTEMBERG produces a wide variety of red, white and rosé wines, but not many are exported. FRANKEN (Franconia), located around the city of Würzburg, is noted for its sturdy white wines shipped in the squat, green BOCKSBEUTEL bottles native to that region.

The color of the traditional, fluted German wine bottle varies by region. Mosel-Saar-Ruwer wines are always shipped in green bottles; Rhine wines and Nahe wines are shipped in brown bottles. Bocksbeutel bottles are always green in Germany.

Gevrey-Chambertin *(Jev'-ray Shawm'-bairtan):* Famous town and red wine commune in the northern CÔTE DE NUITS, Burgundy, since 1847 named after the great CHAMBERTIN vineyard, rated Grand Cru (Great Growth). The equally fine CLOS DE BÈZE vineyard alongside is also named after Chambertin, and is known as Chambertin-Clos de Bèze officially. Other

Grand Cru vineyards in Gevrey-Chambertin include LATRICIÈRES-CHAMBERTIN, CHARMES-CHAMBERTIN, MAZOYÈRES-CHAMBERTIN, MAZIS-CHAMBERTIN, CHAPELLE-CHAMBERTIN, GRIOT-TIE-CHAMBERTIN, and RUCHOTTES-CHAMBER-TIN, though these are considered to be in a somewhat lower class. There are several good vineyards of nearly equal quality, rated Premier Cru (First Growth), the names of which are preceded by Gevrey-Chambertin. The most notable include CLOS SAINT-JACQUES, Veroilles, Gazetiers, Estournelles, and Aux Combottes. Wine not produced from a classified vineyard but from a plot within the Gevrey-Chambertin commune is entitled to a commune appellation. There are 506 acres of vineyard in Gevrey-Chambertin; average annual production amounts to some 133,000 cases of red wine, there being no Gevrey-Chambertin appellation for white wines.

Gewürztraminer (German, *Ge-vertz'-tramme'-ner*; French, *Gevoorts'-tram-me-nair'*): Fine white grape variety, grown widely in Germany and in Alsace, France. Its name means "spicy Traminer" in German, and it is an especially selected strain of the Traminer; its wines have a particularly pronounced bouquet and a characteristically full flavor. Because the Gewürztraminer is recognizably superior to the Traminer, it was recently decreed that no more Alsatian wines are to be labeled Traminer—this distinction being reserved for the Gewürztraminer—although the Traminer is still grown in other parts of the world. Transplanted, the Gewürztraminer has proven very successful in California, and many recent California Gewürztraminers compare favorably with better French and German wines; over 3,600 acres have been planted.

144 **Ghemme** (*Gemm'-ay*): Excellent red wine from the region of PIEMONTE, northern Italy, produced in the northern section of Piemonte known as the Novara Hills. Made primarily from the Nebbiolo grape, usually with an admixture of Bonarda or Vespolina added, Ghemme is a powerful, full-bodied red wine that ages well; by law it must attain at least 12% alcohol. The D.O.C. region of Ghemme covers a relatively small area; production amounts to less than 9,000 cases annually.

Gigondas *(She'-gawn-das):* Wine region in the southern RHÔNE River valley, France, situated in the department of Vaucluse. Gigondas recently received an APPELLATION CONTRÔLÉE rating, primarily on the merits of its excellent and sturdy red wines, though rosés and whites are also produced. The area lies just to the northeast of the famous CHÂTEAUNEUF-DU-PAPE region and the wines are similar, though being less well known, Gigondas wines are apt to be considerably less expensive. The equivalent of about 343,000 cases of wine is produced annually in Gigondas.

Gironde *(She'-rawnd):* Tidal estuary formed by the confluence of the GARONNE and DORDOGNE Rivers north of the city of BORDEAUX, France; also the name of a department or administrative region. The vineyards of the MÉDOC lie on the left bank of the Gironde; opposite, on the right bank, lie the vineyards of BOURG and BLAYE.

Givry *(She'-vree):* Wine region in the CHALONNAIS district, Burgundy. One of Burgundy's lesser known regions, Givry produces red and white wines from the Pinot Noir and Chardonnay; the reds are particularly acclaimed. Certain outstanding vineyards in Givry have been rated Premier Cru (First Growth) under the law of APPELLATION CONTRÔLÉE; they include: La Baraude, Clos Saint-Pierre, Clos Saint-Paul, Clos Salomon, and Cellier aux Moines. About 22,900 cases of Givry are produced annually, reds accounting for about four-fifths of the total.

145

Governo (*Go-vair'-no*): The process of adding a small amount of concentrated must made from dried Colorino grapes to the new wine in the CHIANTI region, Italy. The must ferments and causes a small addition of carbon dioxide to form in the wine, giving it a slight sparkle and added freshness. The process of governo is normally reserved for ordinary Chiantis and is not usually performed on the best wines.

Graach (*Grock*): Little town on the MOSEL River, Germany, with some 250 acres of vineyard. Made from the Riesling grape, the fine wines of Graach are among the Mosel's best, especially in dry years, for the soil consists of thick slate that retains moisture. The leading vineyard (EINZELLAGE) is Himmelreich, but there is one excellent Graach wine from a vineyard owned by the von Kesselstatt family, JOSEPHSHOF, which is not sold as a Graach but is called Josephshöfer. Other good Graach vineyards include Abtsberg and Domprobst.

Graf (*Grof*): German for "earl" or "count."

Grand Cru (*Grawn Crew'*): French for "Great Growth," a wine from an officially classified vineyard (see CRU). As authorized by the laws of APPELLATION CONTRÔLÉE, the usage of this term varies in the fine wine regions of France. In BURGUNDY, a Grand Cru is the very highest rating, applying only to rare and distinguished wines. In BORDEAUX, there are several different categories of Grand Cru, depending on the region. In the MÉDOC district, a Grand Cru applies only to those vineyards classified in 1855, which are divided into five groups of *crus*. In SAINT ÉMILION to the east, a Grand Cru defines a classified vineyard, but officially not one of the best; the finest wines are rated Premier Grand Cru (First Great Growth).

Further north, in ALSACE, a new government decree enacted in 1975 provides that the term Grand Cru shall apply only to wines of at least 11% alcohol made from "noble" grape varieties (Gewürztraminer, Riesling, Pinot Gris, and Muscat) grown in the central and best portion of the Alsatian vineyards. In the French CHAMPAGNE region, a Grand Cru rating applies not to a wine but to the vineyards of a particularly famous village, whose grapes fetch a maximum price each year.

Grands-Échezeaux *(Grawns Esh'-shay-zo):* Outstanding red wine produced in the CÔTE DE NUITS, Burgundy, rated Grand Cru (Great Growth). Located in the commune of FLAGEY-ÉCHEZEAUX, the vineyard of Grands-Échezeaux consists of 22½ acres planted in Pinot Noir that adjoin those of ÉCHEZEAUX, also rated Grand Cru but not considered to be quite as fine. A good Grands Échezeaux is typically very scented and graceful, with a good deal of finesse, and many experts consider it one of Burgundy's very best red wines.

Graves *(Grahv):* French for "gravel"; specifically, a fine wine region located near the city of BORDEAUX, France, on the left bank of the GARONNE River. Graves derives its name from the gravelly soil that dominates the region; both red and white wines of fine quality are made in Graves, though more white is produced than red and it tends to be better-known. The northern portion of the Graves region includes the adjoining communes of Pessac, Talence, Léognan, Villenave, Cadaujac and Martillac, each of which has several famous wine estates or CHÂTEAUX. Probably the best-known château in Graves is HAUT-BRION in the commune of Pessac, which produces some of Bordeaux's finest red and white wines, but Graves has a wealth of other fine wine estates, which were officially classified in 1953: (In the following list, châteaux that produce both red and white wines are marked with an asterisk.) Bouscaut*, Carbonnieux*, Domaine de Chevalier*, Couhins, Fieuzal*, Haut-Bailly, La Mission-Haut-Brion, La Tour-

147

Martillac*, La Tour-Haut-Brion, Laville-Haut-Brion, Malartic-Lagravière*, Olivier*, Pape-Clément, and Smith-Haut-Lafitte*. The Graves region as a whole has over 6,000 acres planted in wine grapes.

Greco di Tufo (*Gray'-co dee Too'-fo*): Fine quality white wine grown in the region of CAMPANIA, Italy, produced from the Greco grape grown predominantly on volcanic soil near the little town of Tufo. Rated D.O.C., Greco di Tufo is one of the few Italian white wines that improves with age; some outstanding examples are produced by the Mastroberardino family, who make a similarly fine white wine called Fiano di Avellino.

Greece: Ancient Greece was one of the birthplaces of viticulture. Wine figures heavily in classical Greek poetry, and was considered a gift of the gods. Today, Greece's warm Mediterranean climate is especially well-suited to grape-growing; in addition to wine, table grapes and raisins are other important products. Currently, Greece has over 420,000 acres planted in wine grapes.

Many Americans associate Greek wines with retsina, or resinated wine, which is white or rosé wine to which pine resin is added during fermentation. The custom of resinating wines dates back to ancient times, when it was thought to give the wines longevity, but retsina wines actually age poorly and should be drunk when very young. To many, retsina is an acquired taste, but it is an ideal accompaniment to Greek food. It is mostly produced around the city of Athens, and is made from the Savatiano grape. The Roditis grape is mostly used for rosés.

The most important vineyard area in Greece is the Peloponnesus in the south, where 33% of the country's wine is produced. The little town of Monemvasia on the Mirtoan Sea, famous for its sweet wine, gave its name to Malvasia (Malvoisie), a sweet grape which is

148

now grown all over the world. The Peloponnesus is also the original home of Mavrodaphne, a dark-colored, sweetish red wine that is one of Greece's most famous.

The Greek islands also produce celebrated wine. The Muscat of Samos is a famous, golden sweet wine made from late-harvested grapes. The islands of Crete and Santorin are also noted for their wines. On the mainland, the areas of Thessalia and Macedonia primarily produce red wine, much of which is used in blending.

Most Greek wines exported to the U.S. are produced by large private firms like Cambas, Nicolaou, and Achaia-Clauss, whose headquarters are in the city of Patras on the Peloponnesus. Their brand names of "Castel Danielis," "Demestica," "Santa Helena" and "Pendeli" are well-known in the trade.

Green Hungarian: White wine grape grown in the cool coastal districts of California. Despite its unusual name, the origins of the Green Hungarian are uncertain. It has a rather neutral flavor, and for this reason it is most often used for blending, but occasionally some pleasant, light white wines are made and sold under its VARIETAL name.

Grenache (*Gren-nash'*): Sweet pink grape, used in blends to make the famous red wine of CHÂTEAUNEUF DU-PAPE and on its own to make the fine rosés of TAVEL and LIRAC. The Grenache is also grown in Spain's RIOJA district (where it is called Garnacha), and is the leading variety. Transplanted to California, the Grenache produces some of the best American rosé wines, usually under its VARIETAL name.

Grèves (*Grev*): Fine red wine vineyard in the commune of BEAUNE, in Burgundy's CÔTE D'OR. Considered to be one of the best in Beaune, the Grèves vineyard consists of 78 acres planted in Pinot Noir, and regularly produces very distinguished wine rated Premier

149

Cru (First Growth). A small quantity of particularly fine wine called "Beaune Grèves de l'Enfant Jesus" is produced exclusively by the Burgundy shipper Bouchard Père et Fils.

Grey Riesling: White wine grape grown in many parts of California. Despite its name, it is not a Riesling but another, unrelated variety known in France as Chauché Gris. The Grey Riesling gives pleasant, rather light white wine, especially when planted in cool climates, but it should not be confused with the true Riesling of Germany, called Johannisberg Riesling or White Riesling in California.

Grignolino (*Grin-yo-leen′-o*): Good red wine grape grown in the region of PIEMONTE, northern Italy, also a wine of the same name. Wine made from the Grignolino is characteristically light in color, but it is full-flavored. Two superior areas where it is made, Asti and Monferrato, were recently awarded a D.O.C. rating.

New plantations of Grignolino have also been made in California, and the wines are very similar to their Italian counterpart.

Grinzing (*Grintz′-ing*): Light, fresh white wine produced north of the city of Vienna, Austria, in the suburb of Grinzing. Made primarily from the Grüner Veltliner grape, Grinzing is very charming when consumed young, and is usually drunk during its first year in many Viennese wine taverns (*Weinstuben*), although it is also exported.

Griotte-Chambertin (*Gree-ot′ Shawm′-beartan*): Excellent red wine vineyard in the northern CÔTE DE NUITS, Burgundy, located in the commune of GEVREY-CHAMBERTIN. Officially rated Grand Cru (Great Growth), Griotte-Chambertin is named after the great CHAMBERTIN vineyard, which lies nearby. It is celebrated for its full, rich red wines, but the vineyard is rather small (13½ acres) and production rarely exceeds 1,000 cases annually.

Gropello (*Gro-pell'-o*): Red wine grape grown on the shores of Lake Garda in the region of LOMBARDY, northern Italy. The Gropello is the principal grape variety used for CHIARETTO wines; light red wines and rosés are also made from the Gropello in other parts of Lombardy.

Gros Lot (*Gro Lo*): Productive red grape grown in the lower LOIRE River valley, France, where it is used to produce the ordinary rosés of AN-JOU. Also known as Grolleau, the Gros Lot is often vinified to retain some residual sugar.

Gros Plant (*Gro Plawn'*): The local name for the Folle Blanche grape in the lower LOIRE River valley, France. One distinguished wine produced near the city of Nantes, Gros Plant du Pays Nantais, has a V.D.Q.S. rating.

Grosslage (*Gross'-log-uh*): German for "collective site." Under the 1971 German Wine Law, a Grosslage is a collective or composite vineyard, made up of a number of different individual vineyards (EINZELLAGEN) within a sub-region or BEREICH. It replaces the former generic sites (*Gattungslagen*), which were used for regional wines.

A Grosslage frequently extends over several different wine villages whose vineyards, soil and climate are judged similar; its size may range from 125 acres to over 3,000 acres. While Grosslage wines will rarely be the best a producer has to offer, they represent a more marketable alternative for the producer in several ways. A Grosslage name may be better-known to the consumer than an Einzellage (ex.: Niersteiner Gutes Domthal vs. Niersteiner Orbel); a producer may also choose to de-classify wine from an Einzellage and sell it in blends as a Grosslage; this allows him to offer it at a lower price, which is advantageous for the consumer since Grosslage wines can be produced in all categories of QUALITÄTSWEIN.

151

Frequently Used Grosslagen

Grosslage Anbaugebiet	OTHER VILLAGES IN GROSSLAGE
Bernkasteler Badstube Mosel-Saar-Ruwer	none
Bernkasteler Kurfürstlay Mosel-Saar-Ruwer	Brauneberg, Lieser, Veldenz, Wintrich
Deidesheimer Hofstück Rheinpfalz	Rupperstberg, Eller- stadt, Meckenheim
Dürkheimer Feuerberg Rheinpfalz	Kallstadt, Ellerstadt, Gonnheim
Forster Mariengarten Rheinpfalz	Deidesheim, Wachenheim
Hattenheimer Deutelsberg Rheingau	Erbach
Hochheimer Daubhaus Rheingau	Kostheim, Wicker, Florsheim
Ihringer Vulkanfelsen Baden	Bickensohl, Bötzin- gen, Endingen
Johannisberger Erntebringer Rheingau	Geisenheim, Mittel- heim, Winkel
Kreuznacher Kronenberg Nahe	Bretzenheim, Harge- sheim
Kröver Nacktarsch Mosel-Saar-Ruwer	none
Niersteiner Auflangen Rheinhessen	none
Niersteiner Gutes Domthal Rheinhessen	Nackenheim, Dal- heim, Friesenheim
Niersteiner Rehbach Rheinhessen	Nackenheim
Niersteiner Spiegelberg Rheinhessen	Nackenheim
Oppenheimer Krötenbrunnen Rheinhessen	Deinheim, Alsheim, Guntersblum
Piesporter Michelsberg Mosel-Saar-Ruwer	Neumagen-Dhron, Trittenheim
Rauenthaler Steinmächer Rheingau	Eltville, Martinsthal, Niederwalluf
Rüdesheimer Burgweg Rheingau	Geisenheim, As- smannshausen, Lorch
Rüdesheimer Rosengarten Nahe	Braunweiler, Rox- heim, Weinsheim
Schloss Böckelheimer Burgweg Nahe	Bad Münster, Nieder- hausen, Norheim
Trierer Römerlay Mosel-Saar-Ruwer	Kasel, Avelsbach, Wald- rach, Mertesdorf
Ürziger Schwarzlay Mosel-Saar-Ruwer	Erden, Enkirch, Traben-Trarbach

Wachenheimer Schenkenböhl Rheinpfalz	Bad Dürkheim
Wehlener Munzlay Mosel-Saar-Ruwer	Graach, Zeltingen
Wiltinger Scharzberg Mosel-Saar-Ruwer	Ayl, Kanzem, Ockfen, Oberemmel
Winkeler Honigberg Rheingau	Mittelheim
Zeller Schwarze Katz Mosel-Saar-Ruwer	Senheim, Kaimt, Merl

Grumello *(Grew-mell'-o):* Sturdy red wine produced in the VALTELLINA district, in the region of LOMBARDY, northern Italy. Made from the Nebbiolo grape, which is called Chiavennasca locally, Grumello is one of Valtellina's best wines. It is slow to mature and can live for decades.

Gumpoldskirchner *(Goom'-polds-keersch-ner):* Popular Austrian white wine, produced near the town of Gumpoldskirchen south of the city of Vienna. Gumpoldskirchner is usually made from a blend of Spätrot and Rotgipfler, blended together in equal proportions; occasionally it may also be produced from Neuberger. A dry white wine that is usually best when consumed young, Gumpoldskirchner used to be available only in the Vienna area owing to its popularity, but some very fine wines have recently been shipped to the U.S.

Gutedel *(Goot-aid'-l):* The German name for the Chasselas grape, which is grown primarily in the MARKGRÄFLERLAND district in the region of BADEN. Wines made from the Gutedel tend to be characteristically mild with low acidity, and are agreeable when drunk young.

Gutturnio *(Goo-toor'-nee-o):* Light red wine produced in the hills south of the city of Piacenza, in the region of EMILIA-ROMAGNA, Italy. Made from Barbera and Bonarda grapes, Gutturnio was one of the region's first wines to receive a D.O.C. rating. Its full name is Gutturnio dei Colli Piacentini.

153

Haardt *(Hart)*: Chain of hills in southern Germany, geologically an extension of the Vosges Mountains in France. The Haardt essentially defines the entire RHEINPFALZ (Palatinate) region; it is divided into three sections: in the south, the Ober-Haardt; in the center, the Mittel-Haardt, and in the north, the Unter-Haardt. The Mittel-Haardt is the most famous for its wines.

Halbstück *(Halb'-shtook)*: Wine cask with a capacity of 600 liters (66.7 cases), used in Germany's RHEINGAU region either as a unit of sale in the trade or, formerly, at wine auctions.

Halbtrocken *(Halb'-trawk-ken)*: German for "semi-dry"; a new category for drier German wines, based on the sugar content expressed in grams of residual sugar per liter. Halbtrocken wines are slightly sweeter than the drier TROCKEN wines; they may have a maximum unfermented residual sugar of 18 grams per liter, compared with 9 grams/liter for Trocken. With Halbtrocken wines, however, the acidity may not be less than 10 grams/liter below the residual sugar content—a wine with 18 grams/liter residual sugar may not have less than 8 grams/liter acidity. Halbtrocken wines are released with a light green seal, the *Deutsches Weinsiegel*, identifying the wine as semi-dry.

In comparison to Trocken wines, which are austerely dry to most palates, Halbtrocken wines may be preferred by those who like a drier wine with meals, but still want some balancing residual sweetness. Beyond 18 grams/ liter of sugar, the wine will be sold as a LIEB- LICH or "mild" wine, without any indication of sweetness.

Hallgarten *(Hahl'-garten)*: Village and wine community in the RHEINGAU district, Germany, with some 500 acres of vineyard, mostly planted in Riesling. An upland commune where the Rheingau reaches its highest point, Hallgarten is distinguished by its full-flavored wines, often the most pronounced of the entire Rheingau. The leading vineyards (EINZELLA- GEN) are: Schönhell, Jungfer, Würzgarten, and Hendelberg.

Haro *(Ha'-ro)*: Little Spanish town on the Ebro River, the center of the RIOJA wine trade.

Hattenheim *(Hot'-en-heim)*: World-famous wine village in the RHEINGAU district, Germany, located on the banks of the Rhine River. Hattenheim has 494 acres under vines; its fine wines are distinguished by their grace and elegance. A portion of the great MARCOBRUNN vineyard extends into Hattenheim from neighboring ERBACH, but under the 1971 German Wine Law all of the wine must be labeled Erbacher Marcobrunn. At a higher elevation, the renowned STEINBERG vineyard lies in its entirety within the Hattenheim commune, but all the wines are only sold as Steinbergers. Besides these two vineyards, Hattenheim has several other fine vineyards or EINZELLAGEN; the most famous are: Nussbrunnen, Mannberg, Wisselbrunnen, Engelmannsberg, Pfaffenberg, and Schutzenhaus.

Haut-Brion, Château *(Oh-bree-awn')*: Famous BORDEAUX wine estate, located in the region of GRAVES. Owned by C. Douglas Dillon, an American banker, Château Haut-Brion regularly produces some of Bordeaux's best wines and was the only red wine château outside the MÉDOC region to be included in the 1855 Bordeaux classification. The vineyard

155

consists of 104 acres, most of which are planted in red grape varieties (Cabernet, Merlot), but a small amount of rare white (blanc) Haut-Brion is also made. Annual production averages about 11,000 cases of the red wine; less than 900 cases of the white.

Haut-Médoc *(Oh May-dawk')*: The central and best portion of the MÉDOC region, north of the city of BORDEAUX. Virtually all of the red wine estates (CHÂTEAUX) that were officially classified in 1855 are located in the Haut-Médoc; for regional wines, Haut-Médoc is also an APPELLATION CONTRÔLÉE, and wines bearing this name will usually be superior to those labeled "Médoc," which normally come from the less favored Bas-Médoc region in the north. The Haut-Médoc district includes the outstanding wine communes of SAINT-ESTÈPHE, PAUILLAC, SAINT-JULIEN, and MARGAUX.

Hectare *(Heck'-tar)*: Metric measure of area, equivalent to 10,000 square meters or 2.471 U.S. acres. For simplicity, hectares have been converted to acres throughout this dictionary.

Hectoliter *(Heck'-toe-liter)*: Metric measure of volume, equivalent to 100 liters or 26.4179 U.S. gallons. A hectoliter is also abbreviated as "hecto." In this dictionary, for simplicity, production statistics specified in hectoliters have been converted into cases of 2.38 U.S. gallons each.

Hérault *(Air-ro')*: Department or administrative region in southern France, located on the Mediterranean coast. A part of the MIDI district, the Hérault is France's largest vineyard area: over 360,000 acres are currently in production. Most of the land is given over to ordinary grape varieties for use in bulk wine production and VERMOUTH bases, but there are a few notable wine regions; the sweet Muscat wines of FRONTIGNAN and LUNEL are world-famous, and the many good red wines of FAUGÈRES and the MINERVOIS are increasingly

156

important in the export trade, being inexpensive and good value.

Hermitage *(Air´-me-tajh)*: Famous wine of the northern RHÔNE River valley, France, produced near the ancient town of Tain, which has assumed its name to become Tain-l'Hermitage. Some good white Hermitage is produced from Roussanne or Marsanne grapes, but the more plentiful red Hermitage is superior, and it is world-renowned. Made primarily from the Syrah grape, usually with a small amount of white grapes added for finesse, Hermitage is one of the most fruity and full-bodied Rhône wines and is exceptionally long-lived. There are 376 acres entitled to the APPELLATION CONTRÔLÉE Hermitage; the area is surrounded by the region of CROZES-HERMITAGE, which produces similar but slightly less distinctive wines. Traditionally, the Hermitage vineyards are divided into little parcels called *mas*, but few of these names appear on labels today and many so-called *mas* are actually trade names. About 40,000 cases of red and white Hermitage are produced annually.

Hessische Bergstrasse *(Hessis´-shuh Bairg´-strass-uh)*: The smallest wine region or ANBAU-GEBIET in Germany, located on the right bank of the Rhine River north of the city of Heidelberg. The region is only about 700 acres large, and Hessische Bergstrasse wines were formerly sold along with those of BADEN before the region was officially delimited in 1971; Bensheim, Heppenheim, Zwingenberg and Auerbach are its most important towns. Hessische Bergstrasse wines are rarely seen on the export market, but the region makes some good white wines from the Riesling; total annual production is about 230,000 cases.

Hochheim *(Hawk´-heim)*: Village and wine region in the most eastern portion of the RHEINGAU district, Germany, with some 470 acres of vineyard. Hochheim is located on the

River Main, a tributary of the Rhine; its fine white wines are celebrated for their characteristic mellowness. Long popular in England, the wines of Hochheim lent their name to the nickname "Hock," a word that now describes Rhine wines in general. The two most famous vineyards or EINZELLAGEN are Kirchenstück and Domdechaney (the latter means "deanery," a name that also applies to an outstanding Hochheim producer, Domdechant Werner'sches Weingut); other fine vineyards include: Stielweg, Hölle, Stein, Hofmeister, Berg, Reichesthal, and Herrnberg. The König-in Viktoria Berg vineyard, named after Queen Victoria of England, is the exclusive property of the Neus company in Ingelheim.

Hogshead: A cask of varying capacity, used for wines, spirits and beers. It applies generally to the *barrique* of BORDEAUX and the pièce of BURGUNDY, each of which hold about 225 liters (25 cases), but the hogshead cask used for sherry, port and whiskey is somewhat larger. The name hogshead is said to derive from *oxhoft*, an old Germanic word, and ordinary wine casks were called hogsheads during the Middle Ages.

Hospices de Beaune (*Awss'-peace duh Bone*): A charity hospital located in the city of BEAUNE, Burgundy, built in 1443 by Nicolas Rolin, chancellor to the duke of Burgundy. The Hospices derives most of its revenues from the wines it sells, produced from a number of fine vineyard holdings throughout the CÔTE DE BEAUNE, with one important acquisition in Mazis-Chambertin. Following each year's vintage, the Hospices sells its new wines at an auction traditionally held on the third Sunday of November, and the prices paid for them are a fairly accurate gauge of Burgundy prices for that year's vintage; the quantity also indicates the size of production. The Hospices' holdings consist of about 140 acres planted in red and white grapes, and typically about 650 *pièces* (casks) of wine are offered at auction, equivalent to about 16,000 cases.

All Hospices de Beaune wines are indicated by the name of the original donor who bequeathed the vineyard to the Hospices. The more important donors are as follows:

Principal Holdings
of the Hospices de Beaune

CUVÉE / RED	LOCATION
Nicolas Rolin	Beaune
Guigone de Salins	Beaune
Charlotte Dumay	Corton
Doctor Peste	Corton
Dames Hospitalières	Beaune
Dames de la Charité	Pommard
Blondeau	Volnay
Brunet	Beaune
Jehan de Massol	Volnay-Santenots
Clos des Avaux	Beaune
Billardet	Pommard
Gauvain	Volnay-Santenots
Hugues et Louis Bétault	Beaune
Général Muteau	Volnay
Maurice Drouhin	Beaune
Boillot	Auxey-Duresses
Arthur Girard	Savigny-les-Beaune
Madeleine Collignon	Mazis-Chambertin
CUVÉE / WHITE	LOCATION
François de Salins	Corton-Charlemagne
de Bahèzre de Lanlay	Meursault-Charmes
Albert Grivault	Meursault-Charmes
Baudot	Meursault-Genevrières
Philippe le Bon	Meursault-Genevrières
Jehan Humblot	Meursault
Goureau	Meursault
Loppin	Meursault
Paul Chanson	Corton-Vergennes

There are some quality differences between the vineyards, depending on the location of the holdings and the vintage in question, but in general most Hospices de Beaune wines are well made. They are not inexpensive, but the

159

buyer is assured that the premium he pays contributes to a worthy cause.

Hungary: Hungarian wines have been famous for centuries, though nationalization of the wine industry following World War II has definitely improved their overall quality. The export of quality Hungarian wines is now in the hands of Monimpex, the state export monopoly, whose central cellars are in Budafok, south of the city of Budapest. Monimpex selects only quality wines for export and stamps each bottle with a government seal of authenticity, with the result that most Hungarian wine shipped to the U.S. is generally quite sound.

Hungarian wines normally take the name of the district where they were grown, plus the grape variety. They are characteristically full-flavored—robust reds (*Vörös*) and sturdy whites (*Fehér*) are ideal complements to the spicy national cuisine. Commercially the most important wine region in Hungary is the Great Plain (*Alföld*), extending over much of the middle half of the country with over 284,000 acres planted in vines. But Hungary's finest wines are produced from vineyards at higher elevations, such as those at TOKAY in the extreme northeast of the country. The most famous Hungarian wine district, Tokay makes a luscious, golden sweet wine from the Furmint, a native variety that is also used to make dry wines. The red Kadarka is Hungary's other leading native grape. It is used for the wines of Eger, produced on the slopes of the Mátra Mountains to the west of Tokay. Eger is celebrated for EGRI BIKAVÉR ("Bull's Blood of Eger"); several other good wines are also made there. Many wine-lovers maintain that VILLÁNY in the south produces the best red wine of Hungary, made from the Nagyburgundi (Pinot Noir). Szekzárd, to the north—and Hajós, in the Alföld—are other leading red wine areas.

Three-fourths of all Hungarian wines are

white. The most widely-grown white wine grape, Olaszrizling (or Wälschriesling), is used for ordinary wine. The Hárslevelü, named for the odd lime shape of its leaves, gives a superior white wine, of which DEBRÖI HÁRSLEVELÜ is an outstanding example, Leányka, another important white grape, is grown in many wine regions—most successfully in Eger. Hungary has the largest lake in Europe, Lake Balaton; on its north shore an extinct volcano, Mount Badacsony, rises up to provide a perfect location for the famous vineyards of BADACSONY. Two particularly good white wines, Badacsonyi Kéknyelü and Badacsonyi Szürkebarát, are among Hungary's most flavorful. The towns of Somló and Mór to the north are other leading white wine areas; the former is famous for its Furmints and Rizlings, the latter for Ezerjó.

Huxelrebe *(Hook'-sel-ray-buh):* New German white grape variety, developed in 1927 by the grower Fritz Huxel in Westhofen, produced from a cross of Gutedel (Chasselas) and Courtillier Musqué. Some 1,300 acres of it have been planted in Germany, particularly in the RHEINHESSEN district; the wines that it gives tend to be full-bodied, with quite a bit of fruit, and are well-suited to the higher categories of QUALITÄTSWEIN MIT PRÄDIKAT.

Hybrid: In viticulture, a cross between two different species or varieties of grapes, with the purpose of creating a new grape variety with especially desirable characteristics. Grape hybridization is a relatively new science: it arose only during the last century in response to the PHYLLOXERA threat in Europe, and when European grape varieties were first crossed with American species, a whole new chapter of viticultural history began.

Grape hybrids fall into three distinct groups. The first is the so-called *producteurs directes*, or direct producers, which are the result of the first grape crossings performed in

161

France around the turn of the century; for this reason they are also occasionally called "French hybrids." Commonly, direct producers are formed by crossing the seedlings of American vines, species *riparia* or *rupestris*, with those of European varieties, with the intent of combining the hardiness and resistance of the former with the taste characteristics of the latter. (A common misconception is that the native eastern American species, LA-BRUSCA, produces a successful hybrid. These were attempted at one time, but the results were poor.) More successful direct producers include (*white*): Seyve-Villard 5276 (Seyval Blanc), Aurora, Vidal blanc, and Ravat or Vignoles. (*Red*): Maréchal Foch, Baco Noir, Chancellor Noir, de Chaunac, Cascade, Rougeon, Léon Millot and Chambourçin. Many of these are the mainstay of eastern and midwestern U.S. wineries, through their innate hardiness to frost damage and disease.

The second group of hybrids, not generally referred to as "hybrids" but as "new grapes" because only varieties and not entire species were crossed, is the result of continuing experiments in Germany at the Institute for Grape-growing in Geisenheim (Rheingau), under the direction of Dr. Helmut Becker. Here, only VINIFERA varieties are crossed, or combined with "second generation" crossings, to produce new grapes with desirable traits. The oldest of these, Müller-Thurgau, was developed in 1882 at Geisenheim; it was followed by dozens of successful new crosses, such as Scheurebe or S-88; other useful new grape breedings include Kerner, Optima, Ehrenfelser, Bacchus, Huxelrebe, Ortega, Siegerrebe, Kanzler, Morio-Muskat, and Reichensteiner. These grapes are finding favor in many German wine districts, but their propagation elsewhere thus far is limited.

162

The third group of hybrids owes its origins to experiments in the U.S. at the University of California at Davis, where popular strains of *vinifera* were crossed to yield new grapes that would be well-suited to warmer climatic zones while producing wines reminiscent of those grown in cooler regions. The oldest of these, Ruby Cabernet, was developed in 1946 and now covers some 17,000 acres in the state; Emerald Riesling, Flora, Carnelian, Centurion, Carmine, Rubired and Royalty are other successful results of the Davis crosses. At other institutes for grape research in other countries, new grapes are constantly being perfected. Austria has produced the Neuburger, Bouvier, and the Zwiegeltrebe, and undoubtedly others will follow.

Hydrometer: An instrument used to measure the amount of sugar in grape musts (see MUST WEIGHT), based on the principle that a sugar solution has a higher density or specific gravity than water. Grape must hydrometers are usually calibrated to indicate the amount of sugar present in grams per 100 grams of solution. The BRIX or Balling scale hydrometer is in general use in the U.S.; in Germany and Switzerland, the ÖECHSLE scale is preferred.

Ihringen *(Ear′-ring-en):* Little town west of the city of Freiburg in the region of BADEN, Germany, with some 740 acres of vineyard. Located in the section of Baden known as the KAISERSTUHL, Ihringen is famous for its fine white wines made from the Ruländer (Pinot Gris) grape, among Baden's best. The leading vineyards (EINZELLAGEN) are Castellberg, Kreuzhalde, Fohrenberg, Steinfelsen, Schlossberg and Winklerberg; one excellent vineyard,

163

the Doktorgarten, is owned by the wine estate of Blankenhornsberg.

Impériale *(Em-pay'-ree-ahl')*: An oversize wine bottle occasionally used in the BORDEAUX district, with the capacity of eight ordinary bottles.

Inferno *(In-fair'-no)*: Outstanding red wine produced in the VALTELLINA district, in the region of LOMBARDY. Made from the Nebbiolo grape, which in the Valtellina is called Chiavennasca, Inferno is the most renowned of the robust Valtellina wines, slow to develop but with impeccable balance at maturity.

Ingelheim *(Ing'-el-heim)*: Town and wine region in the RHEINHESSEN district, Germany, with over 1,000 acres of vineyard. Located on the left bank of the Rhine River and facing the village of JOHANNISBERG, Ingelheim is one of the few regions in Germany that specialize in the making of red wines; some white wine of slightly lesser quality is also made. Kaiserpfalz is the best-known wine name in Ingelheim, but it is important to know that this is a composite vineyard or GROSSLAGE; the leading single vineyards (EINZELLAGEN) are: Horn, Pares, Rheinhohe, Burgberg, and Hollenweg.

Iphofen *(Ip'-hawf-en)*: One of the leading wine villages of the district of FRANKEN (Franconia), Germany. Its 306 acres of vineyard are mostly planted in Silvaner; the wines are shipped in the squat BOCKSBEUTEL bottles native to the Franken region. The vineyards or EINZELLAGEN include: Julius-Echter-Berg, Kronsberg, and Kalb.

Ischia *(Isk'-ee-ah)*: Picturesque little island west of the city of Naples in the region of CAMPANIA, Italy, famous for its good red and white wines rated D.O.C. Certain select Ischian white wines produced in better vineyards are called Ischia Bianco Superiore.

Israel: Wine has been produced in the Palestine region since the dawn of history. The vine suffered under centuries of Moslem rule, but in the 1880s under the direction of Baron Edmond de Rothschild, large-scale vineyard plantings were begun and a developing wine industry sprang up in Israel; with independence in 1948 success was assured.

Israel's mediterranean climate is hot and semi-arid, but modern techniques produce quality wines that rival many others from cooler climates. The new method of drip-flow irrigation introduced in Israel is now in wide use in many parts of the world, and while Israel's vineyards were originally planted in ordinary high-yield varieties, today a trend is developing towards premium wines made from better varieties such as Cabernet Sauvignon, Sauvignon Blanc, Sémillon and Chenin Blanc. Currently there are over 13,000 acres of vineyard planted in wine grapes.

Israel's vineyards are scattered, but many lie near the coast. The largest and most famous is located at Richon-le-Zion to the south of Tel Aviv; another leading area is to the north, at Zichron-Jacob. Together, these two areas produce over 75% of Israel's wine. Their Kosher products are made under Rabbinical supervision, and the U.S. is an important market.

A majority of Israeli wine exported to the U.S. is marketed by the Carmel Wine Co., which offers many good wines. The lower quality grades are not given GENERIC names such as "chablis" because Israel respects the Madrid Convention, restricting these names to the original location. Instead, brand names like "Adom Atic" and "Avdat" are used. A wide range of good VARIETAL table wines is offered, and "The President's Sparkling Wine," bottle-fermented by the traditional Champagne process, is internationally famous.

Italy: Italy's oenological links with the U.S. have become as strong as her ethnic ties. In

165

just under a decade, by 1983 Italy was producing over two-thirds of all the wine imported to the U.S., making her the largest overseas supplier to America by far. Since wine is produced in every part of the country, from the arid barrens of Sicily to the cool alpine regions in the north, this is no accident. Presently, over 4.4 million acres are under vines.

The variety of Italian wines dazzles the imagination. Scores of different grape varieties are grown throughout the country; many indigenous varieties are grown nowhere else in the world. Wine-drinking is a natural part of everyday life in Italy, yet much wine is not even bottled, and is usually and properly consumed before its first year.

Historically, Italy's large domestic consumption worked as a detriment towards export, since not much wine was available for shipment abroad, and winemaking was performed mainly by tradition handed down from father to son. Recently, modern technology has played an important role in improving the quality of Italian wines. In the vineyard, newer vine training systems and a changeover from mixed-farming to grape growing has resulted in a dramatic increase in production, in some areas. In the cellar, skilled oenologists now oversee the quality of Italian wines from a technical perspective. Traditionally, the overall quality of Italian wine exports tended to be very uneven, and a lack of coordinated quality control in some areas tended to compromise Italy's reputation on the world market as a premium wine producer.

But following Italy's membership into the European Common Market, the Italian government took steps to codify wine legislation by enacting the DENOMINAZIONE DI ORIGINE CONTROLLATA (D.O.C.) Laws, which outline specific place-names and delimit viticultural districts according to the best sites. In practice, only potentially fine wines are entitled to D.O.C., and with more recent viticultural areas, an inspection period is required before D.O.C. status is officially granted. Excellent and even great wines were of course produced in Italy long before the D.O.C. laws were enacted, but only a few ever left the country. In the past decade, the overall quality of Italian wines shipped to the U.S. has improved tremendously, and much of the credit can be traced to the D.O.C. laws.

The simplest category of D.O.C. is *simplice* (simple), for wines produced in vineyards not officially entitled to D.O.C. An alternate term is *vino da tavola* (table wine). The next category, *controllata* (controlled), relates to all of Italy's leading wines. Vineyards are officially delimited, their yield restricted, and only approved grape varieties are allowed to be planted. The highest category, *controllata e garantita* (controlled and guaranteed), became official in 1980 when a few very prominent, high-quality red wines were selected to represent the ultimate in Italian wines. To strengthen their claim to greatness in this third category, the government accepts responsibility for the guarantee of the wines' high quality, and affixes a special seal of approval to the bottle. The fact that such provisions exist is indicative of the serious approach towards quality wines in Italy.

The government also recognizes that the Italian winegrowing area is favored climatically over colder growing regions to the north, and unlike most other European countries, sugaring the must to increase alcoholic content (see CHAPTALISATION) is forbidden in Italy. Under D.O.C. law, the wines must also attain a minimum degree of alcohol to qualify for their appellation.

An additional quality control is the national network of *consorzi* (consortiums), which are voluntary organizations in various wine regions that set quality standards for their wines. The most famous is that of the CHIANTI Classico region, which came into being nearly forty

VALLE D'AOSTA

LOMBARDY

TRENTINO-ALTO ADIGE

VENETO

FR

PIEDMONT

EMILIA-ROMAGNA

LIGURIA

TUSCANY

UMBR

L

SARDINIA

N

ITALY

years before the D.O.C. laws were enacted. The *consorzi* have their own seals that are affixed to wine bottles, in addition to a red seal issued by the Italian government which attests that every drop of wine in that bottle is a product of Italy.

Traditionally the most famous Italian wines on the export market have come from PIE-MONTE, where rich, robust red wines are made from the Nebbiolo grape. BAROLO, BARBA-RESCO, and GATTINARA are representative examples; to the east, the VALTELLINA district also relies on Nebbiolo. The TRENTINO-ALTO ADIGE districts in the Italian alps have long been export-oriented, and recently some exceptional wines have been produced in the FRIULI-VENEZIA GIULIA district, near the border with Yugoslavia.

To the south, near the city of Venice, is the VENETO district, the home of SOAVE, VAL-POLICELLA, and BARDOLINO, traditionally popular Italian wines in the U.S. Nearby is the EMILIA-ROMAGNA region, famous primarily for its sweet, semi-sparkling red LAMBRUSCO that is very popular in America. The region of TUS-CANY is well-known for Chianti, but the fine red wines of BRUNELLO DI MONTALCINO and VINO NOBILE DI MONTEPULCIANO have an especially high reputation. The region of MARCHE gives the fine white VERDICCHIO, and UMBRIA to the southwest is noted for ORVIETO, another good white. The Rome region is praised for its light white wines, of which FRAS-CATI and other wines of the CASTELLI ROMANI district are well-known. The region of CAM-PANIA near Naples is famous for LACRIMA CHRISTI and TAURASI; recently the white GRECO DI TUFO has become popular here. Further south, many notable red wines are made: SAN SEVERO and TORRE QUARTO in APULIA, AGLIANICO DEL VULTURE in the Basilicata region, and CIRÒ in CALABRIA.

No discussion of Italian wines would be complete without the fine FORTIFIED WINES of

MARSALA, produced on the island of Sicily. Sicily as a whole, and the island of Sardinia, are expanding their vineyard acreage and increasing their production of quality wines.

Jerez *(Hair-eth')*: Town in Andalusia, Spain, located north of the city of Cadiz; its full name is Jerez de la Frontera. The wines of Jerez have been called "sherries" since the Middle Ages.

Jeroboam: An oversized wine bottle used in the fine wine regions of France. The jeroboam of BORDEAUX has a capacity of six ordinary bottles; in the French CHAMPAGNE district, a jeroboam is equivalent to four regular bottles. No Champagnes are ever aged in jeroboams, however; they are decanted from smaller bottles following the process of DÉGORGEMENT.

Johannisberg *(Yo-hahn'-nis-bairg)*: World-famous wine village in the RHEINGAU district, Germany, with some 450 acres of vineyard. The village is renowned principally for its leading wine estate, Schloss Johannisberg (see JO-HANNISBERG, SCHLOSS), one of the Rheingau's most famous, but Johannisberg has several other fine vineyards or EINZELLAGEN: Klaus, Vogelsang, Hölle, Mittelhölle, Hansenberg, Goldatzel, and Schwarzenstein. Johannisbergers are typically among the best wines of the Rheingau, but it is important to know that under the 1971 German Wine Law, Johannisberg is also the name of a sub-region or BER-EICH, and a wine labeled "Bereich Johannisberg" is simply a regional wine made anywhere in the Rheingau—in all likelihood, not from a

171

vineyard in Johannisberg itself. To be sure of getting the best, one should look for an estate-bottled wine (ERZEUGER-ABFÜLLUNG) from a leading producer.

Johannisberg is also the name used in Switzerland for a wine made from the Sylvaner grape, most often in the canton of VALAIS.

Johannisberg Riesling *(Yo-hahn'-nis-bairg Reese'-ling):* Name given in California and other parts of the United States to the true Riesling of Germany (also called White Riesling), to distinguish it from other grapes that, despite their name, are unrelated. Such varieties include: Franken Riesling (Sylvaner), Grey Riesling (Chauché Gris), Emerald Riesling, and Goldriesling.

Over 10,000 acres of Johannisberg Riesling have been planted in California, and best results are usually achieved in the coolest growing district, which recall the Rhine and Mosel River valleys. California Rieslings have traditionally been somewhat drier and higher in alcohol than their German counterparts, but in the 1970s a whole new generation of Botrytis-infected, LATE HARVEST Rieslings were perfected by a number of producers that truly resembled the great BEERENAUSLESEN of Germany. Some of them have been among the finest sweet wines produced in the state, and undoubtedly more will follow in the future.

Johannisberg, Schloss: Outstanding wine estate in the RHEINGAU district, Germany, producing some of the most famous wines in the world. The estate consists of about 87 acres planted in Riesling, located on a high slope overlooking the Rhine River; the wines are prized for their scent and concentration. Since 1816 the Schloss has belonged to the von Metternich family, but vines have been grown on the property since 871 A.D.

The estate bottles its fine white wines under two different labels: the regular label bears the von Metternich coat of arms against a plain background; the much rarer Schloss label, formerly used to indicate a private reserve or *Cabinet*, is a colored engraving showing a view of the Schloss from across the Rhine. Because the two labels have different colored capsules, the various quality categories and their markings are as follows:

REGULAR LABEL	CAPSULE	COLOR
Qualitätswein b.A.	Gelblack	yellow
Kabinett	Rotlack	red
Spätlese	Grünlack	green
Auslese	Rosalack	pink
Beerenauslese	Rosa-Goldlack	gold with pink stripe
Trockenbeerenauslese	—	—

SCHLOSS LABEL	CAPSULE	COLOR
Qualitätswein b.A.	—	—
Kabinett	Orangenlack	orange
Spätlese	Weisslack	white
Auslese	Himmelblau-lack	sky blue
Beerenauslese	Blau-Goldlack	gold with blue stripe
Trockenbeerenauslese	Goldlack	gold

In addition, some sparkling wine is made under the label of Fürst von Metternich Prädikats-Sekt.

Josephshof *(Yo'-zefs-hof)*: One of the best vineyards in the MOSEL River valley, Germany. The Josephshof is officially located in the village of GRAACH, yet the wines are not sold as Graachs but under the name of Josephshöfer. Owned exclusively by the von Kesselstatt Company, a leading shipper headquartered in Trier, the vineyard consists of 25 acres planted in Riesling, and regularly produces some of the Mosel's best wines—typically full-flavored and very fine.

Juliénas *(Jule-yay'-nahss)*: Wine region in the BEAUJOLAIS district, southern Burgundy; also the name of its fine red wine. Officially classified as one of the *crus* (growths), which regularly produce outstanding Beaujolais, Juliénas is one of the better ones, usually with a char-

173

acteristic firmness that makes it relatively slow to mature. There are currently 1,125 acres of vineyard; average annual production is about 335,000 cases of fine red wine.

Jura *(Shur'-ra):* Mountain range, administrative region (department) and wine region in eastern France, near the Swiss border. The Jura was formerly a large, important wine region, but today there are less than 2,000 acres of vineyard—a fraction of the former total. Its light red, white and rosé wines are not well-known outside the region, but are noted for their quality and variety. Commercially the most important wines are those of ARBOIS, in particular the sturdy rosés; traditionally the rare CHÂTEAU-CHALON, legally required to age six years in cask, is the most famous Jura wine. Another wine, L'Etoile, is equally celebrated but is extremely rare.

Jurançon *(Shur'-awn-sawn):* Wine region in southwest France near the Spanish border, south of the city of Pau. Three grape varieties—Courbu, Gros Manseng and Petit Manseng—are used to make the fine white wines of Jurançon. The vineyards are planted on the slopes of the Pyrénées, and the grapes are often harvested in the late autumn when overripe to make luscious sweet wines; unfortunately, because of high production costs, these excellent wines are now becoming rare. A much larger quantity of less distinguished dry white wine is now produced. The vineyard area of Jurançon extends over about 1,250 acres; average annual production is approximately 191,000 cases.

Kabinett *(Kab-ee-nett')*: German for "cabinet." Under the 1971 German Wine Law, Kabinett is the most basic grade of QUALITÄT-SWEIN MIT PRÄDIKAT (Quality Wine with Special Attributes). Kabinett derives from *Cabinet*, a term coined in the 18th century for special wine reserves at KLOSTER EBERBACH in the RHEINGAU district. The 1971 Wine Law provides that only the spelling Kabinett may be used, and that this term indicates a wine made solely from ripe grapes that have not received any addition of sugar.

The legal minimum MUST WEIGHT requirements for Kabinett vary by area, but in general a Kabinett is the least expensive and driest wine in the *Prädikat* categories that a producer has to offer. See QUALITÄTSWEIN.

Kadarka *(Kah-dark'-ah)*: Red grape variety grown in Hungary and Romania. It is the principal variety used to make EGRI BIKAVÉR, perhaps Hungary's best-known red wine.

Kaiserstuhl *(Kuy'-zer-shtool)*: A hilly volcanic outcropping in the region of BADEN, southern Germany. The Kaiserstuhl (which means "emperor's seat" in German) is part of the BEREICH (sub-region) Kaiserstuhl-Tuniberg. With the exception of Endingen, its northern slopes generally do not yield any wines of great distinction; the southern slopes, particularly the vineyards of IHRINGEN, Achkarren, Bötzingen and Bickensohl, often produce the best white wines of Baden, especially if planted in Ruländer (Pinot Gris).

175

Kallstadt *(Kahl'-shtat):* Noted wine village in the RHEINPFALZ (Palatinate) region, Germany, with 715 acres of vineyard. Kallstadt lies just to the north of DÜRKHEIM, and its fine wines are similar but are not well-known outside Germany. The leading vineyards (EINZELLAGEN) include: Annaberg, Horn, Kirchenstück, Kreidkeller, Kronenberg, Nill, and Steinacker.

Kalterersee *(Kahl'-ter-rer-zay'):* German for CALDARO, a lake located in the region of ALTO ADIGE, northern Italy. This spelling may sometimes be found on wine labels destined for markets where German is spoken.

Kanzem *(Kahnt'-zem):* Noted wine village in the SAAR River valley, Germany, with some 300 acres of vineyard—nearly all of them planted in Riesling. The fresh white wines of Kanzem, usually a bit more full-bodied than others of the Saar, closely rival those of WILTINGEN just to the east. The leading vineyards (EINZELLAGEN) include: Altenberg, Hörecker, Schlossberg, and Sonnenberg.

Kasel *(Kah'-zel):* Little village on the RUWER River, Germany, with 215 acres of vineyard. The largest wine community or *Weinbauort* in the Ruwer district, Kasel is famous for its fine white wines made from the Riesling. The most famous vineyard (EINZELLAGE) is Nies'chen, but Kehrnagel, Herrenberg, Hitzlay, Paulinsberg and Timpert also produce fine wines.

Keller: German for "cellar."

Kelter: German for "wine press."

Kerner *(Kair'-ner):* New German white grape variety, a cross between the Riesling and the Trollinger of WÜRTTEMBERG; unusual in that its color is white and one of its parents (Trollinger) is red. Kerner is rapidly gaining favor as a productive grape variety in many parts of the Rhine district: its high-quality fruit gives powerful, scented wines, with good yields.

176

Kiedrich *(Keed'-rich):* Celebrated wine village in the RHEINGAU district, Germany, with 430 acres of vineyard; most of them planted in Riesling. Often one of the outstanding Rheingau villages in hot years, Kiedrich boasts several fine vineyards or EINZELLAGEN: Gräfenberg, Sandgrub, Wasseros (or Wasserrose), and Klosterberg.

Kir *(Keer):* Refreshing wine apéritif, made with a light, dry white wine and a little crème de cassis liqueur. The classic formula calls for a Bourgogne Aligoté and crème de cassis from Dijon. It is named for the late Canon Félix Kir, former major of the city of Dijon, whose favorite drink it was.

Klevner *(Clayv'-ner):* The local name for the Pinot Blanc grape in the region of ALSACE, France. In BADEN, Germany, under the spelling *Clevner*, this term applies to the Traminer.

Kloster Eberbach *(Klaws'-ter Eh'-ber-bock):* Historic medieval monastery in the RHEINGAU district, Germany, located in the commune of HATTENHEIM. The Kloster was constructed in the 12th century by Cistercian monks, who later planted a walled vineyard nearby: the famous STEINBERG. The Kloster Eberbach presently belongs to the German State, and has been preserved as a wine museum. The Kloster is the location for the annual wine auctions held by the Staatsweingut in Eltville, and bottles that have been sold there at auction often bear a small seal stating: "Ersteigert im Kloster Eberbach" (auctioned at Kloster Eberbach).

K.M.W. (Klosterneuburger Most Waage): The legal standard for various wine quality grades in Austria, used to determine the MUST WEIGHT for categories of quality wines; named for the Klosterneuburg School of Viticulture, located north of the city of Vienna. One degree KMW equals about 5 degrees ÖECHSLE, the scale for must weight used in Germany and Switzerland. Under the Austrian Wine Law, all wines must attain the following minimum standards, expressed in degrees KMW:

Qualitätswein
—Minimum   15°
—Kabinett   17°

Qualitätswein besonderer Reife und Leseart (quality wine from special ripeness and picking techniques)
—Spätlese   19°
—Auslese   21°
—Beerenauslese   25°
—Ausbruch   27°
—Trockenbeerenauslese   30°

Königsbach *(Ker′-nigs-bock)*: Wine village in the RHEINPFALZ (Palatinate) district, Germany, located just to the south of RUPPERTSBERG. Although excellent, the wines are not well-known outside of Germany. The vineyards (EINZELLAGEN) include: Idig, Jesuitengarten, Ölberg, and Reiterpfad.

Kosher Wine: By definition, a wine used for sacramental purposes during Jewish religious services. According to Rabbinical law, all Kosher wine must be pure, unmixed, and produced under strict Rabbinical supervision. There are no restrictions on the type of grape or grapes that go into making it, though in the U.S. most Kosher wines are usually made from the Concord, with cane sugar added to give it characteristic sweetness.

Krems: One of the most famous wine towns in Austria, located in the WACHAU district on the Danube River west of the city of Vienna. A picturesque old village, Krems is noted for its fine white wines made from the Rheinriesling and Grüner Veltliner grapes.

178   **Kreuznach** *(Kroytz′-nock)*: City of some 44,000 on the NAHE River, Germany; the largest Nahe wine community and the center of its wine trade, with over 2,700 acres of vineyard. Because of its famous mineral spas, it is officially called Bad Kreuznach. Its wines are among the Nahe's best, but it is important to know that under the 1971 German Wine Law, Kreuznach also became the name of a sub-region or BEREICH, and that a "Kreuznacher Riesling," without a vineyard name, is merely a regional wine that could come from many villages within the Bereich Kreuznach. The collective site (GROSSLAGE), Kreuznacher Kronenberg, is smaller but still includes many different vineyards. To be sure of getting the best, one should specify one of the leading individual vineyards or EINZELLAGEN: Narrenkappe, Mönchberg, Hinkelstein, Brückes, Krötenpfuhl, Kahlenberg, St. Martin, Forst, Mollenbrunnen, Rosenberg, Osterhöll, Vogelsang, Breitenweg, Steinberg, Galgenberg, Tilgesbrunnen, and Kapellenpfad.

Kröv *(Kruhv):* Little village on the MOSEL River, Germany; also occasionally spelled Cröv. It has achieved considerable fame on account of a comic name given to one of its vineyards, Nacktarsch, which means "naked bottom." The wines bear a label showing a small boy being spanked, with his trousers down, in punishment for drinking wine.

The 1971 German Wine Law authorized Nacktarsch to be the name of a composite vineyard or GROSSLAGE, and while Kröv has six vineyards or EINZELLAGEN (Burglay, Herrenberg, Kirchlay, Letterlay, Paradies, and Steffensberg), the Grosslage name will usually be used because it is better-known.

Labrusca *(La-broos'-ca)*: A species of grape vines native to the American continent; its full name is *Vitis labrusca*. Grown chiefly in the eastern United States, labrusca grape varieties are quite different from the European or East Asian species, Vitis VINIFERA. Concord, Delaware, Catawba, Ives, Noah, Niagara, and others are common examples of labrusca grape varieties.

Lacrima Christi *(La'-creem-ah Kreest'-ee)*: Italian for "Christ's Tears"; specifically, a golden white wine produced on the southern slopes of Mt. Vesuvius near the city of Naples, in the region of CAMPANIA, Italy. A little red wine is also made. Lacrima Christi has been famous for centuries, but has not yet received a D.O.C. rating; its name has often been used freely by producers outside of the original region, for their white wines.

Ladoix-Serrigny *(La-dwah' Serr-een-yee')*: Secondary wine commune with about 340 acres of vineyard in the CÔTE DE BEAUNE, Burgundy, adjoining the commune of ALOXE-CORTON. Very little wine is marketed under the name Ladoix-Serrigny, as most producers prefer to label their wines under the name CÔTE DE BEAUNE-VILLAGES, which is allowed by law. The best wines are generally sold either as CORTON or CORTON-CHARLEMAGNE.

Lafite-Rothschild, Château *(La-feet' Rawt'-shield)*: Perhaps the most famous red wine of BORDEAUX, and one of the most celebrated wines in the world. The Lafite vineyard is many centuries old; it takes its name from the de Rothschilds, a French family of bankers who have owned the property since 1868. The vineyard lies in the MÉDOC district within the commune of PAUILLAC; the area under vines is approximately 200 acres, and production annually averages about 20,000 cases of especially elegant and refined claret, officially rated Premier Cru (First Growth).

Lage *(Log'-uh):* German for "location" or "site," a term used in connection with an officially delimited vineyard. Under the 1971 German Wine Law, an EINZELLAGE denotes an individual vineyard of at least 12 acres in size; a GROSSLAGE is composed of a number of different Einzellagen.

Lagrein *(La-grine'):* Red grape variety grown in the regions of TRENTINO and ALTO ADIGE, northern Italy; used for light red wines and rosés. It is also called *Lagarino.*

Lake: County and emerging wine district in northern California, with over 2,400 acres of vineyard. Named for (and dominated by) beautiful Clear Lake in the country's center, Lake occupies a fairly warm climatic zone and is already noted for its Cabernet Sauvignons and Zinfandels. Many of the vineyards are managed by growers who sell grapes to other wineries, but the new Turner Winery, managed by a family of the same name, now controls over 40% of Lake's vineyards and is rapidly becoming a major producer in the area. Guenoc Winery and Konocti Cellars, a cooperative owned by Lake County Vintners, are other prominent wineries.

Lalande-de-Pomerol *(La-lawnd' duh Pawm-uh-roll'):* Secondary red wine district in the BORDEAUX region, located north of the commune of POMEROL. The many good wines of Lalande-de-Pomerol are similar to Pomerols, but are usually not quite as fine; the leading wine estates (CHÂTEAUX) include: Bel-Air, de la Commanderie, Moulin-à-Vent, Perron, Canon-Chaigneau, and Garraud.

Lambrusco *(Lom-bruce'-co):* Famous sweet red sparkling wine produced near the city of Modena in the region of EMILIA-ROMAGNA, Italy. Lambrusco is made from a grape of the same name in three designated communes: Sorbara, Grasparossa, and Salamino, each of them rated D.O.C. By law the sparkle in a Lambrusco must come from natural fermentation—any addition of carbon dioxide is forbidden. Lambrusco is a light, refreshing and usually inexpensive red wine that should be drunk young.

Landwein *(Lond'-vine):* German for "regional wine." New quality category, established in 1982, for German regional wines—the German equivalent of the French VIN DE PAYS. Its full name is *Deutscher Landwein*, identifying the wine as genuine produce of German vineyards. Under the law, there are fifteen newly-designated Landwein regions within the German winegrowing area:

A. Ahrtaler Landwein
B. Starkenburger Landwein
C. Rheinburgen Landwein
D. Landwein der Mosel
E. Landwein der Saar
F. Nahegauer Landwein
G. Altrheingauer Landwein
H. Rheinischer Landwein
I. Pfälzer Landwein
J. Fränkischer Landwein
K. Regensburger Landwein
L. Bayerischer Bodensee-Landwein
M. Schwäbischer Landwein
N. Unterbadischer Landwein
O. Südbadischer Landwein

As with the French *vins de pays*, Landweine tend to be light, dry and uncomplicated—a step above the most basic German wines (called TAFELWEIN), with more body and character, but lighter and usually less distinctive than QUALITATSWEIN b.A., or quality wine from designated regions. Landweine are usually produced with sugar added, and are thoroughly blended. Since the cost of production of these wines makes them relatively expensive in relation to other imported wine, they are not likely to be seen on the U.S. market.

Languedoc (*Long'-uh-dock*): Old French province, now divided up into five smaller administrative regions or departments: Lozère, Gard, HÉRAULT, AUDE, and Pyrénées-Orientales. The Hérault, Aude and Gard are, in that order, the three largest wine-producing departments in France; most of their output is ordinary wine, either used for VERMOUTH manufacture or for blending purposes, but there are a few exceptions, such as the fine Muscat of FRONTIGNAN and the good red wine of FITOU. See CLAIRETTE, CORBIÈRES, and MINERVOIS.

Late Harvest: Term indicating a wine made from grapes picked especially late in the season, when they have had an opportunity to become particularly ripe. The term late harvest relates to the German word SPÄTLESE, now officially defined under the 1971 German Wine Law; French wines of this type, although considerably rarer than the German Spätlesen, may be termed *vendange tardive* in the district of ALSACE, or, most recently, "sélection des grains nobles."

Technically, late-harvested grapes fall into two groups. The first type is simply grapes that have been picked later than usual, which have gained in sugar and extracts by being left longer on the vine. Timing of picking is very important, because the vine may actually reabsorb some of the material if picking is delayed too long. Most domestic late-harvested wines fall into this group.

183

The second type of late-harvested grape is one that has been subjected to the action of aspecial, beneficial mold, *Botrytis cinerea*, which occurs naturally in many wine districts around the world, including the United States. After warm, moist conditions have prevailed during an especially fine autumn, the mold collects on the grape bunches and increases the sugar content, while lowering the acidity. Not only is this enrichment beneficial in itself, but the mold contributes a special flavor of its own that adds a particular note of distinction to the wine that is produced.

Wines of this type have been the specialty of the Rhine and Mosel districts in Germany for years. In the early 1970s it was demonstrated that the same type of wines could be produced in quantity by American vintners, which initially were released with German names. But since 1975, the U.S. Bureau of Alcohol, Tobacco and Firearms has restricted the use of German names on American wine labels, after incidences where many wines were sold without any clear quality distinction or likeness to the German equivalent. A few American producers, however, specialize in late-harvested wines, and adhere to very strict quality standards for the production of late-harvested wines. Richard Arrowood, winemaker at Château St. Jean in Sonoma County, California, has had particularly wide experience in Botrytis-infected, late-harvest White Riesling, and adheres to the following criteria for production:

GERMAN TERMS	U.S. EQUIVALENT (+ STANDARDS)
Spätlese	Late harvest (minimum sugar: 23° Brix; residual sugar after fermentation: less than 7%)
Auslese	Selected late harvest (minimum sugar: 24.5° Brix; residual sugar after fermentation: less than 13%)
Beerenauslese*	Individual bunch-selected late harvest (minimum sugar: 30° Brix; residual sugar after fermentation: between 13% and 19%)

Trockenbeer-enauslese*	Individual dried bunch-selected late harvest (minimum sugar: 40° Brix; residual sugar after fermentation: greater than 20%)

*grapes qualifying for these grades, in Europe and in California, are assumed to have been subjected to Botrytis.

Latour, Château *(La-tour')*: One of the very greatest red wines of BORDEAUX, officially rated Premier Cru (First Growth). Named for an ancient fortress that still stands on the property, the Latour vineyard consists of some 150 acres of choice land located in the commune of PAUILLAC in the MÉDOC district; annual production averages about 16,000 cases of very distinguished red wine—initially hard and slow to develop, but with incomparable excellence at maturity. The estate also produces a second wine from young vines called Les Forts de Latour, which is somewhat less expensive.

Latricières-Chambertin *(La-treese-yair' Shawm'-bear-tan)*: World-famous red wine vineyard in the northern CÔTE DE NUITS, Burgundy, rated Grand Cru (Great Growth). The Latricières-Chambertin vineyard extends over 17½ acres planted in Pinot Noir, and shares practically the same ideal soil and exposure as the great CHAMBERTIN vineyard, which lies alongside it. About 2,600 cases of especially rich and full-bodied red Burgundy are produced each year.

Lavaux *(La-vo')*: Wine district in the canton of VAUD, Switzerland, located on the north shore of Lake Geneva. Some of Switzerland's best white wines made from the Dorin (Chasselas) grape are produced in Lavaux, particularly those of DÉZALEY and SAINT-SAPHORIN.

Lazio *(Lots'-ee-o)*: Italian for "Latium," the region surrounding the city of Rome. Its vineyards have furnished wine for the capital since the days of the Roman Empire, and are most famous for their fresh white wines that are best consumed when quite young. One of the most

185

famous of all Italian white wines is EST! EST! EST!, made to the north of Rome around the village of Montefiascone. To the south, the many excellent white wines of the CASTELLI ROMANI region—FRASCATI, COLLI ALBANI, Marino, and Colli Lanuvini—are also renowned and have officially been granted D.O.C. status. A good Lazio red wine is Cesanese, produced near the town of Frosinone. The Lazio region as a whole typically produces in excess of 57 million cases of wine, mostly white.

Lees: The residue or gross sediment thrown off by a wine soon after it is made. Most fine wines are allowed to age in cask following vinification, and when most of the lees have settled to the bottom of the cask, the clarified wine is siphoned off into another container during the process of RACKING.

Léognan (*Lay'-own-yawn*): Wine commune in the region of GRAVES, located south of the city of BORDEAUX. Léognan has the highest concentration of classified vineyards of any Graves commune; the foremost wine estates (CHÂTEAUX) are: Domaine de Chevalier, Haut-Bailly, Carbonnieux, Malartic-Lagravière, Olivier, and Fieuzal.

Libourne (*Lee-boorn'*): City in the southwest France, located on the DORDOGNE River twenty miles to the east of the city of BORDEAUX. Libourne is the center of the wine trade for such notable regions as SAINT-ÉMILION, POMEROL, CANON-FRONSAC, FRONSAC, and others.

Liebfraumilch (*Leeb'-frow-milsch*): German for "milk of the Blessed Mother," a trade name for a mildly sweet, blended white wine that has become one of the most widely-used German wine terms. The name Liebfraumilch is said to derive from the Liebfrauenstift vineyard near the city of Worms in the RHEINHESSEN district, but now this vineyard has become an individual site or EINZELLAGE, while Liebfraumilch is essentially a regional wine that has been extensively blended.

Following the first controls over the use of the term Liebfraumilch issued in 1910, many different wines were marketed under this name. The 1971 German Wine Law restricted the legal requirements for wines of this type: all wines sold as Liebfraumilch must meet the minimum standards for QUALITÄTSWEIN, and be the exclusive products of vineyards in the Rhine region. No indication of the grape varieties used may appear on the label nor any of the specific quality categories of QUALITÄTSWEIN MIT PRÄDIKAT, but the wines must be sound and are subject to an official inspection before they are released for sale. In 1982, a new law was passed requiring the growing region to be included on the label, along with the name Liebfraumilch, as an additional quality control and also as a more precise indication of the producing zone.

Wine experts usually disparage Liebfraumilch, perhaps excessively, but they do maintain (with some justification) that to buy Liebfraumilch exclusively is to disregard other fine wines of the Rheinhessen region, which may be superior in quality.

Lieblich *(Leeb′-lish):* German for "lovely" or "delightful"; when applied to wine, one with some residual sugar; also known as *Mild.* Literally a pleasant, easy-drinking wine with a trace of sweetness, a wine sold as *Lieblich* will be slightly sweeter than a HALBTROCKEN, and much sweeter than a wine labeled TROCKEN. See also SÜSSRESERVE.

Light: Term having two different meanings. A light table wine, with an alcoholic content below 14%, generally has a less pronounced flavor and body than a DESSERT WINE, which has been fortified with the addition of alcohol. A wine is said to be light when it has less flavor and extracts than usual, in addition to less alcohol, and recently wines have been sold on

187

the U.S. market using another meaning of the term "light": low in calories.

Wine is a food; and like foods, table wines have a certain calorie content. In acknowledgement of this, some American producers have produced wines that are deliberately lower in alcohol—and in calories—than their usual production. These "light" wines appeared on the U.S. market in the 1980s, and initially there was some confusion over the actual difference. To produce them, wineries harvest the grapes earlier than usual, creating a low-alcohol table wine, or else subject high-alcohol wines to vacuum-heat, where by evaporation the alcoholic content is reduced without appreciably altering the flavor. For a balanced product, some producers blend both wine types together prior to release.

Theoretically, "light" wines are not necessarily preferable or superior to a winery's normal production, although because of their low alcohol content and crisp, subdued flavor, some consumers might prefer them for certain occasions.

Liguria (*Lee-goor'-ya*): One of Italy's smaller wine regions, situated along the Italian Riviera. Its economic and geographic center is the city of Genoa. Although not many of Liguria's wines are exported, they have been famous for centuries—particularly the sweet white wine of CINQUETERRE, which was considered the best Italian wine during the Renaissance; the red DOLCEAQUA, made from the Rossesse grape, is also acclaimed.

Lillet (*Lee-lay'*): The proprietary name for a French wine-based apéritif produced in Bordeaux. In its most usual form it is white and semi-dry, although a less well-known red Lillet is also produced.

188

Limoux (*Lee-moo'*): City in southern France near the ancient fortress of Carcassonne, in the department of AUDE. It is known chiefly for a locally famous, semi-dry white sparkling wine, Blanquette de Limoux, which has an APPELLATION CONTRÔLÉE rating.

Liqueur d'Expédition (*Lee-kerr′ Dex-pay-deese′-syon*): French for "shipping dosage," a mixture of cane sugar, wine, and sometimes brandy, added to wines in the French CHAMPAGNE district following the process of disgorging (see DÉGORGEMENT) before the wines are marketed. The amount of shipping dosage determines the sweetness of the Champagne. See DOSAGE.

Liqueur de Tirage (*Lee-kerr′ duh Teer-rahj′*): French for "bottling dosage," a solution of pure cane sugar mixed with yeasts, added to the wine in the French CHAMPAGNE district so that a secondary fermentation occurs in the bottle, producing a sparkling wine. An essential step in the Champagne process, the bottling dosage is precisely calculated so that just the right degree of sparkle is achieved.

Lirac (*Lee′-rack*): Wine region in southern France, near the city of Avignon in the department of Gard. Lirac lies just to the north of TAVEL, and like Tavel is celebrated for its excellent rosés made from the Grenache grape, though because they are not as well-known, Liracs are usually less expensive. Some red and white wine of lesser quality is also made in Lirac. The equivalent of some 200,000 cases of wine is produced annually.

Listrac (*Leese′-trac*): Wine commune in the HAUT-MÉDOC district, north of the city of BORDEAUX. Though there are no classified growths (CRUS CLASSÉS) in Listrac, there are a number of good estates or CHÂTEAUX that regularly produce fine red wine, entitled to the appellation Haut-Médoc and rated *cru bourgeois supérieur*. Leading estates include Châteaux Fourcas-Hosten, Fourcas-Dupré, Lestage, Sémeillan-Mazeu, and Pierre-Bibian-Darriet.

189

Loire *(Lwahr):* One of France's principal rivers, originating in southern Burgundy and winding across the country for some 600 miles to its mouth in the Atlantic Ocean. An area rich in scenery and history, the Loire valley is also an immense vineyard area. For simplicity, the chief wine regions can be divided into three: upper, middle, and lower Loire.

The upper Loire produces white wines almost exclusively, from the Sauvignon Blanc and Chasselas grapes. The vineyards of POUILLY-SUR-LOIRE and SANCERRE are world-famous. The middle Loire or TOURAINE, around the city of Tours, produces some of the best red wines of the Loire from the Cabernet Franc grape; excellent examples are CHINON and BOURGUEIL. Fine white wines from the Chenin Blanc grape are also a Touraine specialty, such as those produced in VOUVRAY and MONTLOUIS. The lower Loire, between the cities of SAUMUR and Nantes, includes the district of ANJOU, famous for its fine rosés and luscious, sweet white wines, and MUSCADET, one of France's most famous dry white wines. For further information concerning each of these areas, consult their separate headings.

Lombardy: The English spelling of *Lombardia,* a wine region in northern Italy. Its capital is the city of Milan; the area extends east from Lake Maggiore to Lake Garda (Lago di Garda), the largest lakes in Italy. Lake Garda is the source of some attractive light red and white wines, of which LUGANA (white) and CHIARETTO (red) are famous. The sturdy red wines made from the Nebbiolo grape in the VALTELLINA district to the north, near the city of Sondrio, are among Italy's best. Further south, the FRECCIAROSSA wines of the Odero estate are internationally famous. The numerous wines of the OLTREPÒ PAVESE region in the province of Pavia are also renowned. There are several other smaller wine districts in Lombardy—Botticino, Franciacorta, Barbacarlo, etc.—but

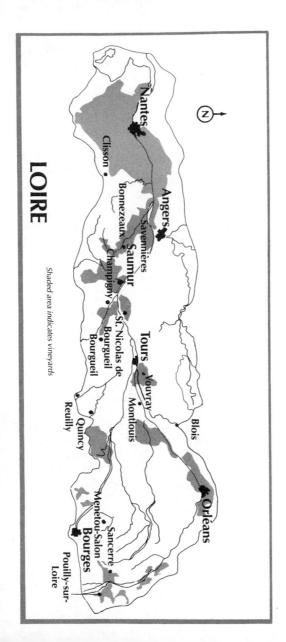

LOIRE

Shaded area indicates vineyards

N

Nantes
Clisson
Angers
Bonnezeaux
Savennières
Saumur
Champigny
St. Nicolas de
Bourgueil
Bourgueil
Tours
Vouvray
Montlouis
Quincy
Reuilly
Blois
Menetou-Salon
Sancerre
Bourges
Orléans
Pouilly-sur-
Loire

they are not well-known outside the region. Total wine production is the equivalent of some 24 million cases a year.

Loupiac *(Loop'-ee-ack):* White wine region in the BORDEAUX district, on the right bank of the GARONNE River near the region of SAU-TERNES. Loupiac forms the northern portion of the SAINTE-CROIX-DU-MONT region, and likewise specializes in sweet white wines made from the Sémillon, Sauvignon Blanc and Muscadelle, similar to Sauternes but generally heavier and less distinguished.

Ludon *(Loo'-dawn):* Wine commune in the HAUT-MÉDOC district, immediately north of the city of BORDEAUX. Although Ludon has one excellent estate or CHÂTEAU, La Lagune, Ludon is not an APPELLATION CONTRÔLÉE and its wines must be sold under the appellation HAUT-MÉDOC. Besides La Lagune, there are several other lesser estates in Ludon: d'Aggasac, Lafitte-Canteloup, Pommies-Aggasac, d'Arches, and Nexon-Lemoyne.

Lugana *(Loo-gahn'-nah):* Light, dry white wine produced near Lake Garda (Lago di Garda) in the region of LOMBARDY, northern Italy. One of the better Lake Garda white wines, Lugana is made from the Trebbiano grape, and entitled to D.O.C.

Lugny *(Loon-yee'):* Village in the MÁCON district, Burgundy; famous for its good white wines, made from the Chardonnay grape and entitled to the appellation Mâcon-Lugny.

Lunel *(Loo-nell'):* Town and wine region on France's Mediterranean coast, near the city of Nîmes in the department of HÉRAULT. Lunel lies 20 miles to the east of FRONTIGNAN, and likewise is celebrated for its sweet FORTIFIED WINE made from the Muscat grape, though Lunel is smaller and less important.

Lussac-Saint-Émilion *(Loo'-sack Sahnt Eh-meel-lyon'):* Red wine commune of secondary importance in the BORDEAUX district, officially part of the region of SAINT-ÉMILION. Lussac lies about 8 miles to the north of the village of Saint-Émilion; the soil is quite different and the wines are generally less fine, but many are quite good and represent excellent value.

Luxembourg (*Lukes'-em-boorg*): The Grand Duchy of Luxembourg has about 3,000 acres of vineyard in the upper Moselle River valley, before the river flows into Germany and is called MOSEL. Light white wines are made from the Müller-Thurgau (Riesling x Sylvaner), Traminer, Riesling, and Ruländer grapes. The east-facing slopes of the Moselle in certain villages—most notably, Remich, Grevenmacher, Ehnen, Wintringen, Wasserbillig, and Wormeldange—can produce some good wines, but few of them are seen on the U.S. market.

Mâcon (*Mah'-cawn*): City in southern BURGUNDY, an important center for the wine trade. Mâcon is also an APPELLATION CONTRÔLÉE for red, white and rosé wines produced in the region around the city; the region is called MÂCONNAIS in French. Usually inexpensive and good value, the Mâcon wines—particularly the fresh, engaging whites—are very popular. They have several quality categories: Mâcon blanc (white), Mâcon rouge (red), and "Pinot Chardonnay-Mâcon," the latter indicating the grape variety from which the wine was made, applies to wines produced anywhere in the Mâcon region. "Mâcon" or "Mâcon Supérieur" indicates wines produced in the *arrondissement*

193

(township) of Mâcon, a much smaller area. The word "Mâcon," followed by the name of the commune where the wine was made, applies to more distinctive white wines; these are also known as "Mâcon-Villages." Particularly outstanding white Mâcon-Villages wines are made in the areas of LUGNY and VIRÉ.

Mâcon-Fuissé *(Mah'-cawn Fwee-say')*: New white BURGUNDY appellation, authorized only since 1976, relating to a dry white wine produced from Chardonnay vines that lie within the township of Fuissé in the MÂCONNAIS district. Permission was recently given by the government to growers who use the name Fuissé in connection with Mâcon-Villages, to identify some 65 acres of vines that were not included in the original delimitation of POUILLY-FUISSÉ. The wine is very similar to a good Pouilly-Fuissé and is considerably cheaper, but since the growing zone is small it remains a rarity on the export market.

Mâconnais *(Mah'-cawn-nay)*: Wine region in southern Burgundy, France, surrounding the city of MÂCON in the department of Saône-et-Loire. The Mâconnais extends southwards from the village of Sennecy-le-Grand down to the BEAUJOLAIS district; the region is celebrated for its fine white wines made from the Chardonnay grape, although some red Mâcon of lesser quality is also made from the Gamay. By far the most famous Mâconnais wine is POUILLY-FUISSÉ, produced in four communes southwest of Mâcon; surrounding Pouilly-Fuissé are the similarly fine regions of POUILLY-VINZELLES and POUILLY-LOCHÉ. A new appellation created in 1971, SAINT-VÉRAN, includes several villages near these areas but without right to their appellation. The total vineyard area in the Mâconnais region extends over some 7,400 acres; the average production is in excess of 1 million cases of wine a year, 66% of it white.

Madeira: Island in the Atlantic Ocean, located some 360 miles off the coast of Morocco; also the name of its wines. Under Portuguese control since 1419, Madeira has been famous for its wines for over 400 years. But in the beginning, Madeira wine was acidic and rather harsh. During the mid-18th century brandy was first added to the wines to strengthen them for long sea voyages, but it was found that the sea voyage itself—with constant motion and exposure to tropical heat seasoning the wines—improved their flavor. Later, Madeira winemakers discovered how to duplicate the effects of the sea voyage with the process of *estufa*, by which the wines are exposed to high temperatures in special warming ovens over a period of 4-5 months, giving them a caramel color and characteristic flavor. Madeira became a national drink in colonial America because the island was Portuguese-controlled and the wines could be carried on American ships. But the Madeira trade with the U.S. declined during the 19th century and is no longer as important today as it once was; western Europe is a more significant market for Madeira than the U.S. Currently, there are about 3,700 acres of vineyard on the island, supplemented by others on nearby Porto Santo island.

Like SHERRY, Madeira is a fortified wine, made with the addition of brandy and blended by the same process used in the Sherry district: the SOLERA system. In Madeira, following fortification and completion of the estufa process, the wines are gradually blended over a period of time with wines from many vintages. In most cases, a vintage date on a bottle of Madeira indicates the date the solera was begun, not the actual age of the wine. Although vintage Madeiras from exceptional years are made on a limited basis, very few are exported.

The different types of Madeira are identified by grades of sweetness, which relates to when the wine is fortified. Sweet Madeiras receive an addition of brandy before the estufa

195

process; the dry wines are allowed to ferment out first, fortification taking place after the estufa process. When all steps are completed, however, the alcoholic content in each case will be the same (18-20%).

The driest Madeira is generally SERCIAL, a scented, pale gold wine made from the Sercial grape—believed to be the same as Germany's Riesling. Grown on Madeira's highest slopes, Sercial is harvested later than other grapes as it is the last to ripen. Being dry, Sercial makes a fine apéritif.

VERDELHO, a slightly darker wine than Sercial, is also a shade sweeter. At one time, an especially light and fragrant blend of Verdelho was known under the trade name RAINWATER and used by a shipper named Habisham in Savannah, Georgia. Today, Rainwater has become a GENERIC name for a fairly light, semi-dry Madeira; the term is now in the public domain.

The next sweetest Madeira is BUAL (or Boal), which, because of its residual sugar, is best served as a dessert wine. The sweetest, richest and fullest of all Madeiras is MALMSEY, made from the Malvasia (Malvoisie) grape that English buyers originally pronounced as "Malmsey."

The port city of Funchal is the center for the Madeira wine trade, where the shippers' offices or "lodges" are headquartered. Leacock, Cossart Gordon, Rutherford & Miles, Blandy's, Welsh Bros., and Henriques & Henriques are among the more important Madeira shippers.

Maderization: The chemical deterioration of a wine, caused either by poor storage or from exposure to heat. Maderization is particularly objectionable in white and rosé wines, causing them to turn brown and take on an unpleasant flat flavor. The word is derived from the wines of MADEIRA, which have a characteristic dark color.

Primarily a process of OXIDATION, maderization gradually occurs in all wines but is most evident when white wines are consumed when too old. Once maderization takes place, the process is irreversible.

Madiran *(Ma-dee-rawn')*: Robust red wine produced in southwest France in the department of Hautes-Pyrénées. One of France's lesser-known wines, Madiran is made from a local grape variety known as the Tannat, usually with some Cabernet Sauvignon added. The wine is particularly rich and full-bodied; not much is exported, but the area has considerable potential.

Magnum: A large wine bottle with the capacity of two ordinary bottles. Besides having extra capacity, a magnum is quite functional: wines age more slowly in large bottles, and fine wines from especially great vintages are often at their best when served from magnums.

Málaga *(Ma'-la-ga)*: Sweet, dark-colored wine produced in southern Spain near the city of Málaga on the Mediterranean coast. Formerly known as "Mountain," the wines of Málaga were popular centuries ago but are now rather rare. They are made principally from Pedro Ximénez and Muscat grapes that are allowed to dry in the sun in order to concentrate their sugar. The wines are aged by the same SOLERA system used in the SHERRY district some 100 miles to the west.

Malbec *(Mal'-beck)*: Fine red wine grape, grown extensively in the BORDEAUX district where it is used in blends to soften the slow-maturing Cabernet Sauvignon. Also known as Cot or Pressac, the Malbec is the principal variety in the region of CAHORS, and is grown to a large extent in South America where it is occasionally spelled Malbeck.

Malconsorts *(Mal'-cawn-sor)*: Excellent red wine vineyard in the commune of VOSNE-

197

ROMANÉE, in Burgundy's CÔTE DE NUITS. Officially rated Premier Cru (First Growth), the Malconsorts vineyard consists of about 15 acres planted in Pinot Noir, which yield especially scented red wines prized for their finesse and breed.

Malmsey: The richest, darkest and sweetest kind of MADEIRA, made from the Malvasia (Malvoisie) grape. The name Malmsey originated from the English mispronunciation of Malvasia, and nowadays applies primarily to the FORTIFIED WINES of the island of Madeira, not the golden sweet wines made in the Mediterranean region from the Malvasia and known by the original name. See MALVASIA.

Malolactic Fermentation: Secondary fermentation by which malic acid is converted into lactic acid through the action of *Lactobacillus* bacteria, an important process that helps reduce much of the youthful harshness in many wines. Malic acid gives the green, unripe quality to wines in their first year, and after it is broken down into lactic acid and carbon dioxide, the wines are usually much more agreeable.

Because carbon dioxide is released during malolactic fermentation, it is best that this secondary fermentation be carried out in cask some time before the wines are bottled, otherwise the wine will become cloudy and fizzy, spoiling both appearance and flavor. Bottled wines suffering from this malady have often been bottled too early, before malolactic fermentation is completed. It has recently been demonstrated that various species of *Lactobacillus* bacteria differ in many wine districts, which could significantly determine the individual character of a region's wines.

198   **Malvasia** *(Mal-va-zee'-ah)*: White grape variety, grown principally in Mediterranean climates and known under several different names. The name originated from the little

Greek coastal town of Monemvasia in the Peloponnesus, where the grape was first cultivated, and it spread throughout the Aegean. Malvasia is the Italian spelling; the grape is called Malvoisie in French, Malvagia in Spanish, and MALMSEY in English, although nowadays the latter term relates to the sweet FORTIFIED WINES of the island of MADEIRA.

Today, the Malvasia is still grown in its original location, and the Greek islands of Crete and Rhodes produce some interesting Malvasia wine. In Italy, Malvasia is grown in many southern wine regions, but the island of Lipari north of Sicily produces what many regard as the best example of Malvasia: Malvasia di Lipari. In France, under the name Malvoisie, the grape is grown in many sweet wine regions—most notably at BANYULS and ROUSSILLON. To a limited extent, Malvasia is also grown in the warmer climatic regions of California.

Mancha, La: One of Spain's largest wine regions, located south of the city of Madrid. There are over 500,000 acres under vines; the climate is very warm, resulting in mostly ordinary wines with the possible exception of the good red wines of the VALDEPEÑAS district, which is included in the La Mancha region.

Manzanilla (Man-than-neel'-ya): An exceptionally light and dry Spanish SHERRY, produced within the Sherry district but specifically around the city of Sanlúcar de Barrameda on the Guadalquivir River, 12 miles to the northwest of the city of Jerez. Manzanilla is usually the driest and most austere of Sherries, comparable to a FINO but lighter in color and with an unusually fragrant, tangy bouquet. It is said that these characteristics derive from the salty air that blows in from the ocean.

Marc (Mar): French for grape pressings or POMACE, consisting of the skins, seeds and pulp remaining after fermentation. Marc can be distilled to make brandy, which is called Eau-de

Vie-de-Marc in French; the marc brandies of BURGUNDY and CHAMPAGNE are famous. In the French Champagne region, however, marc has a slightly different meaning: the capacity of one standard-sized wine press, equivalent to 8,800 pounds of grapes (4,000 kilograms).

Marche *(Mar'-kay)*: Wine region in east-central Italy; the chief city is Ancona, on the Adriatic Sea. By all odds its best wine is the white VERDICCHIO, grown in two D.O.C. regions: Verdicchio dei Castelli di Jesi and Verdicchio di Matelica. The golden BIANCHELLO DEL METAURO, another good white wine, is also rated D.O.C. Red wines of the Marche region are not as famous, though the D.O.C. red Rosso Conero and Rosso Piceno, made from Montepulciano and Sangiovese grapes, have some repute. The Marche region as a whole typically produces in excess of 24 million cases of wine each year.

Marcobrunn *(Mar'-co-brun)*: Celebrated vineyard in the RHEINGAU district, Germany, divided equally between the adjoining wine communes of ERBACH and HATTENHEIM. Its soil and exposure are exemplary; in dry years, its scented and fruity Riesling wines are among the best in the Rheingau. Formerly, the wines were often called "Erbacher Markobrunn" on the Erbach side, and "Marcobrunner" on the Hattenheim side, but under the 1971 German Wine Law, all wines must now be sold as Erbacher Marcobrunn. The leading proprietors are the Staatsweingut, Schloss Schönborn, Langwerth von Simmern, and Schloss Reinhartshausen.

Margaux *(Mar-go')*: Outstanding wine area in the HAUT-MÉDOC district, some 18 miles to the north of the city of BORDEAUX. The area entitled to the APPELLATION CONTRÔLÉE Margaux consists of the associated communes of Margaux, Soussans, Arsac, CANTENAC, and Labarde; the soil and exposure in each of these communes is similar. Largely because of the soil, the fine red wines of Margaux are typically among the most scented and refined in the world. The leading wine estate or CHÂ-TEAU is Château Margaux (see MARGAUX, CHÂTEAU), which is officially ranked as a Premier Cru (First Growth) in the 1855 Médoc classification, but of all the wine communes in the Médoc, Margaux has the largest number of classified growth (*cru classe*) châteaux. *Seconds Crus* (Second Growths): Rausan-Ségla, Rauzan-Gassies, Durfort-Vivens, Lascombes, and Brane-Cantenac. *Troisièmes Crus* (Third Growths): Kirwan, d'Issan, Giscours, Malescot-St. Exupéry, Cantenac-Brown, Boyd-Cantenac, Palmer, Ferrière, and Marquis d'Alesme-Becker. *Quatrièmes Crus* (Fourth Growths):Pouget,Prieuré-Lichine,andMarquis-de-Terme. *Cinquièmes Crus* (Fifth Growths): DauzacandduTertre.

Margaux, Château (*Mar-go'*): One of the finest red wine estates of BORDEAUX, located in the commune of MARGAUX in the HAUT-MÉDOC district. The estate is owned by Mme. Laura Mentzelopoulos, whose husband, the late André Mentzelopoulos, purchased the château in 1977, and is officially classified as a Premier Cru (First Growth), one of only three others in the whole Médoc. In good vintages, the wines of Château Margaux are unsurpassed, characterized by a magnificent bouquet and great delicacy. The estate extends over 650 acres, but only about 160 acres are given over to producing vines; typically, about 20,000 cases of wine are made each year. A small amount of exquisite white wine called Pavillon Blanc du Château Margaux is also made, but it is only entitled to the appellation Bordeaux, there being no Médoc appellation for white wines.

Markgräflerland (*Mark-gray'-flur-land*): Wine sub-region or BEREICH in the region of BADEN, Germany, located between the cities of Frei-

201

burg and Basel. The leading grape variety is the Gutedel or Chasselas, which yields mild, pleasant white wines known locally as Markgräfler; Ruländer, Silvaner and Traminer are also grown. The name Markgräfler derives from *Markgraf*, the German word for count.

Marque *(Mark):* French for "brand." A *marque déposée* is a registered trade mark; a *vin de marque*, however, is merely a branded wine, sold without the restrictions on the use of wine place-names applicable to the laws of APPELLATION CONTRÔLÉE or V.D.Q.S.

Marsala *(Mar-sahl'-la):* The most famous FORTIFIED WINE of Italy, a D.O.C. wine produced in the northwest corner of the island of Sicily. Its center is the coastal town of Marsala, although several Marsala producers have their offices in Trapani to the north.

Marsala may only be made from three grape varieties: Grillo, Catarratto, and Inzolia. Before brandy is added to bring it up to about 18–20% alcohol, the wine is straw colored and full-flavored. Its characteristic sweetness is primarily a result of a grape concentrate made from boiled must, *mosto cotto*, which is added in proportion to the desired sweetness in the finished wine.

Marsala is customarily sold in several grades: *Fine*, the lightest and least expensive, which must attain at least 17% alcohol; *Superiore*, the most usual grade in the export trade, which must be aged in cask for at least 2 years and have at least 18% alcohol; *Vergine* (also called "solera type" because it is made by the same SOLERA system used for Spanish Sherry), which must be aged for 5 years, is light in color and very dry. The terms *Stravecchio* or *Extra* are sometimes used to indicate additional age. *Speciale* or "special" is appropriately named, as it is a Fine Marsala made with a number of different flavors—eggs, strawberry, banana, coffee, etc.

Marsannay *(Mar'-san-nay):* Little town in BURGUNDY, France, just south of the city of Dijon; its full name is Marsannay-la-Côte. Its vineyards usually produce some of the best rosé wines of Burgundy from the Pinot Noir grape, under the appellation "Bourgogne Marsannay-la-Côte." Some light red and white wines are also produced in Marsannay, but the rosés are clearly the best.

Martillac *(Mar'-tee-yack):* Wine commune in the GRAVES district, south of the city of BORDEAUX. The southernmost wine commune in Graves with officially classified *(cru classé)* wine estates or CHÂTEAUX, Martillac boasts several fine châteaux: Smith-Haut-Lafitte, La Tour-Martillac, Domaine de la Solitude, La Garde, Haut-Nouchet, etc.

Mavrodaphne *(Mav-ro-daff'-nee):* Rich, sweet red Greek wine; a specialty of the northern Peloponnesus region, though it is also produced on the nearby island of Cephalonia.

Maximin Grünhaus *(Max'-ee-mean Grune'-house):* Outstanding wine estate in the RUWER district, Germany. Owned by the von Schubert family, the estate consists of 52 acres of vineyard west of the little village of Mertesdorf. Formerly the property of the St. Maximin abbey, the vineyard is divided into three sites or *lagen:* Abtsberg, Herrenberg and Bruderberg, and on each bottle the specific lage will be identified. The lagen names reflect the former church hierarchy: Abtsberg was the reserve of the abbot, Herrenberg belonged to the clergy, and Bruderberg was left to the lay brethren. Of the three, Herrenberg is the largest lage.

The vineyard is renowned for its delicate and scented Riesling wines, though like many Ruwer wines they are generally only at their best in great vintages.

May Wine: A light Rhine wine that has been sweetened and flavored with woodruff herbs

203

(*Waldmeister*, in German). It is usually served chilled in a punch bowl, with strawberries or other fruit floating in it.

Mazis-Chambertin (*Ma-zee' Shawm'-bear-tan*): Renowned red wine vineyard in the CÔTE DE NUITS, Burgundy, located in the commune of GEVREY-CHAMBERTIN and rated Grand Cru (Great Growth). The vineyard adjoins the famous CLOS DE BÉZE vineyard to the south, and consists of about 20 acres planted in Pinot Noir; the wines are noted for their strength and finesse. Average annual production amounts to some 2,600 cases.

Mazoyères-Chambertin (*Ma-zo-yair' Shawm'-bear-tan*): Fine red wine vineyard in the CÔTE DE NUITS, Burgundy, officially rated Grand Cru (Great Growth)—among Burgundy's best. The vineyard adjoins that of CHARMES-CHAMBERTIN, and a Mazoyères-Chambertin, may legally be sold as a Charmes-Chambertin, as some growers maintain that the latter is easier to pronounce, but a Charmes-Chambertin may not be sold as a Mazoyères. Vineyard size and production statistics for the two vineyards are generally combined.

Médoc (*May'-dawk*): World-famous wine region, extending some 50 miles to the north of the city of BORDEAUX on the left bank of the GIRONDE estuary. Its southern half is the HAUT-MÉDOC district: the Bas-Médoc district forms the northern half. All of the most famous Médoc wine estates or CHÂTEAUX lie in the Haut-Médoc, and Haut-Médoc is also an APPELLATION CONTRÔLÉE for regional wines that are generally superior to those labeled "Médoc," which normally come from the less distinguished Bas-Médoc district.

The total area of vineyard in the Médoc is about 17,300 acres, and wine production often exceeds 3.4 million cases a year. But the Médoc is not famous for quantity, rather for superb quality. The region's soil is alluvial, which provides ideal drainage for such noble grape varieties as Cabernet Sauvignon, Cabernet Franc, Merlot, Malbec, and Petit-Verdot. No other varieties are permitted. In most Médoc vineyards Cabernet is dominant, although it is customary for an estate to be planted in several different varieties, adding balance and complexity to the wine. Characteristically firm and tannic in their youth, fine Médoc wines normally require two years of aging in cask and often many more in bottle.

The Haut-Médoc consists of six outstanding communes, which are, from north to south; SAINT-ESTÈPHE, PAUILLAC, SAINT-JULIEN, LISTRAC, MOULIS, and MARGAUX. In 1855 the leading Médoc châteaux were classified into five groups of *crus* (growths), based on the prices that their wines were fetching on the Bordeaux market. Wine estates considered not worthy of classified growth *(cru classé)* status were either rated *cru exceptionnel* (exceptional) or *cru bourgeois* (bourgeois). While any wine from a classified growth château is likely to be distinguished, the 1855 classification has several shortcomings. With only one exception, it has remained unchanged for over a century, and its rigid sequential structure implies that a fifth growth is necessarily inferior to a fourth growth, which is often not the case. Another deficiency with the classification is that it does not include outstanding châteaux from other regions in Bordeaux. For these reasons, a re-classification is possible in the near future.

The Official 1855 Classification of the Médoc (1976 status)

PREMIERS CRUS / FIRST GROWTHS

Château Lafite-Rothschild
Château Margaux
Château Latour
Château Haut-Brion
Château Mouton-Rothschild[1]

205

---

[1] Declared a First Growth in 1973.

SECONDS CRUS / SECOND GROWTHS

Château Rausan-Ségla
Château Rauzan-Gassies
Château Léoville-Las-Cases
Château Léoville-Poyferré
Château Léoville-Barton
Château Durfort-Vivens
Château Gruaud-Larose
Château Lascombes
Château Brane-Cantenac
Château Pichon-Longueville-Baron
Château Pichon-Longueville,
Comtesse de Lalande
Château Ducru-Beaucaillou
Château Cos d'Estournel
Château Montrose

TROISIÈMES CRUS / THIRD GROWTHS

Château Kirwan
Château d'Issan
Château Lagrange
Château Langoa-Barton
Château Giscours
Château Malescot-Saint-Exupéry
Château Cantenac-Brown
Château Boyd-Cantenac
Château Palmer
Château La Lagune
Château Desmirail[2]
Château Calon-Ségur
Château Ferrière
Château Marquis d'Alesme-Becker

QUATRIÈMES CRUS / FOURTH GROWTHS

Château Saint-Pierre-Sevaistre[3]
Château Talbot
Château Branaire (Duluc-Ducru)
Château Duhart-Milon-Rothschild
Château Pouget
Château La Tour-Carnet
Château Lafon-Rochet
Château Beychevelle
Château Prieuré-Lichine
Château Marquis-de-Terme

CINQUIÈMES CRUS / FIFTH GROWTHS

Château Pontet-Canet

Château Batailley
Château Haut-Batailley
Château Grand-Puy-Lacoste
Château Grand-Puy-Ducasse
Château Lynch-Bages
Château Lynch-Moussas
Château Dauzac
Château Mouton-Baronne-Philippe[4]
Château du Tertre
Château Haut-Bages-Libéral
Château Pédesclaux
Château Belgrave
Château Camensac
Château Cos-Labory
Château Clerc-Milon
Château Croizet-Bages
Château Cantemerle

CRUS EXCEPTIONNELS / EXCEPTIONAL GROWTHS

Château Villegeorge
Château Angludet
Château Chasse-Spleen
Château Poujeaux-Theil
Château La Couronne
Château Moulin-Riche
Château Bel-Air-Marquis d'Aligre

---

[2] This vineyard no longer exists; the name is now used as a subsidiary brand by Château Palmer. [3] Formerly two châteaux, Saint-Pierre-Sevaistre and Saint-Pierre Bontemps. [4] Before 1956, known as Mouton d'Armailhacq.

Melon *(Muh-lawn')*: White wine grape, originally grown in the BURGANDY region but now widely cultivated in the lower LOIRE River valley, where it is now called MUSCADET and produces a good dry white wine of the same name.

Mendocino: County and wine district in northern California, wtih some 10,300 acres of vineyard; the most northerly of the "North Coast Counties." Its principal town is Ukiah, along the Russian River—a stream that flows south towards SONOMA and in Mendocino already describes a fine wine district. Mendocino became famous in the 1970s as an emerging wine area, and a number of new wineries

207

were established. One of the most notable of these was Fetzer, since 1968 a producer of some particularly select Cabernet Sauvignon and Zinfandel; Parducci Winery is also famous. The largest cellars in the area are at the Cresta Blanca facilities, now managed by Guild Wineries; recently Edmeades, Greenwood Ridge, Husch, Lazy Creek, Navarro, Milano Winery, Parsons Creek Winery and Tyland Vineyards have contributed to the county's reputation. McDowell Valley Vineyards in Hopland achieved local appellation status in recognition of their superb microclimate, and in 1982 became the first winery in the nation to run on solar power.

Mendoza (Men-doe'-sa): Major wine region and province in western Argentina, producing over 75% of that country's wine. Some 519,000 acres of vineyard are in Mendoza, most of them owned by large wineries or *bodegas* geared to mass production. The Andes Mountains rise up in western Mendoza, blocking rainfall and necessitating irrigation, one factor in the large production. The leading grape variety is Malbeck (Malbec), used to make robust red wines.

Mercurey (Mair'-coo-ray): Wine district in the CHALONNAIS region, southern Burgundy, noted for its good red wines made from the Pinot Noir grape—usually the best of the Chalonnais. Some light white wine is also made from the Chardonnay, but the fruity, rather early-maturing reds are superior. Some 250,000 cases of wine are produced annually.

Merlot (Mair-lo'): Fine red wine grape grown extensively in the BORDEAUX region. The soft, perfumed red wines that it gives are used for blending with Cabernet Sauvignon in the MÉDOC district, or exclusively in the SAINT-ÉMILION and POMEROL districts to the east, where it is the dominant variety. The Merlot is also grown in northern Italy, particularly in the regions of TRENTINO and ALTO ADIGE; across the border in Switzerland it is no less important, particularly in the region of TICINO. In California, major new plantations of Merlot now cover more than 2,600 acres; a number of recent California Cabernet Sauvignons have been markedly improved by a slight admixture of Merlot, which tends to soften the characteristic astringency of Cabernet.

Méthode Champenoise *(May'-toad Shom'-pen-wahz):* French for "Champagne method," the practice used in the French CHAMPAGNE district for sparkling wine whose secondary fermentation takes place in the bottle. The term is often used in other French winegrowing districts, such as Burgundy and the Loire, which produce quality sparkling wines by the same process but which cannot legally sell these wines under the name Champagne. In other countries, these two words may also identify similar wines produced by the same process; in the United States, wines produced by the original Champagne method may bear the label "naturally fermented in *this* bottle." See TRANSFER PROCESS.

Methuselah: An oversized wine bottle with a capacity of eight ordinary bottles, used occasionally in the French CHAMPAGNE district.

Meursault *(Mere'-so):* Outstanding wine commune in the CÔTE DE BEAUNE, Burgundy, famous for its soft, scented white wines made from the Chardonnay. A little light red wine is also produced, but the white is superior and is commercially much more important. Meursault's best vineyards are rated Premier Cru (First Growth); the most famous is PERRIÈRES, which has a central sub-plot, the Clos des Perrières, that is particularly renowned. Other distinguished vineyards include Genevrières, Charmes, La Goutte d'Or, and Poruzots. The Meursault commune includes a small portion of the vineyards of BLAGNY to the south; notable vineyards in the Blagny section include

209

Jennelotte, La Pièce-Sous-Le-Bois, and Dos d'Âne. The total area under vines in Meursault is 1,186 acres; the equivalent of some 150,000 cases of wine is produced annually, over 90% of it white.

Mexico: Spanish settlers introduced the vine to Mexico in the 16th century, but only recently has interest in wine been strong in that country. There are currently over 60,000 acres of vineyard in Mexico, mostly in the north center of the country and to a certain extent in the Baja California region, but not all are planted in quality wine grapes and much is used for brandy distillation. The climate is very dry, and irrigation is necessary in many vineyards. Mexican wines are presently not very significant on the U.S. market, but several well-established wineries like Bodegas de Santo Tomás, Nazario Ortiz Garza, and Bodegas de San Lorenzo (Casa Madero) show considerable promise.

Michigan: The southeastern shores of Lake Michigan have been planted in vines for over a century, though table grapes have traditionally been more important than wine: the state is the nation's fourth largest grape producer. A number of growers make only grape juice in Michigan, but between the cities of Grand Rapids and Benton Harbor, a number of promising wineries have sprung up in the past few years. Fenn Valley Vineyards in Fennville have been particularly successful in wine competitions; Taybor Hill, Bronte Wines and Warner Vineyards nearby are other noted producers in the area. Further to the north, two major producers in the Traverse City district are Château Grand Travers and Leelanau Wine Cellars; Boskydel Vineyard on Lake Leelanau is smaller but committed to high-quality table wines. Many of the biggest Michigan producers specialize in fruit wines and "special natural" wines, but the most successful releases tend to be made from French-

210

American hybrids that are well-suited to the cool growing season.

Midi (*Me'-dee*): French for "the south"; the vast sweep of land along the Mediterranean coast ranging westwards from the mouth of the Rhône River to the Spanish border. It includes the departments of Gard, HÉRAULT, AUDE, and Pyrénées-Orientales. Most of the wine of the Midi is ordinary, but in upland regions where production is restricted, some notable wines are made. See LANGUEDOC.

Mildew: Serious cryptogamic (fungal) disease of the vine, caused by the organism *Plasmospora viticola*; also called downy mildew. Native to North America, mildew was introduced in the late 19th century in the European vineyards, where it was tremendously destructive. Mildew attacks the green portions of vine and cripples it, but it can be controlled with copper sulphate (Bordeaux mixture). See OÏDIUM.

Millésime (*Meal-lay-seem'*): French for "vintage." A non-vintage wine is called "non-millésimé."

Millot, Léon (*Kühlmann 194.2*): Red French HYBRID grape variety, grown in the eastern United States and elsewhere; produced from a riparia-rupestris cross with Goldriesling. It has similar parentage to FOCH, and was developed subsequently by the same hybridizer: the wines that it gives are slightly different, but both grapes are well-suited to cooler eastern climates where winter hardiness is an important advantage.

Minervois (*Mee'-nair-vwah*): Wine region in the old province of LANGUEDOC, southern France, east of the city of Carcassonne. Red, white and rosé wines entitled to the V.D.Q.S. seal are produced in the Minervois region; the reds—made from Cinsault, Carignan and Grenache grapes—are usually the best, and some are among the finest inexpensive wines

211

that France has to offer. About 2.7 million cases of wine are produced annually.

Mis en Bouteilles au Château: see CHÂTEAU-BOTTLED.

Mis en Bouteilles au Domaine: see ESTATE BOTTLED.

Mission: Historic red wine grape, the first VINIFERA variety to be planted in California in the late 18th century by Spanish settlers. In other respects it is less significant: although there are still some 3,600 acres planted in Mission in California, it gives rather common wine, suitable primarily for blending purposes and for making California "sherry" and "port."

Missouri: Wine was first produced from wild grapes in Missouri in 1823, and winemaking has been on a good basis in the state ever since. Several Missouri wineries—Stone Hill Wine Co. in Hermann, Bardenheier's Wine Cellars in St. Louis, and Mount Pleasant Vineyards in Augusta—proudly reflect on a century of winemaking experience. More traditional growing areas lie west of St. Louis along the Missouri River; a few (St. James Winery, Ozark Vineyards) are located further south on the Ozark Plateau. Recently a few wineries have sprung up in the northwest portion of the state, near Kansas City: Bowman Wine Cellars, Kruger's Winery & Vineyards and Midi Vineyards lie in this area. Many of their wines are made from native American varieties—Concord, Niagara, Catawba, etc.— but there is considerable interest in French-American hybrids, which do well in the state.

Mistelle *(Mee-stell')*: French term for grape juice or must that has received an addition of brandy before fermentation takes place, allowing some residual sugar to remain. Mistelles are widely used in the manufacture of VERMOUTH and other wine apéritifs.

Mittelrhein: German for "Middle Rhine," a wine region or ANBAUGEBIET extending southwards along the banks of the Rhine River from near Bonn to Bingen. It includes two sub-regions or BEREICHE: Bacharach and Rhein-burgengau. The most northerly of the German wine regions, the Mittelrhein is one of the smaller and less important; the wines are virtually unknown on the export market. Centuries ago, the region was celebrated for its fine Riesling wines—in particular, those from the villages of Bacharach, Boppard, Oberwesel and St. Goarshausen, but their production is minuscule today. There are 2,110 acres under vines, and in a typical year over 900,000 cases of wine are produced in the Mittelrhein, yet much is consumed by the tourists that visit the region for its scenery.

Monbazillac (*Mawn-ba-zee-yack'*): White wine region in southwestern France, near the city of BERGERAC. Named for the picturesque Château de Monbazillac that overlooks the region, the sweet white wines of Monbazillac have been praised for centuries. They are normally harvested in the late autumn, like the more famous wines of SAUTERNES made some 50 miles to the southwest, though Monbazillacs are slightly drier, less fine, and considerably less expensive. The region extends over some 6,600 acres; annual production averages some 915,000 cases a year.

Monferrato (*Mawn-fair-rot'-toe*): Range of hills in northern Italy, a part of the district of PIE-MONTE. Monferrato has several wine regions; one of them, Barbera del Monferrato, has D.O.C. status.

Monimpex: The Hungarian State Export Agency, which controls the wine and spirit export sales of that country.

Monopole (*Mo-no-poll'*): French for "monopoly"; when seen on a wine label, it indicates that the wine is an exclusive of that producer, signifying either a blended wine sold under a proprietary brand name, or else that the producer owns that vineyard in its entirety.

Montagne de Reims *(Mawn-tahn'-yuh-duh Rans')*: The most northern portion of the French CHAMPAGNE country south of the city of REIMS, with vineyards planted primarily in black Pinot Noir grapes. Beaumont-sur-Vesle, Mailly, Puisieulx, Sillery and Verzenay are its most important towns.

Montagne-Saint-Émilion *(Mawn-tahn'-yuh Sahnt Eh-meel-lyon')*: Secondary red wine commune in the BORDEAUX district, located 3 miles to the north of the village of SAINT-ÉMILION and legally entitled to use its name. Montagne lies in hilly country overlooking Saint-Émilion, and its vineyards do not enjoy the same excellent exposure as those further south, but the wines are similar and are often outstanding value, being considerably less expensive. The leading wine estates (CHÂTEAU) are: Calon, Montaguillon, Plaisance, Roudier, and Vieux-Château-Négrit.

Montagny *(Mawn-tan-yee')*: White wine region in southern BURGUNDY, the southernmost part of the CHALONNAIS district. Montagny is famous for its fresh, light white wines made from the Chardonnay grape, among the best of the Chalonnais. Certain outstanding Montagny vineyards have been rated Premier Cru (First Growth); the more famous include Les Charmelottes, Les Vignes du Soleil, Les Bonnevaux, Les Chanteoiseaux, and Sous-les-Roches. The vineyard area totals about 750 acres, including the communes of Buxy and Saint-Vallerin; average production is about 31,000 cases of wine annually.

Montepulciano *(Mawn-tay-pool-chon'-no)*: Town in southern TUSCANY, Italy, famous for its fine red wine, VINO NOBILE DI MONTEPULCIANO, that is rated D.O.C. Montepulciano is also the name of an unrelated red grape variety grown in the ABRUZZI region, used for making the red MONTEPULCIANO DI ABRUZZO.

Montepulciano di Abruzzo *(Mawn-tay-pool-chon'-no dee Ah-broot'-zo):* Good red wine produced in the ABRUZZI region, southern Italy. Dry and with a fine bouquet, it is entitled to D.O.C.

Monterey: City and county in central California, with more than 32,000 acres of vineyard. One of California's newest and most promising wine regions, Monterey enjoys a temperate climate, owing to cool breezes that blow in from the Pacific Ocean. Because of the cool climate, and that fact that much rainfall is blocked by the Coast Range Mountains to the west, the growing season is exceptionally long in Monterey, and many of the vines have to be irrigated. With most white grapes this presents no problem, but the long growing season occasionally precludes optimum red wine production. The immense new Monterey Vineyard in Gonzales, now owned by the Wine Spectrum in Atlanta, is the production facility for Taylor California Cellars and wines marketed under the Monterey Vineyard label; winemaker Dr. Richard Peterson, who directs this gigantic operation, has much to be proud of. Other major firms like Paul Masson, Mirassou, Wente Bros. and Almadén each have important vineyards in Monterey, although their main offices are located elsewhere.

Because the unique climate in Monterey affords so much possibility for experimentation, many entrepreneur winemakers have come to the county in recent years and have made some outstanding wines. J. Doug Meador's Ventana Winery near Soledad is an exceptional producer of white wines; Jekel Vineyard nearby is similar. Nearer to the coast, Durney Vineyard in Carmel, and the Monterey Peninsula Winery in Monterey itself, are

215

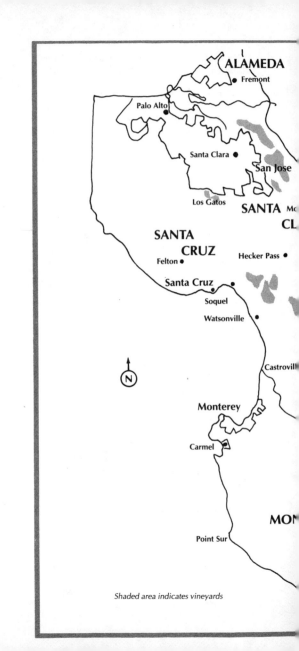

Shaded area indicates vineyards

MONTEREY
(Central California)

Hill

A

Gilroy

Hollister

San Juan
Bautista

Paicines

SAN BENITO

Salinas

Gonzales

Soledad

REY

Greenfield

King City

distinguished by their red wines. Particular accolades go to pioneer winemaker Richard Graff of Chalone Vineyard in Soledad: for decades some of the state's finest Chardonnays have been produced here.

Monthélie *(Mawn'-tay-lee)*: Wine commune in the CÔTE DE BEAUNE, Burgundy, adjoining the famous commune of VOLNAY. Primarily an area for light, scented red wines made from the Pinot Noir, Monthélie is not a well-known Côte de Beaune commune, and many of its fine wines sell for much less than comparable ones from Volnay. There are several good vineyards rated Premier Cru (First Growth); the finest is generally reckoned to be the Clos des Champs-Fulliot, along with the nearby Cas Rougeot, Clos Gautey, and La Taupine. There are some 250 acres under vines; production averages about 30,000 cases a year.

Montilla *(Mon-tee'-ya)*: Sturdy wine from the Montilla-Moriles district in southern Spain, near the city of Córdoba. Montilla is about 250 miles northeast of the SHERRY district, and until recently its wines were often sold as Sherries. Montilla differs from Sherry, however, in that it receives very little addition of brandy—a factor that preserves its unique winey character. The grapes grown in the Montilla district are the same Pedro Ximénez grapes used in the Sherry district, and the identical, special FLOR yeast develops over the wine in cask. Montillas are generally marketed in the same grades as Sherries—Fino, Oloroso, etc., and even the term "Amontillado" is used, although this expression originally arose in the Sherry district to describe wines that took on a Montilla-like character. Montilla is an excellent substitute for Sherry and deserves to be better-known.

Montlouis *(Mawn-lou-wee')*: White wine region in the central LOIRE River valley, adjoining the famous region of VOUVRAY and likewise praised for its fine, scented white wines made from the Chenin Blanc grape. The area of Montlouis is smaller than Vouvray and the wines are generally less costly, being not so well-known. Prior to 1938 Montlouis were often sold as Vouvrays, but since then they have been marketed under their own appellation. There are some 1,230 acres of vineyard, which produce the equivalent of 170,000 cases of wine annually.

Montrachet *(Mon-rah-shay')*: Magnificent white wine vineyard in the CÔTE DE BEAUNE, Burgundy, rated Grand Cru (Great Growth) like a few other outstanding white Burgundy vineyards, but officially the highest ranked of them all. Its 18½ acres, planted entirely in Chardonnay, are divided equally between the adjoining communes of Puligny and Chassagne, which have assumed its name to become PULIGNY-MONTRACHET and CHASSAGNE-MONTRACHET, respectively. Neighboring vineyards have also assumed the name Montrachet to show their relationship with their noble neighbor (see CHEVALIER-MONTRACHET, BÂTARD-MONTRACHET, BIENVENUE-BÂTARD-MONTRACHET, and CRIOTS-BÂTARD-MONTRACHET), and occasionally their wines will challenge Montrachet in a good vintage, though they are almost always somewhat less expensive.

Montrachet has been proclaimed the greatest dry white wine in the world. Pale-gold in color, the wine is succulent, scented and sensational. Unfortunately, total average annual production hardly ever exceeds 3,000 cases, accounting for the rarity and high cost of this exceptional wine.

Morey-Saint-Denis *(Mor'-ray San Duh-nee')*: Notable wine commune in the CÔTE DE NUITS, Burgundy, with some 325 acres of vineyard. It takes its name from the fine CLOS SAINT-DENIS vineyard, rated Grand Cru (Great Growth); the commune's other outstanding Grand Cru vineyards include the CLOS DE TART, CLOS DE

219

LA ROCHE, and a small portion of BONNES-MARES—the bulk of the latter vineyard lies in the neighboring commune of CHAMBOLLE-MUSIGNY to the south. One excellent vineyard rated Premier Cru (First Growth) that is nearly in the same class is the CLOS DES LAMBRAYS, like the Clos de Tart owned by a single proprietor. Other good Premier Cru vineyards in Morey-Saint-Denis include the Clos de la Bussière, Les Ruchots, Clos des Ormes, and Les Fremières. One vineyard, Monts-Luisants, is unusual for these parts in that it is planted in white grapes.

The many fine red wines of Morey-Saint-Denis are not as well-known as those of several other Côte de Nuits communes, and for this reason can offer exceptional value. They typically have an underlying firmness that softens with age, and the best of them rank with the finest red wines of Burgundy.

Morgeot *(Mor-zho')*: Fine red and white wines rated Premier Cru (First Growth), produced in the commune of CHASSAGNE-MONTRACHET in the CÔTE DE BEAUNE, Burgundy. By law the name Morgeot may be substituted for a number of different vineyards in Chassagne-Montrachet. Probably the best-known is the original plot of Morgeot (10 acres); others entitled to this appellation include Guerchères, La Chapelle, Vigne Blanche, Les Petits Clos, etc. The usage is optional, but many growers prefer the name Morgeot because it is so famous.

Morgon *(Mor-gawn')*: Wine commune in the BEAUJOLAIS district, southern Burgundy, and its excellent red wine. Officially one of the nine *crus* (growths), areas that generally produce the best Beaujolais, Morgon is usually one of the fullest and most robust of the *crus*: unlike most Beaujolais, which is best consumed when quite young, Morgon improves with age and is relatively long-lived for a wine made from the Gamay grape. There are 2,026 acres of vineyard; average annual production amounts to some 600,000 cases.

Moscatel de Setúbal (*Mos-ca-tell′ duh Set-too′-bahl*): Sweet Portuguese FORTIFIED WINE produced south of the city of Lisbon. Made from the Muscat grape, it has a pronounced, characteristic Muscat flavor and aroma, a dark color, and good aging potential.

Moscato (*Mos-cot′-toe*): Italian for "Muscat," a sweet wine grape grown in many different parts of Italy. Most Moscatos are white, though one—the Aleatico—is red. Moscato is the variety used for the famous sparkling sweet *spumante* of ASTI in the region of PIEMONTE; elsewhere in Piemonte, Moscato is grown for use in VERMOUTH manufacture, and also near the little town of Canelli to make the interesting Moscato di Canelli. The Moscato Trentino, produced in the region of TRENTINO, is somewhat fuller and sweeter, with a fine bouquet. Further south, Sicily's Moscato di Siracusa, from the town of Siracusa in southeast Sicily, is well-known. The Moscato di Cagliari on the island of Sardinia, and the Moscato di Pantelleria from the little Mediterranean island of Pantelleria, are extremely sweet and high in alcohol—usually over 15%.

Mosel (*Moz′l*): German for *Moselle,* an important European river some 320 miles long. It draws its source in France's Vosges Mountains, continues on through the Grand Duchy of Luxembourg, and winds across Germany until it drains into the Rhine River at Koblenz. Vineyards abound on its banks throughout its eastward journey, but the most famous and important lie in the section in Germany—and in particular in the *Mittel-Mosel,* located between the villages of TRITTENHEIM and ERDEN.

All of the fine wines of the Mosel are white, and almost all are produced from the noble Riesling grape. The soil of the Mosel is predominantly slate, and slate and Riesling partly

221

account for the excellence of the wines. But equally significant is the Mosel's cool climate, which allows the grapes to have optimum sugar-acid balance. The vines cling tenaciously to incredibly steep hillsides, which provide optimum drainage and exposure but necessitate herculean labor to manage the vineyards.

The Mosel has two tributaries, the SAAR and RUWER Rivers, which flow into the Mosel near the city of TRIER. Both rivers also have important vineyard areas. Under the 1971 German Wine Law, the three regions were combined into one wine region or ANBAUGE-BIET: Mosel-Saar-Ruwer. The wines of each region have their own distinct properties, but the best all share a family resemblance: an unsurpassed floral bouquet, coupled with a piquant spiciness. Their delicacy is exquisite: rarely do the wines exceed 11% alcohol.

The 1971 German Wine Law divided up the Mosel into several sub-regions or BER-EICHE: *Bernkastel*, between the villages of Longuich and Zell; *Zell/Mosel* further downstream in the direction of Koblenz, and *Obermosel*, upstream above the city of Trier. Though officially part of the Mosel Anbaugebiet, the Bereich Saar-Ruwer is a separate region, and its wines differ somewhat from Mosels.

Bereich Bernkastel includes world-famous wine villages like BERNKASTEL, PIESPORT, BRAU-NEBERG, GRAACH, WEHLEN, ZELTINGEN, ÜRZIG, and Erden, as well as lesser-known towns such as Klüsserath, Leiwen, Trittenheim, DHRON, NEUMAGEN, WINTRICH, KRÖV and TRABEN-TRARBACH. Bereich Zell/Mosel is much less important, including the vineyards of ZELL, Merl, Edig, Bruttig, Winningen and others. The wines are not often marketed in the U.S. under a vineyard name. Even rarer are the small wines of the Bereich Obermosel, which are even hard to find in Germany.

The best wines from the Mosel villages are sold under the name of the town where they are produced, followed by a vineyard name

(EINZELLAGE). Exceptional vintages accentuate the nuances of the wines, and warm autumn weather also allows the late-harvested grapes to reach full maturity, permitting the fine SPÄTLESE and AUSLESE wines that have made the Mosel a world-renowned wine region. The total area under vines in the Mosel-Saar-Ruwer Anbaugebiet is 28,478 acres; annual production is in excess of 13.7 million cases of wine.

Moselblümchen (*Moz'l-blim'-shen*): German for "little flower of the Mosel," a trade name for a regional wine from the MOSEL district. Under the 1971 German Wine Law, a wine labeled Moselblümchen is a TAFELWEIN, most often a blend of wines from lesser vineyards that have received a large dose of sugar to increase their alcoholic strength. Various brands of Moselblümchen are common on the U.S. market, but they are hardly among the better wines that the Mosel region has to offer.

Moselle (*Mo-zell'*): French for MOSEL, a river originating in France and flowing into Luxembourg and West Germany. Near its source some pale, light wines are produced in the old province of Lorraine: called "Vins de Moselle," they are officially rated V.D.Q.S. but are rarely seen outside the region. In California, Moselle is a GENERIC name occasionally used by some producers to describe a light, semidry white wine.

Moulin-à-Vent (*Moo'-lan ah Vahn'*): World-famous wine commune in the BEAUJOLAIS district, southern Burgundy, and its outstanding red wine. Named for an old windmill that nowadays no longer has its sails, Moulin-à-Vent is one of the nine Beaujolais *crus* (growths), those districts that are apt to produce superior wine. A good Moulin-à-Vent is usually the finest of the *crus*—sturdy, well-balanced, and with great character. The vineyard area of Moulin-à-Vent covers about 1,335

223

acres; average production is the equivalent of some 263,000 cases of wine annually.

Moulis *(Moo-leese')*: Wine commune in the HAUT-MÉDOC district, north of the city of BORDEAUX. Although Moulis has no classified growth *(cru classé)* wine estates or CHÂTEAUX, it has a number of very good ones, two of which are rated *cru exceptionnel* (exceptional growth): Chasse-Spleen and Poujeaux-Theil. Other good Moulis châteaux rated *cru bourgeois* include Gressier-Grand-Poujeaux, Dutruch-Grand-Poujeaux, Poujeaux-Marly, Pomys, and La Closerie du Grand-Poujeaux.

Mourvèdre *(Moor-ved'-ruh)*: Red grape variety grown in southern France; one of the varieties used for CHÂTEAUNEUF-DU-PAPE and other red wines of PROVENCE and the CÔTES-DU-RHÔNE district. Known as Matáro in Spain and California, it is planted in some of the warmer wine districts; about 900 acres are presently under cultivation in California.

Mousseux *(Moo-suh')*: French for "frothy" or "sparkling." Under French law, any sparkling wine produced outside the CHAMPAGNE district—however made—may not be called Champagne, only *vin mousseux* (sparkling wine). Many of them, however, are quite good; some of the best produced outside the Champagne district are made in the LOIRE River valley—most notably at VOUVRAY and SAUMUR—and also in Burgundy (Bourgogne Mousseux). See CRÉMANT.

Mouton-Rothschild, Château *(Moo'-tawn Rawt'-shield)*: World famous wine estate in the HAUT-MÉDOC, located in the commune of PAUILLAC north of the city of BORDEAUX. Owned by the de Rothschilds (a prominent French family of bankers) since 1853, Mouton-Rothschild was ranked as a Second Growth (Second Cru) in the 1855 Médoc classification, but largely through energetic promotion by its present owner, Baron Philippe de Rothschild—and on the merits of its great wines—it was officially promoted to a Premier Cru (First Growth) in 1973. Since 1945 every vintage of Mouton-Rothschild has featured an original work of art on the label. The estate also boasts a splendid museum filled with art treasures, each with wine as a theme.

Usually one of the fullest and most robust of the great Médocs, Mouton-Rothschild takes years and even decades to reach maturity. The vineyard consists of about 150 acres of producing vines; total production in a good year is about 13,600 cases, all CHÂTEAU-BOTTLED.

Müller-Thurgau *(Muh'-ler Tir'-gow)*: White HYBRID grape variety developed in Germany, a cross between the Riesling and the Silvaner; sometimes also designated "Riesling x Silvaner" on a wine label. It is now the most widely-planted wine grape in Germany, accounting for about one-third of the total vineyard area. The grape is hardy and productive, but its wines tend to be rather mild and soft, sometimes lacking in acidity.

Münster *(Minster)*: The name of two wine towns in the NAHE district, Germany. The more famous of the two lies in the BEREICH (sub-region) Schloss Böckelheim and is officially called Bad Münster, on account of its famous mineral spas. The leading vineyards (EINZELLAGEN) are: Rotenfelser im Winkel, Höll, Steigerdell, Gotzenfels, and Königsgarten. The other village with this name lies downstream in the Bereich Kreuznach, and is called Münster-Sarmsheim. Its leading Einzellagen are: Steinkopf, Pittersberg, Dautenpflänzer, Kappellenberg, and Königsschloss.

Muscadelle *(Moos'-cah-dell)*: White wine grape grown in the SAUTERNES and GRAVES regions of BORDEAUX. Grown in conjunction with the more important Sémillon and Sauvignon Blanc, the Muscadelle imparts an agreeable Muscat flavor to the wines, but it is normally planted only in small proportions.

Muscadet *(Moos'-cah-day):* Famous dry white wine produced near the city of Nantes in the lower LOIRE River valley, France; also the name of the informing grape variety, originally called the Melon de Bourgogne, which was brought to the Loire from Burgundy several centuries ago. Muscadet is a wine that should ideally be drunk when very young—within a year or so after it is made. Some Muscadet is kept in barrel on the lees for a short while before being bottled, thus retaining its freshness: this is known as "Muscadet Sur Lie."

There are three APPELLATION CONTRÔLÉE zones for Muscadet: Muscadet, the largest region, south of Nantes; the nearby region of "Muscadet de Sèvre-et-Maine," named after two rivers that flow into the Loire at Nantes; and the "Muscadet des Coteaux de la Loire" further upstream. Each district has its differences; the Coteaux de la Loire usually makes the best wine in hot years. The total vineyard area is in excess of 22,000 acres, mostly consisting of small plots managed by local growers. The production of Muscadet is prodigious, averaging about 3.4 million cases annually.

Muscat: Ancient and versatile grape, used for raisins, table grapes, or wine. It is one of the world's oldest cultivated grapes, originating in the Near East and later planted in warmer climatic regions in Europe. There are many different varieties of Muscat, grown all over the world. The Muscat variety generally best suited to winemaking is Muscat blanc (white Muscat), or Muscat de Frontignan. In warmer climates it produces excellent sweet FORTIFIED WINES, such as in BEAUMES-DE-VENISE, FRONTIGNAN, and LUNEL. In cooler climates, such as in ALSACE, it produces excellent table wines, be st when not too dry. A closely-related variety is Muscat Ottonel, which is supplanting production in Alsace and also in Austria.

Muscat is called MOSCATO in Italy; it is used for making ASTI Spumante, Italy's popular sweet sparkling wine, and also the sweet Muscat di Canelli. Grown in warmer parts of Italy for dessert wines, Muscat gives outstanding results in Sardinia, Sicily and Pantelleria.

In California, better table wines are produced from Muscat blanc, and some 1,400 acres are planted throughout the state. Another Muscat variety, called Muscat of Alexandria, covers about 10,600 acres in the warmer growing districts, but it rarely gives good results for table wine, being better suited to raisins and table grapes. Characteristically, Muscat wines are especially rich in flavor and scent but low in acidity, and must be harvested early to preserve proper acid balance. In all cases, Muscat wines tend to have an intense grapiness, expressed in a powerful bouquet and pronounced grapey flavor.

Muscatel: Any wine made from the Muscat grape. In California, this term is often used for a common FORTIFIED WINE, many poor examples of which have given it a bad name.

Musigny (Mooz'-een-yee): Outstanding vineyard in the CÔTE DE NUITS, Burgundy, which since 1878 has attached its famous name to the nearby town of Chambolle, now called CHAMBOLLE-MUSIGNY. Celebrated for its delicacy and scent, Musigny is one of the most refined wines of the Côte de Nuits. The vineyard consists of three parcels: Les Musigny, Les Petits Musigny, and Combe d'Orveau, planted chiefly in red Pinot Noir vines, although a little is also planted in white Chardonnay to make the rare white Musigny Blanc, equally as fine as the red. Both wines are rated Grand Cru (Great Growth), the highest rank for a Burgundy. Including the plot of Musigny Blanc, the vineyard is about 26 acres large; production in a good vintage is approximately 3,800 cases.

Must: Grape juice, either pressed or crushed, to be made into wine; called *moût* in French.

Must Weight: The number of grams by which one liter of grape juice (must) is heavier than the same quantity of distilled water. Since a solution of sugar has a higher density or specific gravity than water, must weight is a fairly accurate gauge of the sugar content of the must and the alcoholic strength of the wine to be made. A calibrated HYDROMETER is usually employed to determine must weight.

Mutage *(Mew-tahj′)*: French term for the process of adding brandy to partially fermented must to stop it from fermenting, so that residual sugar is retained. Wine that has been subjected to this process is said to be *muté.*

Nackenheim *(Nock′-en-heim)*: Renowned wine village in the RHEINHESSEN region, Germany; with the adjoining village of NIERSTEIN, the finest Rheinhessen wine town. There are 296 acres of vineyard in Nackenheim; a tiny amount of red wine is made, but it is the excellent white wines—made from Riesling and Silvaner—that have made the village famous. The vineyards (EINZELLAGEN) are: Rothenberg, Engelsberg, and Schmitts-Kapellchen.

Nahe *(Nah′-uh)*: River in Germany, a tributary of the Rhine; also a wine region or ANBAUGEBIET, with 10,816 acres of vineyard. Although the many fine wines of the Nahe are not well-known outside of Germany, some of them are among that country's best. The river banks provide excellent exposure for Riesling, Silvaner and Ruländer vines.

The 1971 German Wine Law divided up

the Nahe into two sub-regions or BEREICHE, Kreuznach and Schloss Böckelheim; the former lies downstream, near where the Nahe flows into the Rhine at Bingen; the latter is further upstream, and produces wines that tend to be lighter than those made further downstream. Both Bereiche are named after the two best-known Nahe wine towns, KREUZNACH and SCHLOSS BÖCKELHEIM, and it is important not to confuse regional wines that bear the name of the Bereich with better wines made exclusively in those two towns. Other fine Nahe wine villages include: NIEDERHAUSEN, Münster-Sarmsheim and Bad Münster (see MÜNSTER), NORHEIM, ROXHEIM, Laubenheim, Langenlonsheim, Dorsheim and Rüdesheim (no relation to the more important town of RÜDESHEIM in the RHEINGAU). The equivalent of some 4.5 million cases of wine is made on the Nahe each year, virtually all of it white; various Anheuser family firms are famous producers.

Napa: One of the most famous wine districts of California; also, a fertile valley, county and city located some 50 miles north of San Francisco. Vineyards have been planted in the Napa Valley since the early 19th century; toay, there are over 26,000 acres of vineyard. The city of Napa lies near San Pablo Bay and marks the southern limit of the region; some 25 miles to the north, the town of Calistoga marks the northern limit.

Among the various wine grapes planted in Napa, the area is particularly noted for Cabernet Sauvignon, whose many successes have contributed to the district's great fame worldwide. Over 5,500 acres of it have been planted throughout the valley, making Napa one of America's most important Cabernet regions. Especially when planted in cool upland vineyards, Napa Cabernet Sauvignon ranks among America's very finest red wines. No less important is Chardonnay (also called Pinot

229

Chardonnay). 4,200 acres have been planted, and some superb Chardonnays have firmly established Napa as an equally good growing district for fine white wines. In recent years, Sauvignon Blanc (the drier versions known here as "Fumé Blanc") has become particularly popular, since some excellent examples are somewhat less expensive than Chardonnay. Other grape varieties grown with good results include Pinot Noir, Johannisberg Riesling, Chenin Blanc, Gamay (Napa Gamay), Petite Sirah, Gewürztraminer, and Zinfandel.

The southern section of the Napa Valley, because of its proximity to San Pablo Bay, is cooler and has rather different soil than regions further north. Included here is the Carneros district, a relatively new area in the Napa area devoted to vineyards. The cooler microclimate in Carneros is particularly well-suited to Pinot Noir and Chardonnay. From north to south, the leading towns in Napa include: Calistoga, Rutherford, Oakville, Yountville, and the city of Napa itself; major wineries surround each of these illustrious towns.

Among the oldest and best-known Napa wineries, Beaulieu Vineyard in Rutherford is traditionally famous; it is now owned by the Heublein Corporation and is especially celebrated for its Georges de Latour "private reserve" Cabernet Sauvignons. Also owned by Heublein is Inglenook, which produces a wide variety of quality wines; Beringer Brothers, now under Nestlé ownership, has produced some memorable wines under the winemaking direction of Myron Nightingale. Charles Krug, long the property of the Mondavi family and one of the Napa Valley's established producers, supplants their high-quality line with some good jug wines sold under the "C.K." (Charles Krug) label. Robert Mondavi Winery is run by an innovative family related to the Mondavis of Krug, and since 1966 they have greatly contributed to the world-wide fame and prestige of California wines in general. Louis Martini is one of the most respected California producers for generations; the Christian Brothers nearby is managed by a monastic order originally established in France, and are famous for their brandies as well as their table wines. Sterling Vineyards in Calistoga is now owned by the Wine Spectrum in Atlanta, and for over a decade have specialized in high-quality, premium varietal wines. The new Rutherford Hill Winery occupies the former Souverain premises in Rutherford; it only began operation in the mid-1970s and has already scored some impressive achievements.

Though their distribution is considerably less widespread nationally, the many smaller Napa "boutique" wineries are no less important to the fame of the region—they are perhaps even more significant in terms of the individuality and originality of their releases. Joseph Heitz Cellars produces some of America's finest releases of select Cabernet Sauvignons and Chardonnays, particularly from Martha's Vineyard and Fay Vineyard; Bernard Portet's new Clos du Val Winery is also a top producer of Cabernet Sauvignon and Zinfandel, vinified in a distinctly French style. Diamond Creek Vineyards, owned by Al Brounstein, is particularly famous for single-vineyard Cabernets. Donn Chappellet's impressive winery overlooking Lake Hennessy has made some sensational releases of red wines, as have Caymus Vineyards, Spring Mountain, Duckhorn Vineyards, Joseph Phelps Vineyards, Robert Keenan, Château Montelena, Carneros Creek, and Stag's Leap Wine Cellars (Winiarski)—the latter not to be confused with Stag's Leap Winery (Doumani). Many new, small Napa wineries opened in the 1970s, and are now releasing their wines for the first time: Napa Wine Cellars, Niebaum-Coppola, Markham Winery, Grgich Hills (run by the former winemaker at Château Montelena), Cakebread, Buehler Vineyards, Cassayre-Forni, William Hill, Robert Pecota, Forman Winery (run by the former winemaker at Sterling

231

Vineyards), and Shafer Vineyards. Particularly noted among the smaller "boutique" producers are: St. Clement, Trefethen, Long, Silver Oak Cellars (which specializes in high-quality Cabernet Sauvignon), Mayacamas Vineyards, Château Chevalier, Acacia Winery, Villa Mt. Eden, Stony Hill Vineyard (long noted for Chardonnay), Raymond Vineyard, Stonegate, Mt. Veeder, Conn Creek, and Z. D. Wines. On a somewhat larger scale, Cuvaison, Freemark Abbey, Burgess Cellars and Franciscan Vineyards have produced some notable wines. The French Champagne conglomerate Moët & Hennessy's Napa winery, Domaine Chandon, is an illustrious producer of sparkling wine; Schramsberg Vineyards and Hanns Kornell are traditionally famous producers of domestic champagnes. Sutter Home Winery has been producing fine Zinfandels for over a century; recently, the Charles F. Shaw Winery has developed an excellent Gamay in the French Beaujolais style.

Because it is universally recognized as a prime viticultural area, the Napa Valley has land of inestimable value and worth. Accordingly, the Napa Valley Development Council seeks to limit industrial and residential growth, in order to preserve the integrity of the vineyards.

Nature (Nah-tur'): French for "natural." In the CHAMPAGNE district of France, at the time of final bottling and shipment, it is customary to adjust the final sweetness of a Champagne by means of the shipping dosage (see LIQUEUR D'EXPÉDITION). Commercially, the driest grade of Champagne is "Brut," which receives less than 1½% dosage; nature, theoretically, receives no sugar correction through dosage and is totally dry. Because entirely dry Champagnes are not to everyone's taste, wines labeled nature are relatively rare and are much harder to find than Bruts; the term is occasionally used in the U.S. wine trade for sparkling wines that have not received an adjustment of sugar from the bottling dosage.

Nebbiolo *(Neb-be-oh'-lo)*: Fine red wine grape grown in northern Italy, used to make all the best Italian red wines, particularly those from the region of PIEMONTE (see BAROLO, BARBARESCO, GATTINARA, GHEMME, etc.) and the wines of the VALTELLINA district. Some regional Piemontese wines are also made from the Nebbiolo in the region of Alba and are entitled to the D.O.C. Nebbiolo d'Alba. There are some 500 acres of Nebbiolo planted in California's Central Valley, where the grape thrives in the warm climate.

Nebuchadnezzar: The largest and bulkiest bottle, used rarely—if at all—in the French CHAMPAGNE district, with a capacity of 20 ordinary bottles. Champagnes in such enormous containers have not been commercially exported to the U.S. for many years.

Négociant *(Nay-go'-see-on)*: French for "merchant" or "shipper." In the wine trade, a négociant is usually a buyer who purchases wines from a property or estate and then blends them with other wines to sell them under his own label. He may also qualify himself as a "négociant-éléveur," who purchases the wines in cask during their first year from a grower or *propriétaire*, and then "raises" them in his cellars before releasing them after aging and bottling. A négociant-éléveur may also buy the grapes and vinify the wine himself. Négociants perform a valuable service, both to the proprietors who often find it difficult to produce and sell their wines, and to the buying public who need an experienced intermediary to guide them in their purchases.

Negrar *(Nay-grar')*: Little village located in the heart of the VALPOLICELLA district, not far from Lake Garda, where many of the leading producers of Valpolicella have their cellars.

233

Neuchâtel *(Nuh'-shat-tel)*: City and lake in western Switzerland, also a famous wine region. Like most Swiss white wines, the light, fragrant wines of Neuchâtel are made from the Chasselas grape, and are vinified dry. A little red Pinot Noir is also grown for red Neuchâtel, and the little village of Cortaillod specializes in red wine, but the reds are very pale in color—almost rosé—and are not as well-known as the whites. Some white Neuchâtel is left on the lees *("sur lie")*, which causes a faint sparkle. Including the vineyards on Lake Bienne to the northeast, which form part of the Neuchâtel appellation, there are 1,375 acres under vines; total production of all Neuchâtel is the equivalent of some 346,300 cases annually.

Neumagen *(Noy'-mog-en)*: Wine village on the MOSEL River, Germany, adjoining the village of Dhron to the north. The two villages have been amalgamated under the 1971 German Wine Law into one community, called Dhron-Neumagen. See DHRON.

New York State: The second most important wine region in the U.S. after California, New York State produces some 10% of all the wine annually consumed in the country—in excess of 38 million U.S. gallons, from almost 41,000 acres of vineyard. New York is also the largest producer of sparkling wines in America, which constitute over one-fifth of the total production. After over 125 years of winemaking, the New York wine industry is making sensational strides in quality, derived in large part from a general awareness that many areas within the state are ideal for vineyards. Many new wineries have been established recently, and grape varieties and winemaking techniques are changing in response to the marketplace.

234

Compared to other famous wine regions, the climate in New York State is one of extreme contrasts. The summers are marked with periods of intense heat; the winters are subject

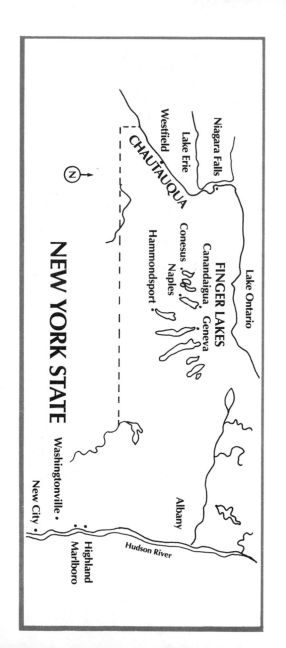

to intervals of severe cold, which often drastically reduce the subsequent crop and occasionally destroy entire vineyards. Thus, native American grape varieties of the species LABRUSCA have traditionally been the mainstay of the New York State wine industry because of their hardiness and productivity. Wines made from labrusca varieties (Concord, Catawba, Niagara, Delaware, Dutchess, Ives, Moore's Diamond, etc.) has a pronounced grapey flavor and aroma that is markedly different from the softer flavor of VINIFERA varieties native to Europe and grown in California. For many years, New York producers found the public receptive to their labrusca wines. Now, faced with a more selective market, many producers are turning to HYBRID varieties (Seyval Blanc, Maréchal Foch, Aurora, Chelois, Chancellor Noir, de Chaunac, Léon Millot, etc.), made from crosses between European and American species of vines and combining hardiness and productivity with improved taste characteristics. The products of this "second generation" are beginning to appear on the market, and they are continually improving.

For years, New York State's climatic extremes were thought to be too inhospitable for vinifera varieties to be successful. In the mid-1950s, Russian-born winemaker Dr. Konstantin Frank emigrated to this country and demonstrated that high-quality wines could be produced in New York from vinifera, if the vines were adequately protected during the winter from frost. The success of his experiments prompted many producers during the past decade to plant vinifera, and some of the wines have proven to be outstanding. Although total acreage of vinifera varieties is still limited in New York, it is steadily increasing. Best results have been obtained with Chardonnay, White Riesling, Sauvignon Blanc, and Pinot Noir.

In order to mute the characteristic, forceful flavor of labrusca wines, New York producers have often blended their wines with those from other regions, most notably California. Federal law allows up to 25% of other wines to be blended with New York wines if sold under this name; if more than 25% is added, the wine must be labeled "American wine." Although such practices tend to diminish the identity of certain New York wines from the largest producers, they have undoubtedly assisted in continuity of supply and taste. As production within the state increases, there will steadily be less of a need for blending with wines produced outside of New York.

Presently, New York State wineries are also moving to expand their output of wines sold under VARIETAL labels, identifying the grape variety used. Traditionally, their wines were usually given GENERIC labels—rhine, chablis, sauterne, etc.—and though generic labeling is still employed by some producers, varietal labeling has become synonymous with the best New York State wine.

When New York's wineries were first established over a century ago, the shores of the Finger Lakes—Canandaigua, Keuka, Seneca, Cayuga, Skaneateles, Owasco, Conesus and others—were a logical location for vineyards. The terrain slopes gently, aiding drainage; the soil in many places is ideal, and the lakes help hold down extreme fluctuations in temperature. Today, the Finger Lakes district has the largest concentration of vineyard acreage in the eastern United States. Of the lakes, Keuka holds much of this acreage in its environs, and near its southernmost tip is the little town of Hammondsport, where several major wineries are headquartered.

The major Finger Lakes wineries include: Taylor, the world's third largest sparkling wine producer and the largest capacity winery in the area; Pleasant Valley Wine Co., now operated in tandem with Taylor by the Atlanta-based Wine Spectrum and noted for its sparkling wines sold under the Great Western brand label; Gold Seal, one of the earliest wineries in the area to achieve success with vin-

237

iferas; Widmer's Wine Cellars, which has been producing wines for over a century; and Canandaigua Industries, which produces the well-known brands of Richard's, Virginia Dare, Mother Vineyard and Wild Irish Rose.

On a much smaller scale, many new producers have emerged on the Finger Lakes wine scene. One of the most visible of them is Walter S. Taylor, originally of the wine family of the same name, who founded Bully Hill Winery in 1970 and now produces wines exclusively from French-American hybrids; his neighbor, Vinifera Wine Cellars, is operated by Dr. Konstantin Frank and serves as a paragon of successful vinifera wine production. Near Hammondsport, little Heron Hill Winery, managed by Peter Johnstone, is a particularly noted producer of white wines from labrusca, hybrids and vinifera varieties. Hermann J. Wiemer, a skilled winemaker who recently established his own vineyard near the town of Dundee, has produced some outstanding vinifera wines, as has his neighbor Stanley (Bill) Wagner, a noted grape grower since 1946. Glenora Wine Cellars and McGregor Vineyard Winery in Dundee, Plane's Cayuga Vineyard in Ovid, and Chateau Esperanza in Bluff Point round out the list of these high-quality "boutique" New York wineries.

The Niagara/Chautauqua districts, located some distance to the west of the Finger Lakes near Lake Erie, have furnished many of the state's table grapes for over a century and are now becoming important new wine production centers. Woodbury Vineyards, Frederick S. Johnson Winery, Merritt Estate Winery, and the new Chadwick Bay Winery in Fredonia best exemplify this trend.

In recent years, the Hudson River valley has reemerged as an important center for viticulture in the state, recalling its origins in the 1840s. Brotherhood, the oldest active winery in the U.S. (est. 1839) is now supplanted by noted producer Mark Miller at Benmarl Vineyards in Marlboro, Walker Valley Vineyards, Cascade Mountain Vineyards, and Clinton Vineyards at Clinton Corners. The Hudson Valley Wine Co. in Highland is another major producer.

The newest area for New York State viticulture appears to be on Long Island, where at the eastern extremes, near Peconic Bay, an ideal combination of soil and predominantly maritime climate have proven that vinifera wines can be grown in the region with good results. Hargrave Vineyard in Cutchogue released their first wine in the mid-1970s, and in recent years have contributed much to the awareness of wine in eastern Long Island.

New Zealand: In addition to being the world's largest dairy exporter, New Zealand is rapidly turning into a wine-exporting nation—the result of thousands of new acres of vines planted during the 1970s that are now in full production. The principal wine regions lie on North Island, near Hawke's Bay and Gisborne, and also further north near the cities of Auckland and Thames. Encouraging results have recently been obtained on South Island, in Marlborough and Blenheim, where the climate tends to be cooler.

The climate throughout the New Zealand wine districts is cool and temperate, similar to many places in northern Europe: good white wines are a specialty. The principal grape varieties presently grown are Riesling, Müller-Thurgau, Sauvignon Blanc, Chardonnay, Cabernet Sauvignon, and Pinot Noir. In the past, New Zealand wineries produced mainly FORTIFIED WINES for domestic consumption, but the trend today is clearly towards high-quality table wines. Montana Wines Ltd. of Auckland is a major producer.

Niagara: White wine grape of the species LABRUSCA, grown primarily in New York's Finger Lakes district and also in the Niagara Pen-

239

insula in Canada. Characteristically fruity, it makes pleasant sweet wines and is generally vinified to retain some residual sugar.

Niederhausen (*Nee'-der-how-zen*): One of the finest wine villages in the NAHE River valley, Germany, with 371 acres of vineyard; most of them planted in Rieslings. Niederhausen's best wines are typically racy and full-flavored, especially those from the leading vineyards or EINZELLAGEN: Hermannshöhle, Hermannsberg, Steinwingert, Rosenheck, Klamm, Kertz, Rosenberg, and Pfingstweide.

Nierstein (*Near'-shtine*): Outstanding wine village in the RHEINHESSEN district, Germany; the most celebrated in the entire area. With over 2,000 acres of vineyard, Nierstein has the largest acreage under vines in Rheinhessen and some of the region's most important cellars. Under the 1971 German Wine Law, however, Nierstein has also become the name of a BEREICH (sub-region), and wines merely labeled "Niersteiner," without a vineyard name, are regionals that can come from dozens of villages within the Bereich. The 1971 Wine Law also substantially delimited Nierstein's vineyards, and three traditionally famous ones—Auflangen, Rehbach, and Spiegelberg—have become composite vineyards or GROSSLAGEN. The most frequently used Nierstein Grosslage name for inexpensive regional wines is "Gutes Domthal," relating to wines that can vary a great deal in quality. But the leading single vineyards or EINZELLAGEN within Nierstein—Hipping, Pettenthal, Hölle, Orbel, Kranzberg, Ölberg, Brudersberg, Glöck, Heiligenbaum, Bildstock, and Patersberg—are deservedly famous. Both Riesling and Silvaner vines produce outstanding wines in Nierstein, especially in vineyards located near the Rhine front.

Norheim (*Nor'-heim*): One of the leading wine towns in the NAHE River valley, Germany, with 138 acres of vineyard planted predominantly in Riesling. The best vineyards (EINZELLAGEN) include: Kafels, Dellchen, Klosterberg, Götzenfels, and Kirschheck.

Nose: An alternate term for BOUQUET.

Nouveau *(New-vo')*: French for "new"; in relation to wine, a light wine, deliberately vinified for early consumption, usually by the method of CARBONIC MACERATION. The term has special significance in the BEAUJOLAIS district of France, where it describes the light, popular "vin de l'année," or new wine, that is consumed within weeks after it is made. The official release date for the *vin de l'année* is November 15, prior to which the wine cannot legally be sold, and on the stroke of midnight at the official release date, thousands of cases of Beaujolais Nouveau set out by road, rail and occasionally air transport to market. Because of public preference for lighter wines that may be drunk young, Beaujolais Nouveau has become extremely popular in recent years. It is alternately termed Beaujolais *primeur.*

Nuits-Saint Georges *(Nwee San Zhorzh')*: Famous wine town on the CÔTE DE NUITS, Burgundy; the medieval city of Nuits gave its name to the Côte, and since 1892 Nuits has added its name to that of its most celebrated vineyard, Les Saint Georges. Many important wine shippers have their cellars in Nuits; the town is celebrated primarily for its many good red wines, though some white wine is also made.

The best vineyards in Nuits-Saint Georges are rated Premier Cru (First Growth), and are located in three different areas. On the border with the neighboring town of VOSNE-ROMANÉE to the north, the most famous vineyards are: Les Boudots, Aux Cras, Aux Murgers, and Aux Thorey. Immediately south of Nuits are the notable vineyards of Les Saint Georges, Les Pruliers, Les Porets, Les Vaucrains and Les Cailles. The adjoining commune of Prémeaux to the south is included in the Nuits-Saint

241

Georges appellation; its best vineyards are: Clos de la Maréchale, Clos des Corvées, Clos des Corvées-Paget, Aux Perdrix, and Les Didiers. There are minor differences between the Prémeaux wines and those of Nuits-Saint Georges; the former are apt to have a slight, characteristic earthy flavor (*goût de terroir*) that is quite agreeable.

Including the vineyards of Prémeaux, the area under vines in Nuits-Saint Georges is 927 acres; annual production averages about 110,000 cases of wine, virtually all of it red.

Oak: The most widely used type of wood for wine cooperage; employed for casks and, in traditional usage, fermenting tanks. Oak is an ideal material for cask aging because it allows air to associate slowly with the wine and mature it; in addition, tannin and oak extract is imparted to the wine, improving the flavor.

While oak is grown in many regions in France, only certain areas produce the qualities that coopers and vintners look for. Limousin (Limoges) and Nevers oak is popular for Bordeaux and Loire Valley vintners; Burgundy growers tend to rely on oak from the Tronçin and Allier districts. After it was demonstrated some thirty years ago that imported French oak could improve the flavor of American wines, many American vintners now import oak barrels from France. In particular, selected French oak improves the quality of Chardonnay, Sauvignon Blanc, Cabernet Sauvignon and Pinot Noir grown in the U.S.

Many areas in the United States also produce high-quality oak that is used for wine cooperage; in particular, Arkansas and Tennessee. A number of domestic vintners prefer the structure and flavor of American oak, and some is even exported as well; with certain red wines like Zinfandel, it tends to be preferred. Yugoslavia is also a major source of quality oak used in wine cask production.

Oberemmel *(Oh-ber-em′-mel)*: Noted wine town in the SAAR region, Germany, with some 200 acres of vineyard—most of them planted in Rieslings. Oberemmel adjoins the much more famous town of WILTINGEN, and its fine wines share many of the same noble characteristics, though they are little-known outside of Germany. The leading vineyards (EINZELLAGEN) include: Hütte, Agritiusberg, Altenberg, Karlsberg, and Rosenberg.

Öchsle: see OECHSLE

Ockfen *(Awk′-fen)*: Outstanding wine village in the SAAR region, Germany, with 158 acres of vineyard; in warm years, often one of Germany's best wine producers. Famous for its fine, well-balanced and perfumed Riesling wines, Ockfen is particularly renowned for one great vineyard, Bockstein; the other leading vineyards (EINZELLAGEN) include: Herrenberg, Geisberg, and Heppenstein.

Oechsle *(Erks′-luh)*: A scale used to measure the sugar content of grape musts, employed in Germany and in Switzerland as a legal determinant for minimum MUST WEIGHT standards. Named for Ferdinand Oechsle, who devised it in the early 19th century, the Oechsle scale relates directly to the specific gravity of the must: as measured by a calibrated HYDROMETER, grape must with a specific gravity of 1.096 would have an Oechsle reading of 96°. The Oechsle reading divided by 8 gives the approximate alcoholic content of the wine after fermentation, so theoretically must with 96° Oechsle would yield a wine of 12% alcohol.

243

However, very high Oechsle readings will result in a wine with considerable residual sugar, because not all the sugar is converted into alcohol, and for this reason many great German wines retain both lightness and unresolved sugar.

Oenology: The science of winemaking, which includes the intricate chemical and technical aspects of vinification. An oenologist is a trained professional who has been certified in the practice of oenology, following his winemaking apprenticeship.

Oestrich *(Uhs'-trich)*: Important wine town in the RHEINGAU district, Germany; with 865 acres of vineyard, one of the largest in the area. Oestrich adjoins the more famous village of HATTENHEIM, but mostly through differences in the soil its wines are quite different, tending to be rather full in body. In good vintages, Oestrich makes some outstanding wines. The leading vineyards (EINZELLAGEN) are: Lenchen, Doosberg, and Klostergarten.

Ohio: In pre-Civil War days, Ohio was America's foremost wine-producing state. Vineyards were first planted in 1823 along the Ohio River near Cincinnati by Nicholas Longworth, the first American to successfully make good sparkling wines from the Catawba grape. Various vine diseases, and then prohibition, dealt severe blows to winemaking in the state, but in the 1970s a number of new wineries were established and the industry is once again important in the state.

Today, Ohio has over forty wineries. Vineyards are still located along the Ohio River in Longworth's "American Rhineland," but the largest properties lie in the north, on the shores of Lake Erie. The largest producer in Ohio is Meier's Wine Cellars in Cincinnati, which owns extensive vineyards on Isle St. George in Lake Erie near Sandusky. Lake Erie's temperate climate is favorable to vineyards, and a number of new wineries became bonded recently: Buccia Vineyards, Cedar Hill (Chateau Lagniappe), John Christ, Grand River, Markko Vineyard, and Chalet Debonne Vineyards. The Dayton/Cincinnati area is experiencing a renaissance of winegrowing, exemplified by Brushcreek Vineyards in Peebles, Colonial Vineyards in Lebanon, Hafle Vineyards in Springfield, Heritage Vineyards in West Milton, Lukens Vineyard in Harveysburg, McIntosh's Ohio Valley Wines in Bethel, Moyer Vineyards in Manchester, and Warren J. Sublette Winery in Cincinnati. Mantey Vineyards in Sandusky, on Lake Erie, was founded over a century ago; Mon Ami Champagne Co. has been producing quality sparkling wines for some fifty years. Tarula Farms in Clarksville, and Valley Vineyards Farm in Morrow, were founded in the 1960s and are gaining in reputation. Traditionally, Ohio has grown native American grape varieties, but these are being supplanted by French-American hybrids and VINIFERA varieties in areas suited to their production.

Oïdium *(O-ee′-dee-um)*: Serious cryptogamic (fungal) disease of the vine, caused by the organism *Uncinula spiralis*; also called "powdery mildew" to distinguish it from "downy mildew," which is of American origin (see MILDEW). Oïdium attacks the green foliage, weakens and often kills the vine, and splits the skins of the grapes. It caused severe damage in Europe in the 1850s, but it can be effectively controlled with finely-ground sulfur powder, which is regularly dusted in the vineyards throughout the summer months.

Oloroso *(O-lo-ro′-so)*: A dark and full-bodied type of Spanish SHERRY, which because it does not mature through the action of the same FLOR yeast as the drier and lighter FINO Sherries, develops a style all its own: noble bouquet, combined with a characteristic "nutty" flavor. Olorosos are used in making sweet

Cream Sherries, though in their natural state they are completely dry—the sweetness is added before the wines are bottled.

Oltrepò Pavese *(Awl-tray-po' Pa-vay'-see)*: Italian for "on the other side of the River Po, in the Pavia area"; a hilly vineyard region in the area of LOMBARDY, Italy, near the city of Pavia. A relatively new wine region in Lombardy, the Oltrepò Pavese area entitled to D.O.C. produces a number of good red and white wines from Barbera, Bonarda, Riesling, Moscato, and Cortese, although Barbera is the most widely-grown variety for red wines. The wines are usually identified by grape variety, as in "Bonarda dell'Oltrepò Pavese." From good vintages, some red wines from the Oltrepò Pavese region can stand among the best in Italy.

Oppenheim *(Awp'-en-heim)*: Famous town in the RHEINHESSEN district, Germany, with 833 acres of vineyard; most of them planted in Silvaner, although Riesling and Müller-Thurgau are also grown. Oppenheim's soft, scented white wines are among the Rheinhessen's best, although much "Oppenheimer" without a vineyard name that is sold in the U.S. is regional wine, not to be confused with the best vineyards or EINZELLAGEN in Oppenheim: Sackträger, Herrenberg, Kreuz, Daubhaus, Schlossberg, Gutleuthaus, Schloss, Paterhof, and Herrengarten.

Optima *(Awp'-tee-ma)*: New white German grape variety, developed from a cross between Riesling, Silvaner and Müller-Thurgau. Its name suggests the "optimum" compromise between an early-ripening, productive grape suited to the very sweet, high-quality AUSLESE wines with flavor characteristics that were formerly the exclusive domain of Riesling.

246 **Oregon**: Large-scale table wine production is new to Oregon, although wines have been made in the state for over a hundred years. The climate in the western part of the state is similar to many fine wine regions in Europe. Many Oregon producers also make fruit and berry wines in regions where grapes cannot grow, but two regions seem especially well suited to viticulture: the Wilamette River valley south of Portland, and the Roseburg area in Douglas County some 200 miles to the south. The Hillcrest Vineyard in Roseburg was one of the state's first major table wine producers; some new wineries are achieving sensational results with Pinot Noir, which is especially suited to the cool climate. Tualatin Vineyards, Knudsen-Erath, Amity Vineyards, The Eyrie Vineyard, Sokol-Blosser Winery, Valley View Vineyard, Ponzi Vineyards, Oak Knoll Winery, Henry's Winery, Elk Cove Vineyards, Bjelland Vineyards, and Adelsheim Vineyard are among the leading producers of table wines in the state.

Original-Abfüllung (*Awr-rig'-in-nal Ab'-fool-ung*): German wine term used before 1971 to indicate a wine that had been ESTATE-BOTTLED by a single producer. Under the 1971 German Wine Law, use of this term is no longer permitted on a German wine label, and in its place the term ERZEUGER-ABFÜLLUNG, or "producer bottling," has been substituted.

Ortsteil (*Orts'-tile*): German for "part of a community." Under the 1971 German Wine Law, an Ortsteil is a vineyard estate that is entitled to sell its wines under its own name, without specifying the town or the vineyard community in which it lies. The STEINBERG, Schloss Johannisberg (see JOHANNISBERG, SCHLOSS) and Schloss Vollrads (see VOLLRADS, SCHLOSS) estates in the RHEINGAU region are Ortsteils; in the SAAR region, the SCHARZHOF-BERG is also an Ortsteil.

Orvieto (*Orv-yay'-toe*): Fine white wine produced in the region of UMBRIA, central Italy, near the city of Perugia. A specialty of the Umbria region that has only recently received

247

D.O.C. status, Orvieto is produced from several different grape varieties—Trebbiano, Verdicchio, Malvasia, Verdello, and Procanico—and is sold in two different forms. When vinified to retain some residual sugar in the traditional manner, it is called *abboccato* or semi-dry, but nowadays the taste is for drier wines, which are labeled *secco*. Orvieto used to be sold primarily in the squat, straw-covered FIASCHI flasks native to central Italy, but with recent high labor costs more and more wine is being bottled in conventional bottles. The wine tends to be fruity, pleasant, and easy to drink.

Oxidation: The reaction of various components in wine (alcohol, tannins, acids, and coloring matter) with oxygen. There is always some dissolved oxygen in wine acquired during fermentation and cask aging, which initially helps to mature it. But in later stages oxidation damages the wine, causing it to turn brown and take on a flat, musty flavor. It is particularly unpleasant in white wines consumed when too old, and an oxidized wine is said to be "maderized" when in this condition. See MADERIZATION.

Paarl *(Parl):* Important town and wine region in South Africa, situated some 40 miles to the northeast of Capetown. Paarl is the location of an immense wine cooperative run by the K.W.V. wine association; some of South Africa's best wines are made there, in addition to superior sherries and brandies. See SOUTH AFRICA.

Palatinate *(Pa-lat'-tin-nate)*: see RHEINPFALZ.

Palette *(Pah-let')*: Wine district in southern France, located in the old province of PROVENCE southeast of the city of Aix-en-Provence. One of the few wine districts in Provence that is rated APPELLATION CONTRÓLÉE, Palette is celebrated for its equally good red and white wines, in addition to fine, sturdy rosés, although the region's production is limited. The principal grape varieties used are Clairette, Grenache, Mourvèdre and Cinsault. One particularly fine estate in Palette is the little Château Simone.

Palomino *(Pal-o-meen'-o)*: White grape variety grown in the Spanish SHERRY district, used for 90% of all the wine produced. Its local name is Listán. There are almost 3,800 acres of Palomino planted in California, mostly in the warm Central Valley, where it is used to make some of the best California sherries; however, it is poorly suited to the making of table wines.

Passe-Tout-Grains *(Pahss Too Gran')*: In the region of BURGUNDY, France, a light red wine produced from a blend of Pinot Noir and Gamay grapes vatted together, with a minimum of one-third Pinot Noir. By law, the wines must attain at least 9.5% alcohol. Passe-Tout-Grains are pleasant light wines, usually inexpensive, which serve an important need in an area so famous chiefly for great wines.

Passito *(Pas-see'-toe)*: Sweet Italian wine made from sun-dried or partially raisined grapes. After the harvest, grapes destined for passito wines are selected and left to dry either in the sun or on special racks, where they lose moisture. A sweet passito wine is the specialty of the little town of Caluso in the region of PIEMONTE (see CALUSO PASSITO); further south, the VINO SANTO of TUSCANY is similar.

249

Pasteurization: Process by which wine is heated briefly and rapidly to a temperature of about 150° F. (65°C.). Named for the great French chemist Louis Pasteur (1822-1895), who discovered its beneficial properties, pasteurization stabilizes wines by ridding them of harmful bacteria and other microorganisms. But because it tends to affect the flavor of the wine as well, it is usually performed only on ordinary wines.

Pauillac *(Poy'-yack)*: World-famous red wine commune in the HAUT-MÉDOC district, located some 30 miles north of the city of BORDEAUX between the celebrated communes of SAINT-ESTÈPHE and SAINT-JULIEN. Pauillac has three of the world's most renowned wine estates: LAFITE-ROTHSCHILD, LATOUR, and MOUTON-ROTHSCHILD; these are rated Premier Cru (First Growth), the highest rating for a Bordeaux wine. Pauillac is also the location of one of the largest oil refineries in southwest France, and its village is the most important in the Haut-Médoc, but its great fame is based solely on its excellent red wines. Made predominantly from Cabernet Sauvignon, Pauillacs tend to be tannic and austere in their youth, but develop into noble and aristocratic Bordeaux wines with sufficient bottle age. The leading wine estates (CHÂTEAUX), as ranked in the 1855 classification of the Médoc, are as follows: *Premiers Crus* (First Growths): Lafite-Rothschild, Latour, and Mouton-Rothschild. *Seconds Crus* (Second Growths): Pichon-Longueville-Baron, Pichon-Longueville, Comtesse de Lalande. *Quatrièmes Crus* (Fourth Growths): Duhart-Milon-Rothschild. *Cinquièmes Crus* (Fifth Growths): Pontet-Canet, Batailley, Haut-Batailley, Grand-Puy-Lacoste, Grand-Puy-Ducasse, Lunch-Bages, Lynch-Moussas, Mouton-Baronne-Philippe, Haut-Bages-Libéral, Pédesclaux, Clerc-Milon, and Croizet-Bages. Note that Pauillac is the only famous Haut-Médoc wine commune with no *Troisièmes Crus* (Third Growths).

Pécharmant *(Pay'-shar-mon):* Red wine region in southwest France, officially part of the BER-GERAC district. Although not well-known outside the region, the fine red wines of Pécharmant tend to be fruity and well-balanced. They evoke the characteristics of those produced in the BORDEAUX region some 60 miles to the west, and the grape varieties used are similar. Average annual production is on the order of some 43,000 cases.

Pedro Ximénez *(Pay-dro He-may'-nays):* Sweet white grape grown in the SHERRY district in Spain, and to an even greater extent in the MONTILLA and MÁLAGA districts to the east, where it is the chief variety. At harvest time, selected Pedro Ximénez grapes are left to dry on mats of straw over a period of about two weeks, allowing the sun to evaporate the moisture and concentrate the sugar. The grapes are then made into a very sweet, concentrated wine used to sweeten other wines, or after an addition of brandy and some cask aging, on its own as a rare and costly wine known as a "P.X." Such wines are hard to come by, but they are unquestionably among the finest and most luscious sweet FORTIFIED WINES made.

Pennsylvania: Much of the land in Pennsylvania is ideal for vineyards, and during the 1970s there was considerable interest in wine-making in the state—a number of new vineyards were established. Between Ohio and New York, along the shores of Lake Erie, a temperate climate provided by the lake combines with good soil to create favorable winegrowing districts; Penn-Shore Vineyards, Heritage Wine Cellars, Presque Isle Wine Cellars and Mazza Vineyards are representative wineries in the North East area. In eastern Pennsylvania, near the Delaware and Susquehanna Rivers, some smaller, family-owned wineries like Buckingham Valley Vineyards, Bucks Country Vineyards, Lancaster County Winery,

251

Mount Hope Estate, Naylor Wine Cellars and Nissley Vineyards are gaining in reputation.

Pernand-Vergelesses *(Pair'-non Vair'-zhuh-less)*: Little hillside town and wine commune in the CÔTE DE BEAUNE, Burgundy, with some 350 acres of vineyard. Pernand-Vergelesses adjoins the more famous commune of ALOXE-CORTON, and its best red and white wines are legally entitled to the name CORTON and COR-TON-CHARLEMAGNE, respectively. The leading vineyard sold under its own name is the Ile des Vergelesses, rated Premier Cru (First Growth); other good vineyards in Pernand Vergelesses include: Les Basses-Vergelesses, Creux de la Net, En Caradeaux, and Les Fichots. Because they are little-known, some red Pernand-Vergelesses wines are excellent value; annual production is the equivalent of some 27,600 cases of wine, about 10% of it white.

Perrière *(Pair-yair')*: French for "rock quarry" or "pebbly soil," a local term used in the BUR-GUNDY region in France to indicate a vineyard situated on or near chalk rubble. Such soil is ideal for white Chardonnay grapes; the Perrières vineyard in MEURSAULT, rated Premier Cru (First Growth), usually produces some of the best white wines of Burgundy. A similarly-named vineyard of comparable excellence lies in the adjoining commune of PULIGNY-MON-TRACHET; to the north in the CÔTE DE NUITS there is a rare white wine vineyard in the commune of NUITS-SAINT GEORGES with this name. Good red wines are produced from the CLOS DE LA PERRIÈRE vineyard in the commune of FIXIN.

Pessac *(Peh'-sock)*: Wine commune in the region of GRAVES, located on the southwestern outskirts of the city of BORDEAUX. Some Pessac wine estates (CHÂTEAUX) are among the most famous in the world, but several are currently threatened by housing developments. The best-known is Haut-Brion (see HAUT-BRION,

CHÂTEAU), but Châteaux La Mission-Haut-Brion, Pape-Clément, and Les Carmes Haut-Brion also produce celebrated wines.

Pétillant *(Pet'-tee-yawn):* French for "semi-sparkling," a term for a wine with residual carbon dioxide, although not to the degree of a fully sparkling wine (see MOUSSEUX). Such wines often develop a faint sparkle through early bottling, when there is some residual sugar. By law, the amount of pressure in *pétillant* wines must not exceed two atmospheres.

Petit Chablis *(Puh-tee' Shab-lee'):* A light, usually inexpensive white wine made in the French CHABLIS district, produced from secondary vineyard parcels along the regional boundary. The minimum alcoholic strength must be 9.5%, and the wine must be made solely from the Chardonnay grape. Petit Chablis was formerly a little local wine that was rarely bottled or exported, but it is now becoming increasingly more important in the trade; in recent vintages, production has increased some 40% over what it was a decade ago.

Petit-Verdot *(Puh-tee' Vair-doe'):* Red grape variety grown in the BORDEAUX district, France, usually used in blends with Cabernet Sauvignon, especially in the MÉDOC region. It adds considerable body to red wines, but because it is susceptible to rot, it is only planted on a limited scale.

Petite-Sirah *(Puh-teet' Seer-rah'):* Red grape variety grown extensively in California, where almost 13,000 acres of it have been planted. The Petite Sirah is named for the robust Syrah grape native to the RHÔNE River valley in France, to which it was originally thought to be related, but grape specialists (ampelographers) have recently determined that it is actually an entirely different variety known in France as the Durif (or Duriff), which is also grown in the Rhône region. Formerly used predominantly in blends to supply needed

253

body and color to GENERIC burgundy wines, it can produce some rather spectacular, full-bodied and fruity VARIETAL wines when grown in cool coastal vineyards.

Pétrus, Château (*Pay-truce'*): Magnificent and full-bodied red wine from the POMEROL district, usually one of the most robust of all BORDEAUX wines. Named for the fisherman apostle Saint Peter, Pétrus is unofficially ranked as the leading Pomerol, and in some vintages it is among the most expensive Bordeaux wines; the estate is only about 30 acres large, and production rarely exceeds 3,500 cases. Its rise to fame was largely the work of its late owner, Mme. Edmond Loubat, whose niece Mme. Lily Lacoste is now co-owner; the estate is managed by Jean-Pierre Moueix, an important Pomerol proprietor. The richness of the wine reflects the very high proportion of Merlot grapes used—over 95%—and it is full of scent, warmth, and finesse.

Pfarrikirche (*Far'-keer-shuh*): German for "parish church," an ecclesiastical order owning a vineyard estate.

pH: A measure of the relative acidity or alkalinity in a solution, known technically as the logarithm of the reciprocal of the hydrogen ion concentration. The pH scale is composed of 14 units: values of 0 – 7 indicate acidity, and values of 7 – 14 indicate alkalinity, with 7 being neutral. Pure distilled water has a pH of about 7; wines with proper acidity should show low pH values. The pH scale is occasionally helpful in indicating the relative acidity of grape musts and finished wine, but it will not necessarily provide a clue to how the wine will taste. See ACIDITY.

Phylloxera (*Fil-lox'-er-ah*): A burrowing plant louse of the Aphididae family (full name: *Phylloxera vastatrix*) that is one of the most serious vineyard parasites. Native to the eastern U.S., phylloxera attacks the roots of the vine and eventually kills it. Introduced accidentally in Europe in the 1860s, the insect laid waste to all major vineyard areas and did millions of dollars worth of damage; various methods of combatting it failed until the technique of grafting the European vines onto American rootstocks (which are immune) was perfected. This is now standard procedure in most of the world's vineyards, for there are few areas where phylloxera has never struck, and the insect remains a constant threat unless grafted vines are planted.

Pichet (*Pee'-shay*): French for "pitcher," a small container, sometimes made of wood or earthenware, used to serve wines at the table.

Picpoul (*Peek'-pool*): White grape variety grown in southern France, used in making Armagnac brandy and light white wines. See FOLLE BLANCHE.

Piemonte (*Pee-ay-mawn'-tay*): Italian for "Piedmont," a wine region in northwestern Italy, at the foot of the Italian Alps. Its capital is the city of Torino (Turin), and wine is one of its foremost products: annual production often exceeds 45 million cases.

A hilly region famous for its outstanding cuisine, Piemonte has two principal centers of wine production. The largest and most important is central Piemonte, due east of Torino around the Monferrato Hills. The other region lies further north in the Novara Hills near the city of Milan, where the Alps begin to rise up to precipitous heights. Along the Swiss border in the extreme northwest is the French-speaking district of the Valle d'Aosta; although this is a separate, autonomous district, its wines share a close similarity with those of Piemonte. Fine Valle d'Aosta wines can be exquisite; unfortunately, these rare mountain wines are encountered only infrequently outside the region.

The chief grape variety in Piemonte is the

255

Nebbiolo, said to take its name from the fog (*Nebbia*) that cloaks the Piemonte hills at harvest time. The Nebbiolo is used for all the best Italian red wines; another important grape is the Barbera, which yields substantial and robust red wine. The best of it is rated D.O.C., and is produced around the towns of Alba, Monferrato and Asti. Other red Piemontese grapes for which D.O.C. zones have been established include Freisa, Dolcetto, and Grignolino. Good but little-known red Piemonte wines include Carema, Brachetto d'Acqui, Fara, Sizzano, and Boca.

Piemonte is also a region of intense white wine production, much of it is used in the manufacture of VERMOUTH, which is a Torino specialty. The sweet Moscato grape is grown for the sparkling wine of ASTI, Asti Spumante, one of the best known Italian sparkling wines. A sweet wine, CALUSO PASSITO, is the specialty of the little town of Caluso north of Torino. The Cortese is another important Piemontese white wine grape.

The noble red wines of Piemonte rank with the world's best—they are heady, robust, and aristocratic. BAROLO and BARBARESCO from central Piemonte are world-acclaimed; GATTINARA and GHEMME from the Novara Hills are less well-known but similar in quality. Even the regional Piemontese wines share many of their superior characteristics, but the best are not always easy to come by outside of Italy.

Piesport *(Peez'-port):* Famous wine village on the MOSEL River, Germany, with 148 acres of vineyard planted predominantly in Riesling. The piquant, scented white wines of Piesport are among the Mosel's best, especially in dry years, for the soil retains moisture. The most famous individual vineyard (EINZELLAGE), Goldtröpfchen, produces especially elegant, scented wines; other fine vineyards include: Schubertslay, Gunterslay, Domherr, Falkenberg, Gärtchen, and Treppchen. It should be noted, however, that the familiar Piesporter Michelsberg is not an Einzellage; under the 1971 German Wine Law, this name has become a collective vineyard (GROSSLAGE), used for regional wines from lesser vineyards in the vicinity of Piesport.

Pineau de la Loire *(Pee'-no duh la Lwahr')*: The local name for the Chenin Blanc grape in the LOIRE River valley, France; also used by some California producers for their wines made from the Chenin Blanc.

Pineau des Charentes *(Pee'-no day Shar-ront')*: A wine apéritif made in the Cognac district, southwestern France, in the departments of Charente and Charente-Maritime. Originally made by accident some 400 years ago, Pineau des Charentes is produced by adding some young Cognac brandy to a partially fermented white wine. Alcoholic strength ranges from 17% to 22%. Pineau des Charentes is pale-gold in color, has a clean, fruity freshness, and is quite popular in France; some very good examples are now being exported to the U.S.

Pinot *(Pee'-no)*: A family of noble grape varieties, widely planted in many of the world's best wine regions. Red varieties include Pinot Noir and Pinot Meunier; white varieties include Pinot Blanc and Pinot Gris. Though they are named Pinot in California, the Red Pinot (Pinot St. George) and White Pinot (Chenin Blanc) are not members of the Pinot family and should not be labeled as such.

Pinot Blanc *(Pee'-no Blawn)*: Fine quality white wine grape, originally native to the Burgundy region in France but now grown in many wine regions. It is being phased out in Burgundy and Champagne in favor of Chardonnay, but still gives excellent results in the district of Alsace, where it is sometimes called Klevner. Pinot Blanc is known as Weissburgunder in Germany and Austria, reflecting its

257

origins in Burgundy, and if fermented dry, the wines recall fine Chardonnays. In northern Italy, the grape is called Pinot Bianco, and is an important variety in the Trentino-Alto Adige and Friuli-Venezia Giulia districts. Over 1,900 acres of Pinot Blanc have been planted in California, where it is currently less fashionable than Chardonnay but often produces comparable or superior wines in certain growing areas: they are less expensive than Chardonnay and are often outstanding. Recent discoveries suggest, however, that the Pinot Blanc grown in California may actually be the Melon from the Muscadet area.

Pinot Chardonnay: see CHARDONNAY.

Pinot Gris *(Pee′-no Gree):* Fine grape variety used to make white wines, although its skins are reddish when ripe. It gives good results in Alsace, where it is classified as a "cépage noble," and produces good, rather full wines under the name Tokay d'Alsace. Across the border in Germany, Pinot Gris is called Ruländer (after a merchant named Ruland, who brought it to Germany from France in 1711); particularly outstanding Ruländers are grown in the Kaiserstuhl-Tuniberg area of Baden, in southern Germany. Called Pinot Grigio in Italian, it is planted extensively in northern Italy and its full, scented wines are quite popular—occasionally in Italy, the fermenting must may receive additional skin contact, so that the wine takes on a slight reddish tinge and picks up extra flavor and body. Although it has nothing to do with Hungarian Tokay, Pinot Gris is sometimes called Tokay or Tokayer because of its characteristic fullness and pronounced bouquet; for the same reason it is called Malvoisie in parts of Switzerland, though the two grapes are unrelated. Pinot Gris is a true Pinot variety and gives a multitude of quality wine types; so far it has only been grown experimentally in the U.S., but deserves to be better known.

Pinot Meunier *(Pee'-no Muhn'-yay)*: Red grape variety grown in the French CHAMPAGNE district, where (as with Pinot Noir, below) it is fermented without the skins so that a white wine is obtained. Its acreage in Champagne is generally decreasing, but it is hardy and productive and adds strength to Champagne blends. The name meunier ("miller," in French) derives from the white, powdery underside of its leaves, which appear to be dusted with flour. In Germany it is called Müllerrebe.

Pinot Noir *(Pee'-no Nwahr)*: Outstanding red wine grape, widely grown in the region of BURGUNDY, France, and to the north in the CHAMPAGNE district. It is called "black" although its berries are deep purple when ripe. Pinot Noir is responsible for all the great red Burgundies, in addition to some fine rosés; in the Champagne district, the grapes are pressed before fermentation to obtain white juice (see BLANC DE NOIRS), and three-fourths of all Champagne is made from Pinot Noir. The grape is grown in many other places in Europe, particularly in Switzerland and northern Italy; because it ripens relatively late and was brought from Burgundy, it is called Spätburgunder in Germany and Austria. Pinot Noir is quite demanding as to soil and growing season; outside of Burgundy the wines' character changes considerably. Some 9,400 acres of Pinot Noir have been planted in California; traditionally California Pinot Noirs have been overly light and lacking in depth, but there has been tremendous improvement recently.

Pinot St. George: see PINOT.

Pomace: The residue of grape skins, seeds and pulp remaining in the fermenting vat after the wine or juice is removed. It can be distilled to make brandy, called *Eau-de-Vie-de Marc* in French and "pomace brandy" in California.

Pomerol *(Pawm-uh-roll')*: Outstanding red wine commune in the BORDEAUX district,

France; one of the smallest wine regions in Bordeaux, with less than 1,730 acres under vines. The generous red wines of Pomerol are similar to those produced in SAINT-ÉMILION, which borders to the east, except that Pomerols are perhaps even fuller in flavor; the region was formerly a part of Saint-Émilion until 1923. The soil is rich in iron and clay, factors that contribute to the distinctive flavor of Pomerols. The equivalent of about 300,000 cases is produced annually.

The dominant vine in Pomerol is Merlot, which imparts a characteristic softness and scent; the other leading variety is Cabernet Franc, locally called the Bouchet. The vineyards are located near the city of Libourne some 20 miles east of Bordeaux; two neighboring districts, LALANDE-DE-POMEROL and NÉAC, lie just to the north and are separated by a small stream. The Pomerols are generally superior to wines from the latter districts, through somewhat better soil and exposure; Pomerol's commune wines are among the best regional wines of Bordeaux.

Pomerol is one of the few Bordeaux wine regions whose wine estates (CHÂTEAUX) have not been classified officially, yet because there are so many good châteaux, some sort of distinction between them is useful. The following unofficial classification is based on the current standing of leading Pomerol châteaux, reflected in the prices they generally fetch in the trade. The single best Pomerol is reckoned to be Pétrus (see PÉTRUS, CHÂTEAU), followed by:

Château Beauregard
Château Certan-de-May
Château Certan-Giraud
Château Clinet
Clos l'Eglise
Domaine de l'Église
Château l'Église-Clinet
Château l'Evangile
Château Feytit-Clinet

Château Gazin
Château Gombaude-Guillot
Château La Conseillante
Château La Croix-de-Gay
Château Lafleur
Château Lafleur-Pétrus
Château Lagrange
Château La Grave-Trigant-de Boisset
Château La Pointe
Château Latour-Pomerol
Château Le Gay
Château Moulinet
Château Nénin
Château Petit-Village
Clos René
Château Rouget
Château de Sales
Château Trotanoy
Vieux-Château-Certan

Pommard (*Po-mar'*): One of the most famous wine communes in the CÔTE DE BEAUNE, Burgundy, and one of the largest, with some 850 acres under vines; total production often exceeds 114,300 cases annually. Since the Middle Ages, Pommard has been celebrated for its fine red wines made from Pinot Noir, prized for their scent and finesse; a tiny amount of white wine is also made, but it is unimportant commercially. The vineyards adjoin those of BEAUNE to the north, and the wines have much in common.

Possibly because the name is easy to pronounce, Pommard is one of the best-known names in the Burgundy wine trade, but there is a big difference between *commune* wines merely labeled "Pommard" and the wines of individual vineyards. Pommard's best vineyards have been rated Premier Cru (First Growth), and in good vintages wines from these vineyards are liable to be very fine. ÉPEN-OTS and RUGIENS head the list; the former is typically graceful and scented, the latter apt to be somewhat fuller. Other good vineyards

261

include: Clos Blanc, Clos de la Commaraine, Les Arvelets, Les Argillières, Pézerolles, Chanlains, Les Chaponnières, and Les Jarollières.

Port: Famous sweet dessert wine; specifically, a product of Portugal named for the city of Oporto, produced from some 61,775 acres of vineyards in a strictly delimited zone in the Alto Douro (Upper Douro) region, from approved grape varieties and by traditional methods. Since 1968 wines shipped to the U.S. from this area must bear the name "Porto" or "Vinho do Porto" to distinguish them from domestic ports produced in California and elsewhere, which are usually made by different methods and often with different grapes.

Port is a rich, ruby-red wine made from several different grape varieties, blended together for complexity. While several dozen different varieties are officially approved for cultivation in the Alto Douro, those that generally give the best results for red wines are Bastardo, Touriga Francesca, Mourisco, Tinto Cão, and Tinta Francisca. White Port, which is not as often seen in the U.S. but is popular in Europe, may be made from Rabigato, Gouveio, Donzelinho, or Malvasia Fina. The vines are planted in amazingly steep, terraced vineyards along a 50-mile sweep of the Douro River; each vineyard estate is known as a *quinta,* the owner of which customarily sells his wine to a shipper for aging and blending. The terraces had to be carved out of solid schist by digging and blasting, and they represent a monumental engineering feat. The delimited region of Port in the Alto Douro was first established in 1756, and it has stayed essentially the same for over two centuries.

The characteristic fruity sweetness of Port derives from the addition of high-proof brandy (known as *aguardente*), distilled from wine and added to the fermenting must before fermentation is completed. At the harvest, grapes are taken to the winery, where they are crushed

262

so that fermentation can begin. For over two centuries, grapes in the Alto Douro district were customarily crushed by treading with the feet, over a period of many hours, but with increased labor costs nowadays mechanical crushing is preferred.

At a predetermined moment, the wine is drawn off into vats, and the spirit is added to arrest fermentation (see MUTAGE). This process of fortification stops fermentation and leaves considerable unresolved sugar in the wine, with a final alcoholic strength of 20%. Almost all Ports are the blended produce of several quintas, which furnish wines with the characteristics desired by the shipper. Commercial grades of Port come from grapes that are sold to larger producers, who use machines of French design to crush the grapes and extract the must; the finer grades still involve the traditional association with winemaking at the quinta.

Though the actual making of Port takes place at the quinta in the Alto Douro, the wine is generally not kept there for more than a few months. Soon after it is made, it is taken downstream to the city of Vila Nova de Gaia, a suburb of Oporto, to the shippers' warehouses or *lodges* for further aging, which can last as long as fifty years. A few *quintas*, such as the Quinta da Vargellas of Taylor/Fladgate and the Quinta do Noval, operate as a single estate that sells the unblended produce of that winery only.

After the new wine has spent some six to nine months aging at a lodge, experienced tasters will have determined its qualities and aging potential. If the quality is exceptional, the shipper will "declare a vintage" and request the Instituto do Vinho do Porto to designate that particular lot of wine as Vintage Port. Less than five percent of the total production in the Alto Douro achieves vintage status— ideal weather conditions that produce such a wine occur only a few times each decade.

263

Usually the fullest-bodied and most long-lived of Ports, Vintage Port is kept in cask only for about two years before continuing its development in bottle, often for decades. During this time it throws a heavy sediment, and before the wine is consumed the mass of sediment must somehow be separated. Usually the sediment takes the form of a cohesive crust, or occasionally a gelatinous mass; the best way of separating a mature Vintage Port is to stand it upright for some time in advance of service, and then carefully transfer most of the contents to another bottle or container (see DECANT). Some wine is lost through decanting and the procedure can be troublesome, but the pleasures of such an exquisite wine reward those with patience.

Very close in quality to Vintage Ports, and even preferred by some, are COLHEITA Ports, also known as "wines with the date of harvest." These Ports bear a vintage date, but instead of being aged in cask for only two years, Colheita Ports remain in wood for at least seven years prior to bottling, thus losing most of their sediment. A similar type of Port bearing a vintage date is a "Late-Bottled Vintage," or "L.B.V.", which is offered by some Port shippers. This is a lighter grade of wine, produced in years not generally declared a vintage, which is aged in cask for six years. When released, the wines are sold with a bottling date on the label, and generally throw little or no sediment with age; they are considerably cheaper than true Vintage Port and much more readily available.

Commercial grades of Port generally fall into two groups. Fuller, sweeter grades are known as Ruby Port, named for the wine's characteristic deep garnet color; lighter and sometimes drier wines are called Tawny Port. The name tawny derives from the fact that as Port wine ages, its rich ruby color changes to a brown, tawny color, and some of its original sweetness evolves into a more complex, delicate flavor. If Port is left to age for long periods of time in wood, as the best grades of Tawny Port are, it becomes an entirely different type of wine—more delicate and subtle than Ruby, with a graceful bouquet. Ports kept in wood in this manner for at least ten and up to forty years are known as "fine old Tawnies," and often cost more than some Vintage Ports, owing to the considerable loss of wine through evaporation over a period of time.

Commercial grades of Tawny can be prepared by blending white Port in with Ruby, thus lightening up the color, but the flavor does not compare with select wines that have been extensively aged in cask. However, this type of wine represents a slightly lighter and drier alternative to basic Ruby, the youngest and least expensive grade of Port.

Finer grades of Ruby Port, which are not marketed with a vintage date, are sometimes sold as "vintage character," in which wines of different vintages are blended together. Occasionally these wines will throw a slight sediment, which may easily be removed by decanting. Another type of wine, less commonly seen nowadays, is "crusted Port," which as its name implies, throws off a sediment in bottle. Sold without any indication of a vintage date, crusted Ports are being displaced commercially by vintage character Ports and Late-bottled Vintage Ports—especially the latter, because modern Port drinkers prefer to see a vintage date on the wines they buy.

Another type of Port, seen less frequently today, is the so-called "Port of the Vintage." The name is misleading, because while the wine may begin its life as the produce of a single year, it is topped up with younger wines during the period of cask aging—similar to the SOLERA process used in Sherry and Madeira. With the increasing proportion of younger wines, the vintage loses its significance and often this invites fraud. The Instituto do Vinho do Porto is suppressing the production of this type of wine in favor of the more controllable Late-bottled Vintages and other types of Port, although there may still be some older bottles in commercial distribution.

White Port is white in name only; more frequently it is amber in color, and may be either off-dry; an ideal aperitif wine, or sweet like Ruby—the latter type is also called *Lacrima*. As Port-drinking is becoming increasingly fashionable in the U.S., there is an occasional call for White Port, but Ruby and Tawny continue to be far more popular at present.

Great vintages of Port during the past few decades have been: 1980, 1977, 1975, 1970, 1967, 1966, 1963, 1960, 1958, 1955, 1950, 1948, 1947, and 1945; a fine Vintage Port is at its best when at least fifteen years old. Among the leading Port shippers to the U.S. are: Fonseca, Taylor/Fladgate, Graham, Croft, Niepoort, Warre, Robertson, Sandeman, Cockburn, Smith Woodhouse & Co., Silva & Cosens Ltd. (Dow), Feist, Burmester, Messias, and the individual Quinta do Noval, which markets its wines independently.

The production of port-type wines in the U.S. in not subject to government control, and the quality is consequently apt to vary considerably. However, a few domestic producers have seriously studied the intricate processes used in Portugal and have succeeded in producing a number of very interesting wines. When the same *tinta* grape varieties are grown in many of the warmer climatic regions, and the highest-quality fruit and production techniques are used, the wines are often excellent and compare favorably to the Ports of the Alto Douro. Among the better California port producers are: Ficklin, Quady, J. W. Morris, Woodbury, and Shenandoah Vineyards in Amador County.

Portugal: The region of what is now modern Portugal was called "Lusitania" by the Romans, who were among the first to appreciate the local wines. Today, wine is one of Portugal's most valuable export products, and the fame of Portuguese wines is world-wide. Though Portugal is only about the size of the state of Indiana, a good deal of the arable land is given over to vineyards, and the Portuguese annually consume over three times as much table wine as is produced in California, despite the fact that the two most famous Portuguese wines—PORT and MADEIRA—are dessert wines and not table wines.

Both Port and Madeira have been subject to strict quality controls for centuries, but only recently has there been government involvement in delimiting other good vineyard areas. The government has classified eight wine regions under the *Denominação de origem* (Denomination of Origin) laws, and several more (Alcobaca, Ribatejo, Lagoa, etc.) are scheduled for approval in subsequent years. Wines entitled to *Denominação de origem* bear a special seal affixed over the neck of the bottle, the *selo de garantia*, guaranteeing their quality and authenticity. Most Portuguese wine destined for everyday enjoyment (*vinho de consumo*) is not subject to these controls, but better quality wine marked for export is, with the result that in England such wines have been called "Europe's best-kept secret."

Most Americans associate Portuguese wines with rosé, which presently constitutes a major portion of Portuguese wine exported to the U.S. No specific region has been delimited, however, for some of the best-known Portuguese rosés on the American market (Mateus, Lancer's, Alianca, etc.), and many excellent Portuguese wines are sold under a brand name, not a place of origin. Besides the fruity rosés, the light, refreshing VINHO VERDE wines—from the Minho and Douro Littoral areas in the north, along the Spanish border—are popular. The "green wines" of the Vinho Verde region are produced from grapes grown on high per-

267

golas, picked before they are fully ripe. High in acidity but low in alcohol (8-11%), they are at their best when consumed rather young.

Most of the best Portuguese wines are red, and they age particularly well. COLARES, produced to the northwest of the city of Lisbon, is traditionally one of Portugal's most famous red wines, but very little is exported, as the wines are becoming rare. A much larger and more promising region is DÃO, located some 150 miles to the northeast, where some outstanding reds and interesting whites are produced. Dão's better producers are becoming increasingly more export-minded, and their wines are gaining in importance. Carcevelos and Bucelas, two wine regions near Lisbon, were at one time celebrated for their red and white wines, but they are not well known outside the region today. The sweet MOSCATEL DE SETÚBAL, produced around the city of Setúbal south of Lisbon, is a fine dessert wine.

Port, produced in the upper Douro (Alto Douro) region—and Madeira, made on the island of Madeira some 530 miles to the west of Lisbon—are the best-known and historically the most famous wines of Portugal. They are of sufficient modern-day importance to warrant separate entries in this dictionary.

Portuguiser *(Por-too-geez'-er)*: Red wine grape grown in Germany, accounting for about two-fifths of all the red wine vineyards in that country. The Portuguiser is widely planted in the RHEINHESSEN and RHEINPFALZ regions, but its wines tend to be rather light, lacking in color and body. Despite its name, it has nothing to do with the wines of Portugal.

Pouilly-Fuissé *(Poo'-yee Fwee-say')*: Outstanding white French wine, produced in southern Burgundy in the MÁCONNAIS region. Made from the Chardonnay grape, Pouilly-Fuissé is now one of the best-known wines in America. Wines bearing this distinguished name may be produced only in four authorized communes:

Fuissé, Solutré-Pouilly, Vergisson and Chaintré; and by law they must attain a minimum alcoholic strength of 11%. There are 1,482 acres under the Pouilly-Fuissé appellation, some more ideally situated than others, and usually the best wines carry some indication of a vineyard name; by law they must attain a minimum alcoholic strength of 12%. The leading vineyards include: Château Fuissé, Clos Ressier, Les Bouthières, Les Clos, Les Champs, Les Vignes-Blanches, Les Menestrières, Les Perrières, and others; however, some names appear to be associated with vineyards but are in fact brand names. The equivalent of some 350,000 cases of Pouilly-Fuissé is produced annually.

Pouilly-Fuissé is a wine to be enjoyed young, and is best when about two years old. It fades soon afterwards, and for this reason should be avoided when older than five years.

Pouilly-Fumé (*Poo'-yee Foo-may'*): Fine white wine produced from the Sauvignon Blanc (*Blanc Fumé*) grape near the village of POUILLY-SUR-LOIRE on the upper LOIRE River valley, France. Despite the similar-sounding name, the wine of Pouilly-Fumé has nothing to do with the Pouilly-Fuissé from the Burgundy region (see above). The word "fumé" means "smoke" in French, and the wines are said to derive their smoky, spicy qualities from the soil on which they are grown. The region adjoins SANCERRE on the other side of the Loire, and the wines have much in common, being made from the same grape variety; however, wines that bear the name "Pouilly-sur-Loire" are *not* made from Sauvignon but rather the Chasselas, and are lighter and fruitier. The area under vines entitled to the appellation Pouilly-Fumé is about 1,975 acres; average annual production amounts to some 180,500 cases. The Château du Nozet (which uses the brand name "De La Doucette") and Château de Tracy are among the leading producers.

269

Pouilly-Loché *(Poo'-yee Lo-shay')*: White wine region in the MÂCONNAIS district, southern Burgundy, located around the little town of Loché. The interesting white wines of Pouilly-Loché are similar to those of the famous POUILLY-FUISSÉ region to the west, but are generally not quite as fine, although they are made from the same grape variety—the Chardonnay—and Pouilly-Lochés are usually somewhat less expensive. The vineyard area is small, however, and only about 8,000 cases are produced annually.

Pouilly-sur-Loire *(Poo'-yee Sir Lwahr')*: Village in the upper LOIRE River valley, France, famous principally for its clean, dry white wine made from the Sauvignon Blanc (*Blanc Fumé*) grape, the fine POUILLY-FUMÉ. A lesser quantity of good but somewhat less distinguished wine called "Pouilly-sur-Loire" is made from the Chasselas, which yields rather light wines that do not always travel well, though they are popular carafe wines in the region. The production zone in Pouilly-sur-Loire includes the communes of St.-Andelin, Tracy, Garchy, St.-Laurent and Mesves; some 25,000 cases of Pouilly-sur-Loire are produced annually, excluding the more important production of Pouilly-Fumé.

Pouilly-Vinzelles *(Poo'-yee Van-zell')*: White wine region in the MÂCONNAIS district, southern Burgundy, located around the little town of Vinzelles. Made from the same outstanding Chardonnay grape used in the famous POUILLY-FUISSÉ region just to the west, the wines of Pouilly-Vinzelles are similar but tend to be somewhat lighter and fruitier. Production is limited to about 17,100 cases annually, but because they are generally inexpensive, some Pouilly-Vinzelles represent excellent value.

Pourriture Noble *(Poo'-ree-tur Nawbl')*: French for "noble mold," the fungus that collects on the skins of the grapes in certain wine regions, concentrating the juice and allowing the making of luscious sweet wines. See BOTRYTIS CINEREA.

Prémeaux *(Pray-mo')*: Wine village in the southern CÔTE DE NUITS, Burgundy, officially part of the commune of NUITS-SAINT GEORGES. The wines of Prémeaux are entitled to the Nuits-Saint Georges appellation and are similar; the best vineyards are: Clos des Corvées, Clos de la Maréchale, Clos des Corvées-Paget, Aux Perdrix, and Les Didiers. Production statistics are combined for the two communes and are listed under Nuits-Saint Georges.

Press Wine: Wine obtained by pressing the skins and pulp remaining in the vat following fermentation, after the FREE RUN wine is drained off. Press wine contains a great deal of tannin and coloring matter; because it tends to be harsh, many producers do not bother with it, but in some regions it is blended with free-run wine to add strength and color.

Prosecco *(Pro-sek'-ko)*: White wine made from the Prosecco grape, grown in the province of Treviso in the region of VENETO, northern Italy. Its full name is Prosecco di Conegliano-Valdobbiadene, after the two communes for which the D.O.C. zone is specified. Prosecco may take several forms; most usually it is a pleasant, light dry wine, but it is sometimes made sparkling or semi-sparkling, and occasionally it is semi-sweet *(amabile)* as well.

Provence *(Pro-vawnss')*: Picturesque old province on the Mediterranean coast in southern France; noted for the local dialect, Provençal (which is still spoken in some regions) as well as lush scenery and delightful wines. Today, Provence consists of the departments of Var, Alpes-Maritimes, Hautes-Alpes, Vaucluse, Bouches-du-Rhône, and Alpes de Hautes-Provence. In relation to its better wines, the most general place-name is CÔTES DE PROVENCE, defining red, white and rosé wines, produced

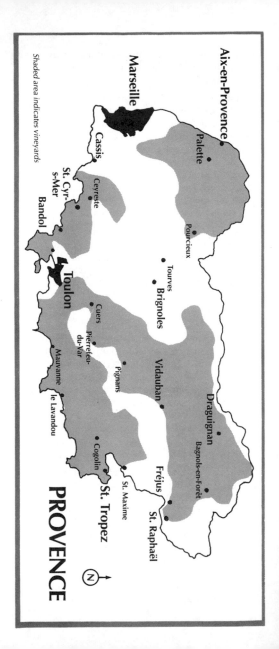

PROVENCE

Aix-en-Provence

Marseille

Cassis

St. Cyr-s-Mer

Bandol

Ceyreste

Toulon

Cuers

Pierrefeu-du-Var

Mauvanne

le Lavandou

Palette

Pourcieux

Tourves

Brignoles

Pignans

Vidauban

Draguignan

Bagnols-en-Forêt

Cogolin

St. Maxime

Fréjus

St. Raphaël

St. Tropez

Shaded area indicates vineyards

N

throughout the region. Provençal red and white wines may be quite good, but in general the rosés are superior. They are often sold in unusual amphora-shaped bottles, which helps to identify them.

There are several wine regions in Provence that have been granted APPELLATION CONTRÓLÉE status, by virtue of their interesting and original wines. Probably the most famous is BANDOL, noted for its sturdy red wines; the little village of CASSIS to the northwest is celebrated both for its seafood and the crisp white wines that complement it so well. PALETTE, further inland, produces a gamut of good red, white and rosé wines. Bellet is another appellation many miles to the east, but its wine production is limited and most of it is consumed on the spot by tourists in Nice, Cannes and Antibes.

Pucelles *(Pew-sell')*: French for "virgins"; specifically, a fine white wine vineyard in the commune of PULIGNY-MONTRACHET, in Burgundy's CÔTE DE BEAUNE. The Pucelles plot consists of about 17 acres planted in Chardonnay, and annually produces exquisite white wines prized for their great delicacy.

Puisseguin-Saint-Émilion *(Pweese'-gan Sahnt Eh-meel-lyon')*: Village and wine commune located some 5 miles to the northeast of SAINT-ÉMILION in the BORDEAUX district. The sturdy red wines of Puisseguin are entitled to the Saint-Émilion appellation; they are usually well-made, which makes many of them excellent value.

Puligny-Montrachet *(Pool'-een-yee Mon-rah-shay')*: World-famous wine commune in the CÔTE DE BEAUNE, Burgundy; like the adjoining commune of CHASSAGNE-MONTRACHET to the south, named for the magnificent MONTRACHET—the most celebrated white wine vineyard in Burgundy, rated Grand Cru (Great Growth). Above it on a slight slope is the

273

equally renowned CHEVALIER-MONTRACHET vineyard, producing white wines of similar quality, and just below Montrachet is the BÂTARD-MONTRACHET vineyard with the associated BIENVENUE-BÂTARD-MONTRACHET parcel. Each one of these Grand Cru vineyards is capable of annually producing some of the greatest white Burgundies, but there is a wealth of similarly fine vineyards surrounding them, rated Premier Cru (First Growth); the better vineyards include: COMBETTES, PUCELLES, CAILLERETS, Clavoillon, Les Folatières, Les Chalumeaux, Perrières, and Les Referts. See also BLAGNY.

Puligny's 578 acres of vineyard are planted almost exclusively in Chardonnay, although there is a tiny amount of Pinot Noir grown as well. The chalk-marl soil and excellent exposure combines to yield succulent, perfumed and flavorful white wines with a lingering aftertaste; production averages about 70,000 cases of wine annually, less than 5% of it red.

Punt: The concave indent on the bottom of a wine bottle, designed to give it added strength and also confine the sediment to a narrow area on the bottom.

Puttonyo *(Poo-tawn'-yo):* In Hungary, a vat, about 8 to 10 gallons capacity, made of wood, like half a barrel, and carried on the back. Used in the vineyards of the Tokay region to collect overripe grapes. The number of puttonyo of overripe grapes added to the standard vat indicates the sweetness and quality of the TOKAY labeled ASZÚ: 3 puttonyos is the lightest Tokay Aszú, 4 puttonyos sweeter, and 5 puttonyos the sweetest wine, made exclusively from overripe grapes. Such outstanding wines are not made every year, and they are necessarily expensive.

Qualitätswein mit Prädikat (*Kval-ee-tates'-vine mit Pray'-dee-kat*): German for "quality wine with distinction." Under the 1971 German Wine Law, a wine labeled Qualitätswein mit Prädikat must be made from sound, ripe grapes in one of the eleven designated wine regions (ANBAUGEBIETE). It is a quality wine or QUALITÄTSWEIN (see above), except that no addition of sugar is allowed. In ascending order of excellence, the quality categories prescribed for Qualitätswein mit Prädikat are as follows: KABINETT, SPATLESE, AUSLESE, BEERENAUSLESE, and TROCKENBEERENAUSLESE; in addition, there is the rare EISWEIN, produced from partially frozen grapes, since 1982 a select wine of Beerenauslese quality.

A wine in any of the *Prädikat* categories will usually be superior to one labeled Qualitätswein, because the requirements for production—in accordance with the legal minimum MUST WEIGHT standards for each category—are more stringent. (For a chart showing these standards, see GERMANY.)

Quarts de Chaume (*Kahr Duh Shome'*): Small but outstanding white wine region in the lower LOIRE River valley, France, located near the village of Rochefort-sur-Loire in the old province of ANJOU. The region is named for an estate originally divided into four parts (*quarts*) near the little hamlet of Chaume; there are some 125 acres of vineyard planted in Chenin Blanc grapes, and in late autumn the grapes are picked when overripe, yielding luscious, naturally sweet wines that are exceptionally

275

long lived; average production is about 6,000 cases a year. The leading vineyard estates are: Château de Belle-Rive, Château de Suronde, Château de Beaumard, and L'Écharderie. See also BONNEZEAUX.

Quincy (*Can'-see*): White wine region in the upper LOIRE River valley, France, situated along a tributary, the River Cher, near the city of Bourges. Quincy has some 495 acres of vineyard planted chiefly in Sauvignon Blanc grapes, and is renowned for its light, clean and fruity white wines; average production is about 35,000 cases annually.

Quinta (*Keen'-ta*): Portuguese for "vineyard estate." In the making of PORT, the wines are made at the quinta, aged briefly, and then are shipped down to the city of Vila Nova de Gaia for further blending and aging.

Racking: The process of transferring new wine from one container to another, with the purpose of separating the wine from the lees and gross sediment. Racking usually results in a slight loss of wine, but it is essential if the wine is to be clear before bottling. The French term for racking is *soutirage*; in German it is *Abstich*. See also FILTRATION and FINING.

Rainwater: A dry or medium-dry MADEIRA, with a golden color and a fragrant bouquet. Originally the proprietary brand of a shipper named Habisham in Savannah, Georgia (who received the nickname "Rainwater Habisham"), Rainwater is now a general term for a type of Madeira, and several Madeira shippers use this name, not always for the same kind of wine. It is said to have originated from a special technique of clarification devised by Habisham, which made the wines clear and brilliant, like rainwater.

Randersacker *(Rahn'-der-sock-er):* Village in the region of FRANKEN (Franconia), Germany, located just to the south of WÜRZBURG. Randersacker has 568 acres of vineyard: the best sites are planted in white grape varieties (Silvaner, Riesling, Müller-Thurgau), although a little red is also grown. In good years Randersacker makes some of Franken's best wine; the leading vineyards (EINZELLAGEN) include: Marsberg, Pfülben, Teufelskeller, Sonnenstuhl, and Dabug.

Rauenthal *(Rau'-en-tahl):* One of the most famous wine villages in the RHEINGAU district, Germany, with 252 acres of vineyard. Rauenthal's vineyards are set back in the hills away from the Rhine, giving finely-scented Riesling wines with a characteristic spiciness. The best-known (and most valuable) Rauenthal vineyard or EINZELLAGE is Baiken, which often makes one of the Rheingau's best wines; other good Einzellagen include: Gehrn, Wülfen, Rothenberg, Langenstück, and Nonnenberg. It should be noted that Rauenthaler Steinmächer is not an Einzellage but a composite vineyard or GROSSLAGE some 1134 acres large; its wines are generally inferior to those from the Einzellagen. The choicest Rauenthal holdings belong to the Staatsweingut, Schloss Eltz, and Langwerth von Simmern.

Ravat 51 *(Vignoles):* White French HYBRID grape variety, grown in the Finger Lakes district of New York and officially named Vignoles in 1970. It was developed from a cross between Seibel 6905, itself a French hybrid, and Pinot de Corton. In cooler growing districts it matures rapidly and is winter hardy;

277

the wines that it gives tend to be fairly full, with a characteristic bouquet.

Ravello (*Ra-vell′-lo*): Little village south of Naples in the region of CAMPANIA, Italy, noted for its wines of the same name. Red, white and rosé wines are produced in Ravello; though not rated D.O.C., the wines are good and are well-known in the U.S. The leading producer in Ravello is Ditta P. Caruso.

Récemment Dégorgé (*Ray′-sem-mawn Day-gor-zhay′*): French for "recently disgorged." In the French CHAMPAGNE district, some producers occasionally set aside a few select bottles of a particularly fine vintage Champagne, and leave them for an additional period of time in the cellars to mature, without disgorging them (see DÉGORGEMENT). These wines, which carry a premium, are usually finer and fuller in flavor than regular vintage Champagnes; they may also be abbreviated as "R.D." The wines are normally disgorged and released for sale about ten years after the vintage, when most of their contemporaries are well past their prime, and they are ready to enjoy immediately.

Recioto (*Ray-chaw′-toe*): A special wine produced in the region of VENETO, northern Italy. Recioto wines are made from the uppermost portions of the grape bunches, which have received a maximum amount of sunshine and are extra high in sugar; the term is derived from the word *recia* (which means "ears," in the local dialect), and thus the wines are made from the "ears" of the bunches. After picking, the grapes are then dried on special wicker racks prior to being pressed. Recioto wines are usually sweet and full-bodied, although dry reciotos are also made (see AMARONE). The most famous reciotos come from the VALPOLICELLA district and are red, called Recioto della Valpolicella, although there is some white recioto from SOAVE as well. Because of their high sugar content, recioto wines are also made sparkling.

Récolte *(Ray'-cawlt):* French for "harvest" or "vintage."

Refosco *(Ray-foss'-co):* Red grape variety grown in northern Italy; the local name for the Mondeuse grape grown in the district of Savoie (Savoy), France. Although little-known, wines from Refosco can be delicious; they are well-balanced and flavorful, and capable of improvement with some bottle age. Especially good ones are made in the district of FRIULI-VENEZIA GIULIA.

Regional: A wine made in a region or district, as opposed to a specific town or vineyard. Regional wines are usually inexpensive blended wines; though they are rarely outstanding, they fill an important need in the trade. Well-known examples include MÉDOC, CÔTES-DU-RHÔNE, and LIEBFRAUMILCH.

Rehoboam: An oversized bottle used occasionally in the French CHAMPAGNE district, with the capacity of six ordinary bottles.

Reims *(Ranss):* City in northern France with a population of some 160,000; occasionally spelled *Rheims,* the old medieval name. Reims is the largest city in the French CHAMPAGNE district, where many of the leading Champagne producers have their offices and cellars. The semicircular sweep of vineyards immediately south of the city, the MONTAGNE DE REIMS, is planted predominantly in black Pinot Noir grapes, and the wines tend to be rich and full-bodied. G. H. Mumm, Veuve Clicquot-Ponsardin, Taittinger, Piper-Heidsieck, Charles Heidsieck, Louis Roederer, Ruinart Père et Fils, Pommery & Greno, Krug and Lanson are among the important Champagne firms with offices in Reims.

Remuage *(Ray-moo-ahj'):* French for "shaking" or "riddling"; specifically, a process employed in the French CHAMPAGNE district for removing the sediment in the bottle, following the secondary fermentation. Remuage was first devised in the 19th century by Madame Veuve Clicquot née Ponsardin (1777-1866), and it is now standard procedure in the Champagne process. The bottles are placed in adjustable, angled racks or *pupitres*, which can be tilted, and skilled workmen twist the bottles regularly over a period of about 90 days, tilting the *pupitres* until the bottles are upside down and all the sediment has collected on the cork. The bottles are then taken to be disgorged (see DÉGORGEMENT).

Reserva *(Ray-sair'-va):* Spanish for "reserve," a selected lot of wine that has been set aside for further aging in cask or in bottle. This term is used most frequently in the RIOJA district.

Retsina *(Ret-seen'-ah):* Greek wine to which pine sap or resin has been added, giving it a woody, pitch flavor. The practice of resinating wines is said to have originated in Ancient Greece when wines were stored in pitched amphorae; such wines are very popular in Greece, though to most Americans they are an acquired taste.

Rheingau *(Rhine'-gow):* Possibly the most famous wine district in Germany, located west of the city of Frankfurt between the villages of Assmannshausen and HOCHHEIM, where the Rhine River takes a nearly straight 20-mile course southwest. From the river, the land rises up to the Taunus Mountains in the north, protecting the region from cold north winds; nearly all the vineyards have an incomparable southerly exposure, resulting in one grand array of well-known wine towns.

Yet the Rheingau is neither the largest vineyard area in Germany nor the most productive, and it is hard to believe that for all their fame, only 7,166 acres are under vines. But the Rheingau is renowned primarily for select bottlings, produced by centuries-old vineyard estates. The nobility still figures heavily among Rheingau producers, and family coats-of-arms appear often on finely-ornamented labels. Four-fifths of the land is planted in Riesling, and from the fine loess-loam soil of the Rheingau, scented and flavorful white wines are the result; a small amount of red wine of purely local fame is the specialty of Assmannshausen.

The Rhine River also contributes to the excellence of the wines: it reflects the sun's rays during the day, and tends to hold the heat at night; in addition, it produces the autumn mists that encourage the formation of what the Germans call *Edelfaüle* or "noble mold" (see BOTRYTIS CINEREA), which, although it does not appear every autumn, allows the making of some of the world's finest sweet wines.

The Rheingau begins upstream at Hochheim, near where the Main River flows into the Rhine, and continues westward past the well-known wine towns of WALLUF, RAUENTHAL, ELTVILLE, ERBACH, KIEDRICH, HATTENHEIM, HALLGARTEN, OESTRICH, Mittelheim, WINKEL, JOHANNISBERG, GEISENHEIM, and RÜDESHEIM; at Assmannshausen, just west of Rüdesheim, the Rhine abruptly shifts north, marking the region's western boundary.

In general, the wines of the Rheingau take the name of the town where they are made, with the exception of some from select estates that are famous enough to be sold under their own name; examples include the STEINBERG and Schloss Vollrads (see VOLLRADS, SCHLOSS). The village of Johannisberg is dominated by one great estate, Schloss Johannisberg (see JOHANNISBERG, SCHLOSS), one of the Rheingau's oldest and most famous, and under the 1971 German Wine Law the entire Rheingau was classified under a single sub-region or BEREICH, Johannisberg. Total annual production averages close to 2.8 million cases.

281

Rheinhessen *(Rhine'-hess-en):* Rheinhessen, or Hessia, is the largest wine region or ANBAU-GEBIET in Germany, with nearly 54,000 acres under vines. The region lies on the left bank of the Rhine River to the north of the RHEINPF-ALZ district, and the vineyards form a vast area beginning south near the city of WORMS, continuing due north along the Rhine as far as Mainz, and then paralelling the RHEINGAU district on the other side of the river, on a south-west course to BINGEN.

The Rheinhessen district specializes in wine for blending sold under regional names; single-vineyard wines are relatively rare. But some Rheinhessen producers produce exceptional, ESTATE-BOTTLED wines that can stand with the best in Germany—especially the luxurious and fruity wines made from LATE-HARVESTED grapes. Rheinhessen wines typically have a characteristic softness—some call them "feminine"—which is a function of the soil and the temperate climate in which they are grown. They are now made mostly from the Müller-Thurgau grape, which now accounts for over a third of the vineyards in the Rheinhessen; a wine for which the grape variety is not specified will probably be made from Müller-Thurgau. Silvaner used to be the dominant variety, but today it is less widely planted. Riesling is relatively rare in the Rheinhessen, but in some better vineyards near the Rhine it produces outstanding wines. Kerner, a new grape variety optimized for production and reliability, is becoming popular, as is Huxelrebe, Bacchus, Scheurebe and Weissburgunder (Pinot Blanc). Some light red wine from Spätburgunder (Pinot Noir) or Portuguieser is made in Rheinhessen, but most of it is consumed locally.

The Rheinhessen is probably most famous for its regional blended wine, LIEBFRAUMILCH, Germany's most popular exported white wine, although not many would suggest that it is Germany's best. The name derives from the Liebfrauenstift church in the city of Worms, and in the past all sorts of wines were openly sold as Liebfraumilch. New regulations recently enacted restrict the name Liebfraumilch to wines from the Rhine region only, which must meet the minimum standards for QUALITÄTSWEIN (quality wine).

The 1971 Wine Law delimited the Rheinhessen region into three sub-regions or BEREICHE. The most important is NIERSTEIN, named for its most famous wine town and better known for its regional wines—usually sold under the name Niersteiner Gutes Domtal—than those of its best vineyards or EINZELLAGEN. Bereich Nierstein includes the celebrated wine villages of NACKENHEIM, OPPENHEIM, DIENHEIM and Bodenheim, which form a chain of well-exposed vineyards at higher elevations along the "Rhine front"—along the river's edge. Gau-Bischofsheim, Harxheim, Lorzweiler, Dexheim, Ludswigshohe, Alsheim, Dalheim and Guntersblum are other prominent wine towns in the Bereich. Further south, Bereich Wonnegau includes the towns of Worms, Alzey, Bechtheim, Weinheim, Westhofen, Osthofen, and Florsheim; much of the wine is used for blending purposes, and only a few producers or shippers market the wines under vineyard names, or under the name of a GROSSLAGE (collective site). The remaining Bereich is Bingen, named after the most western city in Rheinhessen. Included in Bereich Bingen are the villages of INGELHEIM (famous for its good red wine, a rarity in Germany), Gau-Algesheim, Gau-Bickelheim, Sprendlingen, Wöllstein, Bornheim, Wörrstadt, Ockenheim, and Dromersheim. Bereich Bingen extends up to the NAHE River to the west, but the Nahe valley is an independent wine region and its vineyards are discussed separately.

Wine production in the Rheinhessen district is prodigious. Over 22 million cases are typically produced each year, white wine accounting for about 90% of the total.

283

Rheinpfalz *(Rhine'-fahlts):* The Rheinpfalz area, or Palatinate, is the most productive wine region (ANBAUGEBIET) in Germany, and the second largest, with some 51,200 acres of vineyard. Located on the left bank of the Rhine River north of the border with France, the Rheinpfalz region is one of the warmest and driest agricultural areas in Germany. Orchards and vineyards abound in the rolling countryside, and the mild climate assures optimum ripening conditions. The region produces over 27 million cases of wine annually.

The word Pfalz derives from the Latin *Palatium*, for the region was noted for its wine during the Roman Empire, and it was named for the Palatine Hills in Rome, the first residence of the Roman emperors. Some Rheinpfalz wine estates date back to Roman times, with strong traditions for quality.

The area as a whole is shadowed by a rolling mountain chain, the Haardt, which is a geological extension of the Vosges to the south in France. This gives the Rheinpfalz a special climatic advantage. There are three separate sections; in the south is the Ober-Haardt (upper Haardt), which begins at the town of Schweigen on the French border and extends up to the city of Neustadt. The Mittel-Haardt (middle Haardt) continues up about as far as Bad Dürkheim (see DÜRKHEIM), and north of Bad Dürkheim the Unter-Haardt (lower Haardt) extends northwards up to the RHEINHESSEN region.

Over four-fifths of Rheinpfalz wine is white; the light red wine, made mostly from Portuguieser, is primarily consumed locally. A decade ago, 40% of the vineyards were planted in Silvaner, a productive variety, but now almost half the white wine production is furnished by Müller-Thurgau, which has improved flavor characteristics. The ordinary carafe wine in the Rheinpfalz, called *Schoppenwein*, is remarkably good, and still relatively inexpensive by German standards. Some fine, full-bodied white wine is made from Gewürztraminer and Scheurebe, which grow well in the region. The Riesling is not an important variety in the northern and southern sections, but in the Mittel-Haardt contributes to a select part of the production. Some of Germany's most traditionally famous estates rely on this variety. For greater production, growers are turning to new grape varieties like Kerner, Morio-Muskat and Optima, which do well in the climate.

The 1971 German Wine Law divided the Rheinpfalz into two sub-regions or BEREICHE: Südliche Weinstrasse, and Mittelhaardt-Deutsche Weinstrasse. The primary access road through the Haardt is the "Weinstrasse," or wine road, which has been officially designated as such since 1932. The Weinstrasse commences at Schweigen at the immense Weintor (wine gate), and then leads past fields and orchards through the Mittelhaardt, passing by the famous wine towns of FORST, DEIDESHEIM, WACHENHEIM, RUPPERTSBERG, KÖNIGSBACH, Dürkheim, UNGSTEIN, and KALLSTADT. The first four towns are generally considered the most valuable in the entire Rheinpfalz, and their wines fetch high prices in the trade; Riesling predominates among the grape varieties. The three most famous producers in this area— Dr. Bürklin-Wolf, Bassermann-Jordan, and Reichsrat von Buhl—are known colloquially as "the three B's," through their initials; they own some of the most select vineyards in Forst, Ruppertsberg, Deidesheim and Wachenheim. Other leading Rheinpfalz producers include: Dr. Deinhard, Müller-Catoir, Stümpf-Fitz, Carl Jos. Hoch, Dietz-Matti, Johannes Karst & Söhne, and several important wine cooperative associations (*Winzergenossenschaften*).

Rhine Wine: Strictly defined, a wine from the Rhine region in Germany, comprising the present-day regions of the RHEINGAU, RHEINHESSEN, RHEINPFALZ, and MITTELRHEIN. As generally used in the U.S. wine trade, a "Rhine

285

wine" has no specific definition other than a light, semi-dry white wine, and this GENERIC term is used by some producers to identify wines of this type.

Rhône *(Rone):* European river some 504 miles long, drawing its source in Switzerland, flowing through Lake Geneva, and then continuing its journey due south through France to its mouth near the city of Marseilles. Navigable for much of its length, the Rhône is a principal waterway; it is also one of France's leading vineyard areas. The most general term for Rhône wines is CÔTES-DU-RHÔNE, applying to red, white or rosé wines produced from 96,370 acres of vineyards in over 120 communes.

Most of the Rhône's southern journey takes it through hot and dry country, and because the grapes receive a maximum amount of sun, vintages vary less in the Rhône than in other fine French wine regions. The wines tend to be full-flavored—reds are robust and need a long period of time to mature; whites are powerful and long-lived. The lively, stylish rosés are among the best in France.

It is common practice in the Rhône to blend wines of various grape varieties, depending on the district where they are grown. The principal red Rhône grape is the Syrah, a variety used on its own only in a few northern districts; it is normally blended with some white grapes to add finesse. This is standard practice in the famous red wine regions of CÔTE RÔTIE, HERMITAGE and CROZES-HERMITAGE to the north; one white grape, the Viognier, is used for the brilliant white wines of CONDRIEU. Sturdy red and white wines are made in the nearby areas of CORNAS and SAINT-JOSEPH. Further south near the city of Avignon, the famous red wine of CHÂTEAUNEUF-DU-PAPE is made from as many as 13 different grape varieties, of which the Mourvèdre, Syrah, Cinsault, and Grenache are most important. The

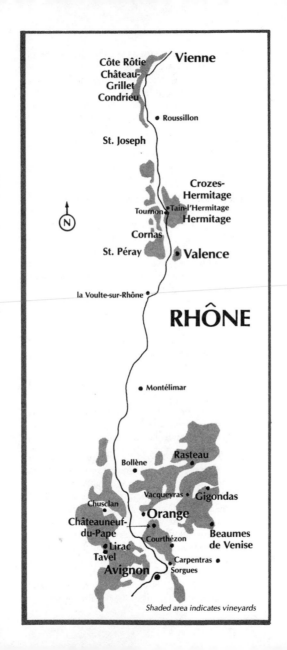

Côte Rôtie
Château-
Grillet
Condrieu

Vienne

• Roussillon

St. Joseph

Crozes-
Hermitage

Tournon • Tain-l'Hermitage
Hermitage

Cornas

St. Péray

Valence

la Voulte-sur-Rhône •

RHÔNE

• Montélimar

Rasteau

Bollène •

Vacqueyras •

Gigondas

Chusclan •

Châteauneuf-
du-Pape

• Orange

Courthézon •

Beaumes
de Venise

• Lirac

Tavel

Carpentras •

Avignon

Sorgues •

Shaded area indicates vineyards

Grenache is also used for the fine rosés of TAVEL and LIRAC. See also GIGONDAS.

In addition, the Hermitage and Crozes-Hermitage regions also make some excellent white wines from Marsanne and Roussanne grapes, and some interesting sparkling and semi-sparkling wines are made in SAINT-PÉRAY and in the village of Die (see CLAIRETTE). The sweet Muscat wine of the BEAUMES-DE-VENISE region is also acclaimed, but it is quite rare in the U.S.

Richebourg *(Reesh'-boorg):* World-famous red wine vineyard in the CÔTE DE NUITS, Burgundy, rated Grand Cru (Great Growth). Located in the celebrated commune of VOSNE-ROMANÉE, the vineyard consists of 19 acres planted in Pinot Noir, and is one of the largest in Vosne-Romanée. Richebourg is usually one of the most full-bodied of the Côte de Nuits Grand Crus; about 3,100 cases are produced annually. The vineyard is shared by several owners, of which Louis Gros, the Domaine de la Romanée-Conti, and Charles Noëllat are the most important.

Ried *(Reed):* Austrian term used to designate an individual vineyard site, the smallest land unit under the 1961 Austrian Wine Law. Used in connection with some traditionally famous vineyards, a Ried is roughly interchangeable with the German EINZELLAGE.

Riesling *(Reese'-ling):* One of the finest white wine grapes, used for the great wines of the Rhine and the MOSEL in Germany, and some of the best white wines of ALSACE in France. Its yield is small and it ripens later than other varieties, but its wines are nobly scented and have great suavity. Because it is grown for the famous wines of Schloss Johannisberg (see JO-HANNISBERG, SCHLOSS) on the Rhine, it is named Johannisberg Riesling in California; over 10,000 acres have been planted throughout the state. The Riesling is also grown in

288

northern Italy, Switzerland, and in many eastern European countries as well. It is one of the few grape varieties susceptible to the "noble mold" (see BOTRYTIS CINEREA), and thus is ideal for superb, lusciously sweet wines made from late-harvested grapes.

There are a number of grape varieties unrelated to the Riesling that have assumed its famous name, and for this reason the true Riesling is called "White Riesling" or "Rhine Riesling" to distinguish it from others such as Wälschriesling, Grey Riesling, Main Riesling, and Emerald Riesling. In California and Australia, a wine may be labeled "Riesling" even if it is made from the more productive Sylvaner or Sémillon. Wines made from these varieties—though they may be similar in style—are generally not quite as fine.

Rioja *(Ree-o'-ha)*: Outstanding wine region in north-central Spain near the French border, named for the Rio Oja River, a tributary of the Ebro, which flows through it. A dry, mountainous region, the Rioja has climatic conditions similar to those in BORDEAUX, France, and shares many of the same winemaking traditions, for in the late 19th century winemakers from Bordeaux came to the Rioja region to escape the PHYLLOXERA, which was then ravaging their vineyards. They brought the same time-honored techniques with them to the Rioja, and many are still in use today.

The Rioja region is divided into three different parts. The upper district, Rioja Alta, has the coolest climate and usually makes the lightest and most refined wines. The wines become more intense in the middle part, Rioja Alavesa, and decidedly coarser in the lower portion, Rioja Baja. The headquarters of the Rioja wine trade is the little town of Haro in Rioja Alta, where many of the leading producers have their cellars or BODEGAS.

Red Rioja is a blend of several different grape varieties: Garnacha (identical to the

Grenache grown in France), Tempranillo, Graciano, and Mazuelo. White Rioja is produced from Malvasia, Viura, and Calagraño. However, more important to Rioja's character than the grape varieties is the amount of time the wine ages in cask. Traditionally, Rioja spends many years in the wood before it is bottled. This is beneficial to the sturdy red wine, making it soft and palatable, but many of the white Riojas suffer from being in cask too long and often tend to turn prematurely brown and flat. New methods of vinification, however, are improving the white wines.

Part of the reason Rioja wines are superior is that the vineyard area of 123,500 acres has been delimited under the *Denominación de Orígen* wine laws, one of the few regions in Spain where this has been authorized. No Rioja is bottled and sold if it does not meet minimum standards, and a small stamp of authenticity on the label, the Certificate of Origin, identifies the wine as genuine Rioja.

Many Rioja producers identify the "style" of their wines by the shape of the bottle: lighter, drier wines are put in Bordeaux-shaped bottles, while fuller, richer wines are put in Burgundy-shaped bottles. The terms *Reserva* or *Reserva Especial* indicate particularly fine wines from great vintages that have spent many years in cask; lighter wines with little cask aging are sold as "clarete." Vintages do vary in the Rioja, but in general a vintage date indicates a good wine, for wine unworthy of a vintage date is not bottled but sold instead as ordinary table wine in the district.

Among the better producers of Rioja are: Bodegas Bilbainas, Marqués de Riscal, Federico Paternina, Marqués de Murrieta, Compañia Vinicola del Notre de España (which uses the brand name C.U.N.É.), R. López de Heredia (Viña Tondonia), Bodegas Muerza, Bodegas Unidas (Siglo), and many wine cooperatives.

Riserva *(Ree-sairv'-ah):* Italian for "reserve," a special lot of wine that has received additional aging, either in cask or in bottle. In certain famous Italian wine regions, usage of the word riserva is legally restricted only to those wines which have been aged at least three or four years before being sold. Such wines are of superior quality, and the prices they command are usually higher than others in their class.

Romanée, La *(Ro'-man-nay):* Tiny but highly-acclaimed red wine vineyard in the CÔTE DE NUITS, Burgundy, located in the famous commune of VOSNE-ROMANÉE and rated Grand Cru (Great Growth). Owned by a single proprietor, the vineyard consists of two acres planted in Pinot Noir, adjoining the great ROMANÉE-CONTI vineyard which lies below it. Average production is a scant 300 cases a year.

Romanée-Conti *(Ro'-man-nay Cawn'-tee):* Perhaps the rarest and most expensive wine of the CÔTE DE NUITS, Burgundy, named for the Prince de Conti, who purchased the vineyard in 1760. Through its fame, the township of Vosne in which it lies is now called VOSNE-ROMANÉE. Officially rated Grand Cru (Great Growth), the vineyard is a mere 4½ acres large, and production averages less than 500 cases a year of intense, satiny and perfumed red wine, all of it ESTATE-BOTTLED. Romanée-Conti is managed by a sole owner, the Société Civile du Domaine de la Romanée-Conti, which has other holdings in some of the best Vosne-Romanée vineyards: La TÂCHE in its entirety, RICHEBOURG, GRANDS-ÉCHEZEAUX, ROMANÉE-SAINT-VIVANT, and a choice section of the great MONTRACHET as well.

Romanée-Saint-Vivant *(Ro'-man-nay San Vee-vahn'):* Famous red wine vineyard in the CÔTE DE NUITS, Burgundy, located in the celebrated commune of VOSNE-ROMANÉE. One of the largest Grand Cru (Great Growth) vineyards in Vosne-Romanée, Romanée-Saint-Vivant

291

extends over some 23 acres of Pinot Noir vines and produces fine, scented red wines with a typically lingering aftertaste; production averages some 3,000 cases a year. The vineyard belongs to several proprietors, the most important being the Domaine de la Romanée-Conti (administrators of the Marey-Monge estate), Louis Latour, and Charles Noëllat.

Romania: The agricultural heartland of Romania is one of the most fertile in Europe, and the climate is ideal for grape growing. Known as Dacia in ancient times, the slopes of the Carpathian Mountains have been a prominent vineyard area for centuries, and it is interesting to note that Romania presently is the sixth largest wine-producing country in Europe, with over 735,500 acres of vineyard.

Like most other key industries, wine-making in Romania was nationalized following World War II, and a governmental export agency called Vinexport was set up to handle the export of Romanian quality wines. Located in the capital city of Bucharest, Vinexport now ships Romanian wines to all corners of the world. France and Germany (two great wine-producing countries in their own right) are among the best customers, and the rest of Europe is an active market for Romanian wines. Romania's wine exports to the U.S. have increased substantially during the past few years, although many of the wines are as yet not well-known.

Traditionally the most famous Romanian wine is COTNARI, a fine sweet white dessert wine produced in the northeast of the country, in the province of Moldavia. Cotnari has a rival in Murfatlar, another good sweet wine grown along the shores of the Black Sea several hundred miles to the south. The Tîrnave vineyard, named for the River Tîrnave that flows westward in the center of Romania, is an important wine area noted for its scented white wines made from Feteasca, Romania's indigenous grape variety. Other good wines are made from Muscat, Cadarca (Kadarka), Cabernet, Pinot Noir, Riesling, and Aligoté. An important wine region east of the Carpathian Mountains is Focşani, the largest new plantation of vineyard in the country, and the Romanian State Government has created a spectacular experimental vineyard just to the south, at Dealul Mare.

Rosato *(Ro-sot'-toe):* Italian for "rosé," or any light pink wine.

Rosé *(Ro-zay'):* French for "pink." A *vin rosé* is a light pink wine, normally produced by crushing red grapes and allowing the juice to remain in contact with the skins only for a very short time—usually 24 to 48 hours—so that the wine obtains a rose-colored tinge. Some well-known and excellent examples of rosé wines are made from the Grenache grape in TAVEL and LIRAC, France; the Grenache is also used for some of the best California rosés. Other good French rosés are made in Burgundy (see MARSANNAY) and in PROVENCE. Rosé wines can also be produced by blending red and white wines, or by pressing red and white grapes together, but the wines are rather different and generally less good than those made by the traditional method.

Rosso *(Ross'-so):* Italian for "red." This term, describing a red wine, should not be confused with *rosato*, which applies to a rosé wine.

Roussanne or **Roussette** *(Roo-sahn'):* White grape variety grown in the RHÔNE River valley, France, used in conjunction with the Marsanne vine to make the fine white wines of HERMITAGE. In the old province of Savoie (Savoy), where it is used for the fine white wine of SEYSSEL. In addition to Seyssel, the grape is grown in other parts of Savoie, and the good white regional wine, Roussette de Savoie, is rated APPELLATION CONTRÔLÉE.

293

Roussillon *(Roo´-see-yawn)*: Wine region in southern France near the Spanish border, in the hilly area around the major city of Perpignan. Noted for its wines since Roman times, the Roussillon area is famous principally for sweet FORTIFIED WINES, some of which are among the best in France. Grand Roussillon is the general name for several associated regions specializing in sweet fortified wines, each of which has been rated APPELLATION CONTRÓLÉE: Côtes du Haut-Roussillon in the south, Rivesaltes in the immediate vicinity of Perpignan, and Côtes d'Agly and Maury to the north. BANYULS, located further south near the city of Port-Vendres, is the most highly acclaimed wine region in the Roussillon area.

Roxheim *(Rawks´-heim)*: Notable wine village in the NAHE River valley, Germany, with 244 acres of vineyard, most of them planted in Riesling. The elegant white wines of Roxheim are among the Nahe's best and share many of the same characteristics as those from nearby KREUZNACH, but they are not well-known outside Germany. The vineyards (EINZELLAGEN) include: Höllenpfad, Birkenberg, Mühlenberg, Berg, Hüttenberg, and Sonnenberg.

Ruby Cabernet: Red HYBRID grape variety, developed in 1946 by Dr. Harold Olmo at the University of California at Davis. A cross between the Carignane and the Cabernet Sauvignon, the Ruby Cabernet was developed to produce quality wines in warm climatic regions; over 16,000 acres have been planted throughout the state, with highest concentrations in the warm Central Valley.

Previously, some wineries produced a VARIETAL wine from Ruby Cabernet and labeled it "Cabernet"; as a result, many people confuse it with Cabernet Sauvignon, which is normally a superior variety in most cooler climatic regions. The B.A.T.F. ruled in 1975 that this practice is no longer permitted, and the abbreviation "Cabernet" now applies only to Cabernet Sauvignon.

Ruchottes *(Roo-shot')*: Excellent white wine vineyard in the CÔTE DE BEAUNE, Burgundy, located in the commune of CHASSAGNE-MON-TRACHET and rated Premier Cru (First Growth). Barely 7½ acres large, the vineyard consists of two parcels, Grands-Ruchottes and Ruchottes, which usually produce some outstanding white Burgundies. The name Ruchottes is said to derive from the French word *ruche*, meaning "apiary" or "beehive," and it is suggestive of the honey-like quality of the wines from this vineyard.

Ruchottes-Chambertin *(Roo-shot' Shawm'-bear-tan)*: Fine red wine vineyard in the northern CÔTE DE NUITS, Burgundy, located in the commune of GEVREY-CHAMBERTIN and rated Grand Cru (Great Growth). Ruchottes-Chambertin is named for the great CHAMBERTIN that lies nearby, though wines from the latter vineyard are usually superior. However, Ruchottes-Chambertin is one of the finest Burgundy vineyards; there are about 8 acres planted in Pinot Noir, and production averages some 1,000 cases annually.

Rüdesheim *(Roo'-dess-heim)*: One of the most famous wine towns in the RHEINGAU district, Germany. The most western village of consequence in that notable stretch of vines, Rüdesheim is located at a sharp bend in the river, where the Rhine commences a northerly direction. The Rüdesheim vineyards or EINZEL-LAGEN are planted on extremely steep, terraced hillsides; the most famous of these—on the steepest terraces—are named "Berg" in acknowledgement of the degree of slope: Berg Rottland, Berg Roseneck, and Berg Schlossberg. The other fine Rüdesheim Einzellagen: Bischofsberg, Drachenstein, Klosterlay, Klosterberg, Kirchenpfad, and Magdelenenkreuz, are located behind the town on less precipitous slopes. Combined, the vineyards extend over 736 acres, mostly planted in Riesling.

Because of Rüdesheim's exemplary soil and location, its wines are usually the most reliable of the whole Rheingau in rainy or mediocre vintages, although the vineyards are apt to lack moisture in dry years. At their best, the Rüdesheimers are superb—typically powerful and authoritative, with a great deal of scent and finesse. Incidentally, it is important to note that there is another wine town called Rüdesheim in the NAHE River valley to the south, but its wines are much less important than the fine Rheingau Rüdesheimers and they are not often sold in the U.S.

Rugiens *(Roo-zhan')*: Notable red wine vineyard in the commune of POMMARD, in Burgundy's CÔTE DE BEAUNE. Officially rated Premier Cru (First Growth), the Rugiens vineyard consists of two associated parcels, Rugiens-Haut and Rugiens-Bas, which extend over about 33 acres; the fine red wines that it gives are characteristically fruity and full-bodied.

Ruländer *(Roo'-lender)*: The local name for the Pinot Gris grape in the region of BADEN, Germany, where over 4,000 acres have been planted. See PINOT GRIS.

Rully *(Roo'-yee)*: Wine region in the CHALONNAIS district, Burgundy, located to the northwest of the city of Chalon-sur-Saône. Rully is famous chiefly for its good white wines made from the Chardonnay grape; in addition, some red wine of lesser quality is also produced, and the area has an important sparkling Burgundy *(Bourgogne mousseux)* industry as well. There are some 26,000 cases of Rully produced each year.

Ruppertsberg *(Roo'-perts-bairg)*: Famous wine town in the RHEINPFALZ (Palatinate) region, Germany, with 939 acres of vineyard. One of the most highly-acclaimed villages in the Rheinpfalz, Ruppertsberg adjoins DEIDESHEIM just to the north, and its fine, scented Riesling wines share many of the same noble characteristics. The vineyards (EINZELLAGEN) include: Reiterpfad, Hoheburg, Nussbien, Linsenbusch, Spiess and Gaisböhl; the latter is owned exclusively by the estate of Dr. Bürklin-Wolf, a top Rheinpfalz producer.

Rust *(Roost)*: Renowned wine village on the western shores of the Neusiedler See (Lake Neusiedl), Austria, in the district of Burgenland. Along with the village of Apetlon on the opposite shore, Rust is the most famous of the Lake Neusiedl vineyards, particularly for sweet wines made from late-harvested grapes—known as AUSBRUCH in Austria. Recent legislation officially delimited the entire wine region (*Weinbaugebiet*) as Rust-Neusiedlersee, in acknowledgement of its importance.

Ruwer *(Roo'-ver)*: Little river in Germany, a tributary of the MOSEL, into which it flows near the city of TRIER. Many famous vineyards are planted along its slate banks; the Ruwer district is considered part of the Mosel area, and the official wine region (ANBAUGEBIET) is Mosel-Saar-Ruwer (see SAAR). Ruwer wines are typically light and refined, though they are generally only at their best in great vintages; in rainy years they are often too acid. The region has over 500 acres of vineyard; the best are planted in Riesling, yielding wines with great class. The two most famous Ruwer wine estates, MAXIMIN GRÜNHAUS in Mertesdorf and the Karthäuserhofberg in EITELSBACH, have been praised for centuries; fine wines are also made in KASEL, AVELSBACH, and WALDRACH.

S

Saar *(Sahr)*: Important river in western Germany, a tributary of the MOSEL; also a world-famous wine region. Saar wines are considered as Mosels, although they tend to be more austere than wines from the Mittel-Mosel. Over 3,800 acres in the Saar River valley are given over to vineyards, where they mingle with orchards and pastures.

Though the Saar's climate varies considerably from year to year, some of Germany's very greatest white wines are produced there. Fine autumn weather brings out delectable subtleties in the Riesling grapes, and certain Saar wines are among the most exquisite and complex white wines in the world. But in many years the weather barely permits any good wines at all, and many have to be made with the addition of sugar.

The most famous Saar vineyard is the SCHARZHOFBERG, producing some of the most prized of all German wines. The Scharzhofberg lies adjacent to the town of WILTINGEN, which also makes fine wines; other famous Saar villages include OCKFEN (especially celebrated for one particular wine, Ockfener Bockstein), AYL, KANZEM, OBEREMMEL, SERRIG, and Wawern. Incidentally, the Scharzhofberg, a specific vineyard or EINZELLAGE, should not be confused with Scharzberg, which under the 1971 German Wine Law has become a composite vineyard or GROSSLAGE that includes all of the vineyards in the Saar region.

Saint Amour *(Sahnt Ah-moor')*: Famous wine village in the BEAUJOLAIS district, southern

Burgundy, with 457 acres of vineyard. Officially one of the nine Beaujolais *crus* (growths), those areas that are particularly noted for their wine, Saint Amour is one of the most popular Beaujolais *crus*, possibly because of its charming name. Most of the vineyards are planted in Gamay, yielding zesty, quick-maturing red wines prized for their fine bouquet, but there are also a few vineyards planted in Chardonnay that produce an equally good white wine, sold under the appellation "Beaujolais Blanc." Total production of both types is some 155,000 cases annually.

Saint-Aubin (*Sahnt Oh-ban'*): Wine village of secondary importance in the CÔTE DE BEAUNE, Burgundy, located near the famous commune of PULIGNY-MONTRACHET. There are some 345 acres of vineyard in Saint-Aubin, which produce few great wines but a generous quantity of good red and white wines; total production averages some 32,500 cases a year. The wines are sold either under the name Saint-Aubin or as CÔTE DE BEAUNE-VILLAGES.

Saint-Émilion (*Sahnt Eh-meel-lyon'*): Picturesque little wine village in the BORDEAUX country, France, located some 25 miles to the east of the city of Bordeaux near the DORDOGNE River. Wine has been made in Saint-Émilion for over 2,000 years; along with POMEROL to the west, Saint-Émilions are usually the most sturdy and full-bodied of the great Bordeaux wines. They are made predominantly from the Merlot grape, with which some Cabernet Franc (locally called Bouchet) is normally blended, and the best Saint-Émilions have a great deal of scent, fruit and complexity.

There are almost 20,000 acres of vineyard that produce wines under the APPELLATION CONTRÔLÉE Saint-Émilion. The central region around the town itself is divided unofficially into two districts, based on differences in the soil: the "côtes" (slopes) Saint-Émilion section is immediately adjacent to the town on mostly

299

chalky slopes, while the "graves" (gravel) Saint-Émilion section is further west, on more gravelly soil. Outside of Saint-Émilion proper, there are six neighboring communes that are legally allowed to use the name Saint-Émilion: MONTAGNE-SAINT-ÉMILION, LUSSAC-SAINT-ÉMILION, PUISSEGUIN-SAINT-ÉMILION, SAINT-GEORGES-SAINT-ÉMILION, Parsac-Saint-Émilion, and the Sables-Saint-Émilion (the latter two are less important). Finally, there are several communes within the central Saint-Émilion district that are not called Saint-Émilion although their wines have legal right to this name; the most important are: St. Sulpice-de-Faleyrans, St. Christophe-des-Bardes, St. Laurent-des-Combes, and St. Hippolyte. These names are included here because they may occasionally be encountered on a wine label.

Saint-Émilion is primarily a region of fine wines, and it has a great number of select estates or CHÂTEAUX. As a result, there is a rather complicated classification of Saint-Émilion wines, which was officially established in 1955. The best estates are rated Premier Grand Cru Classé (First Great Classified Growth) and Grand Cru Classé; other châteaux are either rated "Saint-Émilion Grand Cru" or, for the lowest-ranked châteaux, simply "Saint-Émilion." To qualify for the appellation, all Saint-Émilion wines are annually subjected to an impartial tasting by a professional committee before they are allowed to be sold.

The following is the official list of classified growth Saint-Émilions published by the Syndicat Viticole et Agricole de Saint-Émilion:

PREMIERS GRANDS CRUS CLASSES

Ausone
Cheval-Blanc

Beausejour (Duffau Lagarrosse)
Beausejour (Société)
Belair
Canon
Clos Fourtet

Figeac
La Gaffeliere
Magdelaine
Pavie
Trottevieille

GRANDS CRUS CLASSÉS

L'Angélus
L'Arrosée
Baleau
Balestard-la-Tonnelle
Bellevue
Bergat
Cadet-Bon
Cadet-Piola
Canon-la Gaffelie're
Cap de Mourlin (R. Capdemourlin)
Cap de Mourlin (J. Capdemourlin)
Chapelle-Madeleine
Chauvin
Corbin (Giraud)
Corbin-Michotte
Coutet
Couvent-des-Jacobins
Croque-Michotte
Curé-Bon
Dassault
Faurie-de-Souchard
Fonplegade
Fonroque
Franc-Mayne
Grand-Barrail-Lamarzelle-Figeac
Grand-Corbin-Despagne
Grande-Corbin
Grand-Mayne
Grand-Pontet
Grandes-Murailles
Guadet-Saint-Julien
Haut-Corbin
Haut-Sarpe
Jean-Faure
Clos des Jacobins
Clos la Madeleine
Clos Saint-Martin
La Carte

301

La Clotte
La Clusiere
La Couspaude
La Dominique
Laniote
Larcis-Ducasse
Lamarzelle
Larmande
Laroze
Lasserre
La Tour-du-Pin-Figeac (Bélivier)
La Tour-du-Pin-Figeac (Moueix)
La Tour-Figeac
Le Chatelet
Le Couvent
Le Prieuré
Matras
Mauvezin
Moulin-du-Cadet
L'Oratoire
Pavie-Decesse
Pavie-Macquin
Pavillon-Cadet
Petit-Faurie-de-Soutard
Ripeau
Sansonnet
Saint-Georges-Côte-Pavie
Soutard
Tertre-Daugay
Trimoulet
Trois-Moulins
Troplong-Mondot
Villemaurine
Yon-Figeac

The two most famous Premier Grand Cru Classé Saint-Émilions are AUSONE and CHEVAL-BLANC, which generally fetch some of the highest prices in the Bordeaux wine trade.

Saint-Estèphe *(Sahnt Es-teff')*: Notable wine commune in the BORDEAUX district, France; the most northern of the important MÉDOC wine communes. Located on soil rich in clay, Saint-Estèphe's vineyards give especially robust and full-bodied red wines, perhaps a bit

302

less scented and complex than some other Médocs but possessing a great deal of authority; they age well and are long-lived.

Saint-Estèphe's best wine estates or CHÂTEAUX are traditionally famous and were included in the 1855 classification of the Médoc. *Seconds Crus* (Second Growths): Cos d'Estournel and Montrose. *Troisième Cru* (Third Growth): Calon-Ségur. *Quatrième Cru* (Fourth Growth): Lafon-Rochet. *Cinquième Cru* (Fifth Growth): Cos-Labory. In addition, there are several outstanding châteaux that were not classified in 1855 but which now produce wine worthy of classified growth status, of which perhaps the most notable are: de Pez, Phélan-Ségur, Meyney, Les Ormes-de-Pez, Tronquoy-Lalande, Marbuzet, and Haut-Marbuzet.

Saint-Georges-Saint-Émilion *(San Zhorzh' Sahnt Eh-meel-lyon')*: Wine commune near the SAINT-ÉMILION region east of BORDEAUX, named for its most famous wine estate, Château Saint-Georges.

Saint-Joseph *(San Zho-seff')*: Wine region in the northern RHÔNE River valley, France, noted for its sturdy, full-bodied red wines made from the Syrah grape, there is also some white wine made in Saint-Joseph, but it is less important. The Saint-Joseph vineyards lie on the right bank of the Rhône opposite the famous vineyards of HERMITAGE; total production averages some 98,000 cases annually.

Saint-Julien *(San Jule'-yan)*: One of the most famous wine communes in the HAUT-MÉDOC district, located some 20 miles north of the city of BORDEAUX. Celebrated for its fine red wines, Saint-Julien has the largest number of wine estates (CHÂTEAUX) per square mile of any Haut-Médoc wine commune, although it is the smallest; the equivalent of some 300,000 cases is produced in an average year.

An adjoining commune, Saint-Laurent, lies just to the west of Saint-Julien but its wines

303

may only be sold under the name "Haut-Médoc." In the following list of Saint-Julien châteaux as ranked in the 1855 classification of the Médoc, the Saint-Laurent estates have been marked with an asterisk. *Seconds Crus* (Second Growths): Léoville Las-Cases, Léoville-Poyferré, Léoville-Barton, Gruaud-Larose, Ducru-Beaucaillou. *Troisièmes Crus* (Third Growths): Lagrange, Langoa-Barton. *Quatrièmes Crus* (Fourth Growths): Saint-Pierre-Sevaistre, Talbot, Branaire (Duluc-Ducru), La Tour-Carnet*, Beychevelle. *Cinquièmes Crus* (Fifth Growths): Belgrave* and Camensac*. In addition, there are several outstanding châteaux that were not officially classified in 1855 but now produce wine equal to that of many classified growths; the most renowned is Gloria, followed by du Glana, Peymartin, Larose-Trintaudon*, Terrey-Gros-Cailloux, and Moulin-Riche.

Saint-Laurent: see SAINT-JULIEN.

Saint-Péray *(San Pay-ray')*: Wine region in the RHÔNE River valley, noted for its white wines made from Roussanne and Marsanne grapes. The most famous Saint-Pérays are sparkling wines *(vin mousseux)*, bottle-fermented by the traditional CHAMPAGNE process; there are also good still white wines and some sweet white wines as well. Saint-Pérays are well-known in France but are not widely exported to the U.S.; average production of all types amounts to some 20,000 cases a year.

Saint-Romain *(San Ro-man')*: Secondary wine commune in the CÔTE DE BEAUNE, Burgundy, located in the hilly country near MEURSAULT. Although Saint-Romain is not a well-known wine name, the vineyards are well-exposed and produce good red and white wines from Pinot Noir and Chardonnay, sold either under the name Saint-Romain or as CÔTE DE BEAUNE-VILLAGES. Total production averages some 24,000 cases annually.

Saint-Saphorin *(San Saf'-aw-ran):* Vineyard area in the district of LAVAUX, Switzerland, located on the north shore of Lake Geneva near the city of Montreaux. Along with the vineyards of DÉZALEY just to the west, Saint-Saphorin makes some of the best white wines of Switzerland, produced from the Dorin (Chasselas) grape.

Saint-Véran *(San Vay-rawn'):* White wine district in the MÂCONNAIS region, southern Burgundy; a new place-name created in 1971 by the French government. The vineyard area entitled to the APPELLATION CONTRÔLÉE Saint-Véran includes the wine communes of Chasselas, Leynes and Chânes near the southern border of the famous district of POUILLY-FUISSÉ, as well as Davayé and Prissé to the north; before the name Saint-Véran was adopted, these communes could only sell their wines as "Beaujolais Blanc" or "Mâcon Blanc." Made from the same Chardonnay grape as Pouilly-Fuissé, Saint-Véran has become popular throughout France and the U.S.; it is similar to Pouilly-Fuissé and much less expensive. Some 140,000 cases are produced each year.

Sainte-Croix-du-Mont *(Sahnt Crwa dew Mawn'):* White wine region in BORDEAUX located on the GARONNE River near the famous vineyards of SAUTERNES. Sainte-Croix-du-Mont specializes in sweet white wines made from late-harvested Sémillon, Sauvignon Blanc and Muscadelle grapes; they are similar to Sauternes but are generally less sweet and not well-known outside the region. Total production averages some 166,500 cases annually.

Salmanazar: The largest commercially available wine bottle, with a capacity of twelve ordinary bottles; used by some producers in the French CHAMPAGNE distict.

San Benito: County and wine district in central California, located east of the city of Salinas along the Coast Range mountains. San

Benito was not an important wine region until the 1960s, when urban expansion to the north forced many California wineries to look for new areas for their vineyards. Over 4,500 acres of vineyard have been planted; the largest portion, at Paicines, is owned and managed by Almadén Vineyards. An unusual lime outcropping near the town of Hollister afforded Calera Wine Company the opportunity to make superb Pinot Noir, considered by many experts to be among the state's best. Cygnet Cellars and Enz Vineyards nearby are similarly small but outstanding wineries.

Sancerre (*Sahn'-sair*): Famous white wine region in the upper LOIRE River valley, France, located in the department of Cher near the village of POUILLY-SUR-LOIRE. Made from the same Sauvignon Blanc (*Blanc Fumé*) grape as the celebrated POUILLY-FUMÉ produced nearby, Sancerre is similar and is usually a bit rounder and sooner to mature; very dry and with a fresh, grapey quality, it is usually consumed during its first year. The hilltop village of Sancerre is the region's center, but 14 communes produce wine under the APPELLATION CONTRÓLÉE Sancerre; among the most famous are CHAVIGNOL, Bué, Verdigny, Sury-en-Vaux, Amigny, Menetou Ratel, Crézancy, Champtin, Reigny, and Ménétréol. Combined, there are over 3,000 acres in Sancerre; total production averages some 500,000 cases annually. In addition, some Pinot Noir is also grown in Sancerre, which yields a sturdy red and perhaps an even better rosé wine, which has recently become just as popular as the white wine. Certain outstanding vineyards (*lieux-dits*) produce a finer quality Sancerre than the average, and occasionally these wines will be seen in the United States: Les Monts-Damnés, in Chavignol; Clos de la Poussie, Les Bouffants, Domaine de la Moussière (Mellot), Chêne Marchand, Le Paradis, Cou de Brault, Pain Perdu, Clos de la Perrière (Archambault),

Chémarin, Les Vallées, Côte de Champtin, La Grande Côte, and Cul de Beaujeu.

Sangiovese *(San-gee-oh-vay′-say)*: Fine quality red wine grape grown in central Italy, used in the region of TUSCANY for some of Italy's most famous red wines. In blends it is the principal variety used for CHIANTI and for the VINO NOBILE DI MONTEPULCIANO; a related variety is used for BRUNELLO DI MONTALCINO. In Tuscany this grape is sometimes called "San Gioveto," but Sangiovese is the preferred spelling outside Tuscany. Some experimental plantings have been made in California.

Sangria *(San-gree′-ah)*: Wine and fruit punch, originally native to Spain but now very popular in the U.S. The traditional recipe for Sangria calls for the juice of fresh Valencia oranges blended with a light red wine, which is mixed with a little sugar, lemon juice and soda water and served in a punch bowl garnished with fresh fruit.

San Luis Obispo: City and county in central California, about midway between San Francisco and Los Angeles. A fairly cool area, San Luis Obispo has approximately 4,700 acres under vines and a number of important new wineries. Probably the largest of these is the Lawrence Winery, founded in 1979 and already a major producer in the area; Hoffman Mountain Ranch (HMR), near the town of Paso Robles, is particularly noted for Cabernet Sauvignon and Pinot Noir. York Mountain Winery, and Pesenti Winery, near Templeton, have been producing quality wines for decades. Newcomers to the area include Chamisal Vineyard, Estrella River Winery near Paso Robles, Old Casteel Vineyards, Pendleton Winery, and Mastantuóno.

San Severo *(San Say-vair′-ro)*: Good red, white and rosé wines produced in the region of APULIA (Puglia), Italy, near the town of Foggia. San Severo was originally famous for its white

307

wines, but in recent years the reds and rosés have greatly improved. Made primarily from Bombino and Trebbiano grapes, the white is pale-gold in color and has a clean, fresh taste; the red, made from Montepulciano, is sturdy and ages well.

Santa Barbara: County and city northwest of Los Angeles, California, with over 7,000 acres of vineyard, most of them planted only recently. Santa Barbara's close proximity to the coast makes it a prime viticultural area, especially for white wines; the Firestone Vineyard in Los Olivos, established by Brooks Firestone of the famous tire manufacturing family, is a representative example of the rapid growth and success of many wineries in the area. Zaca Mesa Winery nearby is another rising star, with many notable wines to their credit. In recent years the area has added Brander Winery, La Zaca, Sanford & Benedict, J. Carey Cellars, Copenhagen Cellars, Santa Barbara Winery, Santa Ynez Valley Winery, and Rancho Sisquoc to the roster of notable producers.

Santa Clara: County south of San Francisco Bay, California; historically one of the state's most important wine regions, though today many of the vineyards are seriously threatened by urban expansion—especially around the city of San Jose. Some 1,500 acres of vines endure, however, and from prime hillside vineyards, some exceptional wines are produced. One of the nation's largest and most famous wineries, Almadén, is headquartered in Los Gatos but has most of their vineyards in SAN BENITO to the south; recently, some select wines under their special Charles LeFranc label have been outstanding. Paul Masson Winery, a traditional name in the area, is now owned by Seagram's and is steadily producing some high-quality wines. Mirassou, San Martin and the Novitiate of Los Gatos are other major producers in the area; on a much smaller scale, some of the nation's most celebrated Zinfandels have been produced by winemaker Paul Draper at Ridge Vineyards in Cupertino, and the late Martin Ray, whose family continues his winery near Saratoga, was a legendary producer of Chardonnay and Pinot Noir. Mt. Eden Vineyards nearby enjoys much of the same reputation. Gemello Winery has produced excellent red wines for decades; more recently, Turgeon & Lohr Winery (J. Lohr) in San Jose have looked to MONTEREY in the south for much of their grapes.

In the south section of the county, near Hecker Pass and Gilroy, there is a traditional cluster of wineries, many still family-owned, that have produced wine for decades. Bertero, Fortino Winery, Emilio Guglielmo, Hecker Pass Winery, Kirigin Cellars, Pedrizzetti Winery and Richert Cellars are among the better-known producers in this area. In recent years Thomas Kruse, Congress Springs Winery in Saratoga, and Silver Mountain in Los Gatos have emerged to continue the traditions of Santa Clara as a fine wine region.

Santa Cruz: Small but historic wine-producing county in California southwest of San Francisco—with less than 100 acres of vineyard, but several notable wineries, many of which produce exceptional wines. Santa Cruz overlooks Monterey Bay, and the ocean exerts a strong maritime influence on the area, making the climate cool and temperate. Bargetto Winery in Soquel is one of the nation's most famous fruit wine producers, but they make good table wine also; the late San Francisco attorney Chafee Hall established the Hallcrest Vineyard in the 1940s at Felton, which in 1976 became known as Felton-Empire, now one of California's foremost producers of White Riesling. David Bruce Winery is almost legendary; for decades San Jose dermatologist Dr. David Bruce has made exceptional Chardonnay, Cabernet Sauvignon and Zinfandel. Roudon-Smith Vineyards in Santa Cruz is another

309

outstanding producer. Recently Frick Winery, Grover Gulch, River Run Vintners, Santa Cruz Mountain Vineyards, Sunrise, and Richard Smothers' Vine Hill Wines have added to the county's growing number of wineries.

Santa Maddalena (*Santa Mad-lay'-nah*): Light, attractive red wine from the region of ALTO ADIGE, northern Italy. Produced from the Schiava grape grown near the town of Bolzano, Santa Maddalena is considered one of the best Alto Adige red wines; unlike many northern Italian reds, it is best when consumed rather young—usually before it is three years old. It was rated D.O.C. in 1971.

Santenay (*Sahnt'-nay*): Wine commune in the CÔTE DE BEAUNE, Burgundy, with some 950 acres of vineyard; the most southern of the many important communes along that famous hillside. Both red and white wines are produced in Santenay; the reds are superior and are much more important commercially. Made from the Pinot Noir, red Santenays are generally rather light and should be drunk young; being not as well-known as some other Burgundies, many of them are excellent value. Certain fine Santenay vineyards have been rated Premier Cru (First Growth); the most famous is Gravières, but Beauregard, La Comme, Clos Rousseau and La Maladière also produce good wines. Average production is about 93,000 cases annually.

Sardinia (Italian, **Sardegna**): Mountainous island in the Tyrrhenian Sea, located about 125 miles off the west coast of Italy. Politically a part of Italy, Sardinia has over 150,000 acres of vineyards and grows many of the same fine grape varieties as the Italian mainland. Several of Sardinia's better wines have recently been granted a D.O.C. rating; among the more notable white wines is the firm, dry Vernaccia di Oristano; Nuragus di Cagliari, another good white, is lighter. The seaport town of Cagliari produces an interesting sweet wine, Moscato di Cagliari; the reds—Cannonau and Oliena—tend to be rather heavy and full-bodied. Sardinian wines are not widely-exported, even to Italy, but as a result of the recent D.O.C. approval exports of quality wines are increasing.

Sassella (*Sas-sell′-ah*): Fine red wine from the region of LOMBARDY, Italy; one of the better wines of the VALTELLINA district. Its center of production is near the town of Sondrio, not far from Lake Como. Made from the Nebbiolo grape, which in the Valtellina is called Chiavennasca, Sassella is a sturdy, scented red wine that ages particularly well.

Saumur (*So-mur′*): City of some 33,000 in the lower LOIRE River valley, France; one of the leading wine towns in that area. Dominated by a fine old château that overlooks the Loire, the Saumur vineyards are planted in several different wine grapes. Wines are sold under two APPELLATION CONTRÔLÉES, Saumur and Coteaux de Saumur, of which the former is much more important.

The white Saumurs made from the Chenin Blanc are perhaps the best; they usually have an agreeable trace of sweetness, and are long-lived. Many white Saumur wines are converted into sparkling wines (*vins mousseux*), bottle-fermented by the traditional CHAMPAGNE process, and some are among the best sparkling wines produced outside of the Champagne district. A large quantity of rosé wine made from Cabernet Franc is also produced in Saumur, raising the production of all Saumur wines to more than a million cases.

Just to the west of Saumur is the little village of CHAMPIGNY, where primarily red Cabernet Franc grapes are grown; some of the better red wines of the Loire valley are made there. These sturdy red wines are usually sold as "Champigny" or "Saumur-Champigny," as very little red wine is exported under the name

311

Saumur. About 280,000 cases of Saumur-Champigny are produced each year.

Sauternes (French, *So-tairn'*): Well-known trade name for sweet white wine; specifically, the unique and special product of the vineyards of Sauternes in the BORDEAUX region, France, produced from successive late picking of overripe grapes. The name "Haut-Sauternes" has no legal significance, although some shippers use it to designate a superior wine.

The vineyards of Sauternes are located some 25 miles southeast of the city of Bordeaux, and extend over about 4,700 acres planted in Sémillon, Sauvignon Blanc and Muscadelle grapes. There are several associated wine communes in the Sauternes district; from north to south, these communes include: BARSAC, Preignac, Bommes, Sauternes, and Fargues. Wine from each of these communes is legally entitled to the name Sauternes; however, wine from Barsac is usually sold under the name Barsac. Sweet white Barsacs are generally a shade drier than other Sauternes.

The luscious sweetness of a good Sauternes is a result of the grapes being harvested late, when they are overripe. As the grapes ripen, a mold known as BOTRYTIS CINEREA gradually forms on the skins. This mold is normally destructive in most wine regions, as it causes the grapes to rot. But in the Sauternes district the mold is welcomed, for under the right conditions it does not induce rot but instead causes the grape skins to shrink and the juice to be concentrated. The French acknowledge the beneficial action of Botrytis by calling it "pourriture noble" or "noble mold."

But there are risks in waiting for Botrytis to develop. In many vintages the mold does not develop to the required degree; hence the risk of a failed vintage in Sauternes is very high. The mold also does not mature evenly in the vineyards, and several pickings have to be performed so as to gather all the grapes that have rotted nobly. Only certain estates or CHÂTEAUX have the necessary resources to do this, and often as many as a dozen pickings are required. The grapes are pressed immediately after picking, and after the harvest the wines from each picking are blended and aged before being sold. In the trade, Sauternes can be made commercially by arresting the fermentation before all the sugar is converted into alcohol, either by filtration or by adding sulfur. But the result never equals that of the methodical, successive pickings that only the best châteaux can afford to employ.

The most famous Sauternes châteaux were classified in 1855 into two groups or CRUS (growths), based on the prices their wines were fetching in the trade. The leading château is YQUEM, ranked as a Grand Premier Cru (Great First Growth), which usually produces some of the fullest, sweetest and most expensive of all Sauternes. (In the following group of classified Sauternes châteaux, the Barsac estates have been identified with an asterisk). *Premiers Crus* (First Growths): La Tour-Blanche, Lafaurie-Peyraguey, Clos Haut-Peyraguey, Rayne-Vigneau, Suduiraut, Coutet*, Climens*, Guiraud, Rieussec, Rabaud-Promis, and Sigalas-Rabaud. *Deuxiemes Crus* (Second Growths): de Myrat*, Doisy-Daëne*, Doisy-Védrines*, d'Arche, Filhot, Broustet*, Nairac*, Caillou*, Suau*, de Malle, Romer, and Lamothe.

Outside of France, the name Sauternes has become a GENERIC term describing any sweet or semi-sweet white wine. U.S. labeling law allows American wines to be called "sauterne," but the true place of origin must be specified (e.g., California sauterne) and the name is usually spelled without the final "s."

Sauvignon Blanc (*So'-veen-yawn Blawn'*): Excellent white wine grape, grown in many regions in France and in other countries as well. In BORDEAUX it is used along with the Sémillon for the fine dry white GRAVES and ENTRE-

313

DEUX-MERS; the Sauvignon Blanc is also grown for the famous sweet wines of SAUTERNES, BARSAC, CÉRONS and SAINTE-CROIX-DU-MONT. Further inland, in the upper LOIRE River valley, it gives the dry white wines of POUILLY-FUMÉ and SANCERRE. In the Loire region wines made from Sauvignon Blanc are sometimes called "Blanc Fumé" in the acknowledgement of their faint, "smoky" qualities.

Over 7,200 acres of Sauvignon Blanc have been planted in California, and the grape gives outstanding dry white wines—particularly in cool coastal districts. Good wines from Sauvignon Blanc have been made in other states as well, most successfully from gravelly soil.

Savennières *(Sav-ven-yair')*: Outstanding white wine region in the lower LOIRE River valley, France, near the village of Rochefort-sur-Loire. The vineyards of Savennières produce some of the finest dry white wines of the Loire made from the Chenin Blanc grape; they are similar to VOUVRAYS but are generally drier and perhaps even more scented.

The APPELLATION CONTRÔLÉE Savennières includes three notable vineyards that generally produce wines under their own names: the diminutive Coulée de Serrant, at 10 acres large one of the smallest vineyards in France; the Roche Aux Moines (60 acres), and the Clos du Papillon. The total area under vines in Savennières is about 450 acres; production averages some 10,000 cases annually.

Savigny-Les-Beaune *(Sav'-een-yee Lay Bone')*: Little wine village in the northern CÔTE DE BEAUNE, Burgundy, located along a quaint river valley just to the northwest of the city of BEAUNE. Savigny's vineyards adjoin those of Beaune and share many of the same outstanding characteristics; most are planted in Pinot Noir and produce especially light, fruity red wines, but a little white wine is also made from Chardonnay. The wines typically develop very quickly but age well.

Certain famous vineyards in Savigny have been rated Premier Cru (First Growth); the most celebrated is Les Vergelesses, which extends into the neighboring commune of PERNAND-VERGELESSES, but Marconnets (shared by Beaune), Lavières, Jarrons, Clos des Guettes, Aux Gravains and Dominode can also produce exceptional wines. Because the wines are not well-known outside the region, many Savignys from good producers are often excellent value. The area under vines is about 945 acres, and total production often exceeds some 113,000 cases annually.

Scharzhofberg *(Shartz'-hawf-bairg):* Outstanding vineyard in the SAAR River valley, Germany, located near the famous wine town of WILTINGEN. The vineyard faces south on a steep, slate hillside and has some 30 acres planted in Riesling; in great vintages the finely-scented and complex white wines it produces are without peer. The most famous Scharzhofberg producer is Egon Müller (proprietor of the Scharzhof, an ancient manor house at the foot of the vineyard), but excellent examples of Scharzhofberger are also made by the Vereinigte Hospitien, the Hohe Domkirche of Trier the von Kesselstatt estate, and Van Volxem.

Schaumwein *(Showm'-vine):* German for "sparkling wine." By international agreement, German vintners do not use the word "champagne" to identify their sparkling wines; under the German wine law, they are instead called either Schaumwein or SEKT. At present, there are three classifications in effect for German sparkling wines.

—*Schaumwein:* Base wines must reach a minimum of 8.5% alcohol; the finished product must be 9.5%. Imported sparkling wine must be identified as Schaumwein, followed by the name of the country in question.

—*Qualitätsschauwein* or *Sekt* or *Deutscher Sekt:* Base wines must reach a minimum of 9%

315

alcohol; the finished product must be 10%. Minimum pressure after fermentation must be 3.5 atmospheres. The minimum aging period prior to release is nine months, and the minimum period of fermentation in the presence of yeasts is 60 days. Wines that are the product of Germany may be labeled "Deutscher Sekt." As is the case with QUALITÄTSWEIN, a government taste examination applies, along with an A.P. number.

—*Qualitätsschaumwein b.A.*: 100% of the wine must come from any of the 11 designated wine growing regions (ANBAUGEBIETE). Smaller geographical units, such as BEREICH, GROSS-LAGE, or EINZELLAGE, may appear if desired. Like regular Qualitätsschaumwein, an official taste examination is performed prior to release, except that the minimum test score must be higher.

None of these categories stipulate the three principal methods of sparkling wine production: bottle-fermentation (MÉTHODE CHAMPEN-OISE), TRANSFER PROCESS, or CHARMAT (bulk) PROCESS. If no indication is given, the second fermentation may be assumed to have been bulk process.

Scheurebe *(Shoy'-ray-buh)*: Promising new white grape variety developed in Germany. A cross between the Riesling and the Silvaner, the Scheurebe is planted primarily in the RHEINGAU and RHEINHESSEN districts and gives characteristically full-bodied white wines with a pronounced bouquet.

Schiava *(Ski-ah'-va)*: Red wine grape grown in the TRENTINO and ALTO ADIGE regions, northern Italy, where it is used for the light red wines of CALDARO and SANTA MADDALENA.

Schillerwein *(Shil'-ler-vine)*: Light red wine produced from red and white grapes pressed together, made in the WÜRTTEMBERG region in Germany. The name derives not from the poet Schiller but from the verb *schillern*, which means "shimmer"; the wine is undistinguished and is rarely seen outside Württemberg.

Schloss (*Shlawss*): German for "castle"; in relation to wine, a vineyard estate—roughly equivalent to the French CHÂTEAU.

Schloss Böckelheim (*Shlawss Berk'-el-heim*): Renowned wine town on the NAHE River, Germany; among the best of that district. Its 136 acres of vineyard are mostly planted in Riesling and face south near an old copper mine—identified in the name of one of the leading vineyards or EINZELLAGEN, Kupfergrube, which means "copper mine." Other fine Schloss Böckelheim Einzellagen include: Königsfels, Felsenberg, Heimberg, In den Felsen, and Mühlberg.

Because of the town's great fame, the 1971 German Wine Law authorized Schloss Böckelheim to also be the name of a BEREICH (subregion) including several other wine towns; wines from the best vineyards, therefore, are not sold merely as "Schloss Böckelheimer" but Schloss Böckelheimer followed by the name of the Einzellage in question. A "Schloss Böckelheimer" without this qualification may be assumed to be a blended regional wine, produced from dozens of villages within the Schloss Böckelheim Bereich.

Schloss Johannisberg: see JOHANNISBERG, SCHLOSS.

Schloss Vollrads: see VOLLRADS, SCHLOSS.

Scuppernong: Native American white grape variety of the Muscadine family, belonging to the sub-genus *Rotundifolia*. It is widely grown in the Carolinas and in Georgia to make rather full-bodied sweet wine, although sugar is generally added to give the required sweetness.

Sec (*Seck*): French for "dry." Officially, this term does not mean what it implies: in the French CHAMPAGNE region, a wine labeled Sec is not dry but in fact semi-dry; it may legally contain up to 4% residual sugar resulting from the final shipping dosage (LIQUEUR D'EXPÉDITION). Those who prefer drier Champagnes should select wines labeled BRUT or EXTRA DRY, which contain less than 1% and 3% residual sugar, respectively.

Elsewhere in France, still white wines labeled sec will usually be dry.

Secco *(Say′-co):* Italian for "dry." Wines labeled *secco* will be less sweet than those labeled *abboccato* (semi-dry) or *amabile* (sweet).

Sediment: Deposits in wine usually fall into two categories: precipitated matter in a mature wine resulting from the aging process; and material thrown off by a wine after it has been exposed to extreme temperature changes. The first kind of sediment can be termed normal and appropriate, since through the loss of dissolved, coarse substances mature wine becomes more palatable and pleasant to drink. With the second type of sedimentation, the aging process is quickened and the wine may not exhibit proper shelf life or potential for further development.

The amount of sediment in a wine can be reduced by successive RACKINGS in cask before bottling. Later on, FILTRATION and FINING are also helpful in reducing a wine's sediment. Owing to their greater degree of dissolved tannin and pigments, red wines will throw off more sediment as they age, and the greater degree of extract they contain, the more sediment will be formed. Virtually all fine wines display some sediment after bottle aging.

Chemically, sediment in wine is brought about by the slow reaction and eventual precipitation of fruit acids, tannins, tartrates and other compounds as the wine ages in bottle. Full-bodied red wines usually contain a high degree of tannin, which is shed as a brownish deposit during the aging process. Some wines will occasionally develop chunks or clusters of colorless crystals known as tartrates or bi-tartrates, especially if exposed to cold temperatures. Refrigeration or cold-stabilization of the wine prior to release at the winery will minimize this, even though tartrate crystals are tasteless and harmless, and may redissolve into the wine if it is brought to a warmer environment. Most sediment, however, is unpleasant to the taste and should be separated from the wine before serving. See DECANT.

Seibel (*Sigh'-bel*): Group of French HYBRID grape varieties, produced by crossing European species of VINIFERA varieties with American vines. Each of the more important hybrids is listed in this dictionary, with the official Seibel identification number that relates to the original parents. They are named for the famous French grape hybridizer Albert Seibel (1844-1936), who created hundreds of successful varieties that later became famous under different names.

Sekt: German for "sparkling wine." As with SCHAUMWEIN, German sparkling wines are not called champagne as a result of an international agreement. The term Sekt has become roughly interchangeable with Schaumwein, but technically the latter term denotes a higher quality sparkling wine. Sweetness or residual sugar in Sekt conforms to the following grades: *Herb* (brut), 0 - 1.5%; *Sehr Trocken* (extra dry, extra sec), 1.2 - 2% *Trocken* (dry, sec), 1.7 - 3.5%; *Halbtrocken* (demi-sec, medium dry), 3.3 - 5%; *Mild* (doux), above 5%.

Sémillon (*Say'-me-yawn*): Fine white grape variety grown in the BORDEAUX region, France, and in many other parts of the world. It is one of the few varieties susceptible to the "noble mold" (see BOTRYTIS CINEREA), and is thus ideally suited to the making of luscious sweet wines in SAUTERNES, BARSAC, and CÉRONS. In conjunction with the Sauvignon Blanc it is also used to make dry white GRAVES and ENTRE-DEUX-MERS. Further inland, it is grown

319

ENTRE-DEUX-MERS. Further inland, it is grown for the wines of MONBAZILLAC. In Australia, where it is successful, wines made from Sémillon are often labeled "Riesling," supposedly because they are similar in style. About 3,000 acres of Sémillon have been planted in California, and a wide variety of good dry and semi-dry Sémillon wines are produced there; fine Sémillons have also been made in Washington State.

Sercial *(Sair'-see-al):* The palest and driest kind of MADEIRA, produced from Sercial grapes grown on the uppermost slopes of the island of Madeira.

Serrig *(Sair'-rig):* Little-known but outstanding wine village in the SAAR region, Germany. Its 163 acres of vineyard are planted almost entirely in Riesling and in great vintages its fine white wines are among the Saar's best; in rainy years, however, Serrigers can be rather acidic. The leading vineyard (EINZELLAGE) is Vogelsang, or "bird's song"; other fine Serrig Einzellagen include: Schloss Saarfelser Schlossberg, Antoniusberg, Heiligenborn, Hoeppslei, Herrenberg, and Würtzberg.

Sèvre-et-Maine *(Sevr Eh Main'):* One of the delimited production zones for the MUSCADET region in the lower LOIRE River valley, France; named for two rivers that flow into the Loire near Nantes. Wines from the region are entitled to the APPELLATION CONTRÔLÉE "Muscadet de Sèvre-et-Maine"; the wines differ somewhat from those of the associated "Coteaux de la Loire" region to the east, tending to mature earlier in most vintages.

Seyssel *(Say-sell'):* Light, fresh dry white wine produced in the region of Savoie (Savoy) in northeastern France, near Lake Geneva. Made from the Roussette grape, Seyssel may be either a good still wine or a perhaps even better sparkling wine (*vin mousseux*), bottle-fermented by the traditional CHAMPAGNE process. Some

Seyssel *mousseux* are among the finest sparkling wines produced outside the Champagne region. The equivalent of some 26,000 cases is produced annually.

Seyval Blanc (*Seyve-Villard 5276*): Popular white French HYBRID grape variety, grown all over the eastern and midwestern United States and Canada; originally developed from two Seibel hybrids, S. 5656 and S. 4986. Owing to its winter hardiness and productivity, Seyval Blanc has become one of the most popular French hybrids; it produces a high-quality white wine, with flavor and bouquet.

Sfursat (*Sfoor-tsot'*): Rare and especially full-bodied red wine from the VALTELLINA district in northern Italy, produced from selected Nebbiolo grapes that have been left to dry in airy lofts, for a period of up to two weeks after picking. Also called Sforzato or Sfurzat, these fine wines are similar to the RECIOTOS of the VENETO district, except that they are usually richer, darker in color and more powerful—often 14% alcohol or more. Sfursats take longer to mature than regular Valtellinas and live much longer; since a considerable volume of juice is lost during the drying period, the wines are quite expensive but are well worth it.

Sherry: Internationally famous FORTIFIED WINE; specifically, the product of the seaport city of Jerez de la Frontera in southern Andalusia, Spain, produced from 20,000 acres of vineyard planted on soil unique to the area. The name Sherry is derived from Jerez and hence is a place-name of geographic origin; wines called sherry are made all over the world—notably in Australia, South Africa, and the U.S.—but few are quite like the authentic product of southwestern Spain.

Like several other fine Spanish wines, Sherry is strictly controlled by the laws of *Denominación de Origen*, an official government guarantee of the wine's quality. On most Sherries the *Donominación de Origen* seal is affixed to the bottle, identifying the wine as genuine Sherry. The laws have also delimited the classic production zone according to the soil. The best soils for Sherry are known as *albarizas*, which contain a high chalk content vital to the wine's finesse; certain *pagos* (districts) of albarizas—Carrascal, Macharnudo, Añina, Balbaina, and Miraflores—are famous, but these names rarely appear on wine labels. Soils richer in clay are known as *barros*, which produce a heavier wine; the sandier soils, *arenas*, are the most productive but are on the whole less good than the other two.

Two principal grape varieties are grown in the Sherry country. The most important is the Palomino, also known by its local name Listán, which thrives on the chalky albarizas and produces the best dry Sherries. The other leading variety is the Pedro Ximénez, which is normally set aside after picking to dry on straw mats: the concentrated juice is used for making sweet Sherries.

Like other fortified wines, the alcoholic content of Sherry is largely the result of an addition of high-proof brandy, but several other factors give the wines their unique characteristics. At the time of the grape harvest, the grapes are crushed in large troughs or *lagares*—sometimes still by treading with the feet—and then the expressed must is allowed to ferment. During the winter the wines are stored in *criaderas* or "nurseries," where they are watched carefully; each cask is individually graded by means of chalk marks, or *rayas*. For reasons that are still only partly understood, some Sherries when in cask develop a white, frothy yeast known as FLOR. Occurring spontaneously and only in certain casks, the flor yeast will produce fine, light pale wines; casks of Sherry that do not develop flor will be used for making dark, full-bodied wines. This yeast is only native to a few wine regions, and many

322

other areas that produce sherries from flor must import the yeast.

Another technique used in making Sherry is the long process of blending known as the SOLERA system. Every fall in the Sherry country, the new wines are brought to great warehouses or BODEGAS, where they are set aside to age. But via the solera method the casks are stacked in tiers so that their contents are gradually blended with the wines of many different vintages. The solera system assures that each grade of Sherry will be constant and unchanging year after year. Thus there is no such thing as "vintage Sherry" because through the solera system the casks are constantly being replenished by younger wines as they age. (The year that the solera was established is sometimes specified for a Sherry, but this is of course not the same thing as a vintage year.)

There are five basic types of Sherry. The palest and driest wine is usually MANZANILLA, produced around the associated city of Sanlúcar de Barrameda to the northwest of Jerez. Similar—but generally not quite as auterely dry—is FINO, produced from casks displaying the flor yeast. Fino and Manzanilla are among the few wines whose alcoholic strength actually increases slightly as they age in cask, owing to evaporation, and because they only receive a very small addition of brandy they are especially fragrant and delicate.

Slightly darker and less dry than a Fino is AMONTILLADO, prized for its unique "nutty" qualities; the best Amontillados are Finos that have taken on a darker color and richer flavor. Fuller still is OLOROSO, which comes from casks that did not develop the flor yeast. Olorosos are sweeter than Finos, but in their natural state they are dry; the sweetness is added later. The sweetest Sherries are "Cream" Sherries, which are fine old Olorosos that have been sweetened by a grape concentrate called *dulce*, produced by adding partially fermented grape must into casks containing brandy. Sometimes

323

brandy is added to the juice of selected Pedro Ximénez grapes to make a very sweet wine called "P.X." These special wines are occasionally set aside and sold on their own, rather than being used for Cream Sherries, but unfortunately they are very rare in the trade.

Leading producers of Sherry that export their wines in quantity to the U.S. include: Gonzalez Byass, Williams & Humbert (makers of Dry Sack), Sandeman, Pedro Domecq, Bodegas Osborne (Duff Gordon), Wisdom & Warter, Valdespino, Pemartin, Bodegas Sanchez, and Ferenando de Terry.

Other countries—including the U.S.—make similar kinds of sherry, and California actually produces over four times as much sherry as is made in the Spanish Sherry district. But only a little American sherry is made with flor yeast and aged by the solera system; inexpensive sherries are produced from table or raisin grapes, and the wine is "baked" artificially at high temperature so as to take on a caramel color and a sherry-like flavor. However, quality sherries are produced by many firms, and a new technique called "submerged-culture flor process" is simultaneously reducing the time needed to make a good sherry and improving the flavor. The yeast is introduced into the wine and blended by agitation, rather than being allowed to settle on the surface.

Sicily (Italian, **Sicilia,** pronounced *Si-chee′-lee-ah*): The largest island in the Mediterranean Sea, some 9,680 square miles in size; also a major wine region. There are over 416,000 acres of wine grapes planted in Sicily, and the warm climate is favorable to vineyards, making wine Sicily's second most valuable export, after citrus fruits.

Sicily has only been exporting significant quantities of wines to the U.S. in recent years, but many of her better wines have received D.O.C. listings lately, and exports are sure to increase as a result. Three Sicilian wines are prominent in the wine trade: MARSALA, the most famous FORTIFIED WINE of Italy, produced in the northwest of Sicily around the town of the same name; ETNA, good red, white and rosé wines made on the slopes of Mt. Etna, an active volcano; and CORVO, especially the select bottlings from the estate of the Dukes of Salaparuta. Besides Marsala, Sicily also makes some excellent dessert wines that deserve to be better known. The Malvasia di Lipari, produced on the little Isles of Lipari off the north coast, and the Moscato di Siracusa, grown near the ancient city of Siracusa along Sicily's east coast, have been famous for centuries but were only recently granted D.O.C. status.

Silvaner: The German spelling of SYLVANER.

Soave *(So-ah'-vay):* Perhaps the most famous white wine of Italy, and deservedly so; produced in the region of VENETO to the east of the city of Verona. A wine best consumed during its first or second year, Soave has a pale gold color and a fresh, clean taste; the chief grape variety is Garganega, although a little Trebbiano is customarily added. The region has over 15,000 acres of vineyard.

Soave is traditionally bottled in a green, fluted bottle. If the wine was produced in the central and best part of the D.O.C. region— including the towns of Soave, Monteforte and Costalunga—it is allowed the distinction of "Soave Classico." Soave with an alcoholic strength in excess of 10.5% may also be labeled "Soave Superiore." A major part of the production is controlled by the Cantina Sociale di Soave, one of the largest wine cooperatives in Europe.

Solera *(So-lair'-ah):* A system used in the Spanish SHERRY region for blending the wines of different vintages, so as to insure a uniform output year after year. After various Sherries have been selected according to their quality and characteristics, they are set aside in a three-

325

tiered row of casks: older wines on the bottom, so that the young wines in the uppermost row can be brought down to blend with the older wines. By the nature of the solera system there can thus be no such thing as "vintage sherry," at least commercially, because the wines of different vintages are constantly being blended.

Although it originated in the Sherry district, the solera system is now standard in several other Spanish regions and in many parts of the world. It improves the wines of MÁLAGA and MONTILLA, as well as those of the island of MADEIRA; the better wines of MARSALA also go through a solera, as do some of the best American sherries.

Sonoma: One of California's many fine wine districts; a county and city located just to the north of San Francisco, with much of its boundary bordering the Pacific Ocean. Shaped roughly like a wedge, Sonoma County has a wide diversity of climates, ranging from cool to very warm in summer; the area involved one of the largest expansions in new wineries during the 1970s of any California wine district. Vineyards were first planted in Sonoma over a century ago, and the county now has about 28,000 acres of vineyards. Thus, along with NAPA county, which borders to the east, Sonoma can be ranked in the forefront of California's premium wine production.

Sonoma's climatic diversity results from its proximity to the coast, and also the Coast Range Mountains, which border Napa. Named for Russian fur hunters who combed the area in the 19th century, the Russian River flows through much of Sonoma and follows several climatic changes. Cool winds from the Pacific are blocked in the north, and it is actually hotter in the Alexander Valley between the cities of Cloverdale and Healdsburg than it is further south, near the city of Sonoma. South of Healdsburg, the Russian River flows west and is once again in a cool Pacific climate.

Recently, special appellation status recognizes the uniqueness of several prime Sonoma County viticultural areas: Sonoma Valley, Russian River Valley, Valley of the Moon, and Alexander Valley.

Sonoma's rise to fame as a wine-producing county was largely the work of Agoston Haraszthy, "the father of California viticulture," who in 1856 bought land near the city of Sonoma at what is now Buena Vista Vineyards. Haraszthy was largely responsible for importing thousands of vine cuttings from Europe to California and formally establishing the California wine industry during the 1860s, and his heritage is commemorated at Buena Vista. Neglected for almost a century after Haraszthy's death, Buena Vista was reactivated by a former journalist, Frank Bartholomew, and is now under new ownership. Bartholomew later founded a second winery, Hacienda Cellars, at the edge of the Buena Vista property, which is now producing some outstanding wines from Cabernet Sauvignon and Chardonnay under the direction of winemaker Steve MacRostie.

Many of Sonoma's most famous wineries were founded by Italian immigrants, who brought winemaking techniques from their home country and successfully maintained them during hard times and prohibition. A notable example is the Sebastiani Winery, in Sonoma city. Located on the former site of the capital of the republic of California, Sebastiani grew during the 1970s into one of the state's biggest premium wine producers. This was largely the work of the late August Sebastiani; his son, Sam Sebastiani Jr., continues the family's proud traditions and honors his father with the popularly-priced August Sebastiani line, introduced only recently. Further north is the former Italian Swiss Colony Winery, now managed by United Vintners, which specializes in bulk wines under the new Colony label. Three other wineries of Italian origin are Simi Winery and Foppiano Winery near Healdsburg, and the J. Pendroncelli Winery near Geyserville. Simi is now producing premium wines under the direction of winemaker Zelma Long, distributed nationally by Schieffelin & Co. Foppiano has a new Riverside Farms label, reflecting its great strides in quality recently; the Pedroncelli family continues several decades worth of quality traditions.

The biggest change in Sonoma's long history occurred during the 1970s, when dozens of small, premium quality "boutique" wineries were established and began to fetch rave reviews all over the world. A notable example is Chateau St. Jean, whose winemaker, Richard Arrowood, successfully demonstrated that outstanding Botrytis-infected White Rieslings could be repeatedly produced in California (see LATE HARVEST). The new Jordan winery near Healdsburg has produced some memorable Cabernet Sauvignons, along with Dry Creek, Clos du Bois, and Sonoma (formerly Windsor) Vineyards. Superior Chardonnays have been made by Alexander Valley Vineyards, Kistler Vineyards, Matanzas Creek, Lambert Bridge, and Dehlinger. Zinfandel, which seems to grow expecially well in Sonoma, is the specialty of Hop Kiln Winery, Lytton Springs Winery (from Valley Vista Vineyard), Cambiaso, Davis Bynum, and Trentadue. Near Jack London State Park in the Alexander Valley is Kenwood Winery, a consistent winner at state and local wine judgings, who in 1975 introduced a unique "Artist Series" label for their best Cabernet Sauvignons and also make exceptional single-vineyard wines under the Jack London label. Gundlach-Bundschu, which has been producing wines for over a century and was recently purchased by Jos. Seagram & Sons, has a firm reputation and a fine set of new releases. Other new and very promising Sonoma wineries include: Preston Vineyards, Landmark Winery, J. J. Haraszthy & Son, Balverne Winery & Vineyards, Johnson's Alexander Valley Wines (no relation to the author), Toyon Winery, Field Stone, Sotoyome, de Loach, Mill Creek, Mark West Vineyards, Glen Ellen Winery, Grand Cru Vineyards, and Domaine Laurier.

For over a century, the F. Korbel & Bros. winery at Guerneville, along the picturesque Russian River, has made some of America's best sparkling wines—their new "Blanc de Noirs" (from Pinot Noir) and "Blanc de Blancs" (from Chardonnay) are outstanding. Iron Horse Vineyards nearby specializes in table wines. Souverain Cellars near Geyserville, now under new ownership, makes a wide variety of quality wines; another large operation is Geyser Peak Winery, which augments their offerings with the Summit label. At the other end of the county is the tiny Hanzell Winery, built by the late James D. Zellerbach, former ambassador to Italy, that was among the first of the new "boutique" wineries that have distinguished Sonoma County since World War II.

South Africa: Dutch settlers introduced the vine to South Africa in 1654, and in a short while South African vintners scored some impressive achievements. One particularly famous vineyard was planted at Constantia south of Capetown, and in the 19th century the sweet Muscat wine of Constantia was regarded as one of the world's very greatest wines. This famous property unfortunately makes no wine today, but in its absence the South African wine industry is growing.

Only recently has South Africa been a major table wine producer. Most of the grapes used to be grown for brandy distillation; some South African brandy can be excellent, but in the past it tended to be of poor quality. South African vintners learned how to duplicate the SHERRY process, and South African sherries are now among the best to be found outside of Spain; the latitude of most vineyards is the same as in the Spanish Sherry district. Today the trend is turning to table wines. A new law

329

establishing place-names for wines, the Wines of Origin Law, was passed in 1973, and a government quality seal now appears on bottles of superior South African wines that conform with the provisions of the new law.

There are over 256,000 acres of vineyards in South Africa, and over 6,000 wine growers. Production is largely in the hands of giant wine cooperatives. The South African Wine-Growers' Association (known by its initials, K.W.V.) was founded in 1918 and now controls much of the marketing of South African wines. The K.W.V. owns five important wineries across the country, and one at Paarl 40 miles to the northeast of Capetown is among the largest in South Africa. Eleven miles to the south another cooperative, the Stellenbosch Farmers' Winery Ltd., produces some excellent wines under the "Oude Libertas" label. Further inland in the Little Karoo area, grapes used for brandy and sherry are produced from irrigated vineyards.

South African table wines are usually named after the grape variety from which they are made: leading red wine grapes are Cabernet Sauvignon, Shiraz, Cinsault, and a local specialty called Pinotage, made from a cross between the Pinot Noir and the Cinsault. Good South African white wines are made from Riesling, Colombard, Clairette, and the country's own "Steen"—similar to Riesling but with a style all its own. Occasionally wines made from Steen will be sold as a "Late Harvest," indicating that the grapes were extra ripe at picking, producing a sweeter and richer wine.

Soutirage (*Soo-tee-rahj'*): French for RACKING, the process of transferring new wines from one container to another in order to remove the sediment.

330 **Soviet Union:** In efforts to attract Russians to the pleasures of wine-drinking and draw them away from hard liquor, the Soviet Union authorized an enormous vineyard expansion during the 1950s by which millions of new acres were planted. These immense new plantings made the Soviet Union the third largest wine-producing nation in the world, after Italy and France, and to augment this already prodigious production the Soviet Union imports huge quantities of wine from the west.

Russia is not generally thought of as a great wine producer, though in the beginning the "noble" VINIFERA vines originated in what is now part of the Soviet Union. Grape specialists (ampelographers) have identified the original source of vinifera in modern-day Transcausasia, from where the wine grape was taken throughout the civilized world. Today, vineyards still abound in Transcausasia—the republic of Georgia is one of Russia's foremost producers—and other important wine regions are Armenia, the Crimean peninsula, Moldavia, and the Ukraine.

Grapes do not grow easily in the icy Russian climate. The vines often have to be covered with earth to survive killing winter frosts, and many wineries tend to have primitive equipment. In response to public tastes, over three-fourths of Russian wine is sweet and high in alcohol. But some interesting sparkling wine called "Shampanskoe" or champagne is also made, and there is new interest in table wines. On the whole, Russian wines are improving, and as exports to the U.S. continue to increase, more and more Americans will eventually discover them.

Spain: The vineyards of Spain are among the world's oldest and most important. In the ancient world, Spanish wines were praised long before the wines of other countries became famous, and they are just as fine today. Largely because of the dry climate, however, total wine production in Spain is considerably less than in neighboring countries, even though some 4 million acres are presently under vines.

By far the most famous Spanish wine is

331

Pamplona

Logroño

Rioja

Zaragoza

rid

CATALUÑA

Sitges · Alella

Villafranca **Barcelona**
del Penedés

A NUEVA

Priorato · Tarragona

Mancha

VALENCIA

· Valencia

peñas

· Alicante

SPAIN

ada

(N) *Shaded area indicates vineyards*

SHERRY, the celebrated product of the port city of Jerez de la Frontera in southern Andalusia; yet many Spaniards never drink Sherry but prefer the local wine (*vino corriente*), very little of which is exported. With only a few exceptions, Spain's best known wines are produced primarily for the export market, and in other regions the wines are not so well-known.

Laws relating to wine-making practices in Spain date back to the Middle Ages, but official legislation has only come about recently. The best wine districts in Spain are now subject to the *Denominación de Origen* laws, which authorize place-names and set quality standards for the wines. Not all quality wine in Spain is produced under the laws, nor is all wine entitled to *Denominación de Origen* superior, but the very existence of the laws shows how interested the government is in maintaining the high reputation of Spanish wines.

Spain's climatic regions vary, as do the wines. In general, those made in the cooler districts of northern Spain are light in color and alcohol, while wines produced further south are fuller in body and flavor. Prime examples of the light northern wines are those from the Ribeiro district in northwestern Spain, in the province of Galicia. The pale, fresh Ribeiro wines are produced just to the north of the VINHO VERDE district in Portugal and are quite similar. To the east, the Basque provinces make Chacoli, an even lighter wine.

But just to the south of these cool coastal regions, some of Spain's best wines are made. The RIOJA district near the Sierra Cantabrica mountains is one of the leading red wine districts of Spain, although some good white Riojas are also made; Rioja is probably the best known Spanish table wine that is exported. To the southwest, near the city of Valladolid on the Duero River, another excellent but extremely rare red wine is VEGA SICILIA, made from grape varieties native to France. Select Riojas and Vega Sicilias rank with the world's finest red wines, although the latter is not a wine of *Denominación de Origen*. Two other notable wines from this part of Spain are the sturdy whites of Rueda and, further to the east in Aragón, the full-bodied reds of Cariñena.

Surrounding the city of Barcelona is the region of CATALONIA, which also produces some good wines. Catalonia is noted for Tarragona, a full-bodied sweet red wine, but today the city of San Sadurni de Noya is probably most famous for sparkling wine, bottle-fermented by the traditional CHAMPAGNE process. Alella, produced near the suburbs of Barcelona, is one of Spain's best white wines. Red wine from the Penedés region tends to be sturdy and robust.

Central Spain produces mostly ordinary wine for blending. With over 500,000 acres of vineyard, the LA MANCHA district produces most of the country's bulk wine, although the fruity red wines of the VALDEPEÑAS region in La Mancha are popular and exports to the U.S. are increasing. Good white wines are also made in the Valdepeñas district.

The province of Andalusia in southern Spain is best known for FORTIFIED WINES, of which Sherry is a notable example. Andalusia is also the home of MANZANILLA, one of the world's driest wines—technically a Sherry but with a character all its own. MÁLAGA, the sweet "Mountain" of the Middle Ages, was at one time as famous as Sherry but it is not well-known today. Another wine stripped of its former fame is Alicante, produced on the southeast coast, which used to be known under the curious name of "Tent."

The wines of the Sherry district are famous enough to warrant a detailed separate entry in this dictionary. The wines of MONTILLA, produced 250 miles to the northeast, are similar to Sherries except that they are usually shipped unfortified; they are rapidly becoming popular as less expensive substitutes for Sherry.

Spanna *(Spahn'-na):* The local name for the Nebbiolo grape in the region of Novara, in PIEMONTE, Italy. At least one producer in the GATTINARA district also uses the name Spanna for wines produced outside the D.O.C. limits of Gattinara that do not have right to this famous name; the wines are similar and, in certain cases, even superior to some Gattinaras.

Sparkling Burgundy: In the region of BURGUNDY, France, red, white or rosé wine that has been made sparkling; called *Bourgogne mousseux* in French. Most ordinary sparkling Burgundy is made by the CHARMAT (Bulk) process, but there is a significant production of wine that is bottle-fermented by the traditional CHAMPAGNE process, identified by the words "méthode champenoise" on the label, and some of the better wines are excellent substitutes for Champagne. Sparkling Burgundy is also produced in the U.S., although very little is fermented in the bottle.

Spätburgunder *(Shpate'-boor-gunder):* The German name for the Pinot Noir grape, grown in the AHR River valley and also in the region of BADEN and Austria. See PINOT NOIR.

Spätlese *(Shpate'-lay-zeh):* German for "late picking." Under the 1971 German Wine Law, a wine labeled Spätlese is a QUALITÄTSWEIN MIT PRÄDIKAT, produced from grapes picked later than usual during the harvest that have received extra maturity and are thus riper and richer in sugar. The minimum MUST WEIGHT must be about 80 (varies by area), and the wines may not be made with any sugar added. Wines labeled Spätlese will usually be sweeter and more expensive than those labeled KABINETT, because the requirements for production are more stringent.

The U.S. Bureau of Alcohol, Tobacco and Firearms recently prohibited the use of the word "Spätlese" on American wines, after considerable misuse of this term by several producers for wines that bore no similarity to a true German Spätlese. As a result, wines made from grapes left on the vine longer than usual must be called "Late Harvest" or "Late Picking" to conform with B.A.T.F. laws.

Spumante (*Spoo-mawn'-tay*): Italian for "sparkling" or "frothy." Wines labeled spumante may be produced either by fermenting in large tanks via the CHARMAT (Bulk) process, or in the bottle by the traditional CHAMPAGNE process. The most famous is Asti Spumante, a fruity, semi-sweet sparkling wine from the village of ASTI in the district of PIEMONTE.

Staatsweingut (*Shtots-vine'-goot*): German for "state wine domain." In the 19th century the Prussian government sponsored a general promotion of German viticulture and wine estates were purchased in the MOSEL, NAHE, RHEINGAU and RHEINHESSEN districts. The Mosel estate is located in the city of TRIER; the Nahe estate is in NIEDERHAUSEN. The Staatsweingut in the Rheingau is located in the city of ELTVILLE and is the exclusive owner of the great STEINBERG vineyard. Although officially the property of the German state governments, each estate operates independently and has its own high standards for the wines. All except the Rheinhessen estate (which was recently liquidated) display the state eagle crest on their labels.

Steinberg (*Shtine'-bairg*): One of the most famous vineyards in Germany, a 79-acre expanse of Riesling vines within the commune of HATTENHEIM in the RHEINGAU district. Founded during the 12th century by Cistercian monks, the Steinberg is adjacent to the historic KLOSTER EBERBACH monastery; the vineyard lies at the edge of a forest and sometimes does not dry out in rainy years, but in great vintages the wines are among the finest in all of Germany: they are typically powerful and fruity, with a great deal of class. Like the

Kloster Eberbach, the Steinberg is administered by the Staatsweingut in ELTVILLE and
select bottles are regularly sold at auctions held
at Kloster Eberbach. All Steinbergers are ES-
TATE-BOTTLED and are produced in all categories of QUALITÄTSWEIN, priced according to
their quality.

Sulfur: Non-metallic element widely employed in many stages of wine production. In
its powdered or elemental form (called "flowers
of sulfur") it is dusted on the vines during the
summer to prevent disease such as MILDEW and
ÖIDIUM; by combustion it combines readily
with oxygen to form sulfur dioxide, an indis-
pensable compound used to sterilize casks and
prevent re-fermentation so as to retain residual
sugar in the wine. Sulfur dioxide is used by
the vintner either as anhydrous compressed
gas or as metabisulfite (Campden tablets) to
kill harmful yeast and bacteria. Hydrogen sul-
fide, which gives off an unpleasant "rotten egg"
odor, is both poisonous and objectionable; a
few wines display it after they have been in
contact with sulfur, either in elemental or in
compound form.

Sur Lie *(Sir Lee')*: French for "on the lees." In
certain wine districts, most notably in the
MUSCADET region in France and the NEUCHÂ-
TEL area in Switzerland, some white wines are
allowed to remain in contact with the yeast
and sediment without RACKING; this often imparts a faint, agreeable sparkle to the wine that
adds freshness, and occasionally produces a
wine that is fuller in fruit and flavor than ones
not receiving this treatment.

Süssreserve *(Soos'-reserve)*: German for "sweet
reserve" or "dosage," a small quantity of unfermented grape must, from the same source
and quality grade as the wine to be made, that
is added to the wine once it has fermented out
to dryness. Its intent is to balance the sweetness or residual sugar of the wine, in propor-

tions desired by the winemaker, while avoiding the problems associated with arresting fermentation by other means, such as by adding sulfur dioxide, which could create undesirable flavors or allow re-fermentation. The Süssreserve is withheld entirely, or else is added only in small proportions, to produce the TROCKEN (dry) and HALBTROCKEN (semi-dry) wines that have recently become popular in Germany; a wine with residual sweetness is known as "Lieblich" or "Mild" in German.

Switzerland: The Swiss are great wine lovers. There are few regions in Switzerland suitable for grape-growing that have no vineyards: the country is divided into 22 *cantons* or districts, and only three produce no wine. The Swiss import immense quantities of wine from other countries, most notably France and Italy, but in recent years they have set aside some of their own good wines for export. Few are well-known in the U.S., but many are excellent.

There are some 30,000 acres of vineyard in Switzerland; the largest concentration follows the Rhône River from its source in the Alps and continues along the north shore of Lake Geneva. Two cantons in this area, VAUD and VALAIS, produce three-fourths of all Swiss wine—often the best of the entire country. The lake tends to moderate rapid fluctuations in temperature; protected by high mountains, the Rhône Valley is warm and sunny, allowing the grapes to ripen fully.

The canton of Vaud is divided into two smaller districts: La Côte, to the west of the city of Lausanne, and LAVAUX to the east. Along the shores of Lake Geneva the Chasselas grape, known by its local name Dorin, is grown for a light, fresh white wine. This variety is normally used only for table grapes in most of Europe, but in Switzerland it gives good results and is well-suited to the climate. In La Côte its wines are especially light; one of the best wine towns in this district is Mont-

339

sur-Rolle. East of Lausanne the wines tend to be fuller. Lavaux has two important wine villages: DÉZALEY, just on the outskirts of Lausanne, and SAINT-SAPHORIN, further east. The district of Chablais, part of the Vaud but away from the lake to the southeast, boasts two famous wine towns: Aigle and Yvorne.

The canton of Valais follows the Rhône along a southern slope of vines, and is one of the warmest and driest regions in Switzerland. The Chasselas is called Fendant in the Valais, where it grows well. Some other white grape varieties are grown here that are planted nowhere else in Europe: Amigne, grown near the town of Sion, and Arvine, planted on the unusual salt soil of Fully. The Valais grows several varieties indigenous to France but known by local names: Pinot Gris is called Malvoisie, a strong, scented white variety sometimes used for sweet wines; Marsanne is known as Ermitage in the Valais, where it makes full-flavored white wine with an interesting spicy bouquet. Sylvaner is called Johannisberg in the Valais, and its wines are substantial and flavorful. The best red wine of the Valais is DÔLE, made from the Gamay grape with a little Pinot Noir added; sometimes Petit Dôle, made only from Pinot Noir, is also produced.

Though they are less important commercially, three other regions in Switzerland produce wine. The districts of TICINO (Tessin) in Italian Switzerland grows the red Merlot variety native to BORDEAUX and specializes in a soft, fruity red wine. NEUCHÂTEL to the north along the lakes of Neuchâtel and Bienne makes both red and white wine, though the white is most likely to be seen abroad. The little Herrschaft region in northeast Switzerland near Lichtenstein make light red wines from the Blauburgunder grape, but few are exported.

Sylvaner (*Sil-von'-ner*): Good white wine grape, widely grown in many parts of Europe. Usually spelled "Silvaner" in Germany, it is planted principally in the RHEINHESSEN and RHEINPFALZ districts, in conjunction with the Riesling; though Sylvaner is generally more productive than the Riesling, it can nevertheless match it in certain areas where the grape is best suited: in the region of FRANKEN (Franconia) it is usually a superior variety. The Sylvaner is also grown in ALSACE, France, but there its wines are on the whole less good than the Riesling and it is not classified officially as a *cépage noble* ("noble variety"). Over 1,400 acres of Sylvaner have been planted in California, where its wines are legally allowed to be called "Riesling." California Sylvaners can be quite similar to Rieslings, but those interested in the true Riesling style should look for California wines labeled "Johannisberg Riesling" or "White Riesling."

Syrah *(Sir-rah')*: Excellent red wine grape native to the RHÔNE River valley, France. It gives robust wines with a great deal of color and tannin, and for this reason is normally blended with other varieties to round it out: in CHÂTEAUNEUF-DU-PAPE it is blended with up to 13 different varieties. The wines of HERMITAGE usually have a little white Marsanne added for finesse; in CÔTE ROTIE, a little white Viognier is added. Only at CORNAS and SAINT-JOSEPH is Syrah used almost exclusively. In Australia the Syrah is called "Shiraz" after the area in Persia from where it is said to have been brought during the Crusades; there its wines are similar, among that country's best. The Petite Sirah of California was originally thought to be a related variety, but is not in fact the same grape, although it often produces fine wines.

Szamorodni *(Sam-aw-rawd'-nee)*: Hungarian for "as it comes" or "such as it was grown." In the Hungarian TOKAY district, Furmint grapes not harvested in an overripe condition are made into dry or semi-dry white wine labeled "Tokay Szamorodni," which are normally much less sweet and concentrated than those labeled ASZÚ.

Szekszárd *(Sek-sard')*: Wine village in southern Hungary near the Duna (Danube) River, noted for its red wine, *Szekszárdi Vörös*.

Table wine: By definition, wine with an alcoholic content below 14%, suitable for serving with meals at the table. Wines stronger than 14% alcohol (but not over 24%) must be called DESSERT WINES under U.S. labeling and taxation laws.

Tâche, La *(Tash)*: Outstanding red wine vineyard in the CÔTE DE NUITS, Burgundy, rated Grand Cru (Great Growth). Owned entirely by the Société Civile du Domaine de la Romanée-Conti (See ROMANÉE CONTI), the La Tâche vineyard extends over 17½ acres in the famous wine commune of VOSNE-ROMANÉE; its magnificent and scented red wine is one of Burgundy's very greatest—in some vintages, even superior to Romanée-Conti, though La Tâche is always somewhat less expensive. About 2,500 cases are produced annually.

Tafelwein *(Tof'-fel-vine)*: German for "table wine." Under the 1971 German Wine Law, Tafelwein is the simplest quality category for a German wine. Generally light, inexpensive and suitable for daily consumption, a *Deutscher Tafelwein* must be a product of Germany, originating from the five designated Tafelwein regions: Mosel, Rhein, Oberrhein, Neckar, and Main. Almost always made with sugar added,

Tafelweins are usually bottled in large containers and are rarely exported to the U.S.

Tannin: A group of organic substances present in grape skins and seeds, responsible for the astringent, puckery quality in a young wine. Chemically related to phenols, tannin is present in practically all wines but is more pronounced in red wines because it is extracted from the skins as the wine ferments. Tannin is also introduced into the wine from the oak casks in which the wine ages. The amount of tannin often relates to a wine's aging potential; it is deposited as sediment—along with other substances—as the wine ages in bottle.

Tastevin *(Tat'-van)*: A small metal cup used for tasting wines in the BURGUNDY region of France. In its usual form it is silver, with circular rows of indents along the bottom to catch the light. Its name has been adopted by Burgundy's wine fraternity, the *Confrérie des Chevaliers du Tastevin.*

The term "tastevinage" relates to a special, ornate label used by the Confrérie des Chevaliers du Tastevin for their wine selections. The shipper or producer whose wine is selected pays a small fee to the Confrérie for the privilege of being "tasteviné." Wines sold under the *tastevinage* label are usually superior, though the label implies no quality guarantee.

Taurasi *(Tau-rah'-see)*: Sturdy red wine from the region of CAMPANIA, Italy. Grown in the province of Avellino near the city of Naples, Taurasi is made primarily from the Aglianico grape, sometimes with some Barbera or Sangiovese added. The wine ages slowly and must be at least three years old before it is sold; it is one of the most flavorful red Campania wines, and is rated D.O.C.

Tavel *(Tah-vel')*: One of the best rosé wines of France, produced in the lower RHÔNE River valley near the city of Avignon. Pale orange in color, dry, fresh and scented, Tavel is made from Grenache and Cinsault grapes; by law it must attain at least 11% alcohol. The wine is one of the world's most popular rosés, and is at its best when quite young—usually before it is three years old. There are some 2,000 acres of vineyard in Tavel; about 366,000 cases are produced annually.

Temecula: Wine region in Riverside County, California; located midway between the cities of Los Angeles and San Diego. An inland area with well-drained soil and a long, cool growing season, Temecula became famous in the early 1970s when retired industrialist Ely Callaway established a new winery, called Callaway Vineyards, that has produced some outstanding wines. The area around Escondito to the south has had vineyards since repeal, but Callaway's success prompted several other producers, bonded only recently: Cilurzo & Piconi Winery, Filsinger Vineyards, Glenoak Hills Winery, Mesa Verde, and Mount Palomar Winery. They are clustered in the western section of Riverside County, which now has over 13,000 acres of vineyard, one-fifth of which is planted in wine grapes.

Tenuta *(Tay-noo'-ta)*: Italian for "estate." A "tenuta vinicola" is a wine estate.

Terlano *(Tair-lahn'-no)*: Light, dry white wine produced near the village of Terlano in the ALTO ADIGE district, northern Italy. Terlano is usually made from the Pinot Bianco (Pinot Blanc) grape, but several other grape varieties—Riesling, Sauvignon, and Sylvaner—are also grown in the area for Terlano: if one of these varieties is predominant, it will be mentioned on the label.

Teroldego *(Tair-rawl'-de-go)*: Fruity red wine from the TRENTINO region, northern Italy, produced in the lower part of the Adige River valley. Made from the Teroldego grape variety native to the Trentino region, the wine is full-flavored and ages quite well; it is rated D.O.C.

Tête de Cuvée *(Tet duh Kew-vay′)*: French for "great growth" or "the best barrel," derived from the word *cuve*, or vat (see CUVÉE). Formerly this term was used for the very finest Burgundies from the most famous vineyards, which fetched the highest prices, but since 1935—when the French laws of APPELLATION CONTRÔLÉE were promulgated—tête de cuvée has been largely replaced by the term Grand Cru (Great Growth). Though tête de cuvée is still roughly interchangeable with Grand Cru, it is more correct to use the latter term, since *cru* relates both to the vineyard and its wine, whereas *cuvée* refers only to the wine. See CRU.

Thompson Seedless: White grape variety; the single most important grape variety in California, where over 259,000 acres have been planted. Named for William Thompson, an Englishman who first planted the grape in the Sacramento Valley in 1872, the Thompson Seedless is known as a "three-way" variety: it can be used for raisins, table grapes, or—less successfully—for wine. Being seedless, the grape is ideal for raisins, and 95% of its production is used for this purpose; but the wine that it gives is very neutral, lacking extracts and acidity. In the warm Central Valley of California, Thompson Seedless has traditionally been an important grape for the production of large quantities of bland white wine to be sold as "chablis," but with increased availability of better wine grapes it is used less and less for wine, although occasionally it still may be used to extend the most basic commercial blends.

Ticino *(Tee-chee′-no)*: Name given to the region in southern Switzerland near Lake Lugano and Lake Maggiore, where Italian is spoken; also called *Tessin*. With some 2,750 acres of vineyard, the Ticino area produces an interesting, light red wine from Merlot grapes, called "Merlot di Ticino"; it is one of Switzerland's better reds, with an attractive bouquet. The wine was formerly known only in

345

Switzerland, but some very good Merlots di Ticino are now sold in the U.S.

Tignanello *(Teen-ya-nel'-lo)*: Proprietary brand for a rare, exquisite red wine produced by the Antinori firm in the region of TUSCANY, Italy. The Antinoris are famous for producing a particularly good CHIANTI Classico, sold under the "Villa Antinori" label; in the 1960s they decided to produce a fuller-bodied red wine almost exclusively from Sangiovese, without the customary addition of white grapes to lighten the wine: recently Cabernet Sauvignon has been added for complexity. Since Tignanello does not follow the prescribed formula for grape varieties in the Chianti area, it is sold without a D.O.C. seal, but qualitatively it ranks with some of Italy's finest red wines.

Tinta *(Teen'-ta)*: A family of red wine grapes native to Portugal, used for the wines of PORT and DÃO. The most important Tinta varieties include: Tinta Francisca, Tinta Roriz, Tinta Cão, Tinta Alvarelhão, and Tinta Carvalha. Tinta Madeira is grown in California; over 600 acres have been planted, mostly in the warm Central Valley, where the grape is used for California port. Some superior domestic ports are called "Tinta port" to show that they have been made from this fine grape variety.

Tinto *(Teen'-toe)*: Spanish for "red"; a *vino tinto* is a red wine.

Tocai *(Toe-kie')*: Italian white grape variety, grown in parts of the VENETO district and in FRIULI-VENEZIA GIULIA. Despite the similarity in name, Tocai is unrelated to the Hungarian Furmint grape grown in the TOKAY district. The wines that it gives are fairly full-bodied, with a characteristic flavor and scent.

Tokay *(Toe'-kie)*: Celebrated sweet white wine; specifically, the special product of the Tokay district in northeastern Hungary. The famous wines of Tokay have been produced for nearly a thousand years, and the best has always been rare and expensive. While the name Tokay has been used elsewhere for sweet wines, they are generally quite different than the authentic product of Hungary.

The Tokay vineyards cover some 15,320 acres along the southern slopes of the Carpathian Mountains, on unusually volcanic soil. The chief grape variety is the Furmint, although a little Hárslevelü is also grown. Twenty-nine villages are included in the Tokay district; the most important are Tállya, Sárospatak, Tarcal and Erdöbenye. At the foot of the vineyards flows the meandering Bodrog River, which strongly influences the region's climate. It moderates wide temperature variations and its mists encourage a special mold, BOTRYTIS CINEREA, to form on the grapes in a fine vintage, causing the skins to shrink and the grapes to become overripe. This mold is the same as that in other sweet wine districts—most notably the SAUTERNES region in France—though Hungarian Tokay is made by a somewhat different process.

At the time of the harvest in Tokay, overripe and dried-out grapes known as *Aszú* are placed in tubs and called *puttonyos*. The grapes are then crushed to a pulp and allowed to ferment slowly before being added to a barrel of regular must. Thus the sweetness of a Tokay Aszú relates to the number of puttonyos of overripe grapes in a given vat of wine: 3 puttonyos is the driest Aszú, 4 puttonyos sweeter, and 5 puttonyos the sweetest—made entirely from overripe Aszú grapes. On wines sold as Aszú, the number of puttonyos used will be indicated by a neck band on the bottle.

The wines then age slowly in the cellars for as long as seven years before they are sold. During this time a faint oxidation takes place, causing the wine to turn slightly brown. Before bottling, the wine is pasteurized, adding

347

an imperceptible caramel flavor which is characteristic of a good Tokay.

Only exceptional vintages bring the right weather for Aszú wines; in most years, Botrytis does not form and the very sweetest wines cannot be made. But good dry wine can still be produced; wines not considered up to Aszú standard are labeled *Szamorodni*—Hungarian for "such as it was grown"—which are either dry or semi-dry, depending on the vintage.

Formerly, an extremely rare and exquisite wine called Tokay *Essencia* was made solely from the luscious juice that the grapes exude while waiting to be crushed, but today in Tokay the custom is to blend this nectar into wines labeled Aszú, thereby increasing their overall quality. Tokay Aszú and Szamorodni is sold only by the Hungarian State Export Monopoly, Monimpex, and the wines are put in clear bottles.

Tokay is probably the world's most long-lived wine. Essencia has kept perfectly for more than 200 years, and even older wines are not uncommon. Its fame has lead to many imitations, and a form of Tokay is produced in California in the Central Valley around Lodi, though not by the same process. One popular California table grape is even called "Flame Tokay," but it is not related to the Furmint and has nothing to do with Hungarian Tokay. In the region of ALSACE, France, Tokay is the local name for the Pinot Gris grape, the wines of which are called Tokay d'Alsace. The wines are not at all like Tokay but can be excellent, and the French government in 1975 classified Tokay d'Alsace as a *cépage noble* ("noble variety") entitled to the rank of Grand Cru (Great Growth).

Tonneau *(Tawn-no):* In the BORDEAUX region, France, a quantity of wine equivalent to 900 liters or 238 U.S. gallons, the traditional measure of output in the Bordeaux district. Actually, there is no cask of this size; the standard Bordeaux cask is the *barrique* of 225 liters, equivalent to about 24 cases each: four *barriques* comprise one *tonneau*.

Torre Quarto (*Taw'-ray Kwar'-toe*): Fine red wine from the region of APULIA (Puglia), Italy, produced south of the town of Foggia. Though not officially rated D.O.C., Torre Quarto is one of the finest Apulian wines—it is rich and full-bodied, and has a good bouquet. Torre Quarto is made from a number of different grape varieties, some of which are native to France, and the wines are produced exclusively by the Cirillo-Farrusi estate.

Touraine (*Too-rain'*): Picturesque old French province, located in the central LOIRE River valley. The district includes the present-day departments of Indre-et-Loire and Loir-et-Cher, surrounding the major city of Tours. The Touraine is one of France's most scenic districts, noted for its splendid châteaux; Touraine is also an APPELLATION CONTRÔLÉE for ordinary red, white or rosé wines produced in the district. The region has some 15,000 acres of vineyard; the most important grape varieties are Chenin Blanc and Sauvignon Blanc for white wines, and Cabernet Franc and Gamay for reds and rosés. There is also a large production of sparkling wines in the region. See CRÉMANT.

The best Touraine wines, however, are usually not sold as Touraine (or under the other appellation, Coteaux de Touraine) but under their own names. Perhaps the most famous is VOUVRAY, a scented white wine produced just to the east of Tours; MONTLOUIS, which adjoins Vouvray, is similar. Two outstanding red wines produced further downstream are CHINON and BOURGUEIL. A little regional wine, the best of which is white, is sold under local appellations: Touraine Azay-le-Rideau, Touraine Amboise, Touraine Mesland, etc., but it is rarely seen outside the district.

349

Traben-Trarbach (*Trah'-ben Trahr'-bock*): The names of two associated wine towns on the MOSEL River, Germany, linked together by a picturesque old bridge. The 800 acres of vineyard, mostly Rieslings, lie immediately to the north and south of the towns; those in the Kautenbach valley to the south are superior. Under the 1971 German Wine Law, vineyards in the neighboring towns of Enkirch and Wolf were added to the Traben-Trarbach community. The most famous vineyards (EINZELLAGEN) include: Kräuterhaus, Taubenhaus, Würzgarten, Burgweg, Schlossberg, Königsberg, Hühnerberg, Ungsberg, and Zollturm.

Traminer (German, *Tram-me'-ner*; French, *Tram-me-nair'*): Excellent white wine grape grown in many parts of France, Germany and northern Italy. Its berries are reddish when ripe, and it yields characteristically full-flavored white wine with a remarkable bouquet. The name Traminer derives from the little village of Termeno (Tramin) in the Italian Tyrol, where it was first cultivated; it is still an important grape in the Tyrol, but it produces more famous wines in the region of ALSACE in France and in Germany's Rhine Valley. A selected strain or CLONE of Traminer is called Gewürztraminer, because its wines have an especially pronounced "spicy" quality; in Alsace, where the name Gewürztraminer arose, it was recently decreed that the name Traminer shall no longer be used for Alsatian wines, the name Gewürztraminer being preferable. Elsewhere, Gewürztraminer and Traminer are roughly interchangeable; the shorter spelling is often employed, though technically the Gewürztraminer is a superior strain. Over 3,600 acres have been planted in California.

350   **Transfer Process**: Methods used in sparkling wine production, developed around the turn of the century, by which wines receive their secondary fermentation in bottle and are clarified prior to shipment by special equipment. In its initial stages the method is identical to the Champagne method (see MÉTHODE CHAMPENOISE), but instead of the long, laborious process of riddling and disgorging (REMUAGE), the fermented wine is transferred into a special machine, where through filtration under pressure it is cleared of its sediment. The transfer process saves time and money, but the results are generally not quite as fine as the traditional Champagne process. In the U.S., wines made by the transfer process may bear the label "naturally fermented in the bottle"; as a group, most domestic sparkling wines are produced in this manner. See also CHARMAT PROCESS.

Trebbiano *(Treb-yahn′-no)*: The Italian name for a white wine grape known as Ugni Blanc or "Saint-Émilion" in France. The Trebbiano is important in many Italian wine districts; in the north, it is used in conjunction with the Garganega for SOAVE and on its own for LUGANA; further south, it is one of the varieties used for ORVIETO and EST! EST! EST!

Trentino *(Tren-tee′-no)*: Region in northeastern Italy, forming Trento province around the city of Trento. Although a separate district from the ALTO ADIGE region to the north, the two regions are known collectively as Trentino-Alto Adige, and produce similar wines: one-half of the wine exported from Italy comes from this region. The Alto Adige region ranges over more mountainous country near the Austrian border and acknowledges Austrian influence in its German labels; Trentino is more Italian in outlook.

Trentino is noted for its many excellent red wines. A representative example is TEROLDEGO, a dry, full-bodied red wine made from the Teroldego grape; the superior Cabernet, Pinot Noir and Merlot grapes native to France are also grown in the Trentino region, and are called Cabernet Trentino, Pinot Nero Tren-

351

tino and Merlot Trentino, respectively. The light reds Marzemino, Valdadige and Vallagarina are also good, but they are rarely exported. Fine Trentino rosé wines are produced from Lagarino (Lagrein) and Schiava, as in Alto Adige. White Trentino wines are made from Riesling, Traminer Aromatico, Moscato, and Sylvaner; some excellent sparkling wine is made from Pinot Trentino.

Many of the better Trentino wines have recently received D.O.C. listings. Wines produced in the Alto Adige region are listed under Alto Adige in this book.

Trier (*Tree'-er*): Famous city on the MOSEL River, Germany. Founded in Roman times, Trier is the headquarters of the Mosel wine trade and is the largest city in the area. Though Trier has only a few vineyards of its own, the 1971 German Wine Law included vineyards from many neighboring villages in the Trier wine community, and as a result two of the best wine towns in the RUWER district—AVELS-BACH and EITELSBACH—are now officially part of Trier. Many famous wine producers have their headquarters in Trier, most notably the Vereinigte Hospitien, Bischöfliches Konvikt, Hohe Domkirche, Bischöfliches Priesterseminar, Friedrich-Wilhelm Gymnasium, and Von Kesselstatt estates.

Trittenheim (*Trit'-ten-heim*): Picturesque little wine town on the MOSEL River, Germany, with 741 acres of vineyard. Trittenheim lies at a sharp bend in the river; the vineyards are steep and the wines are generally only at their best in great vintages. The light, stylish Riesling wines of Trittenheim tend to be little known, and many are excellent value. The two most famous vineyards (EINZELLAGEN) are Apotheke and Altärchen; other good Einzellagen are Leiterchen and Felsenkopf.

Trocken (*Trawk'-ken*): German for "dry"; also, a new category for dry German wines, based on the sugar content measured in grams of residual sugar per liter. Officially, there are two separate groups of *Trocken* wines: the driest are suitable for diabetics, and are labeled "Fur Diabetiker geeignet—Nur nach Befragen des Arztes," meaning that diabetics may consume them, but only on the advice of the physician. To qualify for this very dry category, a *Diabetiker* wine may have from 0.5 to 4 grams/liter of residual sugar, and is sold with an analysis certificate detailing the residual sugar and alcohol content, plus a special yellow seal, the *Deutsches Weinsiegel*. Diabetiker wines are austerely dry to most palates, and are not often seen on the U.S. market.

The second category of *Trocken* wines is the regular grade, minus the recommendation for diabetics. The maximum allowable sugar content is 9 grams/liter, with a stipulation that the acidity may not be less than 2 grams below the residual sugar level—a wine with 9 grams/liter sugar may not have an acid level lower than 7 grams/liter. These wines are also sold with the yellow *Deutsches Weinsiegel*, but without the analysis certificate.

The production of *Trocken* wines is fairly simple. Most German wines are produced with the addition of a small quantity of sweet, unfermented grape must, called SÜSSRESERVE or "dosage," that is added to balance out the residual sweetness. Trocken wines, and the semidry HALBTROCKEN wines, are made by simply withholding the Süssreserve and fermenting the wine out to dryness. Although consumption of this type of wine is increasing in Germany, along with a greater variety of German growers and shippers, they have yet to become popular on the U.S. market. They should not be confused with wines labeled TROCKENBEERENAUSLESE (see below), which, being intensely sweet, are their exact opposite.

Trockenbeerenauslese *(Trock'-en-bearen-ouse' -lay-zeh)*: German for "dried berry selection;"

the highest achievement of German viticulture—among the rarest and most expensive wines in the world. During the harvest, a few grapes become overripe through the action of the "noble mold" (see BOTRYTIS CINEREA). If weather permits them to be left even longer on the vine, the skins shrink and the water evaporates so that the grapes appear to be raisins. These are picked individually, berry by berry, and it often takes a picker an entire day to gather enough grapes to make a bottle.

Under the 1971 German Wine Law, only wines with a MUST WEIGHT of at least 150 qualify for the rating Trockenbeerenauslese. The wines are extremely sweet and flavorful, but because of their scarcity they are fabulously expensive; the wines can only be made a few times a decade in most regions.

Tuscany (Italian, **Toscana,** pronounced *Toscahn'-na*): Region in central Italy, surrounding the city of Florence (Firenze); also one of Italy's most important wine areas, with over 560,000 acres of vineyard. A scenic region of rolling hills, Tuscany is most famous for CHIANTI, probably the most widely exported Italian wine. Produced in a large area between the cities of Florence and Siena, Chianti used to be symbolized by the wickered FIASCO flask in which it was traditionally bottled, but now the fiasco is becoming rare. The central part of the Chianti region is called *Chianti Classico.*

Yet Tuscany has several other wines that rival Chianti in quality, although they are not as well-known in the export trade. One of the most celebrated red wines in Italy is BRUNELLO DI MONTALCINO, produced to the south of the Chianti district around the town of Montalcino, which is made from the Brunello grape—actually a variety of Sangiovese. Further to the east, the celebrated red VINO NOBILE DI MONTEPULCIANO is similar; all three of these robust wines are long-lived; and well-made examples are among Italy's very finest wines.

Tuscany produces less white wine than red, and little of it is seen abroad. The renowned VINO SANTO of the Chianti district is a fine dessert wine made from dried grapes; another good white is the Vernaccia di San Gimignano, produced near the Chianti district. The island of Elba is part of Tuscany; Elba makes a good white wine, Procanico, but not much of it reaches the mainland. The remaining Tuscan whites are Montecarlo, produced north of Florence, and Pitigliano, one of the first white Tuscan wines to receive a D.O.C. listing.

Ugni Blanc (*Oon'-yee Blawn'*): White wine grape, widely grown in southern France. Known by its local name "Saint-Émilion," it is the chief variety used for making Cognac brandy; in the Cognac region its pale, acidic wines are ideal for distilling, less so for table wine. However, it gives the fresh, crisp white wines of CASSIS on the Mediterranean coast, and it is grown in many parts of PROVENCE for good white wines. In Italy the Ugni Blanc is called Trebbiano, and is the most widely planted white wine grape in that country (see TREBBIANO). Over 1,100 acres of Ugni Blanc have been planted in California, mostly in the warm Central Valley, where the grape's inherently high acidity is an advantage.

Ullage (*Oo-lahj'*): French term for the air space in a cask or bottle of wine, caused by slow evaporation. Too much ullage is harmful and could promote OXIDATION or ACESCENCE, and so the casks are regularly "topped up" with

355

wine at intervals, a process known as *ouillage* in French. Once the wine is bottled, a pronounced ullage in a very old wine may be a sign that it is no longer fit to drink.

Umbria (*Oom'-bree-ah*): Wine region in central Italy between the cities of Florence and Rome, with some 179,000 acres of vineyard. Land-locked Umbria has only a few well-known wines; by far the most famous is ORVIETO, a fresh white wine that is either dry or semi-sweet; further to the east, the red and white wines of Torgiano, produced south of the city of Perugia, are also celebrated. The local Umbria wine, Colli del Trasimeno, comes from around Lake Trasimeno and was rated D.O.C. in 1972.

Ungstein (*Oong'-shtine*): Wine village in the RHEINPFALZ (Palatinate) region, Germany, with 791 acres of vineyard. Ungstein lies just to the north of Bad Dürkheim (see DÜRKHEIM), and its fine wines are similar; one-fourth of the vineyards are planted in Riesling, and there is considerable red wine production. The best-known wine name is Ungsteiner Honigsäckel, but under the 1971 German Wine Law this has become a composite vineyard or GROSSLAGE; the individual vineyards or EINZELLAGEN include: Herrenberg, Nussriegel, Bettelhaus, Osterberg, and Weilberg; Michelsberg is shared by Bad Dürkheim.

Ürzig (*Ertz'-ig*): Famous wine town on the MOSEL River, Germany, with 885 acres of vineyard planted entirely in Riesling. The steep sloped vineyards produce some of the Mosel's very best wines in hot years; the most famous Ürzig vineyard (EINZELLAGE) is Würzgarten ("spice garden," in German, referring to the wine's characteristics), shared by many proprietors and located on unusual red soil. Under the 1971 German Wine Law this is the only Einzellage in Ürzig; Ürziger Schwarzlay has become a composite vineyard or GROSS-

356

LAGE that includes Einzellagen from several neighboring villages, most of them considerably below Ürzig in quality.

Vacqueyras *(Vok'-kay-rah):* Wine-producing village in the southern CÔTES-DU-RHÔNE district, France; one of the best of the so-called "Côtes-du-Rhône-Villages." Like the district of CHUSCLAN nearby, the wines are often sold under the name Côtes-du-Rhône Vacqueyras; they are generally finer in quality and usually sell for more than most Côtes-du-Rhônes.

Valais *(Val'-lay):* Wine region in southern Switzerland with some 10,900 acres of vineyard, the largest and most important vineyard area in that country. The canton (district) of Valais extends along the Rhône River valley in an east-west direction, and between the towns of Martigny and Brig there is an almost continual wall of vineyard. Being sheltered by high mountains, the Valais is the warmest and driest wine region in Switzerland; the chief grape variety is Fendant (Chasselas), which gives scented white wines. One of the best Swiss red wines is DÔLE, produced from a blend of Gamay and Pinot Noir grapes; some interesting but rather rare Valais wines are produced by grapes grown nowhere else: Arvine, a scented, full-bodied white wine, and Amigne, prized for its fine bouquet. Pinot Gris is called Malvoisie in the Valais, where it is sometimes used for sweet wines. Sylvaner is known as Johannisberg in the Valais; the Marsanne from France is called Ermitage, another exclusive of the Valais.

357

Valdepeñas *(Val-de-pain'-yas)*: Wine region in central Spain, officially part of the La MANCHA district. There are some 51,900 acres of vineyard in Valdepeñas; both red and white wines of good quality are produced, though the light, attractive reds made from Cencibel are superior. Normally a little white wine is blended with the red to make it lighter and earlier to mature; the wines are generally inexpensive and good values.

A grape called Valdepeñas is grown in California, and some 1,800 acres have been planted, mostly in the warm Central Valley; however, it is not the same as the Cencibel grape of the Valdepeñas district in Spain, nor are its wines similar.

Valgella *(Val-jel'-la)*: Red wine from the VALTELLINA district in the region of LOMBARDY, northern Italy. Made from the Nebbiolo grape, which is known as Chiavennasca in the Valtellina district, Valgella is a sturdy red wine that matures slowly; it can be quite good but is generally a little lighter than some other Valtellina wines.

Valpantena *(Val-pon-tay'-na)*: Wine district east of Lake Garda in the region of VENETO, Italy. The Valpantena district adjoins the VALPOLICELLA region, and superior Valpantena wines meeting the standards for Valpolicella are allowed the geographical designation "Valpolicella Valpantena."

Valpolicella *(Val-po-lee-chel'-la)*: Excellent and famous red wine from the region of VENETO, northern Italy, produced north of the city of Verona near Lake Garda. Valpolicella is made primarily from three grape varieties—Corvina, Rondinella, and Molinara—grown in eighteen communes in the province of Verona. The central portion of the Valpolicella district is called Valpolicella *Classico*, which usually produces superior wines; if the wines reach 12% alcohol they may be called "Valpolicella

358

Superiore." A specialty of the district is Recioto della Valpolicella (see RECIOTO), made from dried grapes, which is fuller-bodied than regular Valpolicella.

Valpolicella is a light, fruity red wine that is most enjoyable when quite young—usually before it is five years old—except for the Recioto wines, which are quite long-lived.

Valtellina *(Val-tel-lee´-na)*: Mountainous wine district in the region of LOMBARDY, northern Italy, extending along the Adda River valley east of Lake Como. Though little known, the Valtellina district produces some of Italy's very finest red wines from the Nebbiolo grape—the same outstanding variety grown in other parts of northern Italy—except that here the grape is called Chiavennasca. The grapes are grown on steep Alpine slopes that receive a great deal of sunshine; the wines tend to be hard in their youth but mature magnificently. There are several famous wine regions in the Valtellina district; usually the most celebrated wine is INFERNO, followed by SASSELLA, GRUMELLO, and Fracia; VALGELLA tends to be a little lighter than the others. Castel Chiuro, equally good red and white Valtellina wines, are produced exclusively by Nino Negri, an important grower; SFURSAT (Sforzato), a rich, full-bodied red wine made from dried grapes, is quite high in alcohol (over 14%) and is made by a number of different Valtellina growers.

Varietal: Term used in the U.S. wine trade for wines labeled according to the grape variety from which they were made, as opposed to a region or district. A varietal wine is distinguished from a GENERIC wine, which is labeled according to a "type" or style of wine, in general use. Federal regulations recently increased the minimum for the informing grapes used in a varietally labeled wine, to take effect in January, 1983. Henceforth, varietally-labeled wines in the U.S. must be produced from at least 75% of the variety indicated on the label; for many years the minimum was 51%, and a few producers used this as an opportunity to extend the wine by adding up to 49% of lesser-quality grapes. The new measures make this considerably more difficult, although better producers have been voluntarily complying with the higher requirement for decades. (The 75% minimum is also designed to encourage some helpful blending with other varieties, which when added in the right manner and proportion, greatly assist in balancing the finished wine.)

European wines are not normally named after the grape variety used, because in most regions only approved grape varieties may be planted, in conformity to wine laws issued by the government. Only those varieties that have shown to produce superior wines may be planted in most fine wine regions, and the authenticity of these wines is protected by law. Varietal labeling is therefore significant in areas where there is no restriction as to the grape variety used, and several different types of wines may be produced in these areas.

Vaud (*Vo*): Wine region in Switzerland with some 8,000 acres of vineyard, located along the north shore of Lake Geneva. The canton (district) of Vaud includes three smaller regions: La Côte, west of the city of Lausanne; LAVAUX, to the east of Lausanne; and Chablais, away from the lake along the Rhône River valley. The Vaud is noted for its white wines made from the Dorin (Chasselas) grape, among the best in Switzerland; excellent examples are those of DÉZALEY, SAINT-SAPHORIN, Mont-sur-Rolle, Aigle, and Yvorne.

V.D.P. (Verband Deutscher Prädikatsweingüter e.V.): An association of German vintners that serves to promote the quality and the sale of German estate-grown *Prädikat* wines—the natural, unsugared wines that are representative of their district and their type. Members (*Mitgleider*) in the association include some of Germany's most famous producers. Wines produced by the Verband may be identified by a square black eagle seal appearing on the label, shown with grapes on its breast. Formerly the association was called V.D.N.V. (Verband Deutscher Naturwein Versteigerer), but the association adopted the new title after the enactment of the 1971 German Wine Law, which prohibits the word *natur* to appear on a wine label.

V.D.Q.S. (Vins Délimités de Qualité Supérieur): French for "delimited wines of superior quality." Certain districts in France produce good wines that are nevertheless not considered up to the standards of APPELLATION CONTRÔLÉE, and for these wines the government has established an intermediate quality classification: V.D.Q.S. The laws of V.D.Q.S. resemble those of appellation contrôlée: the wines are produced in officially delimited regions from approved grape varieties that have a restricted yield per hectare. All V.D.Q.S. wines are subject to official approval before being released for sale, and a government seal guaranteeing their quality appears on the label. The law also provides that certain outstanding V.D.Q.S. wines may someday achieve appellation contrôlée status, after they have shown continued improvement in quality. V.D.Q.S. wines are almost always well-made and sound, and because they are usually inexpensive, many are excellent value. Each of the more famous V.D.Q.S. wines is listed in this dictionary.

Vega Sicilia *(Vay'-ga Si-see'-lee-ah):* One of the very greatest red wines of Spain, produced near the city of Valladolid on the banks of the Duero River. Made from a number of grape varieties originally native to France, Vega Sicilia is produced only by one winery, Bodegas Vega Sicilia S.A. Wines labeled Vega Sicilia always bear a vintage date and receive at least 5 years of cask aging prior to their release; the

361

wines then improve for years in bottle. The *bodega* also sells a lesser, non-vintage wine called Tinto Valbuena, which receives less cask aging. Both wines are extremely rare and expensive, but they are among the finest produced in Spain.

Veltliner (*Velt'-leen-er*): A group of grape varieties planted mostly in Austria and other parts of central Europe. The most common variety is the Grüner (Green) Veltliner, grown in lower Austria for a lively, fruity white wine; another important variety is the Frühroter (Red) Veltliner, named for its red berries; this grape is also planted in California.

Vendange (*Von-dahnj'*): French for "grape harvest." This term is used in connection with the process of picking and fermentation, not the wine of a particular vintage; a vintage-dated wine is termed "millésimé."

Vendemmia (*Ven-day'-me-ah*): Italian for "grape harvest." Like *vendange* (see above), this term relates to the harvest, not the wine of a particular vintage. In Spanish, the word is spelled *vendemia*.

Venegazzù (*Vain-nay-got-tsoo'*): Fine red and white wines from the region of VENETO, Italy, produced near the town of Venegazzù del Montello in the Treviso area. The red is made from Cabernet Sauvignon, Merlot and Malbec grapes, and is similar to a good Bordeaux; if the wine has received extra age, it is called "Riserva di Casa." White Venegazzù is made from Riesling and Pinot, and also ages well. Although not rated D.O.C., Venegazzù is among the Veneto region's finest wines; it is produced exclusively by the Conte Piero Loredan-Gasparini estate.

362   **Veneto** (*Vain'-nay-toe*): Region in northeastern Italy, including the major cities of Venice, Verona, Vicenza and Padua (Padova). Veneto's western boundary is near Lake Garda, and

from there the region extends eastwards to the Adriatic; there are over 525,000 acres of vineyard in Veneto, and many fine wines.

The Veneto region divides up into three smaller districts. The most western of these surrounds the city of Verona east of Lake Garda, and boasts the famous red wines of VALPOLICELLA and BARDOLINO and the noted white SOAVE. Middle Veneto, with its gently rolling hills and plains, extends from the city of Vicenza eastwards past Padua; the most celebrated wines of this district are GAMBELLARA, Colli Euganei, Breganze, and Colli Berici. Middle Veneto white wines are generally superior to the reds, and many have received D.O.C. listings. Finally, eastern Veneto (Venetia) includes the suburbs of Venice and the city of Treviso, northwards towards the Italian Tyrol. Near Treviso the River Piave flows down from the Tyrol to the Adriatic; and defines an important wine region; in recognition of their excellence, Vini del Piave (Piave wines) were awarded D.O.C. status in 1971. Piave wines bear VARIETAL labels; better red varieties include Merlot, Cabernet, Pinot Nero, Rubino, and Raboso; superior white wines are made from Riesling, Tocai, Verduzzo and Pinot Grigio.

Other celebrated Venetian wines are PROSECCO, produced near the town of Conigliano, and Verdiso, a Treviso wine. The Veneto region as a whole produces in excess of 97 million cases of wine a year, ranking it as one of Italy's most important wine regions.

Véraison (*Vay'-ray-zawn*): French term for the point during the grape maturation process, when unripe grapes change color from green to purple or translucent green, and their sugar content begins to increase. In many regions the actual time of the harvest can be determined in relation to when véraison occurs.

363

Verdelho (*Vair-dayl'-yo*): A dark, medium sweet MADEIRA, made from Verdelho grapes grown on the island of Madeira. Verdelho is usually a little softer and sweeter than SER-CIAL, but drier than BUAL. This grape is also grown in Portugal to make white Port.

Verdicchio *(Vair-deek'-ee-o):* Famous white wine from the MARCHE region in Italy; made from the Verdicchio grape grown to the west of the city of Ancona. The two D.O.C. regions for this wine are called Verdicchio dei Castelli di Jesi and Verdicchio di Matelica; the former includes the communes of Cupramontana, Monterobero and Castelbellino, and is better known. Verdicchio is either dry or semi-dry, and has a clean freshness; it is one of Italy's finest white wines.

Verdiso *(Vair-dee'-zo):* Light, dry white wine made from the Verdiso grape, grown near the city of Treviso in the VENETO region, Italy.

Verdot: see PETIT-VERDOT.

Verduzzo *(Vair-doot'-so):* Italian white wine grape, widely grown in the VENETO and FRIULI-VENEZIA GIULIA regions of northeastern Italy. It gives dry, scented and rather full-bodied white wines called Verduzzo; good examples are made in the River Piave area in Veneto.

Vermentino *(Vair-men-teen'-o):* White wine grape grown in the region of LIGURIA, Italy for a light, fresh white wine of the same name. The Vermentino is also planted extensively in Corsica and in Sardinia, where it gives similarly fine wines; one particularly good Sardinian wine, Vermentino di Gallura, was awarded a D.O.C. rating in 1975.

Vermouth: A flavored or aromatized wine to which plant extracts and other flavorings have been added. The principal ingredient is worm-wood, and both vermouth and wormwood derive from the German word *Wermut,* meaning the shrub *Artemisia absinthium.* Wormwood leaves are used for French absinthe, but for vermouth the less toxic flowers are substituted.

There are two basic types of vermouth: the dry "French" type, and the "Italian" type, which is sweeter. Both forms of vermouth are named for the places where they were originally developed—Torino, Italy and Lyon, France—but today, dry vermouths are made in Italy and sweet vermouths are produced in France; the most famous producers make both.

Vermouth production begins with a neutral, dry white wine base, such as is produced in the MIDI region in France or in APULIA, Italy. The wines are aged for at least one year before they are blended with a *mistelle*—unfermented must to which brandy is added, thus preserving the sugar and natural flavors. Then plant flavorings are added; the most common are wormwood, quinine, camomile, coriander, cinnamon, orange peel, cloves and hyssop, though each producer naturally guards his own special formula. The flavorings are allowed to mix or infuse with the wine, then the mixture is pasteurized, refrigerated and filtered to remove sediment and impurities. After a final aging period, the wine is ready for sale as vermouth and contains about 19-20% alcohol.

Though vermouth manufacture originated in France and Italy, America is also an important producer; better American vermouths are quite similar to those of Europe. Fine vermouths are also produced in Spain, Portugal, South Africa, and South America.

Vernaccia (*Vair-natch'-ah*): Historic white wine grape; famous during the Renaissance and now grown in many parts of Italy. Both dry and sweet Vernaccias are made; all tend to have a characteristic gold color and full body, and the best are quite sweet and high in alcohol. Better wines that have received official D.O.C. listings include the Vernaccia di San Gimignano of TUSCANY, the Vernaccia di Serrapetrona from the region of MARCHE, and the Vernaccia di Oristano from Sardinia.

365

Verona *(Vair-ro'-na)*: Important city in north-eastern Italy, situated a few miles east of Lake Garda. The Verona district forms the western part of the VENETO region; well-known Veronese wines include BARDOLINO, VALPOLI-CELLA, and SOAVE.

Vidal Blanc *(Vidal 256)*: White French HYBRID grape variety, developed by crossing Ugni Blanc with a Seibel hybrid variety, S. 4986; becoming increasingly popular in the eastern United States. The fine white wines that it gives are full and have considerable character; the grape is quite winter hardy and rapidly develops high degrees of sugar during the growing season.

Vigne *(Veen'-yuh)*: French for "vine," an individual vine in its entirety. Its components include the root-stock, or *cep*, and canes, or *sarments*. Also, a small vineyard holding.

Vignoble *(Veen-yawb'-l)*: French for "vineyard" or "vineyard area."

Villány *(Veel-lahn'-yee)*: Town in southern Hungary near the Yugoslavian border, famous for its red wine, *Villányi Burgundi*.

Vin *(Vahn)*: French for "wine," legally defined as a beverage produced by the partial or complete fermentation of the juice of fresh grapes.

Viña *(Veen'-ya)*: Spanish for "vineyard."

Vin de Paille *(Van duh Pie')*: French for "straw wine," a wine made from grapes that have been left to dry in the sun on mats of straw, or indoors on racks. Since this process causes the grapes to lose water by evaporation, the wines obtained are very sweet and high in alcohol. In France this process is used for the rare wines of the JURA district; in Italy, such wines are called *passito*.

Vin de Pays *(Van duh Pay')*: French for "country wine," the local wines produced in the less famous French wine regions that are not always bottled or exported. Many of these wines can be quite pleasant, however, and in 1974 the French government authorized 44 regions from which *vins de pays* could legally originate; most of them are in the MIDI. The wines are labeled according to their place of origin and the department (administrative region) where they were produced. Few *vins de pays* have been exported to the U.S., but the wines are worth looking for when visiting the regions in which they are made.

Vinho Verde *(Veen'-yo Vair'-day):* Portuguese for "green wine"; specifically, an especially light wine produced in a delimited zone in northern Portugal, in an area bounded on the north by the Minho River and on the south by the Douro. A Portuguese wine region that has been granted *Denominação de origem* (Denomination of Origin) status, the Vinho Verde area has about 61,775 acres of vineyard, and produces red, white and rosé wines.

The Vinho Verdes are not named "green" for their color but rather for the time when the grapes are harvested—before they are fully ripe. The wines have a pronounced but refreshing acidity and are very low in alcohol—rarely above 10%. Because they are made to be consumed young, Vinho Verdes rarely improve with age and should not be stored too long. The whites are superior, and often have a faint, agreeable sparkle; the red and rosé Vinho Verdes are sturdier, and generally taste best when chilled.

Vinifera *(Vin-nif'-fer-ah):* A European or East Asian species of grape vine, the only one of 32 *Vitis* species that gives uniformly good wine—hence the name, which means "wine bearer." Originally native to the region of Transcaucasia on the eastern shores of the Black Sea, varieties of vinifera were transported throughout the ancient world and are now grown in nearly every temperate zone where they are suited.

Vinification: All of the necessary steps by which grapes are made into wine.

Vino *(Vee'-no):* Italian (and Spanish) for "wine."

Vino Nobile di Montepulciano *(Vee'-no No'-bee-lay dee Mawn-tay-pool-chon'-no):* Fine Italian red wine produced in the region of TUS-CANY, near the town of Montepulciano. The wine was called "noble" not for its qualities but for its original clientele, yet its quality is generally superior: produced from a blend of Sangiovese, Canaiolo, Malvasia and Trebbiano grapes, the wine is full-flavored and has a good bouquet. The region adjoins the CHIANTI area, and select Vino-Nobile di Montepulcianos are similar to some Chiantis but are much less well-known. Named for the town of Montepulciano, Vino Nobile di Montepulciano should not be confused with the Montepulciano grape grown in the ABRUZZI region, used for the red wine Montepulciano d'Abruzzo.

Vino Santo: Italian for "wine of the saints," a special type of wine produced in many parts of Italy, especially the TUSCANY region. In the fall, selected Trebbiano or Malvasia grapes are placed in airy lofts to dry during the winter, so that they lose a great deal of water by evaporation. In the spring, they are pressed and the must is allowed to ferment very slowly; Vino Santo is often not put into bottle until its fifth year, and later improves with even more aging. The wine is lusciously sweet, but because so much volume is lost by evaporation, it is produced only in limited quantities and is very rare on the export market.

Vintage: Term having several different meanings. Technically, the vintage is the annual gathering of the grapes during the harvest and the making of wine from those grapes; hence a vintage wine is one from a particular year. During the 19th century, however, producers in the PORT and CHAMPAGNE districts introduced a new meaning of vintage: the selected wines of a particularly good harvest. In these districts, a wine from an especially fine vintage is superior to one not bearing a vintage date—though a "vintage" of course takes place each year in every region where wine is made, without any quality distinction. Many California producers prefer to specify a vintage date only for especially good wines.

In French, the vintage is called *vendange*; in German it is *Weinlese*. *Cosecha* means vintaged wine in Spanish, *Colheita* in Portuguese.

Viognier *(Vee'-awn-yay)*: White grape variety grown in the RHÔNE River valley, France, used in blends for the red wines of CÔTE RÔTIE and on its own for the rare white wines of CONDRIEU.

Viré *(Veer-ray')*: Little village in the MÂCON region, Burgundy, famous for its good white wines made from the Chardonnay grape, entitled to the appellation "Mâcon-Viré."

Viticulture: The science and art of grape-growing, as distinguished from *viniculture*, the science of wine-making.

Vollrads, Schloss *(Fall'-rods)*: Outstanding wine estate in the RHEINGAU district, Germany, located above the village of WINKEL. The estate has some 92 acres of vineyards, mostly planted in Riesling; it is dominated by a massive, picturesque *Schloss* (castle), with a handsome bell-tower and moat that was constructed in the 14th century, and superior wines have been produced on the property for centuries. Schloss Vollrads now belongs to the Matuschka-Greiffenclau family, one of the oldest winemaking families in the Rheingau; the late Count Richard Matuschka-Greiffenclau was former president of the German Vintners Association, and his son, Count Erwein Matuschka-Greiffenclau, presently directs the family business.

Like several other German wine estates,

369

Schloss Vollrads identifies the quality of its wines by means of different colored capsules, in addition to the label bearing the Schloss Vollrads coat-of-arms. No wine below the grade of QUALITÄTSWEIN is sold as Schloss Vollrads; the estate recently introduced a series of drier TROCKEN wines, more suited to accompanying food, which are identified by a special silver stripe on the capsule. The most basic Qualitätswein bears a green capsule, and select lots in the sweeter grades are adorned with a gold stripe. The *Kabinett* has a blue capsule, with superior wines bearing a gold stripe and drier Kabinett wines a silver stripe. The *Spätlese* capsule is pink, and pink with a gold stripe; the *Auslese* is white, and white with a gold stripe. The extremely rare and costly *Beerenauslese* and *Trockenbeerenauslese* both have gold capsules, and may be adorned with a special "moated tower" neck label.

Recently, Schloss Vollrads assumed control of the Fürstlich von Löwenstein estate in Hallgarten, and markets the wine in connection with its own production. In any quality grade, a Schloss Vollrads displays certain noble qualities that define the best Rheingau wines—fine fruit, impeccable balance, and great Riesling character.

Volnay *(Vawl-nay′):* Famous wine commune in the CÔTE DE BEAUNE, Burgundy. Located on a hilly slope between the communes of POMMARD and MEURSAULT, Volnay is celebrated for its excellent red wines made from Pinot Noir; rather light in color, but having much fruit and elegance, they are among the most charming red Burgundies and have been prized since the 12th century. Volnay has several notable vineyards rated Premier Cru (First Growth); the most highly acclaimed is CAILLERETS, but the Clos des Ducs, Champans, Frémiets, Santenots, Clos des Chênes, Brouillards, Mitans, and Chevrets also have wide repute. The total vineyard area in the commune is about 526 acres; production averages about 71,000 cases annually.

Vosne-Romanée *(Vone Ro'-man-nay)*: One of the most celebrated wine communes of the CÔTE DE NUITS, Burgundy, and possibly the most famous of the entire CÔTE D'OR. There are only 593 acres in the whole commune, yet the incomparable red wine produced in Vosne-Romanée is in great demand. The commune is named for the La ROMANÉE vineyard, the choicest portion of which in 1760 was called ROMANEÉ-CONTI: these two great vineyards are rated Grand Cru (Great Growth), the highest rank for a Burgundy. Three other Vosne-Romanée Grand Crus—RICHEBOURG, La TÂCHE, and ROMANÉE-SAINT-VIVANT—produce similarly fine wines. The vineyards of ÉCHEZEAUX and GRANDS-ÉCHEZEAUX are technically not within the Vosne-Romanée commune but are generally included with Vosne-Romanée wines, and if they are declassified they are sold as Vosne-Romanées. Several excellent Vosne-Romanée vineyards are rated Premier Cru (First Growth): the more famous include MALCONSORTS, Suchots, Les Beaumonts, La Grande Rue, and Clos des Réas. Average production for the entire commune rarely exceeds 62,500 cases annually.

Vougeot *(Voo'-zho)*: Wine town in the CÔTE DE NUITS, Burgundy, celebrated chiefly for one famous vineyard, the CLOS DE VOUGEOT. Wines labeled Vougeot, on the other hand, are not the same as Clos de Vougeots but come from lesser vineyards nearby; these are usually not quite as fine as Clos de Vougeots but can nevertheless be distinctive. Some 4,500 cases of red Vougeot are produced annually; there is also a tiny production of superior white wine.

Vouvray *(Voo'-vray)*: Fine white wine region in the LOIRE River valley, France, with some 3,000 acres of vineyard east of the city of Tours in the old province of TOURAINE. The charming, scented white Vouvrays are made from the Chenin Blanc (Pineau de la Loire) grape grown in eight communes—Vouvray, Chançay, Rochecorbon, Noizay, Vernou, Parçay-Veslay, Sainte-Radegonde, and Reugny; occasionally their names will appear on a wine label. There are certain outstanding vineyards in these communes that produce superior wines; among the best are: Le Mont, Les Bidaudières, Moncontour, Le Haut Lieu, and Clos du Bourg. Depending on the vintage, Vouvrays can be dry, semi-dry, or sweet (*moelleux*); the sweeter Vouvrays can improve for decades. In addition to still wines, there is an important production of sparkling Vouvray (*Vouvray mousseux*), bottle-fermented by the CHAMPAGNE process, which are among the best sparkling wines produced outside the Champagne region. Total production of all Vouvray often exceeds 500,000 cases annually.

Wachau (*Vok'-kow*): Wine district in eastern Austria, situated along the Donau (Danube) River west of Vienna. One of Austria's most famous wine regions, the Wachau is one of the designated Austrian *Weinbaugebiete* (wine-growing regions) that includes the important wine towns of KREMS, Dürnstein, Baumgarten and Mautern. The vineyards are planted extensively in Grüner Veltliner, Riesling and Müller-Thurgau grapes.

372

Wachenheim (*Vok'-en-heim*): One of the most famous wine towns in the RHEINPFALZ (Palatinate) district, Germany, with 1,433 acres of vineyard. Wachenheim produces both red and white wines, but the fine white Riesling wines are superior and have fetched world-wide acclaim. Wachenheim lies just to the north of FORST and the wines share many of the same noble characteristics. The best vineyards (EINZELLAGEN) include: Gerümpel, Rechbächel, Goldbächel, Böhlig, Altenburg, Schlossberg, Luginsland, Königswingert, and Mandelgarten; the leading producer is Dr. Bürklin-Wolf, who is the sole owner of Rechbächel.

Waldrach *(Vol'-drock)*: Little wine village in the RUWER district, Germany, with some 297 acres of vineyard. Waldrach is noted for its especially light and delicate white wines made from Riesling, though they are generally only at their best in hot years. The best vineyards (EINZELLAGEN) are Krone, Hubertusberg, Meisenberg, Ehrenberg, and Jesuitengarten.

Walluf *(Vol'-loof)*: Name recently given to two associated wine communities in Germany's RHEINGAU district, Nieder-Walluf and Ober-Walluf, which have now been combined into one municipality. Walluf lies near the Rhine River just below RAUENTHAL, but the wines are generally somewhat heavier and less fine than the Rauenthalers. In fine vintages, however, Walluf can produce some good wines; the vineyards (EINZELLAGEN) include: Berg Bildstock, Langenstück, Walkenberg, Oberberg, and Fitusberg.

Washington State: One of America's newest and most promising wine regions, Washington is the nation's third largest grape-growing state, with over 20,000 acres of vineyard. Grapes were first planted in the Puget Sound area south of Seattle in 1872, but the wines were mediocre and they were only distributed locally. Following repeal, Washington State vintners primarily sold fruit wines and not table wines, but this direction was reversed in the late 1960s when it was demonstrated that

373

outstanding table wines could be made from VINIFERA grape varieties grown in the state.

From west to east, Washington State experiences several extreme climatic changes. The west coast near Olympia is the wettest region in the continental U.S., and a rainforest actually exists there. In the center of the state, the Cascade Range rises up to effectively block most of the rainfall, and in the east it is nearly desert. But since 1906 dam projects in the Cascade Range have allowed irrigation to compensate for the lack of rainfall, and the YAKIMA VALLEY in southeastern Washington is now the state's most important wine region, with 85% of the total vineyard area (over 17,000 acres). Many of the vineyards are still planted in table grape varieties, but acreage in wine grapes is on the increase. The latitude in the Yakima Valley is the same as in the Burgundy region in France, and many of the finer grapes native to France and Germany have been successfully grown there.

The state's major producer is Château Ste. Michelle Vintners, owned by the U.S. Tobacco Co., which produces a complete line of red and white table wines, many of them outstanding. In the 1970s a number of new wineries became bonded: Bingen Wine Cellars, Cedar Ridge Vintners, E. B. Foote, Hinzerling Vineyards, Mt. Rainier Vintners, Preston Wine Cellars, Vierthaler, and Yakima River Winery. Associated Vintners in Redmond was one of the earliest to be successful with table wines, and a number of growers supply wineries in Oregon with their grapes.

Wehlen (*Vay'-len*): World-famous wine town on the MOSEL River, Germany, with some 250 acres of vineyard. Wehlen lies between the celebrated villages of GRAACH and ZELTINGEN and likewise profits from a southerly exposure; the steep vineyards lie on slate soil, and in great vintages the elegant Riesling wines of Wehlen are prized for their great delicacy. The most famous vineyard (EINZELLAGE) is Sonnenuhr, or "sun dial"; other good Wehlener Einzellagen are Nonnenberg and Klosterberg. It should be noted, however, that Wehlener Münzlay is not an Einzellage but a composite vineyard or GROSSLAGE that includes all of the vineyards of Wehlen, Graach and Zeltingen.

Wein *(Vine):* German for "wine."

Weinbauort *(Vine'-bough-awrt):* German for "wine-growing community," an officially delimited township and the surrounding vineyards.

Weingut *(Vine'-goot):* German for "wine estate," a specific winery and its cellars or vineyards.

Weinkellerei *(Vine'-keller-rye):* German for "wine cellar," usually that of the producer and not the consumer.

Weissherbst *(Vice'-hairbst):* German for "white autumn"; specifically, a rosé or pink wine made from black grapes. Under the 1971 German Wine Law, a Weissherbst must meet the minimum requirements for QUALITÄTSWEIN, and must be produced only from one grape variety. Weissherbst can be made in most German wine regions, but much of it comes from the BADEN and RHEINPFALZ areas.

White Riesling: see JOHANNISBERG RIESLING.

Wiltingen *(Vil'-ting-gen):* Famous wine village in the SAAR district, Germany, with 771 acres of vineyard planted mostly in Riesling. The largest and most important town in the Saar, Wiltingen is celebrated chiefly for one great vineyard or EINZELLAGE, the SCHARZHOFBERG, but outstanding wines are also made from other Wiltingen Einzellagen: Kupp, Braunfels, Klosterberg, Hölle, Braune Kupp, Gottesfuss, Rosenberg, Schlossberg and Sandberg. However, under the 1971 German Wine Law, Wiltinger Scharzberg is not an Einzellage but a composite vineyard or GROSSLAGE that includes vineyards from the entire Saar district, and in general the wines will be less good than those from Wiltingen itself.

Wine: As defined throughout this dictionary, and by legal definition in most countries, a beverage produced by the partial or complete fermentation of the juice of fresh grapes. Fermented beverages made from cherries, plums, apples, pears, apricots or other fruits are commonly called "fruit wines" but are not wines in the true sense of the word.

Wines fit into the following categories: *Table wines*, or "still beverage wines," red, white, or rosé wines below 14% alcohol, to accompany a meal; *Fortified Wines*, from 14% to 24% alcohol, to which brandy has been added at some point during vinification; and *Sparkling Wines*, to which a secondary fermentation has been applied to make the wine sparkle.

Winkel *(Vink'-el):* Village and wine commune in the RHEINGAU district, with 687 acres of vineyard. Winkel is famous chiefly for one great wine estate, Schloss Vollrads (see VOLL-RADS, SCHLOSS), which tends to overshadow some of the other fine vineyards or EINZELLA-GEN that often give excellent wines. These include: Hasensprung ("hare's leap"), Jesuiten-garten, Gutenberg, Bienengarten, Dachsberg, and Schlossberg.

Wintrich *(Vin'-trick):* Wine village of secondary importance on the MOSEL River, Germany, with 704 acres of vineyard. The vineyards are planted primarily in Riesling and produce light, scented wines, although they are generally at their best only in great vintages. The vineyards (EINZELLAGEN) are: Ohligsberg, Sonnenseite, Grosser Herrgott, and Stefanslay.

Winzer *(Vint'-ser):* German for "vintner" or "wine-grower."

Winzergenossenschaft *(Vint'-ser-ge-nawss'-en-shoft):* German for "wine-growers' cooperative association." As distinguished from a WIN-ZERVEREIN (see below), a Winzergenossenschaft is usually a wine cooperative on a somewhat larger scale, with facilities for bottling and marketing in addition to wine-making.

Winzerverein *(Vint'-ser-vair-ryne'):* German for "wine-growers' cooperative," an association of growers that have collectively pooled their vineyards and wine-making equipment, so that the wines are sold under one label.

Worms *(Voorms):* Historic old city of some 76,000 on the Rhine River, Germany, near the southernmost limit of the RHEINHESSEN district. A city that played a major role in the Protestant Reformation, Worms is famous for being the original producing zone for the popular white wine LIEBFRAUMILCH. The Gothic Liebfrauenkirche at the edge of the city is surrounded by a 26-acre vineyard, the Liebfrauenstift, which several centuries ago is said to have inspired the name Liebfraumilch. Today, the Liebfrauenstift vineyard is managed predominantly by the P. J. Valckenberg and Langenbach shipping firms in Worms, who market the wines under the name "Wormser Liebfrauenstift-Kirchenstück."

Under the 1971 German Wine Law, the Liebfrauenstift vineyard became an individual site or EINZELLAGE, and others in the area achieved regional status. Since the Einzellagen today cannot produce enough to satisfy demand, the GROSSLAGE Wormser Liebfrauenmorgen includes associated townships that, through skillful blending, produce quality wines consistent with the reputation that Liebfraumilch now enjoys.

377

Württemberg *(Voor'-tem-bairg):* Wine region in western Germany, located along the Neckar River valley around the cities of Stuttgart and

Heilbronn. The fifth largest wine region (AN-BAUGEBIET) in Germany, Württemberg has over 18,000 acres of vineyard and is one of Germany's most important red wine regions, although the wines are not well-known in the export trade. The region consists of three sub-regions or BEREICHE: *Remstal-Stuttgart*, along the valley of the River Rems in the vicinity of the city of Stuttgart; *Württembergisch Unterland*, in the center; and *Kocher-Jagst-Tauber*, to the north, named for three tributaries of the Neckar. Among the more important wine towns are Stuttgart, Heilbronn, Stetten, Kleinbottwar, Schwaigern, and Weikersheim.

The traditional specialty of Württemberg is SCHILLERWEIN, a pink wine made from red and white grapes pressed together, but many of Württemberg's producers are turning away from Schillerwein and are concentrating on quality red and white wines. The most wide-spread grape grown in Württemberg is Trollinger, used for red wine and grown nowhere else in Germany; the Spätburgunder (Pinot Noir) is another important red grape variety. Superior white wine is made from Riesling, Silvaner, Traminer and Müller-Thurgau. Most Württemberg wine is consumed locally, but some better examples are now beginning to appear on the export market.

Würzburg *(Voorts'-boorg)*: City in the region of FRANKEN (Franconia), West Germany. Franconia's capital and largest city, Würzburg is famous for its beer as well as its wines; the wines are bottled in the traditional BOCKSBEU-TEL flask native to Franconia. There are some 988 acres of vineyard; the better sites are planted in Riesling and Silvaner, and produce vigorous and scented wines. One particularly good Würzburg vineyard (EINZELLAGE), Stein, was so famous that Franconia wines are often called "Steinweine" in the export trade, although in Germany this term is restricted to wines produced from the Stein vineyard. Other good Würzburger Einzellagen include: Abtsleite, Innere Leiste, Kirchberg, Stein/Harfe, Pfaffenberg, and Schlossberg.

Yakima Valley: Wine district in southeastern Washington State, located along the lower Yakima River east of the Cascade Range mountains. Principal wine towns in the valley are: Yakima, Richland, Prosser, Wapato, and Grandview. The Yakima Valley has over 15,000 acres of vineyard, but not all are given over to wine grapes; most are Concords that are sold to neighboring states. Nevertheless, the valley lies on the same latitude as do some of Europe's most famous wine districts, and a number of excellent wines have been made from premium varieties grown there.

Yeasts: Single-celled, asexual plant organisms that bring about fermentation in grape juice. Actually, the yeasts themselves do not cause fermentation; an enzyme they secrete, ZYMASE, converts the grape sugar into ethyl alcohol and carbon dioxide by a complex series of biochemical reactions. One particular strain of yeast, *Saccharomyces cerevisae*, is the most useful to the wine-maker because it does the most thorough job of converting the grape sugar.

The selection of the proper yeast is of great importance to the wine-maker. In Europe's traditional wine areas, desirable yeast occurs naturally in the region and collects readily on the surface of the grape skins with the waxy "bloom"; in newer wine regions such as California, harmful wild yeasts collect on the grapes and these must be subdued before fermentation proceeds—most effectively, by adding sulfur dioxide (see SULFUR). Desirable yeast strains are imported from Europe, and are inoculated into the must prior to fermentation.

Yonne *(Yawn):* River and department (administrative region) in northern BURGUNDY, France, in which the CHABLIS district lies.

Yquem, Château d' *(Dee-kem'):* World-famous BORDEAUX wine estate, located in the celebrated commune of SAUTERNES. The château of Yquem was built in the 12th century, and since 1785 has belonged to the Lur-Saluces family; today, it is most renowned for its luscious sweet white wines, considered to be the finest of all the great Sauternes in most vintages. Officially it is ranked as a Grand Premier Cru (Great First Growth) and is among the most costly of all Bordeaux wines: even though there are some 250 acres of Sémillon and Sauvignon Blanc wines, average production is only about 6,700 cases annually, and in unsuccessful vintages the entire crop is declassified and not sold under the château label. In years when the finest sweet wines cannot be produced, the estate also makes an interesting dry white wine known as "Château Y"—pronounced *"Ee'-greck."* Although expensive, Château d'Yquem is among the world's very greatest wines.

Yugoslavia: With over 750,000 acres of vineyard, Yugoslavia is the world's tenth largest wine-producing nation. With a heritage of wine-making dating back some 2,000 years, Yugoslavia has an ethnic and religious diversity reflected in the many different wines she produces. Six different regions—Serbia, Croatia, Slovenia, Bosnia-Herzegovina, Macedonia and Montenegro—make up the federal republic of Yugoslavia, and the wines are as varied as the many ethnic groups.

There are essentially three principal wine regions in Yugoslavia. In the north, bordering

Italy and Austria, is Slovenia; in the center is the rugged Dalmatian coast, and further inland are the mountainous regions of Serbia, Herzegovina and Macedonia. The climate ranges from alpine in the north to mediterranean in the south, and the wines reflect these climatic differences: in general they are lighter and more aromatic in the north, and sturdier and fuller-flavored in the south.

Much quality wine is produced in Slovenia. Grape varieties indigenous to Italy and Austria grow well there; the town of Ljutomer, east of the city of Ljubljana, is particularly noted for its white wines made from Rizling (Riesling), Traminec (Traminer), and Sipon—the latter variety is grown only in Yugoslavia. The Istrian peninsula south of Trieste is another important Slovenian wine district; its red wines from Cabernet, Merlot and Refosk (Refosco) are particularly well-known, as are its white wines from Pinot Blanc and Muscat.

The Dalmatian coast produces an immense variety of red, white and rosé wines, though they are not as widely exported as those of Slovenia. The little islands of Korčula, Hvar and Vis make Grk, Bogdanuša and Plavac, respectively, among the most individual of all Yugoslavian wines. Three Dalmatian specialties are Blatina, a full, soft red wine; Zilavka, a fruity, scented dry white wine, and Opolo, one of the finest rosés in Yugoslavia. As these varieties are native to Yugoslavia, the wines are entitled to a special government *Appellation d'Origine Contrôlée* rating, though this does not correspond to the French wine laws.

The native Prokupac grape furnishes most of the ordinary red wines of Serbia and Macedonia, which are best when drunk quite young. Prokupac rosés are often superior to the reds. This grape is now being supplanted by fine French varieties such as Gamay and Cabernet Sauvignon, as is an indigenous white variety, Smederovka, by important new plantings of Sauvignon Blanc.

Yugoslavian wines are well-represented on the U.S. market. Three major wine cooperatives—Slovin in Slovenia, Navip in Serbia, and Hepok in Herzegovina—have united in a joint effort to export wines under their own brand names; the associated Adriatica brand represents virtually all of the wine regions.

Z

Zell *(Tsell):* Little town on the MOSEL River, Germany, famous for its regional white wine called "Zeller Schwarze Katz" (Black Cat of Zell), sold with a black cat on the label. Because this wine was so well-known, the 1971 German Wine Law authorized Schwarze Katz to be the name of a composite vineyard or GROSSLAGE, and although Zell has several individual vineyards or EINZELLAGEN of its own—Nussberg, Domherrenberg, Kreuzlay, etc.—the Grosslage name is the one most frequently encountered in the trade. Under the wine law, the entire sub-region or BEREICH in which Zell lies is now also called Zell. Despite its great fame, Zeller Schwarze Katz is usually an undistinguished wine and is hardly the best the Mosel region has to offer.

Zeltingen *(Tsel'-ting-gen):* Famous wine town on the MOSEL River, Germany, officially associated with the neighboring village of Rachtig into one municipality, Zeltingen-Rachtig, the largest wine community in the Mittel-Mosel. Zeltingen-Rachtig has 531 acres of vineyard, planted mostly in Riesling; the community adjoins the equally celebrated village of WEHLEN to the south, and its most famous vineyard or EINZELLAGE is likewise named Sonnenuhr ("sun dial"); other fine Zeltingen Einzellagen are Himmelreich, Schlossberg, and Deutschherrenberg. However, under the 1971 German Wine Law, Zeltinger Münzlay became the name of a collective vineyard (GROSSLAGE), describing all of the vineyards in Zeltingen, Wehlen and GRAACH; the leading Einzellagen will generally give more representative wines.

Zinfandel: Fine red wine grape grown extensively in California, where almost 30,000 acres have been planted. It is of the species VINIFERA and consequently was imported from Europe at some time during the 19th century, though experts disagree over its original location and present-day counterpart; the latest theory is that Zinfandel came from Italy and is related to the Primitivo from the region of APULIA. Zinfandel berries are deep purple when ripe, and when the grape is planted in cool coastal districts the wines are full-bodied and fruity, with a characteristic "bramble" or "berry" flavor. Zinfandel is grown in nearly every wine-producing country in California—most extensively in the warm Central Valley—but the greatest success with this grape seems to be in the North Coast Countries, where some producers have made outstanding Zinfandels that rank with America's best wines.

Zymase: Enzyme produced by yeast, which causes fermentation and converts grape sugar to ethyl alcohol and carbon dioxide. The fermentative properties of zymase were first demonstrated in 1896 by the German chemist Eduard Büchner (1860-1917); zymase is now believed to consist of several related enzymes that collectively act as catalytic agents for the fermentation process.

The Varietal Wines

Wines owe their character and taste, in large part, to the grapes from which they are made. There are literally scores of different varieties, each fermenting into wines of different tastes.

Many wines today are labeled for the predominant grape used—Chardonnay, Cabernet Sauvignon, Chenin Blanc, Zinfandel are typical examples. These are called Varietal Wines. On the other hand, European wines are not normally named after the grape variety, but the law requires that specific grapes be used for specific wines of the region stated on the label.

Knowing the leading grape varieties and the character of the wines they make are keys to your selection of wines you'll enjoy. These listings are designed to guide you. They tell you, for example, that a Chenin Blanc wine, produced predominantly from the Chenin Blanc grape, is a soft, scented white wine, generally with slight sweetness. If you are fond of this wine they will also suggest some of the European wines made from the same grape such as the Vouvray, Coteaux du Layon and Savennières from France's Loire region.

WHITE GRAPE VARIETIES

Aligoté: grown in the Burgundy district of France; gives a light white wine called Bourgogne Aligoté.

Aurora: A hybrid grape developed in France, widely grown in the Finger Lakes district of New York State. Gives light, fragrant wines.

Catawba: grown in the eastern United States. Native pink grape of the species *labrusca*; gives a good sweet wine and excellent juice.

Chardonnay: grown in the Burgundy and Champagne districts of France; in California, eastern Europe and in South America. Makes the best dry white wines of California; gives the *Blanc de Blancs* of Champagne. Yields fine, luscious wines; dry, and with great scent and class.

Chasselas: grown in central Europe, chiefly as a table grape. Only gives good white wines in cool districts, such as Vaud and Valais in Switzerland, and Crépy and Pouilly sur-Loire, France; called "Gutedel" in Germany.

Chenin Blanc: grown in the Loire Valley, France; in California and in South America. Fine white wine grape; grown for Vouvray, Coteaux du Layon and Savennières in the Loire. Gives soft, scented wines, generally with a slight sweetness—best when not too dry.

Colombard: grown in the Cognac region of France, and in California. Called "French Colombard" in California; usually produced for blends of inexpensive "chablis," but also sold as a varietal. Standard quality.

Delaware: grown in the eastern United States; chiefly New York State and Ohio. Native white grape of the species *labrusca*; gives scented white wines with a characteristic flavor; best when not totally dry.

Gewürztraminer: grown in Alsace, France; in Germany, Austria, northern Italy, and in California. A superior selection of Traminer; gives full-bodied wines with a characteristic "spicy" flavor. Has reddish berries that give white juice, very full in flavor.

Grey Riesling: grown in parts of France; chiefly in California. Technically not a Riesling, although good for light-semi-dry wines. Its real name is Chauché Gris.

Johannisberg Riesling: grown in central Europe, Australia, and California; outstanding grape, grown for the great wines of the Rhine and Mosel regions in Germany. Also gives excellent results in California, best when not too dry. Also called White Riesling.

Malvasia: grown in the Mediterranean and in California; produced for good dessert wines, but also serves as a fine aperitif. Also used for table grapes.

Müller-Thurgau: grown in central Europe, particularly Germany and Austria; the most widely-grown grape in Germany, developed in 1882 in Geisenheim. Has good yield, gives soft, scented wines, fairly short-lived. Also known as "Riesling x Silvaner" in Germany and Switzerland.

Muscat: grown in the Mediterranean region; also in northern Italy, in France, and California; excellent sweet grape; grown for Asti Spumante, the famous Italian sparkling wine. Known as *moscato*, produces outstanding sweet dessert wines in Italy and in California.

Pinot Blanc: grown in the Champagne and Burgundy districts of France; in Alsace, Germany, Italy and California; very similar to Chardonnay, giving wines of the same character and class, but being phased out generally in favor of Chardonnay. Should actually be more widely planted.

Pinot Chardonnay: see Chardonnay; the accepted, but technically incorrect, name for Chardonnay.

Pinot Gris: grown in Alsace, France; Germany, Switzerland, and northern Italy; a cousin of the red Pinot Noir; not well-known in the U.S. Called Pinot Grigio in Italy, Ruländer in Germany, and Malvoisie in Switzerland. Gives fine, full-bodied white wines, often with a faint tinge of color.

Riesling: See Johannisberg Riesling; the excepted term for Johannisberg or White Riesling, although varietal wines sold under this name may be produced from Sylvaner or Sémillon in California and Australia.

Sauvignon Blanc: grown in the upper Loire Valley, France; in Bordeaux, Chile, Australia, and California; very fine grape, grown for Sancerre and Pouilly-Fumé in the Loire, and Graves blanc and Sauternes in Bordeaux. Gives equally good dry or sweet wines, sometimes called *Blanc Fumé* to identify a deliberately dry style.

Sémillon: grown in the Bordeaux district of France, in South America, Australia, and California; the second important grape in white Graves and Sauternes from Bordeaux; excellent for sweet wines, less successful when totally dry. Often blended with Sauvignon Blanc.

Seyval Blanc: grown in the eastern U.S. and Canada, also in France; a hybrid grape developed in France, gives some of the best dry white wines in the eastern U.S.

Sylvaner: grown in central Europe and in California; companion grape to the Riesling in Germany. Still very important in the Rheinhessen and Franken districts. Productive and agreeable; generally a bit low in acidity; sometimes lacking great distinction.

Trebbiano: grown in Italy and France; some acreage in California; known as Ugni Blanc in France, grown for brandy production; a chief grape used for Soave, Orvieto, Frascati, and other Italian whites. Also known as "Saint-Emilion."

RED GRAPE VARIETIES

Baco Noir: grown principally in eastern U.S.; also in France; a hybrid grape developed in France, named for the botanist who developed it; also called Baco No. 1.

Barbera: grown in Piemonte, northwest Italy; also in South America and in California; usually sold as a varietal. In Italy identified along with the production zone. Gives very full-bodied wine.

Brunello: grown only in Tuscany, Italy, at present; a selection of Sangiovese, grown for one of the best and most expensive Italian red wines, the Brunello di Montalcino.

Cabernet Franc: grown in the Bordeaux district in France, the middle Loire Valley in France, in Italy and recently, in California; related to Cabernet Sauvignon and very similar. Also called "Breton" in France. Generally blended with Cabernet Sauvignon or Merlot in Bordeaux.

Cabernet Sauvignon: grown in the Bordeaux district in France, Provence, Chile, Australia, California and South Africa; practically everywhere; a very fine red wine grape, responsible for the great Bordeaux reds, particularly Medocs. Usually gives the best red wine of California, with great body and long life.

Carignan: grown in southern France, the Côtes-du-Rhône area, and in warm climate regions of California; spelled "Carignane" in California; usually blended and sold as "burgundy" although occasionally as a varietal. Standard quality.

Chancellor Noir: grown in eastern U.S., also in southern France; a hybrid grape, giving medium-bodied wines; well-suited to cool North American climate.

Charbono: grown in California; gives extremely dark and full-bodied red wines, but relatively rare.

Concord: grown in the eastern United States and in Canada. Native American grape of the species *labrusca*; not really suited to wine, has to be heavily sugared to make it palatable. Better suited to juice, jams and jellies.

de Chaunac: grown in Canada and eastern U.S.; a hybrid grape, giving rich wines with plenty of color and substance.

Dolcetto: grown in Piemonte, northern Italy; an agreeable, fruity red grape, giving light, rather soft red wines; usually sold as a varietal.

Gamay: grown in the Beaujolais district of France; in Switzerland, the Loire Valley, and in California. Very important in Burgundy, but not used for the best wines; sometimes blended with Pinot Noir. Gives good, medium-bodied wines, with plenty of fruit, fairly short-lived.

Gamay Beaujolais: grown only in California; originally thought to be the "true" Gamay of the Beaujolais district; now identified as a strain of Pinot Noir. Will be gradually phased out in the future; its wines, however, are generally quite fruity and good.

Grenache: grown in the southern Rhone district of France; in Spain, and in California. Grown for Tavel and Lirac, among the best rosé wines of France; generally has insufficient color for red wines, and is blended with other grapes, as in Chateauneuf-du-Pape. Gives excellent rose wines in California.

Malbec: grown in Bordeaux district in France; in Argentina; tiny quantities in California. Fine quality red wine grape; used for wines of Cahors, blended with Cabernet in Bordeaux. Gives rich, full red wines. Should be more widely planted.

Merlot: grown in the Bordeaux district; in northern Italy and Switzerland, increasingly popular in California; also in South America. Excellent red wine grape; generally not used on its own but blended with other grapes in Bordeaux. Softens Cabernet Sauvignon, and found to improve many California Cabernets.

Nebbiolo: grown in Piemonte and Lombardy, Italy; small acreage in California. Grown for all the great northern Italian reds—Barolo, Barbaresco, Ghemme, Gattinara, and Valtellina. Very fine wines—rich, slow to mature.

Petite Sirah: grown in California and also in parts of France; originally thought to be a strain of Syrah; actually a different grape, known as Duriff. Gives excellent, very rich red wines, increasingly popular as a varietal.

Pinot Noir: grown in the French Champagne district; in Burgundy, Switzerland, Germany, eastern Europe, South America and California. Excellent red wine grape, but not always easy to grow. Vinified as a "blanc de noirs," away from the skins, to make Champagne. Traditionally, California Pinot Noirs have tended to be too light in color, but there has been tremendous improvement recently.

Ruby Cabernet: grown only in California. New grape developed in California in 1948 by crossing Carignane with Cabernet Sauvignon. Best suited to warm climatic regions; has good color and flavor, but not always sold as a varietal.

Sangiovese: grown in Tuscany and in Emilia-Romagna, Italy; important grape used for Chianti, but blended with as many as four other grapes for this purpose. Elsewhere, usually sold as a varietal.

Syrah: grown in the Rhône district of France. Produces the great Rhône reds—Côte Rotie, Hermitage, and Châteauneuf-du-Pape. Recently introduced in California; not to be confused with Petite Sirah. Gives very rich, robust red wines.

Zinfandel: grown chiefly in California; at least, under this name. America's truly unique red grape; of uncertain origin, probably imported from Italy. Gives excellent red wine with a characteristic spicy flavor, in a multitude of different styles and strengths. Best are from the North Coast Counties.

Wine Character Listings

These listings represent groupings of the most popular wines organized in their order, on the basis of body—from light to full—and their degree of sweetness—dry (without sweetness) to off-dry, semi-sweet, and very sweet. To help you select the wine you prefer, begin at the top of the chart and read down as sweetness or fullness increases. Each wine is listed in terms of the general characteristics typical of the wines of the region or the grape variety. When "(var.)" is encountered, this means that the name of the wine indicates the grape variety from which it is made, rather than its place of origin.

WHITE WINES—DRY

Name of Wine Country of Origin / Region	Grape Varieties Used Wine Character
Vinho Verde Portugal, Minho River	various Light-bodied, dry
Chablis France, Burgundy	Chardonnay Light-bodied, dry
Aligoté France, Burgundy	(var.) Light-bodied, dry
Muscadet France, Loire	(var.) Light-bodied, dry
French Colombard various	(var.) Light-bodied, dry
Pouilly-Fumé France, Loire	Sauvignon Blanc Light-bodied, dry
Sancerre France, Loire	Sauvignon Blanc Light-bodied, dry
Bordeaux* France, Gironde	Sauvignon Blanc, Sémillon Light-bodied, dry
· Entre-Deux-Mers France, Bordeaux	Sauvignon Blanc, Sémillon Light-bodied, dry
· Graves France, Bordeaux	Sauvignon Blanc, Sémillon Light-bodied, dry
Sauvignon Blanc various	(var.) Light-bodied, dry
Soave Italy, Veneto	Garganega, Trebbiano Light-bodied, dry
Est! Est! Est! Italy, Lazio	Trebbiano, Malvasia Medium-bodied, dry

*may be red or white

Name of Wine Country of Origin / Region	Grape Varieties Used Wine Character
Verdicchio Italy, Marche	(var.) Medium-bodied, dry
Orvieto Italy, Umbria	Trebbiano, Verdicchio Medium-bodied, dry
Frascati Italy, Lazio	Malvasia, Trebbiano Medium-bodied, dry
Lacrima Christi* Italy, Campania	various Medium-bodied, dry
Pinot Blanc various	(var.) Medium-bodied, dry
Sémillon USA, California	(var.) Medium-bodied, dry
Seyval Blanc USA, New York State	(var.) Medium-bodied, dry
Pinot Chardonnay various	(var.) Medium-bodied, dry
Mâcon* France, Burgundy	Chardonnay Medium-bodied, dry
· Saint-Veran France, Burgundy	Chardonnay Medium-bodied, dry
· Pouilly-Fuissé France, Burgundy	Chardonnay Medium-bodied, dry
Meursault France, Burgundy	Chardonnay Medium-bodied, dry
Puligny-Montrachèt France, Burgundy	Chardonnay Full-bodied, dry
Chassagne-Montrachet* France, Burgundy	Chardonnay Full-bodied, dry
Corton-Charlemagne France, Burgundy	Chardonnay Full-bodied, dry
Montrachet France, Burgundy	Chardonnay Full-bodied, dry

WHITE WINES—SEMI

Riesling France, Alsace	(var.) Light-bodied, off dry
Emerald Riesling USA, California	(var.) Light-bodied, off dry
Johannisberg Riesling USA, California	(var.) Light-bodied, off dry

*may be red or white

Name of Wine Country of Origin / Region	Grape Varieties Used Wine Character
Mosel Riesling Germany, Mosel-Saar-Ruwer	(var.) Light-bodied, off dry
Rhine Riesling Germany, Rhine	(var.) Light-bodied, off dry
Sylvaner France, Alsace	(var.) Light-bodied, off dry
Sylvaner USA, California	(var.) Light-bodied, off dry
Silvaner Germany, Rhine	(var.) Light-bodied, off dry
Chenin Blanc USA, California	(var.) Light-bodied, off dry
Liebfraumilch Germany, Rhine	various Medium-bodied, semi-sweet
Gewürztraminer France, Alsace	(var.) Medium-bodied, semi-sweet
Gewürztraminer USA, California	(var.) Medium-bodied, semi-sweet
Gewürztraminer Germany, Rhine	(var.) Medium-bodied, semi-sweet
Moscato di Canelli Italy, Piemonte	Muscat Medium-bodied, semi-sweet
Saumur* France, Loire	Chenin Blanc Medium-bodied, semi-sweet
Vouvray France, Loire	Chenin Blanc Medium-bodied, semi-sweet
Auslesen Germany, Mosel Rhine	various Full-bodied, very sweet
Barsac France, Bordeaux	Sémillon, Sauvignon Blanc Full-bodied, very sweet
Sauternes France, Bordeaux	Sémillon Full-bodied, very sweet
Tokay Aszu Hungary, Carpathian Mts.	Furmint Full-bodied, very sweet

ROSÉ WINES

Rosé de Marsannay France, Burgundy	Pinot Noir Light-bodied, dry
Grenache Rosé USA, California	(var.) Light-bodied, dry

*may be red or white

Name of Wine Country of Origin / Region	Grape Varieties Used Wine Character
Rosé of Cabernet USA, California	Cabernet Sauvignon Light-bodied, dry
Grignolino Rosé USA, California	(var.) Light-bodied, dry
Lirac France, Rhone	Grenache, Cinsault Light-bodied, dry
Tavel France, Rhone	Grenache, Cinsault Light-bodied, dry
Côtes de Provence* France, Provence	Grenache, Cinsault Full-bodied, semi-dry
Catawba Rosé USA, NY State, Ohio	(var.) Full-bodied, semi-dry
Rosé d'Anjou France, Anjou	Groslot, Cabernet Full-bodied, semi-dry

RED WINES

Bardolino Italy, Veneto	Corvina, Molinara Light-bodied, dry
Valpolicella Italy, Veneto	Corvina, Molinara Light-bodied, dry
Gamay Beaujolais USA, California	(var.) Light-bodied, dry
Beaujolais France, Burgundy	Gamay Light-bodied, dry
· Chiroubles France, Burgundy	Gamay Light-bodied, dry
· Brouilly France, Burgundy	Gamay Light-bodied, dry
· Saint Amour France, Burgundy	Gamay Light-bodied, dry
· Fleurie France, Burgundy	Gamay Light-bodied, dry
· Julienas France, Burgundy	Gamay Light-bodied, dry
· Chenas France, Burgundy	Gamay Light-bodied, dry
· Morgon France, Burgundy	Gamay Light-bodied, dry
· Moulin-à-Vent France, Burgundy	Gamay Light-bodied, dry

*may be red or white

Name of Wine Country of Origin / Region	Grape Varieties Used Wine Character
Côtes-du-Rhône* France, Rhône	Syrah, Grenache Light-bodied, dry
Corbiéres* France, Languedoc	Carignan, Grenache Light-bodied, dry
Rioja* Spain, Navarre	Garnacha, Tempranillo Light-bodied, dry
Bordeaux* France, Gironde	Cabernet Sauvignon, Merlot Medium-bodied, dry
· Médoc France, Bordeaux	Cabernet Sauvignon, Merlot Medium-bodied, dry
· Margaux France, Médoc	Cabernet Sauvignon, Merlot Medium-bodied, dry
· Saint-Julien France, Médoc	Cabernet Sauvignon, Merlot Medium-bodied, dry
· Pauillac France, Médoc	Cabernet Sauvignon, Merlot Medium-bodied, dry
· Saint-Estèphe France, Médoc	Cabernet Sauvignon, Merlot Medium-bodied, dry
· Graves France, Graves	Cabernet Sauvignon, Merlot Medium-bodied, dry
· Saint-Emilion France, Dordogne	Merlot, Cabernet Franc Medium-bodied, dry
· Pomerol France, Dordogne	Merlot, Cabernet Franc Medium-bodied, dry
Chianti Italy, Tuscany	Sangioveto, Canaiolo Medium-bodied, dry
Zinfandel USA, California	(var.) Medium-bodied, dry
Chelois USA, New York State	(var.) Medium-bodied, dry
Cabernet Sauvignon various	(var.) Medium-bodied, dry
Chancellor Noir USA, New York State	(var.) Medium-bodied, dry
Pinot Noir various	(var.) Medium-bodied, dry
Burgundy France, Côte d'Or	Pinot Noir Full-bodied, dry
· Côte de Beaune-Villages France, Côte d'Or	Pinot Noir Full-bodied, dry

*may be red or white

Name of Wine Country of Origin / Region	Grape Varieties Used Wine Character
· Beaune France, Côte d'Or	Pinot Noir Full-bodied, dry
· Chambolle-Musigny France, Côte d'Or	Pinot Noir Full-bodied, dry
· Pommard France, Côte d'Or	Pinot Noir Full-bodied, dry
· Nuits-Saint Georges France, Côte d'Or	Pinot Noir Full-bodied, dry
· Vosne-Romanee France, Côte d'Or	Pinot Noir Full-bodied, dry.
· Gevrey-Chambertin France, Côte-d'Or	Pinot Noir Full-bodied, dry
Chambertin France, Côte d'Or	Pinot Noir Full-bodied, dry
Côtes de Provence* France, Provence	Cinsault, Carignan Full-bodied, dry
Barbera Italy, Piemonte	(var.) Full-bodied, dry
Nebbiolo Italy, Piemonte	(var.) Full-bodied, dry
Gattinara Italy, Piemonte	Nebbiolo Full-bodied, dry
Côte Rotie France, Rhone	Syrah Full-bodied, dry
Hermitage France, Rhone	Syrah Full-bodied, dry
Châteauneuf-du-Pape France, Rhone	Syrah, Grenache Robust, dry
Petite Sirah USA, California	(var.) Robust, dry
Barbaresco Italy, Piemonte	Nebbiolo Robust, dry
Barolo Italy, Piemonte	Nebbiolo Robust, dry
Mavrodaphne Greece, Peloponnesus	various Robust, sweet
Passover Wine USA, New York State	Concord Robust, sweet

*may be red or white

Wine Reference Notes

_____
_____
_____
_____
_____
_____
_____
_____
_____
_____
_____
_____
_____
_____
_____
_____
_____
_____
_____
_____
_____
_____
_____
_____
_____
_____
_____
_____

About the Author

Frank E. Johnson is the contributing wine editor to Beverage Media in New York and the nationally affiliated Associated Beverage Publications network, an organization of leading beverage trade journals in the United States, and since 1974 he has served as east coast editor of Wine World magazine in California. He holds a master's degree in modern European history, and his knowledge of wine in large part relates to his exposure to it during his higher education. He has traveled throughout the world's major wine districts, and has written many articles on the subject in trade and consumer publications. He has translated two books on wine from French into English, and a number of articles in German. He was a cofounder of a professional organization of wine writers, the Wine Media Guild of New York, and currently serves as chairman. With William Kaufman, he edited the *Whole World Wine Catalogue*, was U.S. representative for La Revue du Vin de France in Paris, and is a frequent lecturer on wine. Currently he serves as a consultant and advisor to the American wine industry.